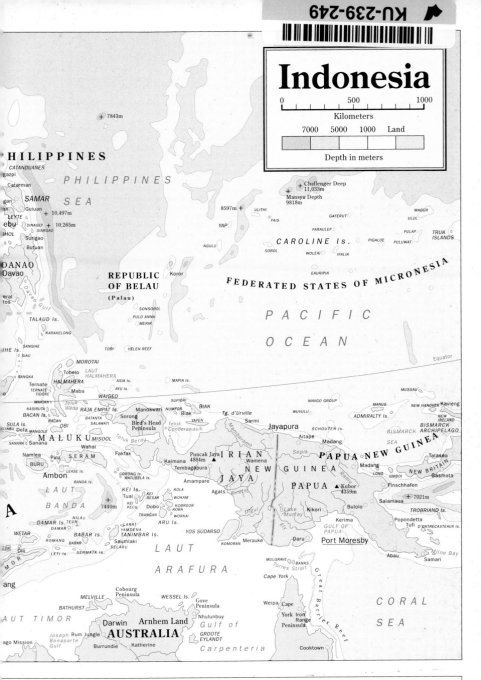

The **Republic of Indonesia**, with 190 million people, is the world's fifth largest country. Originally controlled by several Hindu and Islamic kingdoms, these 13,667 islands attracted the interest of European spice traders beginning in the 16th century. By the 19th century, the East Indies were a colony of Holland. Nationalist sentiment grew in the early 20th century, and after World War II and a difficult Japanese occupation, Sukarno, who was to be Indonesia's first president, declared independence on August 17, 1945. The Dutch were ousted five years later. The Indonesian language is a variant of Malay, long the region's lingua franca. The largest Islamic nation in the world, 88 percent of Indonesians are Muslims. In the more remote parts of the archipelago, traditional lifestyles are still practiced.

Underwater Indonesia

A GUIDE TO THE WORLD'S GREATEST DIVING

KAL MULLER

Edited by David Pickell

PERIPLUS
EDITIONS

The Periplus Travel Guide Series

SUMATRA
Island of Adventure

JAVA

BALI
Island of the Gods

EAST OF BALI
From Lombok to Timor

INDONESIAN BORNEO
Kalimantan

SULAWESI
The Celebes

SPICE ISLANDS
The Moluccas

INDONESIAN NEW GUINEA
Irian Jaya

UNDERWATER INDONESIA
A Guide to the World's Best Diving

WEST MALAYSIA
and Singapore

EAST MALAYSIA
and Brunei

The name PERIPLUS, meaning "voyage" or "journey," derives from the Greek. One of the earliest classical texts to mention Southeast Asia was the *Periplus of the Erythrean Sea*, an Alexandrian sailing manual dating from the first century of the common era. Periplus Editions, founded in 1988 by Eric Oey, specializes in the arts, cultures and natural history of the Malay archipelago— making authoritative information on the region available to a wider audience.

© 1992 by Periplus Editions (HK) Ltd.
ALL RIGHTS RESERVED
Printed in the Republic of Singapore
ISBN 0-945971-14-1

Distributors:
United States of America
Passport Books/NTC, 4255 W. Touhy Avenue
Lincolnwood (Chicago), Illinois 60646

UK/Europe (except Holland)
McCarta Ltd.
15 HIghbury Place, London N5 1QP

The Netherlands
Nilsson & Lamm bv
Postbus 195 1380 AD Weesp

Indonesia
C.V. Java Books
P.O. Box 55 JKCP, Jakarta 10510

Singapore & Malaysia
Periplus (Singapore) Pte Ltd
Farrer Road P.O. Box 115, Singapore 9128

Publisher: Eric Oey
Design: David Pickell
Production and cartography: David Pickell

Cover: A pair of maroon, or spine-cheeked anemonefish, *Premnas biaculeatus,* in their host anemone, *Entacmaea quadricolor.* Photograph by Helmut Debelius of IKAN. Flores.

Pages 2–3: A reef whitetip shark, *Triaenodon obesus,* snatches some food on a reef in the Bunaken group, North Sulawesi. Photograph by Ed Robinson/IKAN.

Frontispiece: Bunaken Island, Sulawesi. Photograph by Ed Robinson/IKAN.

Endpaper: Painting by I. Made Budi, of Batuan, Bali. (Commissioned for this book.)

Contents

Introduction

Java

Bali

See page 46

See page 115

See page 145

Nusa Tenggara

See page 153

See page 66

Sulawesi

Maluku

See page 167

Irian Jaya

Appendix

See page 69

See page 63

Author's Dedication

To my editor, David Pickell

He missed out on the fun part of this effort—the diving—and instead struggled behind his computer to whip the book into shape from the mess of my manuscripts.

Essential to this book were the many dive operators, guides and dive buddies who contributed their time and knowledge, and who made certain I stayed out of trouble underwater (and sometimes above). Very special thanks to **Glenn Barrall**, divemaster of the *Tropical Princess,* for a wealth of much-needed advice, and to my dive buddy on that trip, **Easy Ed Donohue**, who kept a close watch over me in my PC (Pre-Computer) days. Also to **Cody Shwaiko**, a close friend and my most frequent dive buddy, who traveled across Indonesia from his home in Bali several times to join me in the research for this book. And to **Wolfgang Bresigk**, who generously supplied all sorts of information, arranged my diving in Bali, and accompanied me on a series of dives. And to **Wally Siagian**, who stands head and shoulders above all dive guides, who took me to all the right sites in Bali, and found me a cold beer whenever I could not live without one. And to **Graham Whitford**, who, with his sense of humor and never-ending enthusiasm, made my days and dives in Kupang and Roti. And to **Loky Herlambang**, pioneer dive operator, founder of Nusantara Diving Centre, and conservation prize-winner, who did the same in Manado. And to **Jochem and Sabine Dengler**, both superb German dive instructors, who by their example and encouragement helped expand my dive capabilites. And finally, to dive instructor **Raquel Montero**, a faithful companion and dive buddy, who did the dirty work—cleaned equipment and greased O-rings—which allowed me time to write.

Editor's Acknowlegements

Any book of this scope represents the sweat and talent of many people, and an awful lot of both have gone into this one.

The fieldwork for this volume—hundreds of dives, thousands of kilometers of airplane and boat travel, sometimes weeks at a time without a cold beer—was conducted by **Kal Muller**, a strapping and undeniably charming Hungarian polyglot who has spent some 15 years tromping around the archipelago with his cameras and notebook. Kal is a dear friend, a god-awful speller, and probably the most tireless and good-humored person I know.

Dr. Charles Anderson, a marine biologist who works for the ministry of fisheries in the Republic of the Maldives, provided an excellent introduction to the marine life of Indonesia.

Janet Boileau and **Debe Campbell**, both freelance writers living in Jakarta, wrote the Java section. These two were an editor's dream, delivering a quality manuscript on very short notice.

Cody Shwaiko, a very experienced diver and writer living in Bali, provided the Kangean Islands section and parts of the Banda dive narrative. But his influence on this manuscript extends further. The quality of particularly the Bali and Maluku sections can to a large extent be credited to him.

Helmut Debelius—founder, cook and chief bottle washer of the German IKAN photo agency—opened his files to us, not only of his own high-quality work, but also that of **Ed Robinson**, **Jan Post** and **Lionel Pozzoli**. Helmut—the author of *Armoured Knights of the Sea,* a book about crustaceans—also provided a nice anecdote about discovering the beautiful reef lobster that now bears his name.

Photographer **Mike Severns**, who runs a dive operation in Maui with his wife, marine biologist Pauline Fiene-Severns, still calls himself "a beginner" but I'm not convinced. How many beginners know how to call jacks underwater? How many beginners hire six men to haul out a trap set in hundreds of meters of water to get photographs of a nautilus?

I would particularly like to thank Mike for keeping my spirits up during this long, wet winter. Each phone conversation began with: "How are things in New York? The weather here is awful. No clouds, 85 degrees. By the way, we got chased out of the water today by sharks."

Rudie Kuiter, an experienced photographer and the author of *Tropical Reef-Fishes of the Western Pacific: Indonesia and Adjacent Waters* (in publication as of this writing), provided an essay on discovering new species (from a man who should know) and a series of very interesting photographs. These are not only of new species, but also of fish caught in the act of being, well, *fish*—a moray eel eating a cardinalfish, two prawn gobies scrapping.

Kal Muller's photos—excellent, as always—and those of Singapore photographer **Fiona Nichols** also grace these pages.

I would also like to acknowledge dive guide **Wally Siagian** for his excellent and detailed sketch maps of dive sites in Bali and Banda. This is not the most glamorous kind of contribution, but one of the most important.

—**David Pickell**
New York, 1992

Introducing the Indonesian Islands

The islands of Indonesia spread in a wide arc, more than 5,000 kilometers long, from mainland Southeast Asia to Papua New Guinea. Dotted with volcanoes, covered with thick tropical vegetation and bright green rice fields, and surrounded by coral reefs, the Indonesian archipelago is one of the world's most beautiful places.

No one really knows how many islands there are in Indonesia. The most commonly offered figure is 13,677, with some 6,000 of these named and 1,000 inhabited. A more thorough recent survey, however, came up with 18,585—but at what season and tidal stage this count was taken has not been listed.

What can be said reliably is this: Indonesia is the largest archipelagic nation in the world, with more than 80,000 kilometers of coastline (more than any other nation) and 3.1 million square kilometers of territorial waters.

Indonesia is the world's fifth-largest country, with 181 million inhabitants. Most are Muslims, but there are significant Christian and Hindu minorities. Racially the majority of Indonesians are Malayo-Polynesian, with Chinese and Papuan minorities. The capital and largest city is Jakarta, in West Java.

The Indonesian language is a variant of Malay, which, in this nation of hundreds of languages, has long served as the lingua franca of trade.

Seafaring Empires

Indonesians refer to their country as *tanah air kita*—"our land and water"—and have always considered the seas as an integral part of their country. The ancestors of the great majority of Indonesians—the Austronesians—arrived in the archipelago by boat. The invention of the outriggered canoe some 5,000 years ago was as essential a development to seafarers as the wheel was to land-locked people.

Spreading first from the Asian mainland to Taiwan, and then—about 3,000 B.C.—through the Philippines and into the larger islands of western Indonesia, the Austronesians brought with them rice and domesticated animals, and thrived on the rich volcanic soil of the Sunda Islands.

But seafaring skills were not forgotten. Starting in the 4th century, Indonesians from south Kalimantan (Borneo) sailed across the Indian Ocean to settle in uninhabited Madagascar, just off the coast of Africa.

The first great Indonesian empire, the Buddhist Srivijaya, was a maritime empire based around the port of Palembang in southeast Sumatra. The Srivijaya controlled the Straits of Malacca, the key to the crucial China–India trade route, from the 7th to the 13th centuries.

Influences from the Asian subcontinent continued to reach the archipelago, which became increasingly Indianized in culture and religion.

From A.D. 1294 to the 15th century, most of western Indonesia was controlled by the powerful East Java kingdom of Majapahit, the most famous of the archipelago's ancient kingdoms. Majapahit is thought to have exacted tribute from islands as far away as New Guinea.

Above: Many of Indonesia's 13,677 islands are graced with beautiful, palm-lined beaches. This is the south coast of Bali.

Overleaf: A porcelain crab, Neopetrolisthes ohshimai, in Merten's carpet anemone, Stichodactyla mertensii. The porcelain crab is a shy filter-feeder that uses the stinging tentacles of the anemone for protection. Photo by Mike Severns.

Opposite: A black snapper, Macolor niger, and a cloud of peach anthias and lyretail anthias, Pseudanthias dispar and P. squammipinnis, at Mike's Point, on the northwest corner of Bunaken Island in Sulawesi. This site was named after the photographer. Photograph by Mike Severns.

Above: *A fisherman tries his luck off the dock at Ampenan, Lombok.*

Islam and the Europeans

Beginning in the mid–13th century, Indonesian traders and rulers began converting to Islam, for both political and religious reasons. The biggest boost to Islamization of the archipelago came with the conversion of the leader of Malacca, which sat in a very strategic position on the strait between Sumatra and peninsular Malaysia.

Most of these conversions were peaceful—the Sufi doctrine offering a theologically smooth transition for the Hinduized kingdoms—but Majapahit, past its prime, fell by force to the neighboring Islamic kingdom of Demak in the early 16th century.

This was also about the time the Portuguese, seeking spices, arrived in the archipelago, conquering Malacca in 1511. Soon after, the Spanish and English also sought Indonesia's valuable spices, but it was about a century later that Holland, newly independent of the Holy Roman Emperor in Spain, succeeded in controlling the market in cloves, nutmeg and pepper. During much of the 17th and 18th centuries, the Dutch East India Company held a virutal monopoly.

The company went broke in 1799, and in the 19th century, the Dutch concentrated their colonial efforts on Java, leading to a huge increase in the population of this island.

During World War II, the Japanese quickly swept through the Dutch Indies, evicted the colonialists in 1942. At the end of the war, Indonesian nationalist leaders declared independence —on August 17, 1945—but it took five more years to oust the Dutch. Irian Jaya, the western part of New Guinea, was transferred to Indonesia in the 1960s; the former Portuguese colony of East Timor was annexed in 1976.

Lush Islands

The "Ring of Fire" runs through Sumatra, Java, the Lesser Sundas, and then up through the Moluccas. These islands are marked by jagged volcanoes, and the rich, black soil that produces the great rice crops of Java and Bali. Some of the islands—for example, Timor, Seram and Biak—are formed of uplifted coral limestone. Here the soil is poor, and some areas—particularly parts of Timor—exhibit dry grassland that is more reminiscent of Australia than the tropics.

Two seasons of wind sweep through Indonesia each year. The northwest monsoon, usually starting (depending on the area) between late October and late November and ending between March and April, brings rain and wind. The southeast monsoon, with wind but much less rain, begins around late April to late May, and ends in early September. The *pancaroba*—between monsoons—brings generally calm seas and good weather, and falls just about everywhere in the archipelago in October and April.

The worst of the rainy season in most of Indonesia is in the months of December and January. The weather in the island province of Maluku is the most out of step with the rest of the country, and the worst comes in July and August. Some islands— such as Bali—have mountains that block the rains, creating a dry rain shadow in their lee.

Fantastic Diving and Kafkaesque Transport

Indonesia is the least known of the world's best dive locations. The introduction of scuba gear and the beginning of dive operations here are barely a decade old, and new locations are still being explored and opened, albeit slowly.

It will be many years before diving in Indonesia reaches its full potential, which has both great advantages and serious drawbacks. Experienced divers will be excited by the possibility of diving clear, rich waters without being surrounded by hordes of human beings. It is still very possible to dive areas where no one has yet gone. This will be a refreshing change from developed sites like the Caribbean, Hawaii, the Great Barrier Reef, the Maldives and the popular spots in the Pacific Islands.

In all of the huge Indonesian archipelago, containing 10–15 percent of the world's coral reefs, there are currently only eight locations with compressors and dive services, and one year-round live-aboard boat—the *Tropical Princess*—operating out of Biak, Irian Jaya.

The diving is excellent, inexpensive (averaging around $75 a day for two dives) and uncrowded. This does not come without a cost, however: the system of transportation in Indonesia is almost laughably unreliable, the quality of guides is variable, and the weather is often fickle.

Indonesia's Dive Sites

The sites listed below are the only ones in Indonesia as of this writing that have compressors, equipment and other facilities for diving. They appear here in the order they appear in this book, roughly west to east across the archipelago.

West Java. The Pulau-Pulau Seribu—"Thousand Islands"—dive area is quite close to the capital of Indonesia, Jakarta, and many efficient dive clubs provide all the necessary transportation and services to these islands. There is some interesting diving here, but in general coral and fish life is quite limited, and the visibility poor. The clubs will also take you diving off the islands around the famous Krakatau volcano, and off the Ujung Kulon

Above: *Although it makes a heroic effort to connect the archipelago's far-flung islands, Merpati Airlines is often the bane of travelers to Indonesia. Above is one of the airline's rugged Twin Otters in Wamena, in the highlands of Irian Jaya.*

Below: *A diver in the waters off Bali peers into a large barrel sponge, Xestospongia sp.*

HELMUT DEBELIUS / IKAN

Above: *Beautiful Bali cattle wander the rocky beach at Tulamben, Bali, probably the most popular dive site in Indonesia. These placid animals are a domesticated form of the wild cow or banten.*

Nature Reserve on the tip of southwest Java.

If your plans will take you through Jakarta, these dives might be worthwhile, but the diving is much better at points east. If you are coming all the way to Indonesia expressly to dive, your destination should not be Java.

Bali. Bali has more tourist services than anywhere else in Indonesia. It is a beautiful island, and the diving is excellent. There are many different sites here, from the clear water and steep walls of Menjangan to the famous Tulamben wreck to the 4-knot currents and cold water of Nusa Penida. The visibility is usually very good, and the fish and coral life is excellent. One caveat: almost 1 million tourists a year visited Bali at last count, and here is one of the few places where you might find a crowd.

Lombok. The only diving available on this island, just a cheap ferry ride or short flight from Bali, is on the Gilis, three tiny islands off Lombok's west coast. Gili Trawangan and Gili Air have quite good reefs, but even these are far from Indonesia's best. But the Gili islands have fine white beaches and a get-away-from-it-all kind of appeal, and the diving is just off-shore. While you can find luxury accommodations in Senggigi beach on the mainland, this is an hour's ride from the islands. Better to rough it at the small places

on the beach, with the young fris-bee-tossers and sunbathers.

Komodo Island and Labuhanbajo, Flores. The waters between Komodo Island (home of the fabled "dragon," a large monitor lizard) and Labuhanbajo, Flores is literally speckled with small islands ringed with coral. It is also swept by fierce, unpredictable currents. At the time of this writing, there were no "designated" dive spots, and since the compressor (and rental equipment) was still on order, we had to make do with oily air from the compressor used by pearl divers.

Although the compressor in Labuhanbajo should be up and running by the time you read this, do not expect any crowds. In fact, if you go alone, you will be lucky to find a buddy to dive with. Like any unexplored spot, the diving is variable. But it can be superb—witness the fact that internationally known underwater photographers Ron and Valerie Taylor have been coming here every year for 18 years.

Maumere, Flores. Maumere Bay offers a good range of dive locations, suitable for novice, intermediate or expert divers. The visibility is usually excellent. Although the organization had been pretty dismal in the past, during our last visit a new dive instructor had been hired and the owners were investing in new rental equipment and a fast dive boat (the best spots are the furthest). With these changes, Maumere should become a really top dive location. Australian photographer and Indonesian fish specialist Rudie Kuiter has been diving this area regularly for about half a decade. He says he has discovered new fish species on every visit.

Kupang, West Timor and Roti Island. This area provides the closest diving for North Australia–based divers. The marine life is plentiful, and the operators are very enthusiastic. About the only drawback is the visibility, which is poor to just fair by Indonesian standards: 6–12 meters. (According to Australian divers, however, this is still much better than around Darwin.)

Manado, North Sulawesi. The steep coral walls ringing the islands off Manado are some of the very best in the world. The visibility is very good, and the variety of marine life is absolutely superb. The area was pioneered a decade ago by Loky Herlambang, and several operators have since joined him here. Some of the dive operators could use more reliable dive boats, and English-speaking dive masters with international certification.

Ambon. Dive operations in Ambon and the Lease Islands were just beginning in mid 1991. The diving here is very good, however, and there will be no crowds at all. Nor will there be any instructors or guides with certification. New sites here are just waiting to be discovered.

Banda Islands. The Banda Islands are a tiny group rising incongruously out of the middle of the wide Banda Sea—the Hawaii of Indonesia. Some of the dive sites here are fantastic, and large pelagics are commonly seen. English is widely spoken, but there is no one around with any formal dive training. The real problem is getting to these beautiful islands, however. They are really out of the way, and the bottleneck is the final leg on a small plane from Ambon. This flight has a 10-kilo weight limit for baggage (although this is often increased) and leaves—in theory—three times a week. There are no crowds in Banda.

Biak and vicinity. The only diving currently available around Biak, an island off the north of New Guinea that was the site of a famous World War II battle, is off a live-aboard dive boat, the *Tropical Princess*. This takes divers to some small coral islands off Biak, and then in a large circle west and north of the island to the Ayu and Mapia atolls. Packages for the *Tropical Princess* are currently available only for Japan- or U.S.-based divers. At U.S. $250 a day, you certainly get your money's worth, but this is about

Below: *A school of pennant bannerfish,* Heniochus diphreutes. *Swarms of these beautiful butterflyfish are a common sight on Indonesian reefs.*

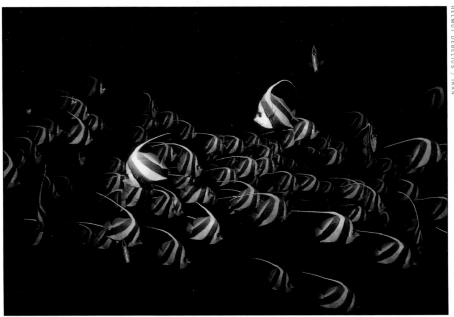

three times the average cost of diving in Indonesia. Still, the very best dives we have ever experienced were off the *Tropical Princess* in the Mapia atoll area.

Exploratory dives

In addition to the few locations in Indonesia where compressors, tanks, weights and guides are available, dozens of others have been prospected, and await investment to be opened. To this list, add hundreds of sites—a few "discovered" but most unexplored—accessible only by liveaboard dive ships, or a chartered craft with a compressor.

Live-aboards are the obvious solution to diving in Indonesia, with its thousands of islands and huge area. But the business has only barely begun. Other than the *Tropical Princess,* P&O Spice Island Cruises also offers diving from two boats that tour the islands of Nusa Tenggara. These are not dedicated dive boats, however, and diving is an extra to their normal cruises. You can, however, join up with one of the *Spice Islander'*s occasional special diving trips.

You can also simply charter a large enough boat, and head off to a location of your own choosing. The problem, of course, is finding a compressor. This may be possible in Bali, however, which would open up locations such as the Kangean Islands, Taka Bone Rate and the Bonerate group. This is territory for real explorers, and if you have the time, patience, and self-sufficiency, this could provide a once-in-a-lifetime experience.

Another way to get access to a compressor is to accompany pearl divers, or to pay them to take a day off and take you out diving. This, while a very romantic experience, and a way to get access to really out-of-the-way places—like Bobale, off the east coast of Halmahera Island's north peninsula, or Lembata, off

eastern Flores—is also fraught with problems.

Pearl divers are working men, and they dive where they can find pearl shells, not where there is good visibility, fish life and reefs. And they are not paid to gawk at every lionfish that swims by. Further, their equipment is used every day, and (apparently) never maintained. The compressors are lubricated with motor oil, and a dive with one of these tanks of "air" can leave you with a major headache, and feeling like you've been breathing from the tailpipe of a Mexico City bus.

Scuba Guides: Variable

Dive services and guides in Indonesia are, to be polite, "variable." Most of these guides have spent more time underwater than their customers, accumulating thousands of dives, and are excellent scuba divers. But this does not make them good guides. They fall short in emergency training and organization.

It best to dive with the foreknowledge that you probably can not expect any help from your guide. Many guides may even have had some theoretical training in emergency procedures. But we have only rarely seen as much as a first-aid kit in any of the local dive boats. Do not expect this man to rescue you if you get into trouble.

This is not much of a problem for well-trained, experienced divers, particularly those who are traveling as a group. In fact, if you fall into this category, Indonesia is going to be a paradise for diving—no crowds, virgin reefs, and a lot of bang for your buck in terms of underwater time.

Beginners, on the other hand, are advised to use extreme caution—especially those who take a resort course after arrival here. Indonesian certification is administered by POSSI, which although under the auspices of the Paris-based CMAS—Confederation Mondiale des Activites Subaquatiques, is not as rigorous or as well-organized as the American or European agencies.

Many of the resort course instructors are not even certified by POSSI. Instructors' command of English is usually incomplete and safety procedures are often neglected. Being "certified" in Indonesia does not make you a competent diver. If a resort course here is your only diving experience, stick to the easy locations, and be very particular in choosing a guide.

In all cases be extremely wary of rental gear. This equipment is very expensive to buy with Indonesian rupiahs, and operators use it to within an inch of its life. If maintenance were regularly scheduled and carried out properly, this wouldn't be a problem. But spare parts are expensive and very hard to get here, and training in repair and diagnostics of dive equipment is basically non-existent.

In most places, dive guides and assistants will ready your gear for you, but we suggest you do this yourself. If you are in the habit of just looking at the pressure gauge to make sure you have a good fill, you better change your way of thinking in Indonesia. Test *everything,* regulator, gauges, BC valves and straps. You should infer from this advice that we highly recommend you bring your own gear.

Indonesia is not the place to push your limits as a diver. We strongly discourage dives below 30 meters, especially if decompression stops are required. Take your dive tables (better yet, a computer) and follow them scrupulously. Don't even think about a decompression chambers being available—they are too few and too far away.

Dive-tour operators, particularly in Europe, are reluctant to send their clients to Indonesia

because of the poor training of local guides. This situation will be remedied only when more dive guides receive adequate instruction in dive planning, emergency procedures and language skills.

Transportation: Kafkaesque

Marine tourism in Indonesia is also stalled by the archipelago's transportation infrastructure. Bali and Java are easy to get to, and so, at least for U.S.-based divers, is Biak (despite its far-off location) because of the regular Los Angeles–Honolulu–Biak–Bali–Jakarta flight.

But particularly at the height of the tourist seasons, July–August and December–January, travel to Maumere, Manado, Banda, and other points in eastern Indonesia can be an exercise in frustration. Delays, overbooked flights, and broken com-

Above: *Since most of the Indonesian dive sites are the steep outer walls of fringing reefs, access is usually just a matter of a short ride by outboard-powered canoe. This is the fringing reef off Bunaken Island in northern Sulawesi.*

puters will make a mess of your schedule. The guilty airport is Ujung Pandang in South Sulawesi. This is the main hub to eastern Indonesia, but too few planes fly to and from Bali.

The scene at the ticket counters of the Indonesian monopoly airlines—Garuda and Merpati—often produces a strange mix of Kafkaesque angst and hilarity (unless you are the suffering party). Frustrated Frenchmen, refusing to speak English and forgetting *fraternité,* brandish Paris-issued confirmations, expecting them to be honored here. Dutch-Ambonese boys in the country of their birth, looking very foreign in long hair and earrings, stand puzzled and mute, unable to speak either enough English or enough Indonesian to be understood. The employees, stolid, with glazed eyes, silently take the abuse that somebody else well deserves.

It's not always this bad. Things are better in the off-peak months, and even during the middle of the tourist rush, only perhaps 25 percent of the confirmed passengers have problems. The basic problem is that Merpati—the internal carrier—has too few airplanes, lacks organization, and owns a computer reservation system that is, in fact, often worse than useless.

Start with the obvious—it can't hurt. Ask the travel agent with whom you made your original booking if the company has a local correspondent. Many have agents in Bali who can re-check confirmations. Even before you arrive, try to obtain something tangible from this agent and/or Merpati airlines, such as a fax or telex showing your confirmed dates. As soon as you get to Bali, re-check your bookings.

As soon as you make it to your destination, confirm your return booking. The dive resorts and many hotels are quite efficient at doing this—they will usually ask you for your plane details right away—but still make sure that it's been done.

If you do all this, it's likely—but not guaranteed—that things will work out as planned. But, just in case, keep some flexibility in your schedule in case there is a day or two of delay. If you have to sit in Bali for a day or two, there are plenty of good day-trips for diving. Unless you are traveling in a large group, go to the airport and try to get on your desired flight, even if you have been told that it's full. We've been on many of these over-booked flights where half or more of the seats are empty.

If you don't get a seat on the plane, forget about lodging an official complaint, getting mad, or punching somebody. If you throw a fit, you will provide a great deal of entertainment to the people waiting around the counter, but such unsavory behavior will inevitably lead to more delays. Sometimes—but not always—it might help to offer to pay "something extra" to get on your flight. It is not unknown that even someone with a confirmed reservation has been "bumped" due to a shady deal.

Are all these potential hassles worth it? You bet. Chances are you won't have problems. We just wanted to warn you—not scare you away. Remember: the diving is great out there. If you can schedule your visit from April through June, or September through early November, planes will be less crowded and everything will be much easier.

When planning your visit, don't try to visit too many places. If you have a week, go just to one place. Otherwise, you can spend much of your precious vacation time contending with the difficulties mentioned above. Add a week for every subsequent location—two days traveling (one there, one back) and five days diving.

Coral Growth and the Formation of Reefs

Diving over a tropical coral reef has been compared to stepping into a time machine. You find yourself in a strange place, 10 million years out of synch with the land. The reef is a reminder of a time when all the life on earth existed in shallow, tropical seas, the original soup of creation.

The myriad fish and invertebrates that shelter among and encrust the rugged surfaces provided by the clumps, shelves and branches of coral are overwhelming in their numbers, shapes and colors. Nowhere else is there such a diversity of animal forms.

Crystal clear tropical water is nutrient poor, an aquatic desert. The strange and varied forms of the members of coral reef communities allow each to fill a niche in a complex nutrient cycle, beginning with the fixing of nutrients by the photosynthesis of algae, and working up to the barracuda that snatches an aging fish from the school. The ammonia and feces secreted by the predator are cycled right back into the reef ecosystem.

Over half a billion years, when the first primitive coral reefs first formed, this community has made a remarkable geological impact. The stony coral skeletons become overgrown and compacted into rock, eventually building up a prodigious thickness of limestone. When forced upward by the buckling of the earth's crust, this old reef rock forms islands.

Distribution of Coral Reefs

Reef-building corals require large amounts of sunlight, and thus are only found in the trop-ics, and even there only in shallow water. The effective limit of coral growth is usually given as 100 meters, although in Indonesia the coral usually stops at half this depth. Corals, even hard corals, are found as deep as 6,000 meters, but these grow slowly and do not form the diverse communities of tropical coral reefs.

The Indo-Pacific region, centered around the islands of Indonesia, harbors most of the world's coral reefs. Of the total area covered by coral reefs, 55 percent is in southeastern continental Asia, Indonesia, the Philip-

Below: *The presence of large gorgonians, crinoids and schools of planktivores like these anthias indicates plankton-rich waters, which can provide a spectacular concentration of marine life. Mike's Point, Bunaken Island, Sulawesi.*

MIKE SEVERNS

pines, North Australia and the Pacific islands; 30 percent is in the Indian Ocean and the Red Sea; 14 percent is in the Caribbean; and 1 percent is in the North Atlantic.

Reef-building corals grow only in water from 18°C (65°F) to 33°C (91°F). And the extremes of this range can only be tolerated for very short periods.

This explains why reefs are generally found only on the eastern coasts of large continents. The wind patterns caused by the rotation of the earth create currents that bring an upwelling of cold water (14°C [57°F]) from the depths at least part of the year to the western coasts of the Americas, Europe and Africa. Thus the Indian Ocean side of Africa has extensive reefs, and the Atlantic side almost none.

No cold currents flow through Indonesia, but even temporary rises in sea temperatures can devastate reefs. In 1983 sea temperatures around the Pulau Seribu islands off western Java rose to 33°C (91°F), killing much of the shallow reef coral there. Fortunately most of the coral has recovered.

Turbid waters, those carrying a great deal of suspended sediment, deter reef formation. This is a very important in South and Southeast Asia, where rivers dump 70 percent of all sediments delivered to the ocean worldwide. (The Ganges is the champion, carrying almost 1.7 billion tons a year to the Bay of Bengal.) In Indonesia, the larger rivers in Kalimantan and Sumatra produce enough sediment to discourage reef formation a significant distance from their mouths.

The Biology of Corals

True reef-building or hermatypic corals are animals grouped in the phylum Cnidaria, order Scleractinia. They all have an indispensable symbiotic relationship with dinoflagellate algae called zoox-anthellae. ("Zooxanthellae and Corals," opposite.) These algae are essential for respiration and nutrient uptake, and the vigorous deposition of calcium.

Coral skeletons are made of aragonite, a very soluble form of calcium carbonate. The material is actually secreted as a way of disposing of a waste product—excess ionic calcium.

Grazing and predation of fish and invertebrates causes portions of the coral skeletons to die, and these are immediately encrusted with algae, sponges, soft corals, or any of a myriad forms of small invertebrates. Over time, these too are grazed, silted over by coral sand, or outcompeted by other organisms, and their remains become part of another compacted layer.

The lithification of coral rock is not well understood, but a fine-grained carbonate cement seems to form in the pores of the old coral, turning it into dense coral rock. This is thought perhaps to result from bacterial action.

The buildup of limestone on the reef is not a simple process of accumulation. It is a cycle just like the nutrient cycle. Scientists studying a 7-hectare reef in the Caribbean measured an annual production of 206 tons of calcium carbonate; they also measured an annual loss of 123 tons. The greatest part of this erosion was produced by boring sponges, and the rest by grazing fishes and echinoderms.

Not all the limestone produced is created by corals, either. In some areas, particularly where there is very strong wave action, calcareous algaes are the primary producers of carbonate, forming algal ridges at the outer edge of the reef.

Coral Reef Architecture

Coral reefs are generally defined as falling into three main types: fringing reefs, barrier reefs and atolls. In a sense, these types also

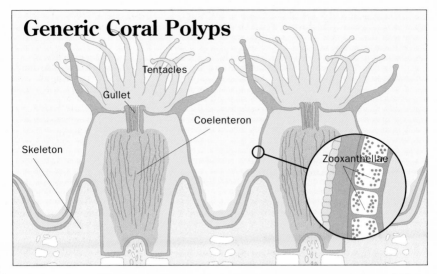

Generic Coral Polyps

Tentacles

Gullet

Coelenteron

Skeleton

Zooxanthellae

Zooxanthellae and Corals

Reef-building corals have evolved an indispensable, symbiotic relationship with a type of yellow-brown algae called zooxanthellae, which is "farmed" in the tissues of the coral polyp. The relationship is mutually beneficial: the coral receives oxygen and nutrients, and the algae receives carbon dioxide and "fertilizer" in the form of animal waste.

The presence of zooxanthellae is so important to the health of the coral that scientists speculate the symbiotic algae must have been present in the polyp tissue almost throughout coral's 50–100 million years of evolution.

The zooxanthellae alga has been dubbed *Symbiodinium microadriaticum,* part of a "supergenus" of marine dinoflagellate algas, but recent research suggests there are more than one species. These algas are dinoflagellates, which have whip-like processes giving them some limited ability to move. This is probably how the cells initially enter the corals, although once they are there they divide vegetatively, and take on a simpler structural form.

Corals are not the only reef animals to have zooxanthellae. Sea anemones and other coelenterates host the algae, as do some molluscs, most famously the giant clams (*Tridacna* spp.). Because zooxan-

thellae is a brown algae, and the host tissues are generally colorless—to pass the greatest amount of light to the algae— zooxanthellae-containing animals are usually a dull color: beige, brown, olive green. There are exceptions, however, including some of the giant anemones and *Tridacna* clams, which can be richly hued. As a general rule, however, brightly colored invertebrates—such as some of the soft corals—do not harbor zooxanthellae.

Coral nutrition

Corals derive their food energy from three sources: plankton captured by their tentacles, organic nutrients absorbed directly from the water, and organic compounds provided by the zooxanthellae. For the reef-building corals, the latter is by far the most important.

In the presence of sunlight, the zooxanthellae produce oxygen and photosynthetically fix nutrients—glycerol, glucose and amino acids—which are "leaked" to the surrounding tissues of the coral polyp. The raw materials for this process are the waste products of the coral animal: carbon dioxide, ammonia, nitrates and phosphates. It is a very efficient, almost self-sustaining partnership.

— *David Pickell*

form a historical progression. As a fringing reef grows outward, a boat channel forms behind. As the reef widens, the boat channel becomes a lagoon, and the fringing reef graduates to a barrier reef. If the fringing reef began around an island, and the island subsequently sinks or the sea level rises, the final result is an atoll, a near circular reef surrounding a central lagoon.

These are not the only forms, and scientists studying reef topography offer many more types. For example, bank reefs, reefs that grow up more or less in patches in open water where the depths are relatively shallow, are an important type in the Coral Sea off Australia. These reefs often form at the edge of undersea plates, and appear when geologic activity causes an uplifting of the bottom. If the bottom is pushed up high enough that sunlight can reach it, a bank reef will form.

Fringing reefs. Most of the reefs a diver will be exploring in Indonesia are fringing reefs, coral formations that grow right up to the edge of an island.

These reefs can take many forms. The steep coral walls for which Indonesian diving is famous are fringing reefs, with sometimes just a few meters of reef flat, and a reef edge that has an almost vertical slope.

Walls, or drop-offs, fascinate divers because these are where deeper dwelling animals come closest to the surface. Semi-precious black coral (*Antipathes* sp.) usually grows far below sport diving depths, but on Indonesian walls can be found at 30 meters. Some of the deep-dwelling dwarf angelfish (*Centropyge* spp.), damsels, and anthias (e.g., *Pseudanthias pleurotaenia*) can be found at comfortable depths only along steep drop-offs.

Generally, a fringing reef consists of a reef edge of stout corals, which absorb the brunt of the waves and current; a reef flat, a shallow area exposed at the lowest spring tide; and perhaps a boat channel or back reef, deeper than the reef flat and quite calm.

The reef edge, and the fore-reef area towards the open sea, are the most rewarding areas for the diver. Here the current is

Below: *On the steep walls of Indonesian reefs, normally deep-dwelling species can be seen at relatively shallow depths. This is a male pink-square anthias,* Pseudanthias pleurotaenia.

strong, bringing plankton and fresh water from the open sea. Here also is where divers will see larger reef fish, and occasional pelagic visitors to the reef. Sometimes the reef edge is indistinct, marked by pinnacles or other formations. And sometimes the area just back of the reef edge will not immediately become part of the reef flat, but instead, protected from the full force of the current, will be rich in more delicate corals and animals.

The reef flat is shallow, and usually light brown with sediment. This is an area of coral sand and detritus, with small boulders of hardy massive corals and clusters of branching *Acropora* coral, growing in pools. Usually there are fewer than a handful of very hardy coral species on the reef flat.

Most divers will walk or wade across this area (wearing an old pair of sneakers, of course) without even looking down. Here there are echinoderms—particularly brittle stars, which sometimes occur in great numbers—small fish, molluscs and soft algaes. Sometimes there will be meadows of the calcareous alga *Halimeda*.

The back reef or boat channel is a deeper area, between the reef flat and the shore. Although often deep enough for swimming, the coral growth here is poor because of sediment run-off from the shore. Resistant *Porites, Acropora* or *Goniastrea* grow in the boat channel in patches. Further inland, there may be beds of turtle grass, a rich habitat for juvenile fishes and many crustaceans.

Barrier reefs. The most famous barrier reefs are the Great Barrier Reef off Queensland, Australia, which is 2,000 kilometers long and 150 kilometers wide, and the large barrier reef off the coast of Belize in the Gulf of Honduras. A barrier reef is a fringing reef where the back

Trepang drying on a dock in Pagimana, Sulawesi

Trepang Fishing

The lowly sea cucumber, a lumbering, inoffensive detritus feeder, hardly looks like something you would want to touch, much less eat. But this homely animal is the target of small-scale fishermen all over Indonesia, and for many it serves as a major source of cash income.

Plucked from the shallow reefs of Indonesia, the sea cucumbers are dried, cleaned and sold in small lots to local businessmen, who ship them to Ujung Pandang, the center of the trade. There they are graded, and sold to the Asian market where this trepang becomes the key ingredient in a Chinese soup.

Most of the collectors are young boys. Wearing homemade goggles made of circles of glass fitted with pitch into carved sections of bamboo, the trepang collectors scan the shallows for their foot-long quarry.

Although the animals are not dangerous, they have an irritating tendency to eject their Cuvierian tubules—long, sticky white strands—when disturbed. Collectors invariably get this goo all over their hands.

Some 30 species of sea cucumber (*Holothuria* spp.) are collected. The inferior, small black ones are sold to the Chinese market, where they fetch up to $2.40 a kilo for the wholesalers in Ujung Pandang. The real prize, however, is *H. aculeata,* fat and whitish when dried. These are saved for the more lucrative Hong Kong market, where they sell for up to $17/kilo wholesale.

Trepang, a Malay word, is also called bêche-de-mer, a pseudo-French word derived from an old English word, derived from the Portuguese *bicho do mar,* "sea worm." The original Latin, however, is more evocative: "little sea beast."
— *David Pickell*

The Biak Fish Bomb Industry

Fish bombing and dynamite fishing are unfortunately widespread in Indonesia. The practice began in earnest after World War II, as wartime construction brought dynamite to Indonesia, the Philippines, and the Pacific Islands. In Indonesia, a flourishing cottage industry has developed to remove the cordite from surplus Allied shells—dumped in the sea at war's end—and distribute it to markets across the archipelago for fish bombs.

Fish bombing is a simple process. A likely spot is located and staked out by a fisherman. A small bomb, usually powder packed into a beer bottle, is stuffed into a cored papaya and thrown overboard. After the explosion, the stunned

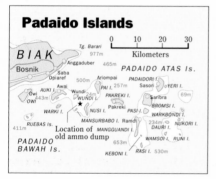

Padaido Islands

and killed fish are scooped up with nets as fast as possible. The papaya helps the bomb sink and muffles the blast; one doesn't want any unsolicited "helpers" when the fish start floating upward.

To a fisherman, who works a long, hard day to bring a few fish to market, the appeal of bombing is obvious. Unfortunately, the impact on the reef is disastrous. Not all the dead fish float, of course, and method is very wasteful. But the most damage is caused by the destruction of the coral by the blast. Fish will essentially reproduce to fill the environment. Coral *is* the environment.

Flourishing Cottage Industry

According to a report by Stephen Nash of the World Wildlife Fund, an old Allied ammo dump in the Padaido Islands has been the source of a cottage industry

supplying the fish bombs used in Biak and the Cenderawasih Bay, and may supply powder to markets as far away as western Indonesia. The report was written several years ago, and at the time the supply of easily-found shells was running out. But the author feared that scuba gear, brought to Biak to equip collectors of tropical marine fish, would make accessible new supplies of bombs.

The Padaido islanders are masters of the very delicate art of live bomb recovery. The shells are found by dragging the sandy bottom with a piece of iron tied to a rope. When it is felt to hit something hard, a diver puts on goggles and dives to the bottom—18 meters—ties the bomb to the rope, and returns to the surface. Then the bomb is hauled up. Once on land, the bomb is carefully opened, and the priming mixture and cordite are extracted for packaging and sale.

The trickiest part of building the fish bombs is constructing the fuse, which is made of the flat, malleable aluminum from a tube of toothpaste. Priming mixture is "diluted" with crushed matchheads and the aluminum sheet is rolled around it like a cigaret. The aluminum makes the fuse waterproof; heat and combustion gases keep the water from rushing in the open end. Different lengths of this waterproof fuse are used depending on how deep the fisherman wants the bomb to go before exploding.

The fuse is attached to a standard beer bottle—or a large ale bottle, or a small medicine bottle—with coconut husk rope and pitch. The whole package is stuffed into a papaya, and thrown overboard. According to the report, fish bombers off the south coast of Biak near the airport time their bombs with the noisy arrival of the Garuda flight, which effectively masks the explosion.

Despite the devastating effect the practice has on the reefs, Nash could not help praising the cleverness of the Padaido entrepreneurs: "This is a terribly warped but remarkably sophisticated appropriate technology!"

— *David Pickell*

reef or boat channel has become a large lagoon. In the case of the Great Barrier Reef, this "lagoon" is in places 100 kilometers wide.

A barrier reef that forms around an island is sometimes called an "almost atoll." There can be multiple barrier reefs, extending outward like ripples, and the large lagoon behind a barrier reef can harbor small patch reefs and sandy cay reefs.

Atolls. Some 425 of these characteristic circular reefs, with a large central lagoon, have been recorded throughout the tropics. The vast majority (more than 300) are in the Indo-Pacific. The largest is Kwajalein in the Marshall Islands, which forms an oval 120 by 32 kilometers.

The largest atoll in Indonesia—and the third-largest in the world, just 20 percent smaller than Kwajalein—is Taka Bone Rate, in the Flores Sea south of Sulawesi. Taka Bone Rate (called Tijger in older texts) stretches 72 by 36 kilometers, covers 2,220 square kilometers, and includes 22 sandy islands. (See map page 178.) "Taka" is a generic term for atoll or bank reef in Indonesian.

The lagoon of an atoll, because it is so thoroughly cut off from the open ocean, forms a unique environment, and is often much richer in life than the lagoon side of, say, a small barrier reef. The level of organic matter in the water inside the atoll's lagoon is considerable higher than outside, allowing it to support as much as 10 times the biomass as the outer reef edge. And, because it is not adjacent to a large land mass, problems caused by of run-off and turbidity are eliminated.

The richness of the lagoon water is thought to be the result of deep ocean water percolating through the walls of the basement structure of the reef, bringing with it nutrients that previously had been locked away in geological storage.

KAL MULLER

The Formation of Reefs

Darwin's theory. British naturalist Charles Darwin first published his theory of coral reef formation in 1842, and it is still the dominant theory today. Darwin, investigating atolls in the South Pacific, suggested that a fringing reef around the edges of an island would gradually grow outward, leaving a lagoon in its wake, and evolving into a barrier reef. If the island, over geological time, subsided, then what would be left would be an atoll:

"Now, as the island sinks down, either a few feet at a time or quite insensibly, we may safely infer from what we know of the conditions favourable to the growth of coral, that the living masses bathed by the surf on the margin of the reef, will soon regain the surface...

"Let the island continue sinking, and the coral-reef will continue growing up its own foundation, whilst the water gains inch by inch on the land, until the last and highest pinnacle is covered, and there remains a perfect atoll." (See diagram at right.)

This, like natural selection, was pure speculation on Darwin's part. Atoll-formation was a phenomenon of history, and not something that he could "prove" with 19th century technologies. In fact, it was not until the 1950s, when the U.S. Geologic Survey conducted an extensive drilling

Above: *In the clear waters of Indonesian reefs, ultraviolet radiation can penetrate several meters underwater. Pigments made up of amino acids shield the delicate growing tips of shallow-water corals such as this* Acropora *sp.*

Step 1. *A fringing reef forms around an island*

Step 2. *The island sinks, and the fringing reef grows into a barrier reef.*

Step 3. *The island sinks below the surface, and only an atoll remains. (After Darwin, 1842)*

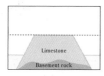

Step 1. *Limestone is exposed by geological forces.*

Step 2. *Rainfall erodes exposed limestone*

Step 3. *Water level rises, and eroded limestone is colonized by coral. (After Purdy, 1974)*

Below: *The emperor angelfish,* Pomacanthus imperator.

program on Pacific atolls, that Darwin's theory was confirmed: deep down, below the layer of coral in the atoll lagoons, the core samples revealed the volcanic rock of a former island.

However, this still did not explain the mechanism for Darwin's "subsistence" of the island. We now know, for example, that the Ice Ages, by locking up much of the earth's water into ice, brought about large changes in the level of the earth's oceans. At the peak of the last Ice Age, 18,000 years ago, the sea level stood almost 100 meters lower than it does today. In some cases, particularly in Indonesia, it has probably been the rising of the oceans and not the sinking of the island that has created atolls.

Karstic saucers. Darwin's is not the only theory of reef formation, and there are some areas where geological evidence does not accord well with his speculations. A newer explanation has been offered, called the karstic saucer theory. "Karst" is the name given to the formations caused by the action of rainwater on exposed limestone—caves, sinkholes and underground channels. (The name comes from the type region around the Dinaric Alps, near the Adriatic coast of Yugoslavia.)

This theory proposes that an area of exposed limestone, acted upon by the weak carbonic acid produced by rainfall, would take the shapes Darwin's theory attributes to reef growth. When the water level subsequently rose, corals would colonize the already shaped and eroded limestone. (See illustration at left.)

One of the great appeals of this theory to scientists is that it can be tested in the laboratory. Weak acid applied to a flat-topped block of calcareous rock will tend to erode it into the shape of a saucer, the acid acting to a greater degree in the center than at the edges.

Products from the Sea

Indonesians have always been sea-farers, and for an archipelagic nation, the ocean is still its greatest resource. Fish provide the main source of protein to Indonesia's 1.8 million people. The waters off Indonesia are

thought to be able to support a fishing industry of 5 million tons a year, with actual catches just 20 percent of this.

Commercially valuable sea products also provide some cash to people living on sandy islands with little or no resources, save perhaps copra from coconuts. Ujung Pandang, the capital of Sulawesi, is the Indonesian leader in the export of sea products, shipping 2,100 tons in 1981. (Surabaya, Java, the next largest exporter, shipped 300 tons the same year.) These included pearl oysters (740 tons), mother-of-pearl or *Trochus* shells (820 tons), other shells (220 tons) and dried sea cucumbers (320 tons). The sea cucumbers, or trepang, are used in Chinese soup. (See "Trepang Fishing," page 27.)

Although collecting these animals provides necessary income to the islanders, over-harvesting by itinerant Bugis and Bajo fishermen has all but wiped out certain species in some areas. Particularly hard-hit are the giant clams (*Tridacna* spp.). The meat is canned and then sold at considerable prices in places like Taiwan, and the shells are made into floor tiles in factories in Surabaya, Java. These clams used to grow in huge "fields" in the reefs of eastern Indonesia. You can now dive in areas and not see a single one.

Triton shells (*Charonia tritonis*), helmet conchs (*Casis cornuta*) and turban shells (*Turbo marmoratus*), which are sold as trinkets, have also disappeared from some areas.

Future of Coral Reefs

Although Indonesia has some of the most untouched coral reefs in the world, even in the remote parts of the archipelago, where industrialization has not yet reached, the reefs are not free of danger. According to officials of the World Wildlife Fund in Irian Jaya, the Indonesian half of the

island of New Guinea, it is the reefs, and not the great forests of that island, that are most at risk.

Even the fastest-growing corals can add new growth only at the rate of 3–4 centimeters a year; and, much like the rain forests, reefs are subject to succession. A diverse, well-populated reef does not just spring from the sandy bottom. Once a reef is wiped out, unprotected wave action and current may prevent regrowth from taking place.

In the more developed areas of Indonesia, dredging of channels, harvesting of coral for construction materials, and filling of estuarial waters has had a devastating impact on the reefs. The Bay of Ambon, in the central Moluccas, once had a reef that moved naturalist Alfred Russel Wallace to write: "There is perhaps no spot in the world richer

Above: *Giant clams like this* Tridacna gigas *were once common on Indonesian reefs. But a market for the canned meat in Asia, and the use of giant clam shells in making terazzo in Surabaya, Java have decimated the population in many areas. This large specimen is still alive and well on a reef off Gili Trawangan, Lombok.*

in marine productions, corals, shells and fishes, than the harbour of Amboyna." During the post-war building boom, the coral was dragged up for building material in Ambon town. Today, the bay is a wasteland.

Also damaging is the continuing practice of fish bombing, in which small powder charges are thrown overboard to stun fish so they can be easily captured for market. (See "The Biak Fish Bomb Industry," page 28). The bombs don't just kill the fish. They create lifeless craters in the reef, deserts where all the coral and the life it supported have been destroyed. In some places this practice has reduced all the nearshore reef to barren rubble.

In the long run, however, the greatest damage to reefs will probably be a result of bad land use: poor farming practices, including overgrazing, public works projects that expose the thin tropical soil to erosion, and deforestation through timbering.

These practices increase runoff and erosion, loading rivers up with silt, which is then carried out to sea. Silt chokes off coral growth, and leads to eutrophication, a great increase in nutrients in the water. This, in turn, causes an algae bloom, which robs the water of oxygen and forms a lethal mat over the coral.

Divers in Indonesia also have a responsibility to keep the country's reefs, many of which truly are in pristine condition, in a continued state of health. This means taking no souvenirs, developing good diving habits so as not to break off or damage fragile corals, and not harassing larger animals like sea turtles.

In many places diving programs are rudimentary, and the guides are not educated in reef conservation. I have been served fresh giant clam after a dive by a guide who took the animal while diving on an Indonesian reef that was a protected marine reserve. He couldn't at first understand why we were upset. As visitors—and customers—divers are in an excellent position to help dive operators develop good conservation habits. I think we owe it to the people and reefs of Indonesia to do at least this much.

— *David Pickell*

Below: *A gorgonian goby (*Bryaninops sp.) *on an antipatharian wire coral. This little animal is no more than 4 centimeters long. Many fishes rely on invetebrates for food, shelter, and protection, but few are as particular as the gorgonian gobies. Some species of* Bryaninops *live and lay their eggs on only a single species of gorgonian or antipatharian.*

Fascinating Inhabitants of Indonesia's Reefs

The waters surrounding the islands of Indonesia form the richest marine habitat on earth. Indonesia lies at the epicenter of species diversity for the entire tropical Indo-Pacific region, which stretches from Madagascar and the Comores islands in the west to the easternmost of the Pacific islands—a vast 12,000-mile sweep through the Indian and Pacific Oceans.

Perhaps 3,000 species of fish, and several hundred species of coral populate the reefs off the larger Indonesian islands. A Dutch ichthyologist cataloged 780 species of marine fish just in Ambon Bay alone, almost as many as can be found in all the rivers, lakes and seas of Europe. (Alas, this reef has been destroyed, dredged after World War II to provide building materials for booming Ambon town). Even the healthiest Caribbean reef has just 10–20 percent of the species diversity of a comparable Indonesian reef.

The islands that now make up Indonesia are likely to have been the genetic "source" of Indo-Pacific marine life. This region has remained tropical for 100 million years, exposed to the strong sunlight that makes tropical waters so much richer than temperate waters, giving the animals a long time to diversify.

Although ocean currents distribute fish widely, the further across the Pacific one goes from Indonesia, the fewer species will be found. For example, 123 species of damselfish are found in Indonesia.* (see note at right.) In the Philippines, 118. In Papua New Guinea, 100. In Fiji, 60. In the Society Islands, 30. In the

Galapagos, just 18. The entire Caribbean holds just 16 species.

One million years ago the Ice Ages began, periodically tying up much of the earth's water in ice. This lowered sea levels by as much as 130 meters, reducing the tropical Atlantic to a small refuge in the south Caribbean, decimating the animal population. The Indo-Pacific never suffered such an extinction.

But volcanism and continental drift caused similar disruptions in Indonesia, and it is probably because the islands provide such a wide variety of habitats—deep sea trenches, rocky shores, sand and mud flats, sea grass beds, mangrove swamps and, of course, coral reefs—that the fauna here is so diverse.

While muddy turtle grass beds, mangrove swamps and estuarial waters are of immense interest to the biologist, divers usually find little in these shallow, turbid waters to hold their attention. When divers talk about tropical water diving, they mean coral reefs.

A Compendium of Reef Life

There are so many species present on the Indonesian reefs that even specialists can not give an exact tally of their numbers here. With this in mind, the aim of this chapter is to provide an introduction to the major groups of animals that will be seen when diving on Indonesian reefs. No attempt at comprehensive coverage is made.

Algae

Although people often mistakenly think of many of the reef animals—corals, gorgonians, sea

Above: *A long-nosed hawkfish,* Oxycirrhites typus, *sitting among the lacy gorgonians encrusting a wreck, just off Molas beach near Manado, Sulawesi.*

Australia, chiefly because due to its location it includes both tropical and colder-water habitats, hosts the most damselfish species, 132.

Above: *Turtle grass,* Thalassia *sp., is one of the very few true marine plants. Although not found on reefs, back-reef areas may have beds of turtle grass, which nourish crustaceans and juvenile fishes as well as the green turtle.*

Below: *The marine algas* Udotea *(top) and* Halimeda *can both be occasionally found on the reef.* Udotea *is only lightly calicified, but the calcium carbonate disks of* Halimeda *are in some areas a major component of the reef substrate.*

"anemones"—as plants, what is perhaps most striking about the coral reef is the apparent lack of plant life. Other rich coastal marine environments, for example the kelp forests off California or the sea-grass beds and mangrove swamps off some of the Indonesian islands, are obviously based on the photosynthetic production of oxygen and nutrient-fixing by algae or higher plants.

On the reef, however, despite its teeming life, plants seem absent. In fact, plants are the primary producers on the reef, just like every other environment. Most of the algae found on the reef grows as a short "turf," a fine carpet of hairs that is a mix of dozens or hundreds of species of brown, red and green algaes. While diving, look closely at an area of bare coral rock and you will probably see a fine carpet of "hairs" growing on it.

The algal turf grows at a prodigious rate, but a herd of grazers—tangs, parrotfish, damselfish, sea urchins, snails and many others—keeps it clipped short. If an area of reef were caged off to prevent the entry of herbivores, the turf would quickly sprout into a thicket. The farmerfish damsel (*Stegastes lividus*) does just this, by force of personality keeping out all intruders from his own luxurious green patch of hair algae.

Some reef algaes, the so-called coralline algaes, are calcified, providing them with protection both from grazers and physical damage by surge. These appear as small pink "trees," or flat, encrusting pink or lavender growths on old chunks of coral. Some of the coralline algaes grow in areas of very high wave action, indeed they prefer areas that are too turbulent for even corals to survive.

On reefs facing the open ocean, it is a ridge of coralline red algae that receives the full force of the crashing ocean waves, dissipates their energy, and allows less robust organisms including corals to thrive. Other varieties of coralline algae grow deep on the reef, below the level at which reef-building corals can survive, where they contribute significantly to reef growth and sand production.

One recognizable green macro-alga that can sometimes be seen on shallower reefs is *Halimeda,* a heavily calcified alga made up of chains of green disks, each the size of a small button. These disks are calcium carbonate, like coral, and in some areas *Halimeda* rubble is a major component of the reef substrate.

Sometimes an inshore reef will merge with shallow beds of turtle grass, one of the very few true marine plants. These grassy beds provide an environment for seahorses, pipefish, damselfish, wrasses, and the young of some reef fishes, including butterflyfish, as well as small crustaceans, mollusks and worms. The sea grass also provides forage for the rare dugong (*Dugong dugon*), or sea cow, which ranges across Indonesian waters.

Plankton

The diver will rarely *see* plankton, and if he or she does, it will usually be apparent as a cloudiness of the water, or an irritating backscatter in photographs. But plankton is an important link in the reef food chain. Reef areas rich in plankton will be characterized by an abundance of filter-feeders, animals that have evolved methods of sifting or snaring plankton from the current—including soft corals, mussels and oysters, anemones, crinoids, gorgonians and sponges.

Plankton consists of both "plants"—phytoplankton—and "animals"—zooplankton, and the larger zooplankters are predatory on the diatoms and algae of the phytoplankton. The plankton also contains some temporary

HELMUT DEBELIUS / IKAN

members, the meroplankton, which consists of the larval stages of fish and invertebrates. As these grow, they settle out of the plankton stream to become part of the swimming nekton (fish, jellyfish) or the crawling or fixed benthos (sea urchins, gorgonians).

Sponges

Indonesian reef sponges vary in size from tiny to huge, from the small patches of color provided by encrusting sponges (family Clionidae) to the meter-high barrel sponges (*Xestospongia* spp.). All sponges are members of the phylum Porifera, "the hole-bearers," and their porous, "spongy" nature is crucial to their mode of feeding. Sponges are the archetypal filter-feeders, straining plankters from the water through myriad microscopic pores.

A cross-section of a sponge shows a very sophisticated system for moving water. Small intake pores lead to an internal system of tiny canals and chambers lined with cells bearing whip-like processes. Beating constantly, these cells create a cur-

rent through the sponge that moves its own volume of water every 4–20 seconds. Even a relatively small sponge can circulate as much as 5,000 liters a day. The chimney or barrel shape of many larger sponges helps increase surface area and the water flow through the animal.

Sponges are notoriously difficult to identify from photographs or on the basis of external characteristics. Colors vary and even the shape or size of a sponge does not necessarily mark its species; sometimes shape is just a response to local conditions.

Scientists rely on detailed examination of the internal "skeleton" to identify sponges. Sponges are made of a proteinaceous secretion called spongin. This fibrous net forms the useful part of the bath sponges (*Spongia* and *Hippospongia*) harvested in the Mediterranean and Caribbean. Many sponges also contain spicules of silica or calcium carbonate, or both, bound together with spongin.

There are hundreds of species of sponges in Indonesia. The giant barrel sponges are

Above: *A school of sapphire damsels, Pomacentrus pavo, takes shelter in a sponge. Halmahera, Maluku.*

Below. *Marine dinoflagellate plankters, top to bottom: Gymnodinium, Gonyaulax, Peridinium, Ceratium.*

most impressive to divers, but the smaller tube sponges and vase sponges also create colorful and aesthetically pleasing forms.

Like many invertebrates, sponges can grow to a remarkable age. Experiments with commercial farming of bath sponges in the Caribbean have led researchers to estimate that larger specimens are as much as 50 years old.

Reef sponges create an environment that is exploited by a variety of other creatures. Small crabs and shrimps and even fish hide in the tubes and cavities. Crinoids perch on upright sponges to filter plankton from the current. And sea cucumbers and other detritus feeders graze on the organic material that collects on the sponge's surfaces.

Corals and their relatives

Corals, soft corals, sea anemones, gorgonians, hydroids, jellyfish and the other members of the phylum Cnidaria (formerly Coelenterata) cause a great deal of confusion for the diver trying to identify the teeming mass of branched and tentacled life he sees attached to the reef. Taxonomists identify these animals by their stinging cells, nematocysts, and simple coelenteron, literally "hollow intestine." All have the form of a polyp at some stage in their lives. Other than these shared characteristics, the form of these animals varies widely.

Aristotle considered them an intermediate form between plants and animals, and they were first placed by taxonomists in a group called Zoophyta, "animal-plants." Only in 1723 were the corals and their relatives properly identified as animals, and Jean André Peyssonel, the naturalist who proposed this to the French Academy of Sciences, was laughed at and quit science in disgrace.

Phylum Cnidaria is usually divided into three classes: Antho-

zoa, the corals and anemones; Hydrozoa, hydroids and fire corals; and Scyphozoa, the jellyfish. Anthozoa, in turn, is split into two sub-classes: Alcyonaria (Octocorallia), containing the soft corals and gorgonians; and Zoantharia (Hexacorallia), containing the stony corals and anemones.

The Stony Corals

The stony or hard corals are the reef-builders. They are in the order Scleractinia, and are sometimes called scleractinian or "true" corals. The skeletons these animals secrete range in shape from the massive, smooth boulders of *Porites* and stout-branched *Pocillipora* that take a pounding at the reef edge to the finely foliated needle coral (*Seriatopora* spp.).

These corals are colonies, comprised of thousands of individual coral animals, or polyps. Each polyp, upon close examination, will be seen to have much the same shape as a sea anemone, with tentacles ringing a central mouth. What makes the stony coral polyp distinctive, and so ecologically important, is that it deposits calcium carbonate (limestone) around its lower part, forming a skeletal cup. The skeleton is essentially formed of

Right: *The presence of whip coral gorgonians often indicates very clean water and plenty of plankton. Bunaken group, Sulawesi.*

repeated casts of the tiny polyp.

Most reef-building corals are nocturnal. During the day, the polyps are retracted, drawn down into the skeletal cup. At night, these corals are transformed from dead-looking lumps of rock into miniature forests thick with polyps, which expand to feast on the abundant night plankton. Tiny plankters are snared by the polyp's tentacles, which are armed with stinging nematocysts. Although they feed on plankton, the vast majority of the nutrition of reef-building corals is provided by the symbiotic zooxanthellae in their tissues. (See sidebar, "Zooxanthellae and Corals," page 25.)

Corals, like other reef animals, also spawn at night, releasing pink clouds of sperm and eggs. To increase the chances of fertilization, corals of the same species tend to coordinate the release of their eggs and sperm. Many reef animals spawn around the time of the full moon, when tidal currents are strongest, to ensure wide dispersal of the larvae. On the Great Barrier Reef of Australia the majority of corals spawn 4–5 days after the November full moon. Some corals in Indonesia spawn at this time too, but the full pattern of coral spawning has not yet been determined here.

According to travel brochure clichés, corals are supposed to be "kaleidoscopic" with color. Divers, of course, know that at least for the reef-building corals, this is not at all the case. Most shallow water corals are a dull brown color, a consequence of the pigments in their zooxanthellae. Still, some are blessed with subtle pastel tints. In particular, the growing tips of *Acropora* can be colored with a pinkish or purplish pigment, a group of amino acids called S-320 which serves as an ultraviolet filter to protect the still-young polyps.

The shape of stony corals,

rather than their color, is their most salient characteristic. The form the coral will take is strongly influenced by wave action and currents, and even the same species may take different forms under different conditions. A specimen of the distinctive palmate Caribbean elkhorn coral (*Acropora palmata*) placed in a research ecosystem at the Smithsonian Institute in Washington, D.C. sent up new growth in the bushy form of *A. prolifera*. This, it would seem, further complicates the already difficult project of stony coral identification.

Massive forms. In general, massive, boulder-like forms grow in shallow water where light is plentiful, and along the reef edge where the current is strong. These include the common *Monastrea, Pocillopora,* and *Porites.* In the shallow, often turbid water of the back reef, the more robust branching forms (*Acropora* spp.) often out-compete the massive forms, which are more vulnerable to siltation.

Massive corals sometimes form "micro-atolls" in relatively calm backreefs and reef flats. These are flat-topped forms in which the center has been killed by excessive siltation or regular exposure by low tides. The sides continue to grow outward, demonstrating Darwin's theory in miniature.

Goniopora is an unusual massive coral that extends its polyps

KAL MULLER

Above: *A detail of the eponymous vesicles of the bubble, or grape coral,* Plerogyra sinuosa. *These sacs, called acrorhagi, possess stinging nematocysts. During the day they are inflated with water and protect the polyp tentacles. At night they shrivel, and the polyps are extended to snare plankton. The acrorhagi also discourage other corals from overgrowing* Plerogyra, *blocking its sunlight and supply of plankton.*

during the day. These are also usually large, reaching 20–30 centimeters in length. The effect is of a round stone, covered with little brown flowers.

Branching forms. Deeper in the reef, or in protected parts of the shallows, the diver will encounter finely branched and "leafy" forms. These more delicate structures cannot withstand strong wave action, and the added surface area of their shapes serves to better expose their zooxanthellae to the diminished sunlight of deeper waters.

The most common is the fast-growing and ubiquitous *Acropora*. This genus (there are some 100 species) takes a variety of forms, ranging from branching thickets to table-like formations. The tables are considered to be a defense mechanism, as the *Acropora* quickly grows outward, shading any other corals that might try to overgrow it.

Another branching coral often recognized by divers is the needle coral *Seriatopora hystrix,* sending up delicate, pointed branches of cream, blue or pink. *Seriatopora* is usually found in quiet, rather shallow water.

Smaller corals. Some of the smaller coral colonies have distinct, interesting shapes. These corals are not primary reef builders, but colonize already established areas of the reef.

The mushroom corals (*Fungia, Heliofungia* and *Herpolitha* spp.) are common in Indonesia. These form carbonate skeletons that are flat and oval-shaped, perhaps 15–30 centimeters inches long, with fine, radial structures reminiscent of the "gills" of a mushroom cup. The skeletons are not attached to the reef, and particularly on drop-off reefs, are often knocked upside down by currents. They often look like they were just dumped there. Some long tentacled species can be mistaken for sea anemones.

The flower corals (*Euphyllia* spp.) are not as common as *Fungia,* but can be quite beautiful. They form a maze of flat plates that stick up vertically 10–20 centimeters and cover an area 50 centimeters or more in diameter. These corals have long, colorful tentacles, which they extend during the day. *Euphyllia* tolerates turbid water, and can be found growing on patch reefs in back reef channels.

The very bright orange polyps of the coral *Tubastrea* (and the similar *Dendrophyllia*) can be seen in small clusters, usually in low-light areas such as deep on the reef or under overhangs. These finger-sized polyps can easily be mistaken for anemones. They are true scleractinian corals, however, and secrete a very fragile internal skeleton. *Tubastrea* contains no zooxanthellae and receives all its nutrition by capturing plankton. At night, you can watch the polyps feeding by using your light to attract the plankton within reach of the polyps' tentacles. (If your light is very bright, shade it so it will not cause the polyps to retract.)

Anemones

Despite their soft and fleshy appearance sea anemones (order Actinaria) are more closely related to the stony corals than the soft corals. The giant anemones commonly encountered in Indonesia contain symbiotic algae and are most abundant in relatively shallow areas. They can be seen tucked into the coral rock in the shallows and at the lip of drop-off reefs.

Like the corals, color and even shape varies widely in the giant anemones, and they are often very difficult to identify. In Indonesia, one can find the long-tentacled *Heteractis* spp., the short-tentacled carpet anemone, *Stichodactyla* spp., and the unusual *Entacmea* sp., with bulbous-tipped tentacles. These

Discovering New Species

For the diving scientist, Indonesian waters are the most exciting in the world. Not only can "new" species be found on just about every dive, but so much of the behavior of these animals is still unknown that underwater observations are full of surprises.

Scuba has radically changed the way scientists study marine animals. No longer is it necessary to collect everything to study in an aquarium, an artificial environment that often produces artificial behavior, or to collect species the old way—netting, trapping, or even poison. A diver can collect very selectively, and make observations without interfering with the animals' ways of life.

Innumerable small crustaceans and other benthic creatures living in the cracks and crevices of Indonesian reefs go undescribed by science. Even among the best-known reef animals—the fishes—new discoveries are made regularly.

The Grandfather of Ichthyology

To find new species of fish, a good eye and thorough knowledge of the literature serves one better than an academic degree. The grandfather of Indonesian ichthyology was Pieter Bleeker, a Dutch army doctor with a keen interest in fishes. He arrived in Jakarta in 1842, and over the following 30 years produced some 500 papers that became the foundation of his famous, nine-volume *Atlas Ichthyology* (1862–78).

Unlike many 19th century scientists, who were for the most part simple taxonomists, Bleeker had a very modern understanding of the inter-relationship of species. His work is highly respected by today's scientists.

Finding New Species

Bleeker's work was so good that species described 100 years ago are still waiting to be "re-discovered." It is amazing how many deep-water fishes were collected in those days and never seen again. But scientists tend to concentrate on these, and the intertidal areas are often overlooked.

Above: *The red-headed wrasse,* Halichoeres *sp., is sexually dichromic (the male is at top). This beautiful wrasse was discovered by Kuiter in 1986 in Maumere Bay. Common there, it has not been seen anywhere else.*

A knowledgeable diver, with sharp powers of observation, has a very good chance of finding an unknown animal on just about any dive in Indonesia.

I have been visiting the Flores Sao Resort on a regular basis since 1986, photographing and observing the animal life of Maumere Bay. Despite my many dives in these waters, new species turn up on every trip. Often a "new" species looks very similar to a well-known one, and thus has been overlooked. But in other cases the new species is so spectacular one wonders how it could possibly have ever gone unnoticed.

I started underwater photography 20 years ago, and even among my first dives with a camera, I photographed things that I have never seen since. I always take the picture first, and try to sort out the story later. The underwater world is so diverse you may never see it again.

—*Rudie Kuiter*

anemones are large, sometimes growing to half a meter or more in diameter, although what at first seems to be one anemone is sometimes a group of several.

Giant anemones are easy to spot because they nearly always host a pair, or small group of clownfish (*Amphiprion* spp. and *Premnas* sp.). (See "Clownfishes and their Sea Anemone Hosts," page 46.) These fish are not the only animals to take advantage of the security of the anemone's stinging tentacles. Porcelain crabs (*Neopetrolisthes* spp.) and various shrimp are also commensals of anemones.

Cerianthids. In some areas, particularly with sandy bottoms, one can find cerianthids or tube anemones. Cerianthids have very fine tentacles arranged in two concentric bands, and secrete a horny tube into which they can retract if disturbed. Tube anemones (Cerianthidae) are in a separate order from true anemones, and have a more potent sting.

Corallimorphs. These animals (order Corallimorpharia) have some of the characteristics of anemones, and others of corals. In fact, however, they look like small anemones. They are mostly colonial, and consist of flat disks, 2–4 inches in diameter, with a smooth, napped or tentacled surface. One genus, *Discosoma,* is particularly colorful, overgrowing rocks with its bright blue, purple or red disks.

Soft corals and gorgonians

These animals (subclass Alcyonaria) are among the loveliest of the cnidarians. In the clean, plankton-rich waters of Indonesia, soft corals and gorgonians— sea whips or sea fans—are common. Some contain zooxanthellae, but many frequent the deeper parts of the reef, where they filter plankton from the water. Semi-precious pink "coral" is a gorgonian (*Corallium*), harvested from deep waters off Japan and in the Mediterranean.

Soft corals. Soft corals, as the name suggests, lack the hard limestone skeletons of their reef-building relatives. Instead, the numerous polyp animals that make up the colony are supported by a fleshy central "body"; in some cases strengthened by spicules, little spines of silica or calcium.

Soft corals (order Alcyonacea) have few obvious defense mechanisms, and might seem to be vulnerable to attack by predators and parasites, or to fouling by overgrowth. The animals avoid these problems by secreting various bioactive substances, a kind of chemical defense. Substantial efforts are being made by biochemists and pharmaceutical companies to identify compounds in soft corals—and also sponges—that may have properties useful in medicine. Since many of these compounds have evolved to prevent alien growths, they are receiving attention as potential anti-cancer drugs.

A very common group of soft corals in Indonesia are the leather corals (*Sarcophyton* spp. and *Sinularia* spp.) so-named because of their color and texture. These corals grow as wrinkled lobes in well-lit, shallow areas of reef. Because of their symbiotic zooxanthellae, they are a dull brown, sometimes with a slightly green or yellow tinge. When their white polyps are extended for feeding they are easy to identify as soft corals, but when their polyps are retracted they could be mistaken for sponges. The leather corals, however, have a much smoother surface than sponges.

Perhaps the most beautiful of the soft corals is *Dendronephthya,* a soft coral with fuzzy branches of vivid pink, white, orange, red, red-and-white, and a variety of other colors. The main "stem" is normally translucent and contains numerous white spicules, which offer some structural support. Most of the color comes from the polyps, which also contain sharp spicules to deter browsing by fishes. *Dendronephthya* grows deeper on the reef and in areas of low light, and always where currents can provide it with abundant plankton.

Xenia, particularly common in Indonesia, has perhaps the largest individual polyps of any soft coral, perhaps 6–8 centimeters long. The white (also tan, or light blue) polyps grow in clusters, and the tentacles at the end of each are feathery. These continually open and close, like numerous grasping hands. In *Xenia* one can easily count eight tentacles, which is one feature that distinguishes soft corals (Octocorallia) from hard corals and anemones (Hexacorallia) which have six, or multiples of six, tentacles.

Gorgonians. Gorgonians (order Gorgonaceae) have a strong, horny skeleton, which gives strength and support without sacrificing flexibility. They tend to grow on the deeper parts of the reef, away from strong wave action. They live by filter feeding, and to maximize the water flow across their surfaces always grow at right angles to the prevailing current. Where the tidal current flows along the reef, gorgonians grow out from the reef with their long axis vertical. Sometimes, however, particularly on some of the big walls in Indonesia, large sea fans can be seen growing horizontally out from the reef wall, to take advantage of the current upwelling.

There are many species of these animals. Some have a twig-like structure, like a branch from a delicate tree. Many are brightly colored. The sea fans (*Gorgonia* spp.) are flat nets, growing in some cases to three meters across. The skeleton of a sea fan is coated with a kind of "rind," which is sometimes a delicate shade. When you see a big sea fan it is worth spending a few moments looking closely at its surface because they often host an assortment of small symbiotic animals.

Sea pens. These animals (order Pennatulacea) are filter-feeders related to the gorgoni-

Below: *Closeup of the lovely soft coral* Dendronephthya *sp. In this photograph the strengthening spicules are clearly visible in the animals' transparent tissue.*

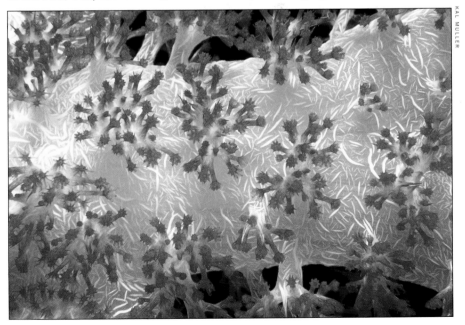

KAL MULLER

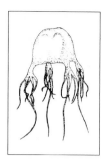

Above: *The poisonous sea wasp, Chironex. This animal has been responsible for human fatalities in Australian waters.*

ans. Their common name comes from their resemblance to the old-fashioned quill pen. Although common in Indonesia, they are not really reef dwellers, and will usually only be seen by night divers who venture out over mud or sand bottoms. Sea pens, sometimes growing in large fields, rotate gently back and forth with the current, their "feathers" sifting plankton from the current.

Black corals. Black coral (order Antipatharia) looks to the diver like a gorgonian, although it is more closely related to the stony corals and anemones. In Indonesia, one can see whip corals (*Stichopathes* and *Cirrhipathes*), and the bushy black coral trees (*Antipathes*).

The polished skeleton of the latter, particularly the thicker branches, is the precious black coral. Black coral is scarce, and its export from Indonesia and import into many other countries is prohibited by laws.

Above: *A pair of Chromodoris willani, perhaps mating. All nudibranchs are hermaphrodites, although they require a partner to produce viable offspring. Bunaken group, Sulawesi.*

Fire coral and hydroids

All cnidarians have stinging cells on their tentacles with which they can defend themselves and immobilize their prey. In most cases, however, these are rather weak and are usually not capable of penetrating human skin. One group, class Hydrozoa, which includes the fire corals and their relatives, has members capable of inflicting very painful stings.

The notorious Portuguese-man-of-war (*Physalia physalis*) is a hydrozoan, and not, despite its appearance, a jellyfish. Fortunately for divers this animal is more of an open ocean dweller.

Stinging hydroids. A far greater nuisance to divers in Indonesia are the feathery hydroids *Aglaophenia* and *Lytocarpus*. Despite their delicate, fern-like appearance, these colonial animals can deliver a burning sting that raises a welt on bare skin. They are fairly common on many Indonesian reefs, and their presence prompts divers to wear Lycra or thin neoprene suits even in the warmest of conditions. The stinging hydroids are sometimes called sea ferns, or sea nettles.

Fire corals. Somewhat less virulent are the fire corals of the genus *Millepora*, but as their name suggests they too should be treated with respect. These hydrozoans are members of a group called hydrocorals for their superficial resemblance to the true corals. Hydrocorals secrete a limestone skeleton, and form colonies that are usually a dull-yellow brown in color (*Millepora*) although some species (*Distichopora*) can be brightly colored. The unusual blue coral (*Heliopora coerulea*), is a fire coral which has a skeleton that when dried displays a light blue tint. Fire corals have very small polyps, and a smooth surface.

Some hydrocorals are important reef-builders, particularly *M. platyphylla,* which can be found growing with massive scleractinian corals at the pounding edge of the reef.

Jellyfish

These familiar animals (class Scyphozoa) are characterized by a dominant medusa stage. Like all cnidarians they form a polyp for part of their lives, but for the jellyfish, this is just temporary. Occasionally, large jellyfish can

ED ROBINSON / IKAN

be seen while diving in Indonesia, particularly in areas of rich plankton. These can be quite beautiful to observe. More bothersome are the cubomedusae, or sea-wasps, tiny jellyfish that can have an irritating sting. Members of the genus *Chironex* have even been responsible for human fatalities in Australia. Because they tend to inhabit the surface layer during the day, they are more of a bother for snorkelers. The lights of night divers, however, can often attract an unwelcome swarm of these creatures.

Worms

Although the word conjures up a dull, and faintly repulsive animal to many people, the worms found on the reefs of Indonesia show a diversity of form and color that often astounds the observer.

There are many different sorts of worms, but most likely to be seen by divers on Indonesian reefs are those in the following phyla: the flatworms (phylum Platyhelminthes); the ribbonworms (phylum Nemertina); the tongueworms (phylum Echiura); and the segmented worms (phylum Annelida).

Flatworms. Flatworms often have the strikingly beautiful colors divers associate with nudibranchs, or sea slugs (which are molluscs). The species seen on Indonesian reefs rarely grow longer than 10 centimeters, and feed on sessile animals such as tunicates and sponges. Flatworms move by gliding over the bottom, or by muscular undulations. This latter waving action is characteristic, and mimicked by the juveniles of several species of fish. This mimicry and the worms' bright colors suggest the presence of a noxious chemical to deter would-be predators.

Ribbonworms. These animals are longer than flatworms, and not as showy. Many are white, with dark stripes or bands. They tend to live under rocks

and corals or in the sand, and are most likely to be seen by divers at night. Some can grow to astonishing sizes, as much as several meters. They feed on molluscs and other worms.

Tongueworms. The tongueworm *Bonellia* can be seen on reef slopes. However, it hides its sac-like body in a crevice, with only a forked proboscis protruding, and can be easy to overlook. These animals have an unusual

sex life. All the fully formed *Bonellia* are females; if a larva settles into an area where there are no worms, it becomes a female. If there are already *Bonellia* established in the area, the larva passes into the body of an adult, becoming a dwarf male, which lives like a parasite on the female "host."

Segmented worms. The segmented worms are the most abundant and diverse of all the

Above: *Two dorid nudibranchs,* Notodoris citrina *(top) and* Nembrotha sp. *Nudibranchs tend to be very prey-specific.* Nembrotha, *as is shown here, feeds only on hydroids.* Notodoris *was photographed in Halmahera, Maluku;* Nembrotha *in Flores.*

groups of reef worms. Divers are familiar with the feathery feeding parts of the tiny Christmas tree worms (*Spirobranchus*) which extend from lumps of living coral. The body of the worm is hidden in a tube within a *Porites* coral head. The similar, but larger fanworm, or feather duster worm (*Sebellastarte*), secretes a tube of flexible parchment to protect its soft body. From its tube, it periodically extends a crown of colorful "feathers" to collect plankton. These worms make good subjects for macrophotography, but any sudden movement will cause them to withdraw their crowns.

Some of the segmented worms have evolved unusual reproductive strategies, perhaps the most famous being that of the *palolo* worms, (*Eunice* sp.). Called *nyale* in parts of Indonesia, these worms spend their lives in coral crevices, but one night a year, their tail parts metamorphose into a sexual form, containing either eggs or sperm.

These sexual forms, called epitokes, break off and swarm to the surface. The timing of the event is set by the moon, and in parts of Indonesia, most notably western Sumba and southern Lombok, the appearance of the epitokes is an important event in the ritual or cultural calender. It is also a great culinary event, as the rich-tasting epitokes are highly prized for eating.

Molluscs

Molluscs are one of the largest and most familiar groups of invertebrate animals, and thousands of species live in Indonesian waters. The phylum is organized into either five or eight classes, the main ones found on Indonesian reefs being: Gastropoda (univalves—single shells), including snails, cowries and conches, as well as the shell-less sea slugs; Pelecypoda (bivalves—two-part shell),

Above: *The triton shell,* Charonia tritonis. *This gastropod preys on crown-of-thorns starfish.*

Above: *The helmet conch,* Casis cornuta. *Indonesians call this shell* kima kepala kambing, *the "goat's head."*

including clams, oysters and mussels; and the Cephalopoda, including octopi, squid and cuttlefish. Despite their differences, animals in these three groups all possess a soft, fleshy body (mollusc means "soft") and most—octopi and nudibranchs are exceptions—have the ability to produce a calcareous shell.

Nudibranchs and snails

Gastropods are abundant on Indonesian reefs, but they are easily overlooked because most are small, many are nocturnal, and some are very well camouflaged. Nevertheless the diver who develops the habit of carefully scrutinizing the reef surface will soon find many of these delightful creatures.

Nudibranchs. Nudibranchs, the "naked gilled" sea slugs, are the most interesting to the diver. Like common garden slugs, they are snail-like animals that have lost their shells. Nudibranchs are often strikingly colored.

In some species the coloration is clearly cryptic, allowing them to blend in with their chosen prey. Nudibranchs are carnivorous, and most are very prey specific, feeding for example only on particular types of soft coral or sponges. Since these prey animals are often very colorful, so are the nudibranchs.

In other species, it seems certain that coloration serves as a warning to would-be predators that the animals are foul-tasting or poisonous. Nudibranchs are known to produce some very concentrated toxins. Some even have nematocysts, which they obtain from their cnidarian prey and concentrate in the outer layers of their own skin.

Most nudibranchs are small, although a few mainly nocturnal forms grow to 20 centimeters or more in length. One of the largest and certainly the most spectacular nudibranch found in Indonesia is the Spanish dancer,

Hexabranchus sanguineus, a beautiful, crimson-colored animal. This nudibranch only wanders out at night, and if it is found and gently picked up, it will begin its "dance." The wild undulations of its body and surrounding skirt are thought to serve as part of a warning display. Like many nudibranchs, Spanish dancers lay their eggs in huge numbers, in spiral ribbons that can look like flowers.

Rock shells. The rock shells or murex (*Murex* spp.) feed heavily on small bivalve molluscs such as oysters. This is not an easy task, because the bivalves clamp their shells shut when attacked. A murex shell overcomes this resistance by chipping away at the edge of the oyster with its sharp radula or mouthpart, and then pokes its proboscis into this opening to feed on the fleshy tissues within. Another species, with similar tastes in prey, is the drill (*Thais*). This small gastropod literally drills a hole through the oyster's shell. The large number of bivalve shells with neat holes drilled in them that are washed

up on Indonesian beaches testifies to the efficiency of this feeding method.

Tritons. The triton shell (*Charonia tritonis*) is famous as a predator of the troublesome crown-of-thorns starfish, which has devastated Australian reefs. This large shell (to more than 30 cm.) is a popular souvenir, and over-harvesting has been blamed for population explosions of the crown-of-thorns. The helmet conch (*Casis cornuta*) is another large, predatory gastropod found in Indonesia. Because of collectors, both the triton and helmet conch are endangered in parts of Indonesia.

Cone shells. Cone shells (*Conus* spp.) are even more rapacious predators. Their radulas are modified as barbs, with which they stab their victims. They then immobilize their prey by injecting a neurotoxic poison. Most cone shells eat worms, although a few are piscivorous. The poison of some of the fish-eating *Conus* species is powerful enough to kill a human, so treat them with respect.

Cowries. Cowries (*Cypraea*

Above: Tridacna gigas *is the largest of the seven species of giant clams. It can be distinguished by its size and the pebbly texture of its mantle. Scientists believe these to be among the longest-lived animals, some surviving as long as 200 years. A specimen as large as the one pictured here is probably well over 50 years old.*

Above: *A predatory gastropod prying open a bivalve.*

MARINE LIFE   **45**

Clownfishes and their Sea Anemone Hosts

ED ROBINSON / IKAN

Above: *The colorful giant sea anemone* Heteractis magnifica. *Although not visible here, this particular specimen hosts the pink anemonefish,* Amphiprion perideraion.

Below: *Juvenile Clark's anemonefish,* Amphiprion clarkii, *in the anemone* Entacmaea quadricolor. *This distinctive anemone can be recognized by its bulbous-tipped tentacles. 15 meters, Bunaken Island, Sulawesi.*

There is perhaps no sight more charming than a pair of bright clownfishes nestled in one of the colorful giant reef anemones. Although known to possess powerful stinging cells, the anemones clearly don't harm the clownfishes, which look downright snug tucked into the soft tentacles of their host.

The relationship between the fish and the actinian is commensal; the anemonefishes clearly benefit, receiving protection for themselves and their offspring. They even pluck at the tentacles and oral disk of the anemone, eating the organic material that has collected there. The benefit to the anemone is less clear. The constant prodding, cleaning and stimulation provided by the fishes certainly *seems* enjoyable, but this may be just pathetic fallacy. Anemonefishes are never found without anemones; anemones, however, are sometimes found without the fish.

A Delicate Operation

It had been thought that clownfishes were somehow immune to the anemone's stinging nematocysts. Close observations, however, have shown this not to be the case. The fish, through a series of brief—and careful—encounters with the actinian, picks up a substance in its mucous that the anemone recognizes as its own. The nematocysts don't fire when touched by the fish for the same reason one tentacle doesn't sting another.

Some cold-hearted experimenters tested this theory by scraping the mucous off a clownfish and placing it back with its anemone. The hapless fish was immediately and unceremoniously stung.

Clownfishes are protandrous

MIKE SEVERNS

hermaphrodites; that is, all mature as males, and then a few sex-reverse to females. A typical anemone will contain a pair of clownfish, and perhaps a few young ones.

The largest fish in the group is the female. If she should die, the reigning male sex-reverses, and the dominant juvenile becomes the functional male. Juveniles sharing an anemone with an adult pair are hormonally stunted, and remain small.

Although clownfish are the only fishes to require an anemone host, other small damsels will opportunistically occupy anemones as juveniles, especially the three-spot dascyllus, *Dascyllus trimaculatus.*

Sea Anemones

Some of the giant reef anemones can reach a meter in diameter. All have zooxanthellae, and are thus found in relatively shallow water. They derive most of their nutrition from the algae, but also consume plankton and any other small animal unlucky enough to blunder into their tentacles.

Anemones can live to a ripe old age. In the 19th century, British naturalist John Dalyell kept a coldwater *Actinia* sp. anemone for 66 years. Over this period, it produced 750 young (by budding), 150 of these after the age of 50. The anemone eventually outlived the scientist.

Some 10 species of Indonesian anemones, in three families, host clownfish.* The systematics of this group was in some confusion until Dr. Daphne Dunn reorganized it in 1981.

Cryptodendrum adhaesivum. Lies flat; very short tentacles. Hosts only Clark's anemonefish.

Entacmaea quadricolor. The bubble anemone. (See photo at left.) Hosts 11 species.

Macrodactyla doreensis. Very

Left: *Young Clark's anemonefish,* Amphiprion clarkii, *in the distinctive sand anemone,* Heteractis aurora.

Left. *The spine-cheek anemonefish,* Premnas biaculeatus, *in* Entacmaea quadricolor. Premnas *varies from red to almost black.*

Left: *A pair of common anemonefish,* Amphiprion ocellaris, *in Merten's anemone,* Stichodactyla mertensii.

long, widely spaced tentacles. Usually dull color, buries column in sand. Hosts 2 species.

Heteractis aurora. Dull color, buries column in sand. Distinctive tentacle shape (see top photo above.) Hosts 7 species.

H. crispa. Long, thin, almost pointed tentacles that often seem tangled. Hosts 11 species.

H. magnifica. Brightly colored column, blunt tentacles. Often photographed. (See small photo opposite.) Hosts 10 species.

H. malu. Like *H. magnifica,* but peach-colored. Hosts Clark's.

Stichodactyla haddoni. Haddon's carpet anemone. Short-tentacles. Grey, with white radial stripes. Hosts 6 species.

S. gigantea. Bludru anemone. Longer tentacles, larger than Haddon's. Hosts 6 species.

S. mertensii. Merten's anemone. Colorful; largest carpet anemone, to 1m across. (See bottom photo above.) Hosts 10 species.

— *David Pickell*

*All these anemones are widely distributed across Indonesia except *Heteractis malu,* which ranges from Australia to Hawaii and is likely to occur only in eastern Indonesia.

Above: *One of the piscivorous cone shells (Conus sp.) devouring a small goby. Most cone shells eat worms, but the relatively few fish-eating species are very dangerous.*

Below: *The octopus has highly developed eyes and a very sophisticated nervous system. It is thus considered "intelligent," and people find it hard to believe that it is a mollusc.*

spp.) are common, small (most just a few cm.) gastropods with a smooth shell that is completely covered by the animal's fleshy mantle. Both the shells and mantles can be beautifully marked, often with very different patterns. The cowries are omnivorous, feeding on algae as well as a variety of sedentary animals such as soft corals.

Trochus. Top shells (*Trochus* spp.) are relatively large (6–8 cm.), and conical. Before the advent of plastics they were widely collected for the manufacture of buttons. Removing the grubby outer layer of shell reveals the lustrous nacre, or mother-of-pearl beneath. Until the invention of Bakelite, and the many plastics that followed, shell nacre for buttons was an important business in Indonesia. Today they are still collected, most to be used in souvenirs and to supply the small market for "real" buttons.

Clams and Oysters

The bivalves include such familiar forms as clams, oysters, mussels and scallops. All have two articulated shell halves that can

be closed with a large muscle. It is this muscle that makes bivalves so prized as seafood. With a very few exceptions, bivalves cannot move, like gastropods, and thus most have adapted to filter-feeding. They draw water in through one tube or "siphon" and pass it out through another. This stream of water passes through the animal's gills, which serve the dual purpose of respiration and filtering out food particles.

All bivalves must hold their shell halves at least slightly ajar to maintain water circulation through their bodies. But when danger threatens they are clamped shut. Some Indonesian bivalves gain further protection by boring into corals and reef rock, so that predators cannot reach them. The boring is achieved by a combination of chemical action and rasping with the two shell haves. Eventually, reef bivalves become so encrusted with sponges, coralline algae, bryozoans and cnidarians that they are barely visible.

Giant clams. The giant reef clams, *Tridacna* spp., have a dif-

ferent means of feeding. Like reef-building corals, *Tridacna* clams harbor zooxanthellae in their fleshy mantles, and can thus "manufacture" most—or perhaps all—of their own food. Like corals, they require lots of light, and tend to be found in the shallows. They grow with the hinge of their shells down, and their rippled gape facing the sun.

There are seven species of *Tridacna*, of which the giant clam, *T. gigas,* is the most dramatic. These animals can reach a meter and a half in diameter. An animal that big could be a century old. Although smaller than *T. gigas, T. squamosa* has a beautiful ruffled shell. The fleshy mantles of *Tridacna* clams are beautiful, varying in color from brown to yellow to green to blue, with contrasting spots or mottling.

Tridacna clams are a great delicacy in Asia, particularly in Taiwan, and their shells are made into terrazzo in factories in Surabaya. Over-harvesting has greatly reduced their numbers throughout Indonesia. Shallow reefs in Eastern Indonesia that used to support literally fields of giant clams have been stripped in just the past few years. There is fear that the population in many areas is no longer at a self-sustaining level.

Recently, however, researchers at the Micronesian Mariculture Demonstration Center in Palau, headed by Gerald Heslinga, have discovered a method of "farming" giant clams by inoculating the veliger larvae with zooxanthellae. Once the symbiotic algae is in place, the clams need only a good supply of seawater and plenty of light to thrive. The farming operation requires little room, and the clams reach 10 centimeters across in just two years. Because of the commercial potential for these clams, a number of pilot farms have recently been established in the Pacific region.

HELMUT DEBELIUS / IKAN

Oysters. A number of oysters can be found on the reef, in many cases so well camouflaged with encrusting growths that they are at first invisible. The cock's comb oyster (*Lopha cristagalli*) has a distinctive sharp, zig-zag opening, and is often covered by encrusting sponges.

The colorful mantle of the thorny oyster (*Spondylus aurantius*) stands out, although its rough shell is usually overgrown with algae, sponges, and small cnidarians.

Pearl oysters are grown in many parts of Indonesia by Japanese companies. The secret of inserting the "seed" around which the oyster will secrete its pearl is very tightly guarded, and the Japanese defend their valuable crop with small private armies.

Cephalopods

These animals, despite their close relationship to the snails and clams, are active, "intelligent" predators with highly developed eyes and sophisticated behaviors. The octopus has eight suckered arms, while squid and cuttlefish have an additional two grasping tentacles. Both octopi and squids have a hard, chitinous beak. The nautilus—of which only one genus is extant—differs markedly from the other cephalopods. It has 90 arms, without suckers, and a well-developed shell. Unlike other

Above: *The thorny oyster (*Spondylus sp.) is often so encrusted with sponges, algae, tunicates and other organisms that only when it is agape with its bright mantle showing (as here) can it be seen. Halmahera, Maluku.*

cephalopods, the nautilus has very primitive eyes, lacking a lens and open to the water.

Octopi. These familiar animals can be found on the reef, although they normally hide in small caves or crevices. They have no internal skeleton so are able to squeeze into surprisingly small spaces.

Chromatophores on their skin give octopi remarkable abilities able to change color, which they do either to blend in with their surroundings or to display emotion. They can also change their surface texture, from smooth to lumpy and back, presumably for the same reasons.

Octopuses are particularly fond of eating crabs and other crustaceans, and a pile of shells often marks a hole where one is resident. Normally an octopus crawls rather slowly across the reef, but it can also swim by contractions of its legs, much like an umbrella opening and closing. If disturbed, it can produce a short burst of speed by squirting water out of its large gill cavity through a muscular siphon.

Beware of the common, small blue-ringed octopi (*Hapalochlaena* spp.) which can be found under rocks on the reef flats in Indonesia. Do not pick one up. Some species possess a very toxic poison, and not all are as distinctively marked as the often photographed *H. maculosa*.

Squid. Squid are free-swimming animals, usually seen in groups in shallow lagoon areas or along the reef edge. They have perfected the mode of jet-propelled movement. While stationary they maintain position with gentle undulations of their lateral fins. Movement, either forward or backward, is achieved by the highly maneuverable water jet. Like the octopus, squids can change their coloration, adopting a sparkling array of brilliant colors and patterns.

Squid have a rudimentary internal "shell," actually a non-calcareous strengthening device called a pen. It is of a clear, flexible substance that looks and feels like a piece of plastic.

Although you will never see one on the reef, the largest cephalopods by far are the giant squids (*Architeuthis* spp.), which can reach a length of 18 meters. These animals frequent very deep water, and little is known of their habits. They are the preferred prey of the sperm whale.

Cuttlefish. Cuttlefish (*Sepia* sp.) superficially resemble squid, but can be distinguished by their generally larger size and more robust shape. Unlike squid, which often travel in large groups, lone cuttlefish can often be seen foraging on the reef slope, and are the most frequently encountered cephalopods.

Like the other cephalopods, cuttlefish can squirt out a blob of ink if threatened. The shape of this blob, roughly the size of the animal that ejected it, and its strong smell, distracts the would-be predator while the cuttlefish jets away. In earlier times, this ink was used for writing, as is suggested by the cuttlefish's genus name, *Sepia*.

Instead of the squid's flexible pen, cuttlefish have a "cuttle-bone," a calcareous structure perhaps most familiar for its use as a dietary supplement for cage birds. Although it provides some stiffness, the most important use of the porous "bone" is for buoyancy control, balancing the animal's vertical movements across the reef face.

Nautilus. These animals, with their distinctive spiralled shell, are the most unusual of the living cephalopods. The chambered shell serves as a form of buoyancy control, like the cuttlefish bone, but much more sophisticated. This control is necessary as the animals undergo a considerable daily vertical migration. During the daylight hours, the

Opposite: *A mantis shrimp,* Odonto-dactylus scyllaris. *These animals are fierce predators, using their modified front claws to seize or bludgeon prey in the manner of their namesake, the praying mantis.* Odontodactylus *is the most colorful and one of the larger mantis shrimps—it is said to be able to cut a four-inch crab in half with one strike. Some divers call these animals "thumb-splitters" and with good reason. Do not try to touch one! Tulamben, Bali.*

nautilus stay at 1,000–1,500 meters, and only rise into relatively shallow water at night. Only rarely are they found in depths a sport diver could reach. In this way they avoid predators, and perhaps also are able to more easily find their food—carrion and, particularly, the molts of crustaceans.

There are several species, but the most common on Indonesian reefs is the pearly nautilus (*Nautilus pompilius*).

Crustaceans

The jointed-foot animals—Arthropoda—is the single most successful phylum of animals. On land, the insects and spiders dominate; in the water, the subphylum Crustacea is king, with almost 40,000 species. Crustaceans—crabs, shrimp and lobsters—are very abundant on Indonesian coral reefs, but many keep themselves well-hidden, particularly during the day. They are most likely to be seen by night divers.

The largest commonly seen crustaceans are the spiny lobsters, *Panulirus* spp. By day spiny lobsters hide in caves and crevices, often in small groups, with only their long antennae protruding. But at night they venture out of their retreats in search of food. If surprised out in the open, spiny lobsters can swim backwards with great speed using powerful flicks of their tail.

These lobsters, of course, make very fine eating, but visiting divers should resist the temptation of trying to catch a lobster for the table. Removal of animals from a dive site is short-sighted, and lobster catching is quite a skilled operation. An unpracticed diver who attempts it is likely to be left only with painful cuts and a handful of antennae.

Shrimps

On night dives large shrimps can sometimes be spotted out in the open where their reflective eyes catch the light and stand out as two bright red spots. But even by day the careful observer should be able to spot several species of small shrimp.

Commensals. A variety of sometimes colorful shrimp associate with anemones, coral and echinoderms for protection, making them easy to spot. The tiny bumble-bee shrimps (*Gnathophyllum* spp.) associate with sea urchins. Various species of *Periclimenes,* some quite colorful, associate with anemones, gorgonians and sea urchins. One, *P. imperator,* lives in the folds of the Spanish dancer nudibranch.

Cleaner shrimps. Also easy to see are the cleaner shrimps, protected from predation by the services they offer. These cleaners pick parasites and bits of dead tissue from fish, and can all

Below: *A dispute developed between these two prawn gobies,* Mahidolia mystacina, *when the yellow goby and its shrimp wandered into the grey goby's territory. When the grey fish came out of its burrow, the sand started to fly. Both of these gobies are females. Tulamben, Bali.*

RUDIE KUITER

INTRODUCTION

be recognized by long, white antennae.

The candy shrimps (*Lysmata* spp.) are beautiful red striped or spotted cleaners. The coral shrimps, *Stenopus* spp., live in pairs in small caves or holes, with their large white antennae extended to attract the attention of passing fish.

The common banded coral shrimp, *Stenopus hispidus,* has well-developed front claws, and is sometimes called the boxer shrimp. Various species of *Periclimenes* also serve as cleaners.

Cleaner shrimp often set up a "station," that fish visit repeatedly. It is quite a sight to watch a tiny shrimp crawl into the mouth and gills of a grouper or large angelfish. If approached slowly enough cleaner shrimps will climb onto a diver's outstretched hand, to see if it too needs cleaning, or even into his mouth.

Pistol shrimp. These animals (*Alpheus* and *Synalpheus* spp.) have well-developed pincers, one much larger than the other. By some means that is not well understood, the pistol or snapping shrimp is able to create an audible clicking sound with its large claw.

Some of the blind or near-blind pistol shrimp have developed interesting relationships with small gobies. In lagoons and on sandy patches around the reef you can see these small fish sitting up on their fins outside a small burrow. Next to the fish will be one or more pistol shrimps. The shrimps rely on the gobies, with which they keep in contact by their long antennae, to warn them of the approach of any danger. The gobies benefit from this relationship by having a safe burrow dug for them.

Crabs

Many species of crabs live on Indonesian reefs, but they are not always easy to find. Crabs would soon be eaten by strong-jawed fish such as wrasses if they ventured out boldly by day. Many species are therefore only seen at night when they come out under the cover of darkness to feed. If you look closely at a well-protected coral thicket, however, you will likely see a few small crabs safely wedged in.

Hermit crabs. These familiar, and comical creatures use the discarded shells of gastropods as portable refuges. Some of these small animals are very colorful, particularly *Calcinas* and the demon hermit crabs, *Aniculus.* A few species of hermit crabs go one stage further, carrying small sea anemones (with stinging tentacles) on their shells as additional discouragement to potential predators.

The large terrestrial coconut or robber crab (*Birgus latro*), a delicacy in the Moluccas and other parts of Indonesia, is actually a hermit crab that abandons its shell when it reaches adulthood. Small land hermit crabs (*Coenobita* spp.) are common along the high tide line on some Indonesian beaches.

Decorator crabs. These are types of spider crabs that protect themselves by sticking live sponges, gorgonians or other material onto their fuzzy or spiny backs as camouflage. Small decorator crabs may be spotted at any time on sea fans or black coral trees. But look out for the large nocturnal species that carry massive chunks of soft coral or sponge on their backs, held on with their last pair of legs.

The small and colorful boxer crab, *Lybia tesselata,* grasps a pair of tiny sea anemones in its claws which it then uses for both defense, and to collect food.

Porcelain crabs. The porcelain crabs (*Neopetrolisthes* spp.), so-named for their smooth, colorful shells, are sometimes called "half-crabs," for they are structurally similar to prawns and lobsters. They are commensals on the giant anemones where, protected from predators, they strain plankton from the water with mouthparts that have been modified for filter-feeding.

Echinoderms

Everyone is familiar with the common starfish or sea star. But starfishes are only one of five groups that together form the Echinodermata, "hedgehog-skinned" animals. The others are the sea urchins, the brittle stars, the feather stars and the sea cucumbers. Most echinoderms have a skeleton of spiny plates—most developed in the sea urchins, and least developed in the sea cucumbers—and five-sided symmetry.

Starfish. The five-sided symmetry of the echinoderms is clearly displayed in the starfishes. Most Indonesian species have five arms, although some individuals may have one arm more or less. The common cobalt-blue starfish *Linckia laevigata* is particularly variable in this regard. Some of the larger starfishes may have a great number of arms.

Starfishes are predators, feeding on a wide variety of bottom-dwelling animals, or detritivores. A feeding starfish envelops its prey with its arms, then actually pushes part of its stomach out through its mouth over the victim, digesting it externally. Starfishes are able to hang on to even actively struggling prey with their myriad tube feet, tiny suckers that cover the undersides of their arms. The gripping power of these animals is considerable, and over time they can even overpower the strong muscle of a bivalve. The tube feet are also used for locomotion.

Some starfish have very thick arms, particularly the pincushion starfish (*Culcita* spp.) common on Indonesian reefs. These animals can inflate their bodies to the point where they become almost spherical. *Culcita* normally have tiny symbiotic shrimps living on their lower surfaces.

The most notorious starfish in Indonesian waters is the crown-of-thorns, *Acanthaster plancii,* which is found throughout the tropical Indian and Pacific Oceans. This animal feeds exclusively on coral polyps.

Normally the crown-of-thorns, large, multi-armed and bristly, occurs in very low numbers on coral reefs—divers usually see perhaps one per dive. But population densities have occasionally reached plague proportions, and at these times whole reefs can be destroyed. Some of the greatest damage has been on the Great Barrier Reef of Australia and on the reefs of southern Japan, but *Acanthaster* outbreaks have occurred throughout its range, including Indonesia.

These plagues have been the subject of a long and heated debate by reef scientists. Some argue that over-fishing, over-harvesting of predators like the triton conch, and agricultural runoff have contributed to the disastrous outbreaks. Huge coral heads, hundreds of years old, have been destroyed by the ravages of the starfish. These scientists argue that control measures are necessary, and advocate the removal of *Acanthaster* whenever seen by divers. (Note: The crown-of-thorns is spiny, and some people have a toxic reaction to its thorns. Do not touch one unprotected.)

Another opinion suggests that the outbreaks are a natural phenomenon, and point to core samples taken on the Great Barrier reef that show periodic accumulations of *Acanthaster* spines. These scientists say the outbreaks remove dominant coral species, and may be necessary to increase the species diversity of tropical reefs. They note that the reefs have recovered relatively rapidly from the outbreaks, and suggest removal of crown-of-thorns would in the long run be counter-productive.

Brittle stars. Brittle stars are quite similar in appearance to starfish, but have thin, flexible arms. These arms are easily broken off, hence the name. While starfish move mainly by the action of the tiny tube feet on the underside of their arms, brittle stars move by movements of the whole arm.

Many brittle stars have spines on their arms which are very sharp and can give the unwary diver a nasty sting. Despite these spiny defences and their unappetizing appearance, brittle stars are preyed upon by several species of fish, and thus tend to remain well-hidden.

On the shallow reef flats one can sometimes find literal "fields" of brittle stars, their bodies flat on the bottom and their arms wriggling in the water, filtering plankton and debris. On the reef, these animals are less bold, and extend just an arm or two from the safety of their crevices.

Serpent stars are brittle stars with smooth arms, and often very striking colors. These animals can sometimes be seen with their arms coiled in tight loops around gorgonians.

Basket stars are the most highly developed filter-feeding brittle stars. They only come out to feed at night, when they extend their branched arms to capture planktonic animals drifting past. Basket stars are beautiful creatures to watch, and they are particularly common on Indonesian reefs where they can grow to over a meter across.

Crinoids. The crinoids or feather stars are survivors of the sea lilies, animals that once were among the most common in the seas. Although there are still some stalked crinoids extant, those seen on Indonesian reefs— *Amphimetra* spp. and *Himerometra* spp.—are unstalked. They perch on the edge of sponges or gorgonians with a set of small clasping legs, and deploy their delicate arms—of which they have 30 or more—to strain plankton from the water. Feather stars can also walk on these long arms, and if dislodged may swim

Below: *Many species of shrimps act as cleaners. This is a* Leandrites *sp. at work on the mouth of a coral grouper,* Cephalopholis miniata.

with them in a beautiful but rather inefficient manner.

Food filtered from the current by the fine hairs on the crinoid's arms are passed down a channel to the central mouth. Crinoids sit "upside-down" compared to other echinoderms, and the mouth is on top the animal. Many feather stars are nocturnal and hide by day in reef crevices. As night falls they come out of hiding and climb up onto prominent blocks of coral or other high points where they are exposed to the strongest current flow.

Sea urchins. Sea urchins are important and abundant grazers on Indonesian coral reefs. Even the spiniest of urchins may be attacked if they venture out into the open by day, so they tend to confine their activities to the night. By day they wedge themselves into crevices or hollows to avoid the attentions of predatory fish. Sea urchins have a very sophisticated feeding apparatus which they use to scrape at the

JAN POST / IKAN

reef, removing not only algae but also quantities of coral rock. In fact, some small species actually excavate their own daytime hiding places out of the soft coral rock by the constant scraping of their jaws and spines.

On shallow, quiet reefs in Indonesia one can often see the black, long-spined urchin *Diadema* sp., so-named for the cluster of glistening "jewels" set into its upper body. This urchin has very long and brittle spines, and stepping on one would be a disaster. In harbors and other disturbed areas of reef, large numbers of these animals can be found.

The slate pencil urchin (*Heterocentrotus mamillatus*) is a distinctive species, with thick, red spines. No longer used as chalk, the unfortunate animals' attractive spines are now being made into wind chimes.

The bodies of most sea urchins seem roughly spherical, but in fact they are made up of five radial segments, in typical echinoderm fashion. Sea urchins develop a calcareous skeleton or test, which contains the feeding apparatus, the intestines, and the gonads. Prior to reproduction the gonads expand to fill the whole shell, and it is this rich substance that make sea urchins so attractive to hungry fish despite their spiny defences.

The ripe gonads of the sea urchin *Hemicentrotus pulcherrimus* are prized in Japan for sushi; the taste of this *uni* is strong, but delicious.

Sea cucumbers. Though at first they look just like loose sacks, or large worms, sea cucumbers (class Holothuria) are constructed with the same five-sided symmetry typical of the echinoderms. Because they are so elongate, they have a "head" and a "tail," unlike the starfish or urchins. The head of a sea cucumber is not, however, particularly well developed, consisting of little more than a ring of tentacles around the mouth. Sea cucumbers are an important trade item in Indonesia. (See "Trepang Fishing," page 27.)

Most species are detritus feeders, the tentacles being used to pick up sand and pass it into the mouth. Organic matter is digested and the undigested remains are passed out through the anus. Sea cucumbers have to eat a lot of sand in order to obtain enough food, so they often leave a continuous trail of sandy feces behind them. A few species are filter feeders. They hide their bodies in reef crevices and hold their tentacles up in to the water current to feed. The tentacles are rapidly withdrawn if disturbed.

Sea cucumbers appear as elongated and somewhat flaccid forms lying among coral rubble or sea grass, moving slowly in a worm-like way by contractions of their bodies. These are usually black or dull-colored. A few species, such as the sea apple (*Pseudocolochirus*), are very colorful, however.

Many sea cucumbers are active by day. Since they are not attacked by predatory fish it would seem that they must have some efficient means of defense. Some species can discharge sticky white threads if molested, and most tropical sea cucumbers contain toxins.

Sea Squirts

The sea squirts or tunicates are an entirely marine group of animals, and are unfamiliar to many people. Despite their unimpressive appearance, they are chordates, and—technically—are more closely related to human beings than to any of the invertebrates listed above. They have a notochord, a primitive backbone, only in their larval form. Once they settle out of the plankton and become sessile filter-feeders, the backbone is unceremoniously shed. (So much for the vaunted evolutionary superiority of "higher order" forms.)

The tunicates seen on Indonesian reefs are all in the class Ascidiacea, a name derived from the ancient Greek word for leather bottle. They are rather like little bottles, with (usually) two openings rather than just one. Water is drawn in through the uppermost of these siphons, filtered through a basket-like arrangement internally, and then passed out through the lower siphon. Peer into the opening of a large tunicate and you may be able to make out the fine sieving apparatus within. Many tunicates have stout spikes projecting from the inner wall of their siphons, to thwart small fish or other unwanted intruders.

One of the most common and conspicuous tunicates on Indonesian reefs is the beautiful white,

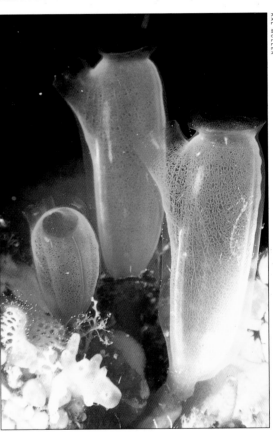

KAL MULLER

purple and yellow *Polycarpa aurata*. These creatures are about the size of a man's thumb, and have a tough leathery outer coating, or tunic. *Polycarpa* is a solitary and very distinctive animal and easy to identify underwater. But many tunicates are colonial, and can easily be mistaken for sponges. If the siphons of a sea-squirt are touched (gently so as not to harm the animal)

Above: *A cluster of unidentified tunicates. Water enters through the uppermost opening, is filtered of plankton and nutrients, and then passed out the lower opening. Bunaken group, Sulawesi.*

Above: *The blue ribbon eel,* Rhinomuraena quaesita, *is one of the most attractive moray eels. Young eels are black, and don't turn electric blue until they reach a bit over a half-meter in length. Bunaken group, Sulawesi.*

they will squeeze shut. Sponges do not react to touch. If a tunicate is lifted out of the sea this same contraction will cause water to be squirted out of its siphon—hence the common name sea squirt.

Most colonial tunicates are overlooked because they tend to be tucked away in dark corners. An exception are the marble-sized, white-and-green grape ascidians, *Diademnum molle,* a colonial tunicate that is very common on shallow reefs in Indonesia. Diademnid tunicates have a single large inhalent opening, and many small exhalent openings around their globular tunics.

Their green color comes from a symbiotic algae living within its tissues, much like the zooxanthellae of stony corals. The relationship between this tunicate and its algae is one of mutual dependency, neither party being able to survive alone. *Diademnum* larvae even carry samples of the algae with them to ensure that the relationship is continued in the next generation.

The Fishes

Corals and other invertebrate animals can provide a lifetime of interest for a diver in Indonesia, but the fish are what really grabs one's attention. On most reefs, brightly colored and beautifully patterned fish are everywhere, darting among the corals or lying sedately in mid-water. It would

be impossible in the space available here to offer a complete description of the thousands of fish species found on Indonesian reefs, so all that will be attempted is a brief survey. Consult "Further Readings" page 272 for more complete resources.

Elasmobranchs

Sharks and rays are elasmobranchs, and differ from true bony fishes by having a cartilaginous skeleton, only parts of which are calcified (e.g., the jaws of a shark). Gill structure—elasmobranch means "plate-gilled"—and other physical features differ between bony fish and sharks and rays, which are considered a more primitive form.

Sharks. There are many species of sharks in Indonesian waters, but those most commonly seen by divers are the reef white-tip shark (*Triaenodon obesus*), the gray reef shark (*Carcharhinus amblyrhynchos*), and the reef black-tip shark (*C. melanopterus*).

The reef white-tip shark grows to 1.7 meters, and is a thin, gray fish with white tips to its dorsal and tail fins. This is the most commonly seen shark on the Indonesian reefs. This small shark can be seen plucking fish and crustaceans from crevices in the reef, or can be found hiding under overhangs.

The gray reef shark grows up to 2.3 meters, and has a very dark trailing edge to its tail. Although this animal is known to be aggressive in some areas, it is not considered dangerous in Indonesia.

The reef black-tip shark grows to 1.8 meters, and is pale gray or brown with distinct black tips on all its fins. This shark sometimes comes up into very shallow water on reef flats and in lagoons to look for food.

The largest fish extant is the whale shark (*Rhincodon typus*), a harmless animal that strains krill and small fish from the water. Growing to more than 12 meters in length (although specimens of 5–7 meters are more common), the whale shark is not a reef fish, although it can be found seasonally off some reefs in Indonesia.

The only really dangerous sharks a diver might encounter on an Indonesian reef are the tiger shark (*Galeocerdo cuvieri*), a large—up to 5.5 meters—scavenger that sometimes comes up onto the reefs at night, and the unusual hammerhead sharks (*Sphyrna* spp.), which grow to 3–4 meters and are known to be beligerent. These sharks, however, are very rarely seen.

Rays. Structurally, rays are essentially flattened sharks. The stingrays have one or two stout spines at the base of their tail, which are their main means of defence. They will not normally be used against divers, although you should always take care to avoid stingrays while walking in shallow water.

Stingrays are bottomfish, and have strong teeth which they use to crush shellfish. In areas where stingrays are common you may see large craters in the bottom, caused by their feeding activities. Perhaps the most common stingray in Indonesia is the blue-spotted stingray (*Taeniura lymma*), which is frequently seen on sandy patches under coral overhangs. It grows to a span of about a meter.

A much larger animal is the spotted eagle ray (*Aetobatis narinari*), which can sometimes be seen cruising the reef edge looking for crustaceans. Eagle rays can reach 2.3 meters across.

The largest ray, however, is the manta (*Manta alfredi*). Like the whale shark, mantas are essentially open water fish, but they are regularly seen by divers in Indonesia. The manta ray, growing up to 6.7 meters across and weighing 1,400 kilos, is a planktivore. Both whale sharks and mantas occur only seasonally in different parts of the country, as they migrate to the areas where the plankton is thickest. (Mantas are much more commonly seen than whale sharks.)

Because they are found in areas dense with plankton, mantas tend to be seen at times when visibility is relatively low. This, however, is a small inconvenience when weighed against the pleasure of swimming with such magnificent creatures.

Bony Fishes

Eels. The moray eels (family Muraenidae) are common both in folklore and on the Indonesian reef. Although not as dangerous as movies like *The Deep* would have us believe, they have sharp teeth and should not be provoked. A hand dangling carelessly in front of a moray's lair could

Below: *The ornate ghost pipefish,* Solenostomus paradoxus. *This strange animal is a relative of the seahorses and pipefishes, however in* Solenostomus *the female broods the eggs. Although this juvenile stands out here against the brilliant red crinoids, the coloration and growths are probably cryptic. Tulamben, Bali.*

RUDIE KUITER

be mistaken for a prey animal, and would receive a nasty bite. The largest species, the giant moray (*Gymnothorax javanicus*), can reach more than two meters in length, and weigh 35 kilos. Many morays are nocturnal hunters, resting in holes by day and prowling the reef by night. They feed on dozing fish which they detect by smell.

A very beautiful eel, related to the morays but more delicately built, is the blue ribbon eel (*Rhinomuraena quaesita*). The adult coloration of this animal is electric blue and yellow, although adult females can turn bright yellow. Juveniles are black.

Several species of the unusual garden eels (a subfamily of the conger eels) can be found on sandy bottoms in Indonesia. They live in burrows in often large groups, and the sight of all their thin bodies waving in the current gives them their common name. They have small mouths, and pluck plankton from the current. If you swim over the "garden" the eels will slip back down into their burrows, disappearing in a wave before you.

Although garden eels are usually found in deeper water, particularly the sandy channels between reefs, they can sometimes be seen in very shallow sand patches on the reef. There is a colony of garden eels in shallow water on the approach to the popular wreck at Tulamben, Bali.

Seahorses and pipefish. These fishes (family Syngnathidae) are generally slow-moving and secretive, and are not often easy to find. They are planktivores, and can be found in sea grass beds and estuaries as well as in coral reefs. In fact, their fins are poorly developed, and they shun areas of high current or surge. Seahorses (*Hippocampus* spp.) can be highly camouflaged, some exactly matching a single species of gorgonian.

The master of camouflage, however, is the ghost pipefish (*Solenostomus cyanopterus*), an animal whose shape and color precisely duplicate a blade of turtlegrass. A strikingly colored relative is the ornate ghost pipefish, *S. paradoxus*.

Pipefish (*Syngnathus* spp.) are long and thin, and superficially

Below: *A school of shrimpfishes,* Aeoliscus strigatus. *The shrimpfishes always swim with their noses pointed downward, and can often be found using the long, black spines of the jeweled sea urchin* Diadema *for protection. In the process of evolution their dorsal, tail and anal fins have migrated to a position on the side fo the body, where they can produce lateral motion while the animal is oriented vertically.*

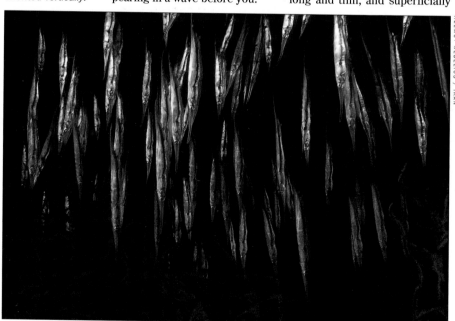

appear quite different from sea-horses. In fact, structurally they are quite similar, the pipefish just being a stretched-out version. The male incubates the eggs in a pouch on its stomach, and the young are born "live."

The large trumpetfish (*Aulostomus chinensis*) looks like a pipefish on steroids (these can be a half-meter or longer) and feeds on small fish. It has the curious habit of hiding behind larger fishes until it comes within range of its prey. One color morph is bright yellow.

Scorpionfish. The most commonly seen of this family (Scorpaenidae) are the lionfishes (*Pterois* spp. and *Dendrochirus* spp.). During the day these lavishly colored fish can be seen perching on coral heads. Perhaps because of their poisonous fins, they are relatively unperturbed by the presence of divers.

Lionfishes feed mainly at night on shrimps and small fishes. They use their elaborate fins to shepherd their prey into a suitable position, whereupon they shoot forward and inhale it whole into their large mouths.

Scorpionfish are less commonly seen, chiefly because they are so well camouflaged. Covered with folds and flaps of skin, they blend right in with the algae and other growths.

The scorpionfishes and lionfishes have a row of poisonous spines along their backs. So, despite their usually benign behavior these fish should be treated with some respect. More than one underwater photographer has been stuck by a lionfish while trying to encourage it into position for that perfect photograph. Lionfish poison is not strong enough to kill an adult, but it will certainly give you many hours of acute pain. .

Some victims have required hospitalization. The best treatment is to immerse the affected part in very hot water, as heat breaks down the venom.

Much more dangerous is the stonefish (*Synanceia verrucosa*), which carries a toxin responsible for several well-publicized deaths. These animals are masters of disguise, and encrusting algae and bryozoans actually grow onto their skin. When a small fish or crustacean absently wanders within range, it is engulfed by the animal's formidable mouth.

Groupers. The groupers (family Serranidae), are a common family on Indonesian reefs, ranging in size from more than a meter to the tiny dottybacks or pseudochromids, colorful planktivores no larger than a man's little finger.

Most of the larger groupers are plainly marked, but some, most notably the bright red and blue-spotted coral grouper (*Cephalopholis miniata*) and the flagtail grouper (*C. urodeta*) are exceptions. One of the largest fish on the reef is the giant grouper (*Ephinephelus lanceolatus*), which can reach 3 meters and weigh 400 kilos.

The fairy basselets or anthias (subfamily Anthiinae) are also groupers. Anthias, which hover in large schools around coral heads and soft coral colonies, picking plankton from the water, are very beautiful, and staples of underwater photography. Their names—the peach fairy basslet (*Pseudanthias diaspar*), the purple queen (*P. pascalus* and *P. tuka*) and the pink square anthias (*P. pleurotaenia*)—hint at their lovely colors.

Anthias are protogynous hermaphrodites, meaning that the fish all mature as females, and then a few undergo a terminal sex-change to male. These terminal males exhibit distinct, and very striking colors.

· The dottybacks (Pseudochromidae), also among the real jewels of the reef, are tiny, secretive fishes that hide in caves and under ledges.

Another unique member of the grouper family is the comet (*Calloplesiops altivelis*). This small fish has long, black fins covered with a multitude of white spots. Because of the ocelli on the fins, and the fish's movements, it is thought to be a Batesian mimic of the juvenile spotted moray eel (*Gymnothorax meleagris*). A Batesian mimic

Ciguatera Poisoning

Ciguatera is a toxin produced by a tiny dinoflagellate alga, *Gambierdiscus toxicus*. The alga itself is harmless enough, living around rocks, seagrass and filamentatious algae. The quantities of poison in each organism are minute.

But the dinoflagellates are eaten along with the algae in which they live by herbivorous fish and invertebrates. These herbivores are then eaten by larger, carnivorous fishes, and these are in turn are eaten by even larger, and more voracious predators. Since the ciguatera is not broken down, it concentrates in the tissues of these higher order predators.

A human being who eats a ciguatoxic fish will experience numbness in hands and feet, disorientation, weakness, vomiting, diarrhoea, shortness of breath and even cardiac arrest. The poison is very serious. People have died from ciguatera and there is no available cure.

The greatest danger comes from fish at the highest levels of the food chain: snappers, groupers, large jacks, barracuda, some triggerfish and moray eels. For reasons not well understood, certain species are more frequently ciguatoxic than others: particularly the red snapper (*Lutjanus bohar*), and also the giant moray (*Gymnothorax javanicus*), the saddleback grouper (*Plectropomus laevis*) and the giant grouper (*Epinephelus lanceolatus*).

Open-water fish (tuna, mackerel, etc.) are not part of the same food chain and are not affected, but any large, predatory reef fish is a candidate.

— *David Pickell*

uses its resemblence to a known dangerous animal to protect it from predation.

Hawkfish. Hawkfishes (family Cirrhitidae) get their name from their predatory habits. These small fish (6–10 cm.) perch on coral heads or sponges—anything that gives them a good lookout—and when a small crustacean or fish comes within range, they swoop down on it like a hawk. Because they are so sedentary, they make very easy photo subjects. Some species are also quite colorful—particularly the large Forster's hawkfish (*Paracirrhites forsteri*)—and the long-nosed hawkfish (*Oxycirrhitus typus*) has an interesting, pointed "beak."

Jacks. The jacks or trevallies (family Carangidae) are often seen patrolling the upper reef slope in small groups. They are among the most active predators on the reef. Jacks are always on the lookout for a meal, and groups regularly interrupt their steady cruising with powerful bursts of speed as they chase unwary smaller reef fish. Sometimes a few jacks will make a sortie into a lagoon in search of prey. If they find and attack a school of fish the sea surface erupts as the hunted fish desperately try to escape, sometimes throwing themselves onto the beach in the attempt.

Snappers and sweetlips. Snappers (*Lutjanus* spp.) are common predatory fish around deeper reefs, and are an important food fish. The red snapper (*Lutjanus bohar*), although delicious, is one of the most frequently ciguatoxic fishes (see "Ciguatera Poisoning," at left.)

Perhaps the most commonly seen reef fish in Indonesia is the yellow-backed fusilier (*Caesio teres*), a streamlined, 20–30 centimeter fish marked with bright blue and yellow. These planktivores, related to snappers, travel in large aggregations that provide a measure of protection against predators such as jacks.

Sweetlips (*Plectorhinchus* spp.) are medium-sized, strikingly marked fish related to the snappers. They are common in Indonesia, where they can often be seen in mixed schools. The juveniles are especially attractive, with bold stripes and dots of white against a brown or black background.

Batfishes. The batfishes (*Platax* spp.) are common inhabitants of Indonesian reefs. As adults, these animals take the shape of a large, silvery platter, as much as half a meter in length, with two or three broad black vertical bands. Traveling about the reef in small groups, they have a reputation for being very "intelligent," and seem to regard divers with curiosity.

There are three species in Indonesia, the orbiculate (*Platax orbicularis*), the round-faced (*P. tiera*) and the pinnate (*P. pinnatus*). As adults, orbiculate and round-faced batfish are almost impossible to distinguish. The pinnate batfish can be recognized by its long snout.

As juveniles, the fish are very different in shape, with greatly elongated dorsal and ventral fins. Juvenile orbiculate batfish are mottled brown, which is though to be a cryptic coloration to match a dead blade of sea grass. Round-faced batfish (the juveniles are sometimes called longfin batfish) are black and white and have very long fins.

The most beautiful as a juvenile is *P. pinnatus*, which has a band of electric orange all around its body and fins. This juvenile, sometimes called the orange-rimmed batfish, is thought to mimic a toxic flatworm.

Butterflyfishes. The butterflyfishes (family Chaetodontidae) are beautiful, delicate looking fish that feed on small benthic animals. Some species feed heavily on coral polyps. They have laterally compressed bodies, and snouts and teeth adapted to their particular feeding habits, enabling them to pick up their preferred prey deftly. In particularly, the

long-nosed butterflyfishes (*Forcipiger* spp.) have long, thin mouths perfect for snatching small animals from cracks and crevices in the reef. These bright yellow fish will be seen hovering under overhangs in the reef, often upside down.

Some species, occur singly or in pairs, e.g. *Forcipiger*. Others are schooling fish. The black, white, and yellow pyramid but-

HELMUT DEBELIUS / IKAN

terflyfish (*Hemitaurichthys polylepsis*), for example, occurs in massive aggregations along the walls in Manado and other parts of eastern Indonesia. Other common schooling butterflyfish include the bannerfish (*Heniochus* spp.), the most distinctive of which is the pennant butterflyfish (*Heniochus diphreutes*), which have very elongated dorsal fins and bright yellow, white

Above: *The twinspot lionfish, Dendrochirus biocellatus, is one of the most attractive of the dwarf lionfishes. It is much smaller than* Pterois *sp., growing to just 8 centimeters. Halmahera, Maluku.*

and black markings.

Angelfish. The angelfishes (family Pomacanthidae) probably make it onto more postcards than any fish other than the Moorish idol. They browse the reef for sponges, algae and occasional small crustaceans. Adult angelfish, some of which can reach 30 centimeters, are truly magnificent animals.

In Indonesia, one can often see emperor angelfish (*Pomacanthus imperator*), with thin, horizontal stripes of blue and yellow; blue-girdled angelfish (*P. [Euxiphipops] navarchus*), with a deep blue "girdle" against bright orange; and regal angelfish (*Pygoplites diacanthus*), the most shy of the bunch, with vertical stripes of yellow, white and blue.

All *Pomacanthus* species have very similar juvenile coloring, a series of thin white or light blue stripes against a dark blue background. Two fish with dramatically different adult coloration, for example the blue-girdled and emperor angelfish, look so similar as juveniles that only an expert could tell them apart.

Damselfish. These small, ubiquitous fish (family Pomacentridae) are members of one of the largest groups of tropical reef fish. In addition to the reef itself, they occur along rocky shores, algal flats, and even in silt-choked harbors. The damselfish feed on plankton and algae, some even setting up small territories from which they aggressively keep all herbivores away, "farming" the algal turf that then grows on the coral rock.

The black and white three-striped damselfish (*Dascyllus aruanus*), the blue devil (*Chrysiptera cyanea*), and the blue damsels (*Pomacentrus* spp.) are common among the coral heads and rubble of the shallow reef. The pugnacious black farmer fish (*Stegastes lividus*) also defends its patch of algae in the shallows. Deeper on the reef, the planktivorous blue-green chromis (*Chromis viridis*) is common, occurring in large schools like anthias, which it superficially resembles.

Favorites among divers are the anemonefish (*Amphiprion* spp. and *Premnas biaculaeatus*). These beautiful and plucky little fish will even nip a diver to defend their anemone home. (See "Clownfishes and their Sea Anemone Hosts," page 46.)

Wrasses. The wrasses (family Labridae) are a large and successful family on the coral reefs. Most are small, elongated fishes, with a distinct swimming style that depends more on the pectoral fins than the tail. Many are colorful, and inhabit the shallow parts of the reef and reef flats, although some (such as the hogfishes) are characteristic of the deep reef.

Wrasses undergo sometimes dramatic color changes as they pass from juveniles to adults. Many of these predators on worms and small crustaceans bury in the sand at night to sleep, or dive into the sand to escape predators.

Most familiar to divers is the blue-streak cleaner wrasse (*Labroides dimidiatus*), which set up stations to clean small parasites and pockets of decay from the skin, mouth and gills of larger reef fish. Some wrasse act as cleaners only when young (for example, the colorful lyretail hogfish, *Bodianus anthoides*).

The largest of the family is the Napoleon wrasse (*Cheilinus undulatus*), which can reach 1.8 meters. This is one of the largest fish a diver will see on many dives. These stately animals, also called the humphead wrasse, have a prominent forehead and formidable-looking snout and cruise the outer edge of the reef in loose groups, with one large male and a few smaller females. Although wary of divers, at some localities they have been "tamed"

sufficiently to allow hand feeding. Hard boiled eggs are a favorite.

Parrotfish. The parrotfishes (family Scaridae) are among the most important herbivores on the reef. They get their name from their bright colors, curious flapping "flight" (much like wrasses), and their strong, bird-like beaks, which they use to scrape algae and other living matter from rocky surfaces. In so doing they inevitably take in great quantities of coral rock. This is ground down by powerful sets of teeth in the throat so that the organic material can be more easily digested. The waste product of the feeding activities of parrotfish is coral sand—a major component of Indonesian beaches especially on the offshore islands.

Parrotfishes are protogynous hermaphrodites that undergo a series of color changes with age and sexual status. Primary phase parrotfish—whether males or females—are exceedingly difficult to identify, all being relatively drab grey or rust-colored. The terminal males are striking, however, usually green with bright markings, particularly around the cheeks and eyes. In most species the primary phase is made up of mixed males and females (diandric); in others the primary phase is all females (monandric).

One notable exception to this pattern is the bumphead parrotfish (*Bolbometopon muricatum*). All bumphead parrotfish (males, females and juveniles) are a dull green in color. Although parrotfish have popularly been considered coral-eaters, they are chiefly herbivores, scraping the reef surface to extract the algal turf, not to eat coral polyps. The bumphead parrotfish is an exception, and feeds for the most part on living coral. They are massive beasts which grow to over a meter in length and travel along the reef in groups looking for all the world like squadrons of army tanks, leaving clouds of coral sand in their wakes. Sometimes their crunching can be heard underwater.

They should not to be confused with the Napoleon wrasse (see above), a superficially similar fish. The bumphead parrot-

Above: *The Napoleon wrasse, or humphead wrasse, Cheilinus undulatus, is the largest wrasse and—at up to two meters— often the largest fish of any kind one will see on a given dive. This predator on crustaceans, gastropods, fishes and echinoderms is usually a solitary rover, but sometimes a pair or a small "squad" will be seen. Australians call this fish the Maori wrasse.*

fish has a more rounded head.

At night, parrotfish secrete a transparent cocoon of mucus in which to sleep. At first glance such a fragile structure would seem to offer little protection against predators, but at night, most predators hunt with their sense of smell, not their eyes, and the cocoon is an effective defense against this.

Barracudas. These familiar

ED ROBINSON / IKAN

Above: *The bump-head parrotfish,* Bolbometopon muricatum. *This, the largest parrotfish, is also one of the few true coral feeders. With its impressive fused "beak" it can crunch on corals like they were pretzels. It is sometimes confused with the Napoleon wrasse, but a comparison of this photo with the one on the previous page should make clear the physical differences between them.*

fish (family Sphyraenidae) are one of the most important predators on the reef, but their reputation for ferociousness is exaggerated. Despite their formidable teeth, they are not known to attack divers. Small barracudas often occur in schools, sometimes numbering many hundreds of individuals. In contrast, large barracudas (which may grow up to 1.7 meters) tend to be solitary. Such giants may be quite old, so are less likely to be seen near heavily populated areas where there is a lot of fishing pressure.

Blennies. These little fishes (family Blenniidae) often go unnoticed by divers. They are most abundant in shallow waters, and can also be found on back-reefs and in murky estuarial waters. Most are not very colorful. Some have interesting "faces," although these are only really visible to the macro lens.

The mimic blenny (*Aspidontus taeniatus*) mimics the color

and even the movements of the blue-streak cleaner wrasse *Labroides dimidiatus.* However, instead of cleaning parasites from the larger fish, the mimic blenny bites off a tender chunk of scales and flesh, and then beats a hasty retreat.

Dartfishes. One group the diver will notice, because of their striking colors and their habit of hovering in small groups above the coral sand, are the firefishes (*Nemateleotris* spp.), particularly *N. magnifica,* a beautiful fish with a greatly elongated dorsal fin which it flicks in nervous little movements.

Gobies. These fish (family Gobiidae) are small, usually dull-colored, and often remain hidden in crevices and the branches of coral. There are many hundreds of species and perhaps 100 genera in the Indo-Pacific, making them the single most successful family on the coral reefs. Identifying these fishes is very difficult, and there are probably hundreds still undescribed.

Although not reef-dwellers, the curious mudskippers (*Periophthalmus* spp.), which can be found in Indonesia on the brackish mudflats around mangrove swamps, are also gobies. As long as their gills and skin remain wet, these small brown fish can hop about on land.

Related to the gobies are the little dragonets. These are found in weedy areas and sea grass beds as well as the reef itself. Perhaps the most spectacular is the mandarinfish (*Synchiropus splendens*), with a pattern that could have come off a bright paisley silk tie.

Surgeonfish. The surgeonfishes and tangs (family Acanthuridae) are a particularly important group of herbivores. They are often seen singly, in shallow water over coral flats. Since single grazers are often chased by damselfishes protecting their territories, surgeonfishes sometimes form large feeding aggregations.

Despite their apparently destructive feeding habits, herbivorous fish are of immense value to the coral reef community. By breaking down hard-to-digest plant material they make the nutrients in it available to other animals. Furthermore, by limiting the growth of plants they may actually enhance that of corals. Without grazing, the plants would grow to such an extent that they would soon cover the reef, making new coral settlement virtually impossible.

The surgeonfish family includes some of the most exquisitely patterned and colored of all reef fishes. But one feature that is common to all is that they all have one or two pairs of scalpel-like blades on the sides of their tails. These give the family its name and can inflict serious cuts if the fish are handled carelessly.

The orangespine unicornfish (*Naso lituratus*) with its bright orange spots warning of its spines; the hepatus tang (*Paracanthurus hepatus*) with its electric blue and black body, and the clown surgeonfish (*Acanthurus lineatus*), orange-and-blue striped, are just a few examples.

Moorish idol and Rabbitfishes. The Moorish idol (*Zanclus cornutus*) and the rabbitfishes (*Siganus* spp.) are close relatives of the surgeonfishes. The Moorish idol is for many people the quintessential reef fish; with its bright, contrasting yellow, white and black color, prominent snout, and long, thin dorsal fin, it is indeed an elegant-looking animal. They are fairly common grazers, and can be found all the way from the east coast of Africa to the west coast of Central America.

The rabbitfishes look much like surgeonfish or Moorish idols, although with the exception of the foxface (*Siganus volpi-*

nus) and the coral rabbitfish (*S. corallinus*), not as brightly colored. They have no "scalpels," but they do have a very strong poison in the short spines of their fins, and should not be handled.

Tuna and Mackerels. Although one or two members of the family Scombridae patrol reefs—particularly the dogtooth tuna (*Gymnosarda unicolor*)—most are true pelagics, living in

ED ROBINSON / IKAN

the open sea, and will only occasionally be seen on the outer reef edge. When traveling by boat between islands or to offshore dive sites it is not unusual to see big schools of tuna splashing at the surface, often with attendant flocks of seabirds overhead. These schools are usually composed of skipjack tuna, although there are several other species found in Indonesia.

Above: *A school of pyramid butterfly-fishes,* Hemitaurichthys polylepsis. *These plankton feeders gather in large groups around the lip of drop-off reefs in eastern Indonesia. The Bunaken group, Sulawesi.*

Above: *Indonesian flashlighfishes.* Anomalops katoptron, *top, is the more common of the two.* Photoblepheron palpebratus *tends to be found in smaller groups in rather deep caves. Both species grow to about 10 centimeters long.*

Skipjack (*Katsuwonis pelamis*) grow to just under a meter in length, and are plump and streamlined, with a characteristic series of about five black lines on their bellies. They will not be seen on the reef itself, however, although there will be plenty in the fish market.

Triggerfish. Triggers (family Balistidae) are common fish at moderate depths on the reefs, where they hunt spiny crustaceans and echinoderms. Shaped like a compressed football and often exquisitely marked, they use powerful jaws to dispatch their hard-shelled prey. Large schools of the black triggerfish (*Odonus niger*), which is actually more blue in color, can be seen hovering off the reef walls, swimming with characteristic undulations of their fins. This fish is sometimes called the red-toothed trigger, although you have to look very closely to see that its teeth are, indeed, red.

Some distinctively marked triggers include the Picasso trigger (*Rhinecanthus aculeatus*), so-named for its cubist markings, and the undulate trigger (*Pseudobalistes fuscus*), covered with wavy markings. The largest trigger you will see on the Indonesian reefs is the Titan triggerfish (*Balistoides viridescens*), a downright ugly and beligerent animal that grows to more than 60 centimeters.

The most dramatic of the family is the clown triggerfish (*Balistoides conspicullum*), with its bright orange snout, blue body, and white-spotted belly. The clown trigger is very territorial, and will patrol the same area of reef. When threatened, a clown trigger will wedge its body headfirst into a crack in the coral wall, and extend its dorsal spine. The first spine, once raised, is locked in place by the second, making it impossible to pull the fish out of his hole. A diver who knows what he is doing can reach in and

gently push back the second spine, unlocking the fin. He can then extract the irritated fish.

Puffers. The curious pufferfishes (family Tetraodontidae) are solitary omnivores, often seen wandering about the reef in their slow, almost clumsy way and plucking at algae, crustaceans, molluscs, worms and sponges. When threatened they inflate themselves with large quantities of water, which either locks them into a coral crevice, or makes it impossible for a predator to swallow them. In addition to this protection, the skin and most of the internal organs of puffers contain a deadly poison. This poison is absent from the flesh, which in Japan is the highly prized *fugu*.

A common puffer on Indonesian reefs is the dog-faced or black-spotted puffer (*Arothron nigropunctatus*), which exhibits a great deal of color variability, from the usual dull brown to bright yellow, always with many small black spots.

The related porcupinefishes (family Diodontidae) possess the same defenses as the puffers, with the addition of numerous spines, which become erect when the animal is inflated. The common porcupinefish (*Diodon hystrix*) is often seen. Boxfishes (family Ostraciontidae) are similar to puffers, except their protection comes in the form of a hard, roughly cubical external covering.

Nocturnal fish. At night the schools of day active species break up and the fish take refuge in holes in the reef. They are replaced by nocturnal species such as the cardinalfishes (family Apogonidae), bigeyes (family Priacanthidae), and squirrelfishes or soldierfishes (family Holocentridae), which feast on the abundant night plankton.

One of the most interesting families of fish to come out at night are the flashlight fishes

INTRODUCTION

(Family Anomalopidae). These delightful little black fish have special organs under their eyes which contain millions of light-producing bacteria. The fish are able to cover and uncover these organs to produce characteristic flashes of blue-green light. The function of these lights is not fully understood, but they are probably used to communicate, to see by, and perhaps to confuse predators.

Two species of flashlight fish are found in Indonesia. The most often seen is *Anomalops kataptron*, a 6–8 centimeter fish that forages for plankton in shallow reef waters, often in large schools. (*Anomalops* also occurs in a much larger—27 centimeters—deepwater form that lives in up to 400 meters of water.) *Photoblepharon palpebratus* is rare and tends to occur in relatively small groups in deep caves.

Marine Reptiles

Sea turtles. One of the most delightful experiences a diver can have is swimming with turtles, and in Indonesia such encounters are quite common.

Six species of marine turtles are found in Indonesian waters, but the two most likely to be seen by divers are the hawksbill turtle (*Eretmochelys imbricata*) and the green turtle (*Chelonia mydas*).

They are not always easy to distinguish underwater, although the hawksbill has a distinct beak, and the trailing edge of its shell is jagged. The hawksbill is also generally smaller, and is tortoiseshell brown (instead of olive green) although such relatively minor color differences are very hard to determine underwater. A third species that may be seen by divers is the loggerhead (*Caretta caretta*), which is much like the green turtle, except it has a massive head.

The green turtle feeds almost entirely on sea grass, while the hawksbill and loggerhead are both largely carnivorous. The shell of the hawksbill is covered with large horn-like scales, the source of "tortoiseshell." Tortoiseshell products—and even stuffed and varnished hawksbill turtles—are offered in Indonesian markets, although import into most Western countries is

Below: *A bluestreak cleaner wrasse,* Labroides dimidiatus *picks at the eye of a bright, terminal male purple queen,* Pseudanthias tuka. *The little cleaners provide an essential service and are never molested by their "customers." Manado, Sulawesi.*

MIKE SEVERNS

KAL MULLER

Above: *Traditional whaling still takes place in two villages east of Flores. These men, from Lamalera, Lembata, are flensing a sperm whale they caught with a hand-hurled spear from their small wooden boat. The men catch no more than 15–20 small whales a year, although they will also harpoon whale sharks, marlin or any other large fish they come across.*

strictly prohibited.

Marine turtles spend nearly all their lives at sea, but their eggs have to be laid on land. At certain secluded beaches females regularly haul out at night to deposit their eggs above the high water mark.

Sea snakes. Most sea snakes (family Hydrophiidae) never come onto land at all, even giving birth at sea. There are some 60 species of sea snakes in the world, over half of which are found in Indonesia. They tend to be patchily distributed, very common in some areas and absent from others. As reptiles, they must come up for air, although they have a very large lung and can stay under for many hours.

Sea snakes can be seen underwater poking their small heads into cracks and crevices, searching for small fish and crustaceans. The head of a sea snake is often difficult to distinguish from the tail, as both are blunt, although the head is always smaller, and the tail is flattened somewhat, to aid in swimming.

Sea snakes are equipped with extremely toxic venom which can be delivered through two short fangs on the upper jaw. The venom is used to subdue prey such as spiny fish or moray eels, which could cause the snake considerable damage if not killed very quickly. Since fish are quite resistant to most toxins, it is not surprising that sea snake venom is so strong.

Sea snakes are rarely aggressive towards divers, however, and unprovoked attacks are virtually unknown. They are sometimes inquisitive, however, and may inspect a diver.

The grey-and-black banded colubrine or amphibious sea snake (*Laticauda colubrina*) is common around Manado. This animal—collected in huge numbers in the Phillipines for its skin—It is an inoffensive creature, and slow to anger. Guides often catch the animals for their clients to pose with. We don't suggest you try this, however.

The yellow-bellied sea snake (*Pelamis platurus*) is the most numerous reptile on earth. This colorful animal is so well-adapted to an aquatic life that, if washed ashore, it will die. It cannot even crawl back to the water.

Crocodiles. One marine reptile that is truly dangerous is the salt water crocodile (*Crocodylus porosus*). These monsters can grow to many meters in length, although real giants are very rare these days. Fortunately for divers they usually live in murky estuarine areas, not on coral reefs. Saltwater crocodiles are found in Irian Jaya, and in scattered locations in Maluku.

Marine Mammals

Swimming with dolphins or other marine mammals is always a memorable occasion for a diver. Unfortunately, while common enough in Indonesian waters, mammals are rarely seen while diving.

Dolphins. Schools of dolphins are a frequent sight while traveling out to dive sites by boat. Sometimes their "whistling" can be heard during a dive (a sound that is sometimes uncannily like a leaking air cylinder) but they will normally stay well beyond the range of visibility. The best way to see them underwater is to snorkel from the dive boat when a school is encountered in deep water. Usually they will move away, but you could get lucky.

There are several dolphin species in Indonesia and identifying them at sea is a far from easy task. Common species here include the spinner dolphin (*Stenella longirostris*), so-called because of its characteristic high, spinning jumps; the common dolphin (*Delphinus delphis*), which has a black-tipped snout, and a crisscross pattern on its flanks; and the spotted dolphin, with a pattern of fine spots on its sides.

Whales. Several species of large whale also occur in Indonesia, some arriving seasonally from polar regions, others being year-round residents. Like dolphins they are best watched from a boat rather than the water. Some whales breed in Indonesian waters, so it is very important not to harass them by chasing them in boats.

Most of the species seen are plankton-eating baleen whales which have vertical spouts and a small, but distinct, dorsal fin. They might be distinguished on the basis of size, but this requires some experience. The blue whale (*Balaenoptera musculus*) is known in Indonesian waters, as are several smaller but very similar species, including the fin whale (*B. physalus*) and minke whale (*B. acutorostrata*). The humpback, (*Megaptera novaeangliae*), is easier to identify.

The sperm whale (*Physeter catodon*), of *Moby Dick* fame, is a very different animal. These are toothed whales, which feed on giant squid and fish snatched from great depths. The sperm whale has a characteristic forward pointing spume and hump-like ridges rather than a dorsal fin on its back. Two species of dwarf sperm whale (*Kogis* spp.) also inhabit Indonesian waters.

Dugong. It is very unlikely that a diver will see this rare animal. The dugong or sea cow (*Dugong dugon*) is a slow-moving animal, up to 2.5 meters long, that looks like a walrus without the tusks. There are only three other members of order Sirenia, manatees from Florida, the Amazon basin and West Africa.

The dugong is the only herbivorous marine mammal, and is strictly aquatic. The animals can eat 10 percent of their body weight a day in sea grasses, and are found mainly in sheltered bays where these plants grow.

Dugongs are threatened throughout their range, because they are slow-moving, easy targets for hunters, and because they take so long to reproduce. Calving takes place only once every 3–7 years, and a dugong takes 15 years to reach maturity.

—Charles Anderson and David Pickell

Introducing the Island of Java

Lush and populous Java—perhaps the most familiar of Indonesia's thousands of islands—is the political, cultural and industrial heart of the island nation. Some 115 million people live on Java, almost two-thirds of Indonesia's total population on just 7 percent of the nation's land area.

The island is rugged and volcanic, and its rich soil makes it one of the world's most productive agricultural regions. In Dutch colonial times, Java was called "The Garden of the East."

Jakarta

The Ibu Kota—literally "Mother City"—of Indonesia is Jakarta, on the northwest coast of Java. With 9.48 million inhabitants, it is one of the world's premier cities. Jakarta is the fourth most dense city in the world, more dense, even, than Bombay. This richness of humanity—or crush, depending on your outlook—is essential to Jakarta's bustling (and hustling) charm.

History of Java

Java, which until 20,000 years ago was connected together with Sumatra and Borneo to the southeast Asian mainland, is one of the world's earliest populated spots. In 1894, Dutch naturalist Eugène Dubois announced that he had discovered a "Java apeman," the first known fossil remains of what scientists now call *Homo erectus.*

Between "Java Man," who lived as much as 1 million years ago, and the first Bronze Age Javanese, who lived 2,000 years ago, there is little surviving archaeological record on Java. The ancestors of modern-day Melanesians and the Australian aboriginals are thought to have passed through Java some 30,000 years ago. But the ancestors of today's Javanese were the Austronesians, the region's great seafarers and most successful settlers, who moved into Java about 5,000 years ago.

Java is most famous for her great Indianized kingdoms, which developed out of trading contacts with India, beginning in the first millennium A.D. The Hindu and Buddhist kingdoms of central Java produced the largest Buddhist stupa extant, Borobudur on the Kedu plain, and the many Hindu monuments of Prambanan, including the 47-meter high Loro Jonggrang.

East Java's Majapahit, which lasted through the 14th and 15th centuries, was the most successful of the early Javanese kingdoms. According to an old manuscript, Majapahit claimed an area under its control greater than that of present day Indonesia.

By the 16th century, Islam had displaced the old Indianized kingdoms and at the same time, European traders seeking spices began arriving. The Portuguese were first, but it was the Dutch East India Company, the infamous Vereenigde Oostindische Compagnie, that established a chokehold on the spice trade. After the V.O.C. went bankrupt in 1799 the Dutch government ran Indonesia as a colony.

With the imposition of the "Culture System" in Java, Dutch planters grew wealthy, and the Javanese worked as near slaves growing export crops like coffee and sugar. Resentment grew and nationalism boiled at the turn of

Overleaf: *A school of sleek unicornfish,* Naso hexacanthus. *Photograph by Ed Robinson of IKAN. Manado, Sulawesi.*

Opposite: *A pink clownfish,* Amphiprion perideraion, *in front of its host anemone,* Heteractis magnifica. *Because the anemone is partially contracted, its bright column is visible. Bunaken Island, 3 meters. Photograph by Mike Severns.*

the 20th century.

After World War II and a cruel Japanese occupation, the nationalists declared independence in 1945. The Dutch were unwilling to relinquish their colony, however, and it took five years of fighting and mounting international opposition to the Dutch to drive them out. The Republic of Indonesia was officially born on August 17, 1950.

People and Culture

The great majority of the Javanese—88 percent—are Muslims, and in fact Indonesia is the largest Muslim country in the world. Still, older threads of Hinduism, Buddhism and many regional ethnic cultures are deeply woven into Javanese culture. Hindu epics, the *Mahabharata* and *Ramayana,* are still the chief source of material for the very popular shadow puppet theater, *wayang kulit*, and drama, *wayang orang.*

Javanese music, played on the famous gamelan orchestra of metallophones, brass drums, gongs and other mostly percussion instruments, is a famous holdover from the days of the Hindu courts.

Batik, fabric that has been patterned through repeated dyeings over a wax resist, is sometimes considered a Javanese invention, although it is perhaps more likely that the techniques came from India. Whatever the source, Javanese batik is today very popular, both as art and a source of everyday clothing.

Geography

Several of Java's volcanoes are still active, and Kelud erupted as recently as early 1990, killing 31 people. Java's most famous eruption occurred in 1883, when Krakatau exploded.

The Java Sea to the north of the island is quite shallow, less than 200 meters. But to the island's south is the Java trench, where the Indian Ocean reaches its deepest point, 7,450 meters.

Much of the island's forest has been given up to cultivated land. The last wilderness area is Ujung Kulon National Park on Java's westernmost peninsula.

— *Janet Boileau and Debe Campbell*

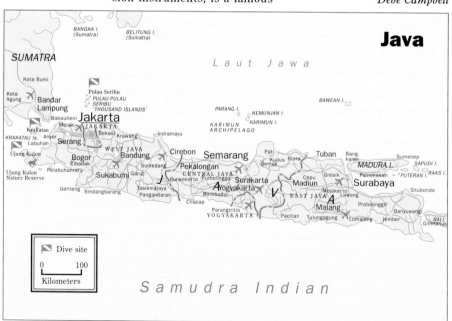

Diving Krakatau and Ujung Kulon Park

Diving in the waters off Krakatau, the rocky islands forming the crater of an underwater volcano in the Sunda Strait off West Java, or in the waters around the Ujung Kulon peninsula in southwest Java, is not the best to be found in Indonesia. But the seascape of cracked volcanic rock around Krakatau, and the caves and tunnels around Ujung Kulon provide an interesting underwater experience.

Reaching either of these sites requires some patience and initiative. There is little chance of making a day of it from Jakarta. One must overland to Anyer or Labuhan, and then take a boat to the dive sites.

Recent road repairs make the trip from Jakarta to Anyer quite pleasant. From there, a boat will take you the 50 kilometers to the Krakatau group, a 4-hour crossing (see map page 78). To reach Ujung Kulon, one can go either by train or car to Labuhan, and then by boat to Ujung Kulon.

We strongly suggest that you organize your jaunt with a Jakarta dive outfit. (See "Java Dive Practicalities" page 85). You can either go with your own group, or hook up with one of the many weekend dive excursions. It can be a challenge to find a seaworthy boat, and strong and unpredictable winds in the strait could prove quite troublesome to an inexperienced captain.

If our warning does not deter you, you can charter a boat through the ranger stations at Labuhan, Carita, or Ujung Kulon Park, or through one of the many small hotels scattered along the way. Alternately, a tour agent in Jakarta could arrange a boat charter for you. In any case, do not expect a purpose-built dive boat with an attached Zodiac. What you will likely find is an older wooden *pinisi,* a traditional sailing craft that has been converted to diesel power.

Krakatau

The famous eruption of Krakatau on August 26, 1883 sent up a plume of ash and pumice 26 kilometers high and 6,000 kilometers wide, and the explosion could be heard from Myanmar to Australia. The huge tidal waves created by the explosion destroyed 165 villages in Sumatra and Java, killing more than 36,000 people.

The original caldera collapsed in on itself, leaving three islands remaining of its rim: Sertung, Panjang and Rakata. In 1928, Anak Krakatau—"Child of Krakatau"—appeared. This still active daughter cone continues to eject tephra and lava, growing

---

AT A GLANCE

Krakatau and Ujung Kulon

Reef type:	Volcanic rock slabs and formations, some reef
Access:	4 hrs from Anyer by boat for Krakatau; Ujung Kulon sites 15–30 min from ranger station
Visibility:	Fair to good, 10–20 meters
Current:	Gentle, to 1 knot; swells and 1.5 knot current at Ujung Kulon sites
Fish:	Fair to good variety
Highlights:	Strange underwater landscape at Krakatau; rock tunnels at Karang Copong; good coral at Tg. Jajar.

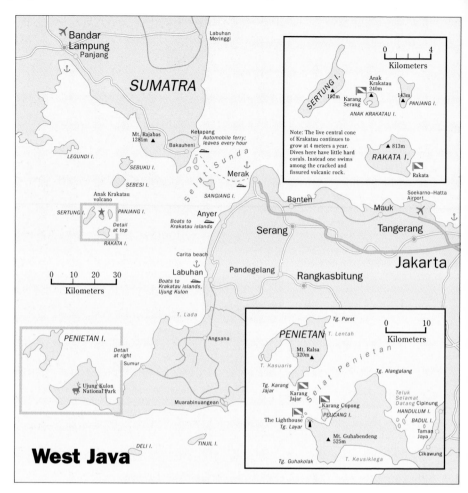

Inset map (top right, ANAK KRAKATAU detail):

0 — 4
Kilometers

SERTUNG I.

Anak
Krakatau
240m

182m
Karang
Serang

143m

PANJANG I.

ANAK KRAKATAU I.

Note: The live central cone
of Krakatau continues to
grow at 4 meters a year.
Dives here have little hard
corals. Instead one swims
among the cracked and
fissured volcanic rock.

813m

RAKATA I.

Rakata

Main map:

Bandar
Lampung
Panjang

Labuhan
Meringgi

SUMATRA

Mt. Rajabas
1281m

Ketapang
Automobile ferry;
leaves every hour

Bakauheni

LEGUNDI I.

SEBUKU I.

Merak

SEBESI I.

Anak Krakatau
volcano

SERTUNG I.

PANJANG I.

Detail
at top

RAKATA I.

SANGIANG I.

Anyer

Boats to
Krakatau islands

Serang

Banten

Mauk

Tangerang

Soekarno–Hatta
Airport

Jakarta

0   10   20   30
Kilometers

Carita beach

Labuhan

Boats to
Krakatau islands,
Ujung Kulon

Pandegelang

Rangkasbitung

T. Lada

PENIETAN I.

Detail
at right

Sumur

Ujung Kulon
National Park

Angsana

Muarabinuangean

DELI I.

TINJIL I.

West Java

Inset map (bottom right, PENIETAN detail):

Tg. Parat

0 — 10
Kilometers

PENIETAN

T. Lentah

Mt. Ralsa
320m

T. Kasuaris

Tg. Karang
Jajar

Karang
Jajar

Karang Copong

PEUCANG I.

The Lighthouse
Tg. Layar

Mt. Guhabendeng
525m

Tg. Guhakolak

T. Keusiklega

Tg. Alangalang

Teluk
Selamat
Datang Cipinung

HANDULUM I.

BADUL I.

Tamaa
Jaya

Cikawung

at the rate of 4 meters each year,
now having reached 240 meters.

A rocky, wide skirt of black
sand rings the island. Being so
new, Anak Krakatau has provided a perfect laboratory for scientists studying early colonization
of islands by plant and animal
life. So far, 120 species of plants
have found their way to the little
island. The shoreline is dominated by feathery casuarinas, and a
few tough succulents have found
a niche further up the slope.

It takes just 20 minutes to
climb the 150 or so meters to the
rim of the new crater. Inside, the
steaming cone is surrounded by
a lunar landscape of fumaroles.
Looking outward, one can see
the surrounding island remains

of the once-massive original
Krakatau. The descent is easy,
and is best finished with a
refreshing swim along the black
sand beach.

Karang Serang Rocks

These rocks, painted white by
the sea birds, mark the site of a
dive off Anak Krakatau. The
underwater scenery consists of
large blocks of volcanic rock,
seemingly sheered off by the
blast. The cracked and sharp-
edged rocks make a west-facing
submarine cliff look like the ruin
of an ancient Greek temple. In
the crevices of the rock, coral
growth is beginning.

The visibility is fair to good,
10 to 20 meters. Schools of Moor-

ish idols and other reef fish inhabit the area, and one occasionally sees reef whitetip sharks. The bright colors of emperor angelfish stand out starkly against the background of dark rock.

On the south end of the site, the slab scenery is interrupted by growths of staghorn and table *Acropora,* some with blue-tinted tips. Around the rocks to the east grow an astonishing number of orange fan coral gorgonians. The smallest covered three square meters, and the largest, five square meters. The visibility drops here, because of the sandy bottom. Reef blacktip sharks patrol this area.

Rakata

This site, off the southeast end of Rakata, offers a nice drift dive. The steep sides of the island prevent access. The depths here are modest, to just 25 meters, and the gentle current carries you east. The underwater scenery is, again, slabs of volcanic rock.

A decent variety of small reef fish populates the shallower depths, and some of the crevices have been claimed by moray eels. Green turtles are numerous at this site. In the 19th century, before it exploded, Krakatau island was a common stop for sailors, who loaded up on turtles.

An unusual feature of this dive are the many underwater trees, which have been cast from the island cliffs by landslides. These attract large schools of fusiliers and jacks.

Ujung Kulon

This park, covering the peninsula at the southwest tip of Java and Penietan Island (the Krakatau group is also part of the park), is a rich area of lowland tropical rainforest. On these 420 square kilometers are hornbills and mynahs, wild boar and rusa deer, macaques and monitor lizards. The most famous inhabitants,

however, are the last wild Javan rhinos. These animals, of which only 57 are still believed to exist, are so elusive that even some park rangers have not seen one.

Accommodations at the Pulau Peucang ranger station, Taman Jaya, and Pulau Handeuleum run $10–$80 a night. There is even a new restaurant at the ranger station on Peucang. The station's 16 units attract surfers, who frequent the peninsula's south side, known for its great waves. Peucang Island also has some beautiful beaches, but beware of the nosey macaques. They will rummage through unattended bags and take to the trees with whatever strikes their fancy.

The Lighthouse

Tanjung Layar lighthouse on the tip of Ujung Kulon is the landmark for triangulating a rocky

Above: *The common lionfish,* Pterois volitans. *Although the dorsal and pectoral spines of this fish carry a potent venom, it is not an aggressive creature. The lionfish's lavish finnage and lazy disposition make it a favorite with photographers. Maumere Bay, Flores.*

island. The highlight of this shallow (to 12 meters) dive are tunnels in the rock that lead to caves in the island. Seeing schools of fish swimming in and out of these tunnels is a surprisingly breathtaking experience. Visibility is 20 meters.

The surge here is quite strong, and you are rocked back and forth as the prevailing current carries you from the tunnels across some sandy mounds, where the sea life is abundant—including some nice soft corals—but visibility is quite reduced, to less than 10 meters. This site makes a fine night dive.

Karang Jajar

This site is on the rocks off large Penietan Island's Karang Jajar cape. It is an hour's sail from the ranger station at Peucang. If conditions are right, a drift dive off the south stretch offers a good, and very colorful growth of coral. You drop to 15 meters, and then drift east with a gentle current to a maximum of 20 meters. Below you, the wall plunges to past 40 meters. Turtles frequent the area, and we saw too many stingrays to count.

Badul Island

Tunggal Jaya is a sleepy community on the northern side of the isthmus of the Ujung Kulon peninsula. Just offshore here is a tiny, sandy island, Badul, which is surrounded by a good reef. You enter the water from about 15 meters off Badul's west shore, and an easy drift dive takes you about 3/4 of a kilometer before your air runs out.

Coral growth around the island is not spectacular, but the variety of both hard and soft corals was good. Visibility during our dive was less than 8 meters. Schools of bannerfish and fusiliers inhabit the reef, and we saw some bright nudibranchs.

—Janet Boileau and Debe Campbell

Above: *The Thousand Islands archipelago is very close to Jakarta, Indonesia's largest city, and many of the islands, such as this one, have been developed into fancy resorts providing weekend getaways for rich city dwellers.*

dive location off the west point of the peninsula. Expect swells to rock your dive boat, heavy surface current, and unusually cool water temperatures.

Beneath the surface, however, the sea is surprisingly calm. The visibility is quite good, around 20 meters. The rocks that jut just above the water plunge underneath the surface to 30 meters, looking just like submerged mountains. Coral is scarce, but in the underwater valleys there were large barracuda, schools of fusiliers and other medium-sized fish, and platoons of bumphead parrotfish. We also saw turtles circling the submerged rocks and a fat, nosey reef whitetip shark.

Karang Copong

This is a small island within sight of the northwest tip of Peucang

Diving on Java's 'Thousand Islands'

Pulau-Pulau Seribu

While not noted for Indonesia's best diving, Pulau-Pulau Seribu —the "Thousand Islands"—can be a good choice because of its proximity to Jakarta, and because of the great number of available sites. The islands, which actually number about 110, are scattered in a vertical group north from Jakarta in the shallow Java Sea.

Some 12,000 people live on Pulau-Pulau Seribu, more than half of them on the island of Pulau Kelapa.

With some advance planning, it is quite easy to get to the islands from Jakarta. Boats, ranging from inter-island shuttles to large cabin cruisers, ferry passengers to and from the various islands for $3.50 to $50, depending on the comfort of the craft and the distance to the island. The nearest islands are just 10 minutes from shore; the furthest can take nearly two hours by speedboat.

Accommodations on the islands also vary dramatically. International standards accommodations that cater to divers can be found on the islands of Putri, Pelangi, Sepa, Kotok, Pantara (Barat and Timur) and Matahari. Each of these also has a shop offering dive equipment rentals and compressors.

Transportation, and bookings for accommodations and dive trips, may be made at the departure pier in Ancol Marina, or through Jakarta travel agents or certified dive centers, such as the Jakarta Hilton's Dive Masters. Also check the English language daily newspaper, the *Jakarta Post,* for trips and special offers. Mid-week diving and accommodations are usually easy to arrange, but be aware that Pulau Seribu is very popular among Jakartans for weekend jaunts.

Popular Resorts

Some of the islands have resort type accommodations, and they may provide some music or a bar at night. On the less "civilized" islands, nighttime entertainment might be limited to the buzzing of mosquitoes.

Upmarket resorts, built in cooperation with Japan Airlines, have gone up on Pantara Timur and Pantara Barat islands. These are very posh, with all the comforts one might expect from a fine hotel in Singapore or Hawaii.

Pelangi and Putri islands offer somewhat less toney accommodations. Putri has small bungalows, a restaurant and bar, and sailboats and sailboards can be rented. Pelangi is a larger resort, and boasts fancy cottages, tennis courts, and a popular restaurant out over the water. Shops here

---

AT A GLANCE

Pulau-Pulau Seribu

Reef type: Coral slopes

Access: 45 min to 2 hrs by boat, depending on location and type of vessel

Visibility: Poor to fair, 8–15 meters

Current: Quite gentle

Coral: Can be very good

Fish: Good varieties and numbers

Highlights: Wooden shipwreck at Pulau Piniki; excellent coral at Pulau Kotok and Pulau Gosonglaga.

Pulau-Pulau Seribu

Reef

Dive site

0   5   10
Kilometers

DUA ISLANDS
DUA BARAT I.
DUA TIMUR I.

PETELORAN Kcl. I.
PETELORAN Bsr. I.   PENJALIRAN TIMUR I.
JAGUNG I.   PENJALIRAN BARAT I.

NYAMPLUNG I.   RINGIT I.
ALIMAN I.   SEBARU Bsr. I.
BUNDER I.   SEBARU Kcl. I.
HANTU Bsr. I.
HANTU Kcl. I.   GOSONGLAGA Kcl. I.
YU Bsr. I.
YU Kcl. I.   GOSONGLAGA Bsr. I.
JUKUNG I.   SATU I.
           CINA I.
MALINJO I.   SEPA Kcl. I.
MELINTANG Bsr. I.   SEMU Is.   SEPA Bsr. I.   *TONDAN ISLANDS*
MELINTANG Kcl. I.   PETAK I.   PAPA THEO (TONDAN TIMUR) I.
PANJANG I.   PELANGI (TONDAN BARAT) I.
TANGKIN I.   PUTRI TIMUR I.
MACAN Kcl. I.   PUTRI BARAT I.
MACAN (MATAHARI) I. PUTRI GUNDUL I.
                 BIRA Bsr. I.
GENTENG Bsr. I.
GENTENG Kcl. I.   BIRA Kcl. I.
PANJANG Kcl. I.   PEMEGARAN I.
PANJANG Bsr. I.   RAKITTIANG I.
              PALEMPARAN I.
KALIAGEH Bsr. I.
KALIAGEH Kcl. I.   OPAK Bsr. I.
SEMUT I.   OPAK Kcl. I.
KOTOK Kcl. I.   KARANGBONGKOK I.   PINIKI I.
KOTOK Bsr. I.
KARANG PANDAN I.   GOSONGCONGKAK I.
                SEMPIT I.
SEMADAUN I.   KARYA I.
LAYAR I.   PANGGANG I.   PRAMUKA I.
          AIR I.
               SEKATI I.
KARANGBERAS I.

TIDUNG Bsr. I.
          TIDUNG Kcl. I.
AIR BESAR Is.   PAYUNG Kcl. I.
       PAYUNG Bsr. I.   *TIDUNG ISLANDS*
                    JONG I.
       TIKUS I.   PARI I.
          TENGAH I.

                        DAPUR I.

     LANCANG Bsr. I.
                 BOKOR I.
     LANCANG Kcl. I.
LAKI I.
                  RAMBUT I.
                   UTUNGJAWA I.
                  UBI Kcl. I.
Tg. Kait   Tg. Pasir   UBI Bsr. I.
         Tanjungpasir   ONRUS I.
Karangserang   Fish   CIPIR I.
Mauk   Kramat   Ponds

J A V A   Teluk Naga

         Soekarno-Hatta
         International Airport

and at the other resorts offer basic items like toothpaste and suntan lotion.

Resorts on some of the nearest islands have been in use since Dutch colonial times, and some of the islands have historical interest. Pulau Onrust, just off Tanjung Pasir and 1/2 hour from Ancol by ferry, is where Jan Pieterszoon Coen, the head of the Dutch East India company, planned his final, successful attack on the town of Jayakarta in 1619. Afterward, he named the town Batavia, which it was to be called until 1942, when the invading Japanese renamed it "Jakarta," a name the Indonesians kept.

Diving Pulau Seribu

The dive possibilities are almost countless here. The reefs around many of the 110 islands are excellent in terms of coral growth and fish life. What makes the diving here just fair by Indonesian standards is the visibility, which usually hovers around 10–15 meters. It sometimes improves, but even then only reaches 20 meters.

Daily rainfall here determines how good the visibility will be, but it is generally best in the middle of the dry season, typically May through September.

With few exceptions, the marine life at most Pulau Seribu locations will include an abundant variety of hard and soft corals, a good variety of reef fish and some pelagics, turtles and an occasional shark.

Unfortunately, at some sites the deterioration of marine life is increasingly noticeable. Like the dwindling reef in the Florida Keys, Pulau-Pulau Seribu has suffered for its proximity to a large population center. Pollution, and in some cases, mismanagement, is killing off the coral.

Pulau Piniki

This is an oblong island (see map opposite), oriented along a north–south axis. A few people live here, and the island is marked by a transmission antenna. There is an interesting reef off the western side of Piniki. The reef starts at 5 meters, but has its best coral growth and fish life at around 20 meters.

At the southwest point is the wreck of a 20-meter wooden cargo ship. The ship's cargo of cement has solidified, but the weakened wooden structure is not safe to enter.

Schools of barracuda, batfish, large parrotfish and moray eels have made the wreck their home. There is also a particularly large number of anemones and anemonefish here.

Pulau Papa Theo

This island, formerly called Pulau Tondan Timur, was renamed when the *Papa Theo,* a cargo vessel, sank on the reef here in 1982. The vessel, about 20 meters long, rests now with its port side facing the reef. The bow is at 20 meters, and the stern at 30 meters.

Until April 1991, the ship stood almost upright, but then its stern collapsed, spilling its until then intact cargo of paper products and pharmaceuticals, including condoms.

Until the cargo spilled, the beautiful reef was a favorite dive spot with Jakarta residents. Once the debris has been washed away, the reef may again become a popular spot. All the fittings and other items of value have been removed from the *Papa Theo.*

It is a simple wreck dive, with lots of marine life and an occasional shark in the deeper waters at the stern end. There are parrotfish, some resident groupers, many morays and a particular abundance of stingrays. The north reef is often chosen for night dives.

Papa Theo island is a very pleasant island hideaway, even for non-divers. The simple huts are clean and comfortable, and a basic Indonesian *mandi* or splash bath is provided. The generator shuts down at dark, and then one hears only the sound of the waves through the thatch walls. A candle-lit restaurant serves very fresh fish and standard Indonesian dishes.

Below: *A juvenile pinnate batfish,* Platax pinnatus, *examines a diver in an underwater grotto off Maumere, Flores. At right is a regal angelfish,* Pygoplites diacanthus.

KAL MULLER

KAL MULLER

Above: A hawksbill turtle, Eretmochelys imbricata. Hawksbills, the smallest of the sea turtles, are also the most commonly seen on Indonesian reefs. Their shells provide the raw material for tortoiseshell, although the importation of such products is banned in many countries, including the United States. In Indonesian markets, one can see small hawksbill turtles, stuffed and varnished, offered as souvenirs, and even live ones, which are destined for the stew pot.

Kuburan Cina

This very small island is among the best diving sites in Pulau-Pulau Seribu. The good reef begins due west of the island, continues around the south, then east. There is a small bit of reef at the north tip. Excellent coral growth provides the backdrop for a good drift dive in 8–20 meter depths. In areas, the coral is good to almost 30 meters.

Low tide exposes a wide expanse of reef flat. At high tide, the island shrinks dramatically, with only a sand bank showing.

Pulau Malinjo

A very good reef extends from the west around to the north, and along the south–southwest edge of the island. The best diving is at 8–12 meters.You can find lobsters here up to 30 centimeters long. The reef is also home to a great number of moray eels.

Pulau Kotok

This island sits on the western edge of the Pulau-Pulau Seribu group, and thus offers some of the best coral growth. The undamaged reef here is good for snorkeling as well as diving. Pulau Kotok is the best in the islands for snorkeling and off-the-beach diving. The west, north and east reefs are good to 20 meters.

Because it faces the open sea, Kotok is the place to see schools of sweetlips, turtles and sharks. Small manta rays have been seen here. The area is abundant in gorgonians and soft corals.

Pulau Gosonglaga

This island is basically a small sandbank surrounded by an immense reef. The entire circumference of the reef is good, and in areas good coral growth extends down to more than 20 meters. Since the island is on the fringe of the Pulau-Pulau Seribu group, it is one of the best places to see larger reef fish and occasional pelagics.

— *Janet Boileau and Debe Campbell*

Note: The authors would like to thank PADI Dive instructor Vimal Lekhraj of Dive Masters, Jakarta for his invaluable help in preparing this article.

Java Dive Practicalities

All prices in U.S. $ unless otherwise noted. Telephone code for Indonesia is 62, city code for Jakarta is 21.

Jakarta, with its 9.5 million people, is the center of Indonesia's government and commerce. It is beyond the scope of this book to give a complete description of all the lodging and transportation possibilities there. If you are going to be in Jakarta, you will need a good guidebook. Instead, this section will offer just the practical information relating to diving Pulau Seribu and West Java.

Dive Operators

There are many dive operators in Jakarta who take divers to Pulau Seribu and the West Java sites. Here are a few of the most reliable:

Dive Masters Indonesia

Jakarta Hilton International Hotel
Indonesian Bazaar Shop 31
Jl. Jend. Gatot Subroto
Jakarta 10002 Indonesia
Tel: 570 3600 ext. 9037, 9036
Fax: 420 4842
Contact: Vimal Lekhraj
  Equipment sales, rentals and repairs. Dive Masters has a 5-star PADI training facility, and its own dive boat. The outfit offers dive trips to Pulau Seribu nearly every weekend and special charters throughout the year. This is the most professional, reliable full-service facility.

Dive Indonesia

PT Diveindo Sindhutama
3d floor, East Wing, Shop 34
Hotel Borobudur Inter-Continental
Jl. Lapangan Banteng Selatan 1
Jakarta 10710 Indonesia
Tel: 380 5555 and 370 3333,
ext. 76024, 76025
Fax: 380 9595
Telex: 44156 BDOIHC IA
Contact: Andre Pribadi

Equipment sales, rentals and repairs. Dive travel, dive boat, u/w photography, deep sea fishing. Affiliated with Jakarta Dive School.

Jakarta Dive School and Pro Shop

Jakarta Hilton International Hotel
Indonesia Bazaar Shop 32
Jl. Jend. Gatot Subroto
Jakarta 10002 Indonesia
Tel: 570 3600 ext. 9008, 9010
Telex: 46673, 46698 HILTON IA
Contact: Andre Pribadi
  Equipment sales, rentals and repairs. Dive travel, air fills, u/w photography, PADI 5-star training facility.

Stingray Dive Centre

Gedung Mangal Wanabakti
Wisma Rimabawan 2d floor, room 4
Jl. Jend. Gatot Subroto
Jakarta Indonesia
Tel and Fax: 570 0272
Contact: Andi
  PADI instruction, dive tours.

Pulau Seribu

These islands are a favorite place for Jakartans to spend a relaxing weekend, so you should definitely book ahead. Ferries depart daily around 7 am from the Ancol Marina, usually without prior booking. The trip takes about 2.5 hours—depending on the island—and the return ferry leaves the islands around 2:30 pm. By speedboat and hydrofoil, the same trip can take one hour. Inquire at Putri Pulau Seribu Paradise office in Djakarta Theatre building.

Dive charters

It is far less complicated to book your entire trip with one of the above listed dive outfits. Dive weekends to sites in Pulau Seribu average $100–$125. This includes round trip transportation, 4 boat dives, and one night in basic, air-conditioned, twin-share accommodations. Afternoon meals are included, although full board may be extra.

West Java

Travel to Krakatau or Ujung Kulon is more of an effort than Pulau Seribu. It requires an overland journey to Anyer or Labuhan, and then a fairly long boat ride. Again, it is much better to organize such a trip with a reliable Jakarta dive outfit.

Krakatau

Boats can be chartered from Labuhan or Carita beach, just 8 kilometers north of Labuhan. A forestry official in either town can help arrange boats for up to 20 people—about $100—or local fisherman can be contacted to charter a smaller vessel, about $50. It is impossible to determine the seaworthiness of these boats, or just how reliable are their motors. Remember, this is a 4-hour crossing over rather unpredictable seas. Too many stories circulate of foreigners adrift on crippled boats for days or even weeks for them all to be apocryphal.

Ujung Kulon

The peninsula can be reached only by boat, or by a lengthy hike—good for seeing wildlife, but not practical for diving. You can arrange a boat at Labuhan, but again, it is best to organize the whole thing with a Jakarta dive agency. A government forestry boat at Labuhan will run about $100 for the 9-hr. trip to Peucang Island or Taman Jaya. To reach the actual dive sites, figure on some intense bargaining with local fishermen.

Weather

Diving is generally best during the dry season, which varies but generally takes place March through November. The very best time is from May to September.

— Janet Boileau and Debe Campbell

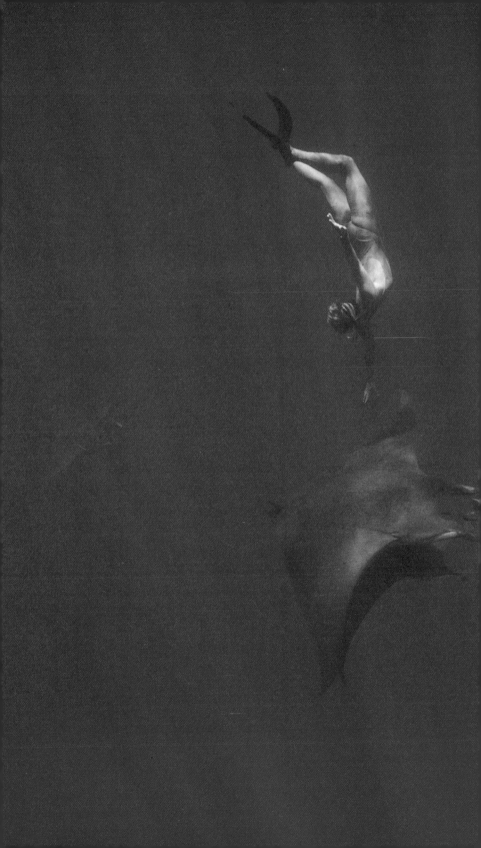

Introducing The Island of Bali

The tiny volcanic island of Bali is one of the most physically beautiful and culturally rich places in the world. The balmy climate, lush, green ricefields and lavish productions of the Hindu-Balinese cultural calendar never fail to charm visitors. Although writers continue to flatter Bali with adjectives, none has surpassed Indian prime minister Pandit Nehru, who called the island "the morning of the world."

Much of the mythology erected around this "paradise" is more revealing of its western authors than of the island itself—*South Pacific*'s silly "Bali-Hai" comes most immediately to mind—but visitors find themselves persistently drawn here. Today, some 1 million tourist a year visit Bali.

Balinese Culture

Indonesia is the largest Islamic country in the world, but the 2.5 million Balinese are overwhelmingly Hindus. *Agama Hindu Dharma* as practiced in Bali is a philosophy, religion and cultural organizing principal that has resulted from Buddhist and Hindu doctrines and practices arriving from India—partly through Java—between the 8th and 15th centuries. It is a uniquely Balinese meld.

Balinese cultural life cycles according to the Pawukon, a complex 210-day ritual calendar. Holiday celebrations—New Year, temple anniversaries, Galungan—and rites of passage—tooth filings, weddings, cremations—are scheduled according to the Pawukon. These ceremonial events, marked by bright costumes, lavish offerings of food, and dance performances,

leave visitors with some of their fondest memories of Bali.

Bali has been famous for her art since the arrival of the first European tourists in the early 20th century. Balinese masks are now almost *de rigueur* on the walls of fashionable apartments in uptown Manhattan. The island's artists turn out painted Hindu icons like Garuda, whimsical animals, and unfinished abstract and surrealistic figures. Most of Bali's painters work in watercolor, producing intricate and detailed group scenes.

Balinese dance ranges from stately processionals to wild leaping and posturing. In general it is more lively than the very refined Javanese court dances, which are considered ancestors to Balinese dance. Some of the most popular forms—such as the monkey dance or *kecak*—are purely secular events, hybrids of old court dances and modern, western-influenced sensibilities.

Dance is accompanied by the *gamelan,* an all-percussion orchestra of metallophones, gongs and cymbal-like instruments. Rhythm is everything in gamelan music, and the musicians' overlapping runs on their bright-sounding instruments creates an unforgettable sound.

History of Bali

Before about the 9th century, when writing and other Indian influences made their way to Bali, little is known of the island's history. Stone altars and sarcophagi, dating back to several centuries B.C. have been found on the island, and these suggest a Bronze Age culture of herders and farmers who practiced a

Above: *Rangda, the antagonist in Bali's famous Barong drama. Rangda is a powerful sorceress.*

Overleaf: *Snorkeling with manta rays, Manta alfredi. Mantas, the largest rays, are harmless plankton-feeders. They are wide-ranging pelagic fish, and show up seasonally in areas accessible to divers, including Bali's Nusa Penida. Bunaken group, Sulawesi. Photo by Ed Robinson of IKAN.*

Opposite: *A diver feeds a banana to the fish at the Tulamben wreck off Bali's northeast coast. The damselfish are the Indo-Pacific sergeant-major, Abudefduf vaigiensis. Photo by Kal Muller.*

form of ancestor worship.

From the 9th century onward, Bali had regular contact with Java, at the time being influenced by Indian cultural practices. During the 14th and 15th centuries, East Java was dominated by the Majapahit empire, of which Bali became a colony in 1365.

This event and date—though by no means certain, as its source, the *Negarakertagama,* is something of a panegyric—marks the point when the Hindu caste system, court culture, performing arts and other Javanese influences came to Bali.

For the next several centuries Bali was ruled by a single court, but factions developed, and by the time the Dutch arrived in the 19th century, Bali was made up of nine realms: Badung, Gianyar, Bangli, Klungkung, Karangasem, Buleleng, Mengwi, Tabanan and Jembrana.

Although they had been in the archipelago since the turn of the 17th century, the Dutch avoided Bali at first. The Balinese had a reputation of being quite fierce, and the fractious internal politics of the little island were considered too great an obstacle to Dutch rule there. Besides, the only important trade item it offered were slaves.

The Dutch finally subjugated Buleleng (now Singaraja) on the north coast and established a colonial center there in 1849. Then, some 50 years later, a Dutch ship ran aground on the reef off Sanur. The disappearance of the cargo to freelance salvage operators served as a pretext for an armed invasion of the south. The Badung court expired in 1906 in a *puputan,* a ritual mass suicide.

Geography and Climate

The island of Bali was shaped by the action of volcanoes, which produced the rich, black soils that nourish Bali's beautiful and productive rice paddies.

Just 8°–9° south of the equator, Bali is always warm—a mean 27.2°C, although the highlands are about 6° cooler. Humidity is an almost constant 75 percent. Most of Bali's annual 2,500–3,000 millimeters of rain falls from November through March.

—*David Pickell*

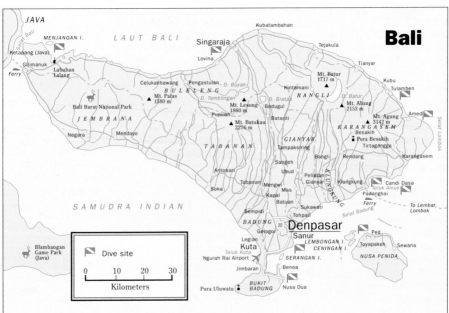

Splendid Wreck, Fine Walls and Varied Sites

Bali is one of Indonesia's most beautiful islands, and always a favorite with tourists. Although it looks small on the map, Bali's winding and narrow roads can eat up a lot of your underwater time. So, before arriving, think a bit about how much time you want to spend diving, and how much sight-seeing.

Most tourist accommodations are in the south, in the Kuta—Nusa Dua—Sanur triangle. (See map opposite.) If you stay here, there is one interesting, unde-manding dive nearby, on the reef off Tanjung (Cape) Benóa, that can give you an introduction—but no more—to Bali's underwater world. The best dive sites require several hours driving from the southern tourist center.

Serious divers should find accommodations close to the best dive spots: at Candi Dasa, Tulamben, or Lovina beach. None of these has the range of *losmen,* restaurants, tourist services and shops as does Kuta Beach or the other resort areas of the south, but they are much closer to the good diving.

Where to Stay

Candi Dasa, in the old Karang-asem Regency on the island's east coast, is the best compro-mise between comfort and prox-imity to good diving: Cemeluk and Tulamben are within an hour's drive, the little islands of Tepekong and Mimpang are just offshore, Padang Bai is just across the bay, and Nusa Penida is a fairly short boat trip away. Only Menjangan Island, off the far western tip of Bali, is distant.

And Candi Dasa, particularly in recent years, has become quite a bustling little town. There are plenty of accommodations and good restaurants. People have compared it to Kuta beach before the big boom in tourism.

For diving on the Liberty wreck off Tulamben, we suggest staying in Tulamben itself—if you can get a room. There are few accommodations, and these are often booked up, especially during the two high seasons, July–August and around Christ-mas and New Year.

For the dives off Menjangan Island, stay at Lovina beach, a bit over an hour's drive away. There is a small and very basic *losmen* less than two kilometers from where the boat leaves for Men-jangan, but the closest compres-sor is in Lovina.

Dive Operators

Unless you are planning just a few, casual dives in Bali, contact one of the dive operators before you arrive and plan a series of dives with them. They can book a hotel for you in your price range, and plan a diving program that matches your interest and experience. (See "Bali Scuba Tour Operators," page 125.)

At this same time—well before your arrival—request a good, English-speaking dive guide. Don't wait until you arrive to do this, or you may end up with someone you will be giving English lessons to. The very best guide in our experience is Wally Siagian of Wally's Special Tours, available through Baruna Water Sports. There are other compe-tent guides as well, but if you wait until the last minute, the best will be booked up.

If you have made plans with

Temperature

Water temperature in Bali is normally quite comfortable, from 24° to 26°C (75°–79°F).

During July and August, the temper-ature drops to 21°C (70°F), and some-times as low as 19°C (66°F) at the following sites: Nusa Dua, Nusa Penida, Padang Bai and Tepekong.

—*Wally Siagian*

Some Tips

1. The best sites to do your open water certification are Cemeluk and Tulamben.

2. Your most memorable night dive will be on a full moon at Tulamben wreck.

3. When the wind is from the north, it is difficult to dive Cemeluk, Tulamben and Menjangan.

4. During the rainy season (January through March), the visibility at Nusa Dua, Padang Bai and Cemeluk will be reduced. Your best diving will be at Nusa Penida and Menjangan in these months.

—*Wally Siagian*

an operator, an itinerary will be worked out for you ahead of time. If not, contact the operators when you arrive—at hotel counters, or at their office. You will be diving with whomever else signs up. Pickups at your hotel are fairly early in the morning, and drop-offs late in the afternoon.

The tours are usually all-inclusive, including tanks and belts, guides and lunch. If you need other equipment, such as a BC and regulator, check to make sure that they are available. It is also a very good idea to take a close look at the equipment the day before the dive. We would.

Bali's Dive Sites

There are five main areas for diving in Bali, working counter-clockwise around the island from the airport in the south: Nusa Dua and Sanur; Nusa Penida; Padang Bai and Candi Dasa; Cemeluk and Tulamben; and Menjangan Island.

Each area offers dive locations for novice, intermediate and advanced divers—except for Nusa Dua and Sanur, where no location requires more than a little experience. (Diving is also available at Lovina. It is not really worth a special trip, but if you are staying there you might want to take a look. See "Bali Scuba Tour Operators," page 125.)

At most sites, you can plan a dive to match your degree of experience—just try to be with divers whose level is similar to yours. It is no fun for either beginners or experts to be lumped together just to convenience the tour operator. Currents of 2–2.5 knots are not going to disturb an experienced diver, but for your first drift dive a half a knot is quite sufficient.

We found very little of interest on Bali's reefs beyond the safe sport diving limit. The best diving in Bali—and in Indonesia generally—lies between 5 and 20 meters.

Nusa Dua and **Sanur**. The dives here are along the outer edge of a reef that runs from below Nusa Dua to Sanur. Operators ferry their clients over wide, shallow reef flat to the dive site. The passage is difficult or impossible at low tide. The dives are drop-offs, but to only about 15 meters. Coral cover is poor, but fish life is fair to good.

Nusa Penida. The dive sites off Nusa Penida, and nearby Ceningan and Lembongan islands, require the longest boat rides and strong currents and surge make conditions tricky, although a good guide can usually find an alternate site. These are drop-off dives, and the fish life and coral variety is excellent. The water can be quite cold because of upwelling.

Candi Dasa and **Padang Bai.** The coastal sites in Amuk Bay are shallow and undemanding, with only occasional, mild currents. Visibility can be quite poor. The islands in front of Candi Dasa—Tepekong, Gili Mimpang, and Gili Likuan—offer excellent diving with a great variety of fish life, including many larger species. Temperatures are usually low, and a 3mm wet suit is almost essential. Currents can be strong and unpredictable, including downdrafts and surge.

Cemeluk and **Tulamben.** These areas have excellent coral walls with many species of fish. Some sites also have a great diversity of corals. The Tulamben shipwreck is the area highlight, offering unlimited photo opportunities at shallow depths. There is very little current here. The beach entry over rocks at the wreck dive site can be difficult if the surf is high.

Menjangan Island. An undemanding dive with excellent walls and very clear water—up to 50 meters visibility. There is also an old wreck at 40 meters, and superb coral gardens in just 5–7 meters of water.

NUSA DUA AND SANUR
Convenient and Undemanding Dives

The dives just beyond the reef line east of the northern part of Tanjung Benoa peninsula, or in front of Sanur, are not the best in Bali. But the sites are easy to get to, and there is quite a good variety of reef fish to see. These dives serve perfectly as a quick refresher if you haven't dived in a while, or as your first dive if you have just completed a dive course. (See map page 94.)

An outboard-powered outrigger canoe takes you the few hundred meters from the beach to the dive location, just beyond where the waves break. The only way out is over very shallow reef flat, so the tide must be in to make the trip. Be prepared for a bit of spray during the ride out or back and when crossing the (usually low) breaking waves.

On the reef face off Tanjung Benoa, we dropped down to 8–9

AT A GLANCE
Nusa Dua and Sanur

Reef type: Drop-off to moderate depth
Access: 5 minutes by small boat
Visibility: Low, 6–8 meters (can reach 15 meters on occasion)
Current: Very gentle
Coral: Limited coverage, few species
Fish: Surprisingly good variety
Highlights: Feeding frenzy on a fresh spawn
Other: Nusa Dua has slightly better coral cover than Sanur

meters on a slightly sloping bottom with scattered coral formations. Visibility (late September) was just 6–8 meters, but we were told that it is usually twice this. The majority of the fish were at

Below: *A swarm of anthias, mostly red-cheeked fairy basslets,* Pseudanthias huchtii. *Nusa Penida, Bali.*

HELMUT DEBELIUS / IKAN

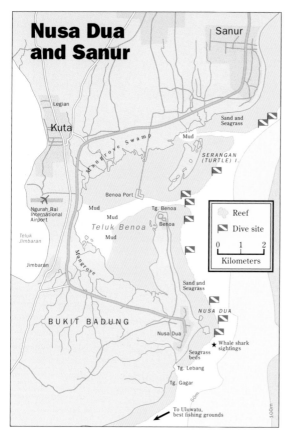

Nusa Dua and Sanur

Sanur

Legian

Kuta

Mangrove Swamp

Mud

Sand and
Seagrass

SERANGAN
(TURTLE) I.

Benoa Port

Ngurah Rai
International
Airport

Mud

Mud

Teluk Benoa

Tg. Benoa

Benoa

Teluk
Jimbaran

Mud

Mangrove

Jimbaran

Reef

Dive site

0   1   2
Kilometers

Sand and
Seagrass

NUSA DUA

BUKIT BADUNG

Nusa Dua

★ Whale shark
sightings

Seagrass
beds

Tg. Lebang

Tg. Gagar

To Uluwatu,
best fishing grounds

8–10 meters. We made a couple of quick dips to 14 meters, and saw nothing.

Good Variety of Fish

The coral cover here is not fantastic, but for still the few mini-pinnacles drew plentiful fish life with a good variety of species. We saw several 50–75 centimeter fish glide by, but visibility was too restricted to make an identification. Our guide found a giant moray and pointed him out to us. This big fellow lives in a coral cave with several openings, and for a while he played hide and seek, popping his head out of three different holes.

We saw a fairly large group of yellowtail fusiliers, a nicely compacted hovering mass of blue-lined snappers, a few red bigeyes and several small aggregations of bigeye soldierfish.

Fairy basslets hovered over almost every coral outcrop. Damsels were present in a variety of species. The butterfly fish were well-represented, but the only schooling species we saw was a small group of masked bannerfish (*Heniochus monoceros*). Groupers were common, especially the white-lined grouper (*Anyperodon leucogrammicus*), which we saw in both color morphs: white, and brown-green.

Parrotfish were present in good variety, but the only species we noticed more than once was the blue-barred parrot (*Scarus ghobban*). The only angelfish we saw were the dwarf bicolor angel (*Centropyge bicolor*) and several big emperor angels. Surgeonfish were common, particularly the spotted unicorn fish (*Naso brevirostris*). We saw pairs of rabbit-fish of at least three species, and a single pair of Titan triggerfish.

A Feeding Frenzy

The highlight of the dive came when we saw a furious cloud of several dozen fish of various species whirling around what looked like a bare patch of dark, reddish coral. Caught up in a feeding frenzy, the small fish allowed us to approach as close as we wished. We could even touch them, they were so intent on their meal. We never did identify what it was they were eating, although it is likely it was a fresh spawn of some kind.

Dives off Nusa Dua will probably not offer such a show very often, but are still worth making for the variety of fish here. The reef to the north, off the Sanur coast, is similar—wide tidal flats behind the reef front—and access is also impossible at the lowest tide. The variety of fishes is quite good in Sanur, but there is even less coral cover than at Nusa Dua. If you are a serious diver, either of these dives will just whet your appetite for more challenging locations.

Abundant Pelagics, Some Fierce Currents

Nusa Penida, across the Bandung Strait from Bali's southern tip, offers some of the best diving to be found anywhere. But conditions around Penida and its two small sister islands—Nusa Lembongan and Nusa Ceningan—can sometimes be difficult, with unpredictable currents reaching four or more knots. This is not a place for beginning divers, inexperienced boatmen, or engines in less than perfect condition. Also, upwellings from the deep water south of Bali, which keep visibility here clear, can also make the water uncomfortably cold.

Even if you are an expert diver, contract with one of Bali's well-organized diving services to dive Nusa Penida, and make sure that you get a reliable boat and a guide with plenty of experience. The currents in this area can usually be predicted from the tide tables, but they can increase, decrease or shift direction with no advance notice, and vary dramatically with depth. We recommend that your guide bring a buoy, and that you do not wander off by yourself. The dive locations are all close together, and an experienced guide can easily shift you to an alternate site if the conditions at your planned location are unsatisfactory.

Dive boats to Nusa Penida leave from Nusa Dua or Sanur, or from Padang Bai. (See map page 97.) From either of the resorts the 34-kilometer (18-nautical-mile) trip takes 1.5 hours; from Padang Bai, just 17 kilometers (9 nautical miles) from Penida, it takes 45 minutes to 1 hour, depending on the boat. You can also rent a speedboat at Padang Bai (about $110 round-trip) to shave trip time to the minimum, but if you do, make sure your dive guide knows the boatman. The chap could fall asleep while you're under and be out of whistle range when you come up with the current. It has happened.

Coral Walls and Pelagics

Most of the dive spots are around the channel between Nusa Penida and Nusa Ceningan. The standard reef profile here has a terrace at 8–12 meters, then a wall or steep slope to 25–30 meters, then a fairly gentle slope to the seabed at 600 meters. Pinnacles and small caves are often encountered. At 35–40 meters, long antipatharian whip corals are common, spiraling outward more than 8 meters.

Pelagics are the main attraction here, and you have a good chance to see jacks, mackerel and tuna. Reef sharks are so

Tip

The quickest transfer to Nusa Penida is from Padang Bai, using the "Express" ferry, which has twin 85hp engines. This takes 26 minutes to Toyapakeh.

—Wally Siagian

AT A GLANCE
Nusa Penida

Reef type:	Drop-offs, steep slopes
Access:	45 min to 1.5 hrs by boat
Visibility:	Good, 15 meters
Current:	Moderate to very strong (4+ knots)
Coral:	Very good variety of hard corals; excellent stand of *Dendronephthya*
Fish:	Excellent variety; many pelagics
Highlights:	Large school of sweetlips, very large hawksbill turtle. Site also hosts sharks, mantas, and even oceanic sunfish
Other:	Can be very cold; currents are unpredictable and often fierce

and southwest coasts of Penida, but these areas, swept by tricky currents, require an experienced guide and more time than is available in a daytrip to reach.

A Dive off Penida

We were staying at Baruna's Puri Bagus Beach Hotel in Candi Dasa when the opportunity came to dive Nusa Penida. One of the hotel's minibuses picked us up early, and after a 15-minute ride dropped us off at Padang Bai, where the large diesel-powered *Baruna 05* dive boat was already waiting for us. We waded through waist-high water to load our gear, and were soon on our way for the hour-and-a-half trip.

The boat anchored off the Ped/S.D. area, and we dropped into a practically currentless sea. From an initial 7 meter depth, we followed the slope of 45 degrees down to 37 meters. There was good hard coral cover, and an occasional pinnacle reared up 5–6 meters from the slope. We crossed a big school of black triggerfish mixed with a few sleek unicornfish.

A small cave in one of the coral knolls held a densely packed school of pygmy sweeps (*Parapriacanthus ransonetti*). These greenish, semi-transparent fish feed at night on small plankton attracted by the bioluminous organs located just in back of their pectoral fins.

Early in the dive we crossed paths with a large black-spotted stingray. He allowed us to approach to within just over a meter, but after just one photo flew off to his next appointment. Shortly after we met the ray, we saw a hawksbill turtle, one of the largest we have ever seen. This 1.3–1.5 meter animal flippered off before I could approach within decent camera range.

The rest of our dive passed through busy schools of yellowtailed and lunar fusiliers, and occasional schools of longfin ban-

Above: *Two clown anemonefish,* Amphiprion ocellaris, *in the host anemone* Heteractis magnifica. *Bali.*

common that after a while you stop noticing them. Mantas are frequently sighted. Perhaps the most unusual pelagic visitor to Nusa Penida is the weird molamola or oceanic sunfish (*Mola mola*), a mysterious large, flattened fish with elongate dorsal and ventral fins, and a lumpy growth instead of a tail fin.

Dive guide Wally Siagian says he has seen a mola-mola here about once every 15 dives. On two occasions he has been able to swim up and touch the bizarre, up to 2-meter-long animals.

The most common dive spots are just south of the dock at Toyapakeh, or a bit further east, at Ped, the site of an important temple of the same name, Sampalan Point, and "S.D.," named for the *sekolah dasor* or primary school there. There are other dive spots down the northeast

nerfish. We saw several groupers and even more sweetlips, and an occasional clown or Titan triggerfish. A good-sized barracuda observed us from above. Visibility was good, in the 15-meter range.

When we ascended we noticed the surface current had increased markedly since we began our dive. Wally complained that we had not spotted any big sharks, which are common in this area.

Toyapakeh

We motored a bit further west along the coast of Nusa Penida, and dropped anchor a few hundred meters from the dock at Toyapakeh. We descended through a slight current (less than 1 knot) into veritable clouds of peach fairy basslets (*Pseudanthias dispar*), each the exact color of a blue-eyed Nordic tourist who had done too much time in the sun. The anthias were mixed with large aggregations of firefish, which are more often seen in pairs or small groups.

A long stretch of our dive route—this at 25–30 meters—consisted of an almost unbroken thicket of pastel-tinted *Dendronephthya* soft corals. A school of two dozen or more greater amberjacks swam several lazy circles around our group, mixing sometimes with a larger school of bigeye jacks. As we started upwards, we saw a huge black-

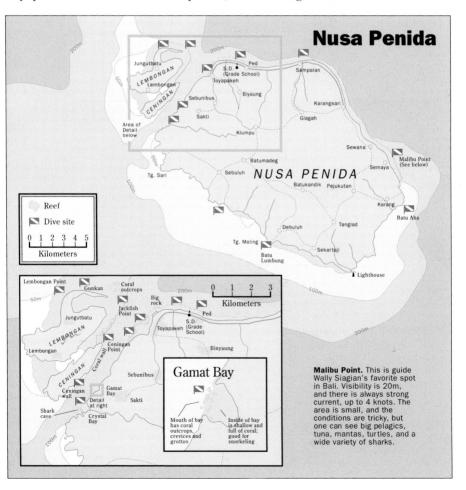

Nusa Penida

Reef

Dive site

0 1 2 3 4 5
Kilometers

Jungutbatu

LEMBONGAN
Lembongan

CENINGAN

Sebunibus

Sakti

S.D. (Grade School)
Toyapakeh

Ped

Biyaung

Klumpu

Sampalan

Karangsari

Glagah

Sewana

Area of Detail below

Tg. Sari

Sebuluh

Batumadeg

NUSA PENIDA

Batukandik Pejukutan

Semaya

Malibu Point
(See below)

Karang

Batu Aba

Debuluh

Tanglad

Tg. Moling

Batu Lumbung

Sekartaji

Lighthouse

Lembongan Point

Gunkan

Coral outcrops

Big rock

Jackfish Point

Toyapakeh

S.D. (Grade School)

Ped

0 1 2 3
Kilometers

Jungutbatu

LEMBONGAN

Lembongan

CENINGAN

Ceningan Point

Coral wall

Ceningan wall

Gamat Bay

Detail at right

Sakti

Binyaung

Sebunibus

Gamat Bay

Shark cave

Crystal Bay

Mouth of bay has coral outcrops, crevices and grottos

Inside of bay is shallow and full of coral; good for snorkeling

Malibu Point. This is guide Wally Siagian's favorite spot in Bali. Visibility is 20m, and there is always strong current, up to 4 knots. The area is small, and the conditions are tricky, but one can see big pelagics, tuna, mantas, turtles, and a wide variety of sharks.

WALLY SIAGIAN
The Best Dive Guide in Bali

Take a group of the most experienced divers in Indonesia and ask them who they think is the best dive guide in the islands. Wilhelm Siagian—"Wally," to one and all—will be at the top of the list, every time.

Wally has shown off his Balinese reefs to top underwater pros, including Rudie Kuiter, John E. Randall, and Roger Steene—the leading authorities on the archipelago's marine life and some of the world's top underwater photographic professionals. As a result, Wally has become an informal student of Steen and Kuiter, learning the Latin names of the fish with which he is so familiar.

Wally was born in Bandung, Java in 1960 of Sundanese, Batak and German blood-lines. He was 16 when he first started diving, with a CMAS certificate from Jakarta's Ganesha Diving Club. After some 200 dives around Pulau Seribu and about 30 off Ujung Kulon, he left for a bit of travel. Stints of working and diving around Sorong, Irian Jaya and Balikpapan, East Kalimantan led Wally to decide that diving was all that really mattered in life. (It was while diving near an oil rig off Balikpapan that Wally saw the biggest barracuda of his career—more than 2 meters and fa-a-a-t.)

After Kalimantan, Wally decided to settle with his Swiss wife in Bali. Times were difficult for a while, until he landed a miserably paying job with Baruna in 1985. Since then, he has made more than 1,500 dives around Bali, pioneering new sites and working his way up at Baruna and the diving ranks: Dive Master rating in 1988 from CMAS, Open Water Instructor from SSI in 1990, and Advanced Open Water Instructor with Dive Control speciality, also from SSI, in 1991.

Though training is important, it is his experience and motivation that makes Wally a superior guide. He knows the Latin and English common names of hundreds of fish in the reefs around Bali. He really knows the dive locations, and can set up a sequence of dives to suit the interest and level of competence of any divers in his charge. If necessary, he can cure wounds with traditional medicine and even deliver an excellent massage. A true Renaissance Man.

He has an open personality, a sense of humor and an infectious enthusiasm for diving—and he'll find a cold beer in the most unlikely places. He is my friend, drinking buddy and, of course, my favorite guide.

— Kal Muller

spotted moray, with about 1 meter of its snaky body sticking out of its lair.

We surfaced just at funnel mouth of the channel between Nusa Penida and Nusa Ceningan. The local fishermen were unfurling the sails of their *jukung*s, and we climbed back on board just as the current began to pick up speed.

The *Baruna 05* tied up to the dock at Toyapakeh, and Wally borrowed a bystander's bicycle to go fetch us some food. While he was gone, a fisherman pulled up in his outrigger, and we bought a just-caught 20-kilo yellowfin tuna for dinner.

Sunset Show

Just before sunset, the current picked up to 5–6 knots. We watched the *jukung*s literally shoot through the channel on their way out for a night's fishing. Others, taking advantage of the wind and a back current, headed for "mainland" Bali in the direction of towering Gunung Agung. This was one of the finest sunset shows I had ever admired in Indonesia.

The tuna we bought ended up as sashimi and charcoal-grilled tuna steaks, and combined with a lobster Wally had snatched from a grotto on our first dive, we had a splendid supper. We then spread our mattresses on the top deck, and settled down to drinking beer. A few little boats fished around us with bright pressure lamps, and we drifted off to sleep.

The night was surprisingly cool, and I woke up at midnight to a sky full of stars. I quickly discarded all thoughts of a night dive as I heard the current rushing by the boat. The beer had taken its usual route, and I relieved myself overboard, creating swirling bioluminescence on the water's surface.

Another Dive at S.D.

The next morning, after the sun

had warmed us thoroughly, we headed back east along Nusa Penida's coast to begin our next and last dive where we had ended the previous morning: in front of the long, red-roofed elementary school.

This was a drift dive, in a 1.5 to 2 knot current that occasionally "gusted" to 3 knots. The fish hovered effortlessly in the current as we sped by. Swimming diagonally, we approached two large map puffers, and several smaller, but exquisitely patterned cube trunkfish. We also took a closer look at a hallucinogenic scribbled filefish.

Between two coral knolls we came on an aggregation of some 40 sweetlips. The fish were split into four groups, all facing the current. The sight of these attractively patterned fish was too much to just pass by, so we carefully grabbed onto some hard corals and crawled along the bottom for a closer look at the sweetlips show.

Perhaps feeling there was safety in numbers, these magnificent animals allowed us to approach to within 2 meters

HELMUT DEBELIUS / IKAN

before they drifted off to find a new spot just a bit further away. While we watched our sweetlips, a turtle rose up just ahead and, with no effort at all, swam off straight into the current.

Then, a huge grouper, well over a meter long, appeared out of nowhere, buzzing one of our group before disappearing just as suddenly. Consulting the fish books later, we came to a consensus that our visitor was likely to have been a blotchy grouper (*Epinephelus fuscogattus*).

We later saw triggerfish, a barracuda and a reef white-tip shark; still, it was anticlimactic.

Above: *The argus comet,* Calloplesiops argus. *When alarmed this fish will duck into a crevice, but instead of hiding, will display its long fins and tail, in this way mimicking a moray eel. The ocelli near the argus comet's tail serves as the eel's "eye."*

Below: *Guide Wally Siagian gets his teeth cleaned by the shrimp* Lysmata amboinensis.

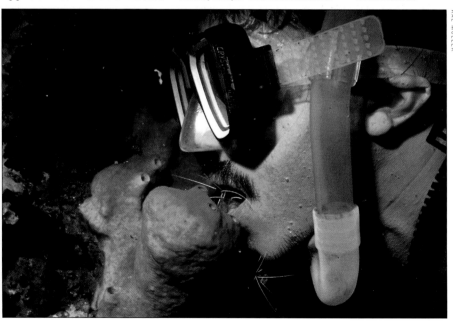

KAL MULLER

PADANG BAI

Good Diving Along the Coast of Amuk Bay

There are two main dive spots at Padang Bai: Pura Jepun and Tanjung Bungsil. We rate these sites as slightly better than those off Nusa Dua or Sanur, but a damn sight colder. Bring a wet suit if you're going to dive this area. A good, deep chill can take the pleasure out of any dive.

The ride to Padang Bai from the Kuta–Nusa Dua–Sanur triangle is a long, traffic-clogged 60 kilometers. Padang Bai is the port for the five-times-a-day Lombok ferry run, and things can always get a bit congested near the dock area. It's far more convenient to dive this spot from Candi Dasa, just 15 minutes away.

Before diving, you will suit up on the beach, at the restaurant favored by your dive operator. Most small dive groups are taken to the site in little local outriggered fishing canoes powered by small outboard motors. It's usually just two divers per craft, so if you have a large group, the little armada plays follow-the-leader to the site. There will probably be some spray just as you leave the harbor, and it may follow you further on if the wind is up. Both dive sites are a short 10–15 minutes away. (See map page 102.)

Pura Jepun

We started our first dive about 50 meters from shore, just opposite a small temple shrine (*pura*) called Pura Jepun, after the Balinese word for frangipani, although no flowers were in evidence along the stretch of coast leading to our entry point. (The shrine sits on a little cape, also called Jepun, so the site is sometimes called Tanjung Jepun.)

After leaving the harbor, we headed northeast along the coast, passing Blue Lagoon Bay with an idyllic white sand beach at its back. A rocky point, against which some pretty large waves crashed, marked the end of Blue Lagoon, and from there to the Pura Jepun site the steep hills ended in small cliffs. These look like they drop straight down to the depths, but unfortunately continue only 2–3 meters underwater. At this point the bottom levels off quickly to a wide terrace at 6–10 meters.

We jumped overboard and began our drift dive, pushed back the way we came by a slight, less than one-knot current. Further out from the initial, 6–10 meter terrace, a slight slope eases down to 15–20 meters, followed by flat sand at 40 meters.

After a very quick look in the deeper areas, we restricted ourselves to 6–12 meters, where we had determined most of the animal life was to be found. Coral formations were scattered, although there were quite a num-

AT A GLANCE
Padang Bai

Reef type:	Flat-bottomed mixed reef and sandy bottom, some wall
Access:	10–15 min by small canoe
Visibility:	Variable; poor to fair, 6–15 meters
Current:	Gentle, less than 1 knot
Coral:	Scattered outcrops, fair variety
Fish:	Good variety and numbers
Highlights:	Large feeding Titan triggerfish, blue-spotted stingrays

ber of giant anemones, crinoids of varying colors, odd clumps of tunicates and a few sponges. The bottom remained quite flat across our "flight path" until we reached the rocky point that marks the entrance to Blue Lagoon Bay, where a sheer wall drops close to 40 meters. Visibility throughout the dive was a decent enough 10–12 meters.

Since we remained in quite shallow water during most of the dive, we were treated to several schools of elongated surface feeders: silvery, pencil-thin keeled needlefish (*Platybelone platyura*) and halfbeaks (*Hemiramphus* sp.), and only slightly more substantial arrow barracuda (*Sphyraena novaehollandiae*).

I disturbed a peacock flounder (*Bothus manchus*), delicately patterned to blend in with the sand, quite unlike its namesake. It is only when the fish swims slowly that one can appreciate its colorful back pattern and strangely positioned eyes. The dive's other highlights included a playful few minutes with a cuttlefish, and two small lionfish cowering in a vase sponge. Two blue-spot-

ted stingrays also made a brief appearance but disappeared quickly.

Otherwise, the dive was basically average for Indonesia, which is to say not bad at all. We saw lizardfish, hawkfish, a bright yellow trumpetfish, the odd small grouper, a few oriental sweetlips, goatfish, parrotfish, wrasses, butterflies, emperor and blue-faced angelfish, damselfish—especially plucky sargeant-majors—foxface and lined rabbitfish, a cubefish, a dog-faced puffer, Moorish idols, surgeonfish—including clown surgeonfish and a single electric-blue hepatus tang—and several species of triggerfish. Although the hard coral was not plentiful, we saw a fair number of anemones, crinoids and sponges. Even though I was not carrying a macro set-up, and was looking for overview shots, I noticed a very beautiful nudibranch.

Blue Lagoon

When we arrived off the wall below the rocky point at the end of Blue Lagoon, we dipped down just far enough (25 meters) to see a few larger predatory jacks:

Above: *Photographer Rudie Kuiter caught this moray eel at night in the act of snatching a cardinalfish. The eel is the undulate moray,* Gymnothorax undulatus; *the cardinalfish is an unidentified* Apogon *sp. Tulamben, Bali.*

rainbow runners, a couple of black jacks, and blue-lined sea breams. There are said to be occasional strong down-currents towards the base of this wall, but we felt no pull whatever.

When we were almost out of air, we surfaced and, not seeing our boat around, snorkeled to the beach at Blue Lagoon, stopping along the way to check out a few coral outcrops in the sandy bottom. When we clambered out of the surf in our gear, we were the sunbathers' center of attention. These included four very pretty Italian girls, but unfortunately our boatman showed up immediately, apologizing profusely for the delay. Arivaderci.

Tanjung Bungsil

After a quick lunch, we headed for Tanjung Bungsil, on the south side of Padang Bai harbor. This dive was to be even shallower than the morning's—at the end my computer showed a maximum depth of 10.2 meters. The very slightly sloping bottom was a bit rockier here than at Tanjung Jepun, with corals growing to within a few meters of the sur-face. Some large carpet anemones grew here in the shallows. In places the visibility dropped to a very poor 5–6 meters.

The good variety of fish life here was similar to the morning's dive. We also saw several six-banded angelfish, and a little group of the curious, headstanding shrimpfish. As I tried (unsuccessfully) to sneak up on a clown triggerfish, a very attractively marked ringtail wrasse (*Cheilinius unifasciatus*) swam up and insisted on posing for a portrait.

The dive's highlight was a Titan triggerfish, doing a headstand while furiously snapping away with its strong teeth at a patch of coral rubble, apparently trying to dislodge an irresistible hors d'oeuvre.

This big boy's energetic activities attracted a host of camp followers looking for a free snack: angelfish, butterflyfish, wrasses, goatfish and even a pair of Moorish idols.

Unfortunately, the triggerfish did not allow human beings into his circle of friends, and abandoned his activities as soon as we approached to within 3 meters.

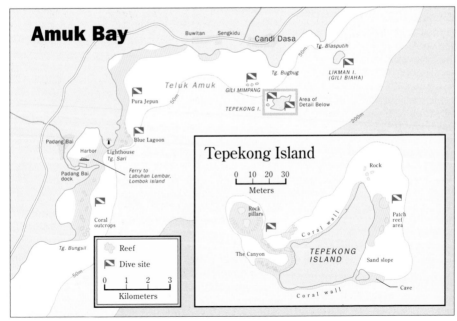

Swirling with the Fish in Tepekong's Canyon

Just offshore from Candi Dasa is tiny Tepekong, a little outcrop that offers some spectacular diving. The coral walls are steep, the water is cold, and the current can be strong. But for an experienced diver, drifting with a 3-knot current through The Canyon offers an outstanding underwater experience.

You can reach Tepekong from anywhere along the southeast coast, but access is easiest from Candi Dasa. There are actually three dive sites here: Tepekong (sometimes called Kambing—"Goat"—Island); Gili Mimpang (three mini-islands sometimes called Batu Tiga, "Three Rocks"); and Biaha Island, sometimes called Likuan Island. (See map opposite.)

Your ride to the dive site is a fishing boat or *jukung,* fitted with a tiny outboard. Two or three divers at most will fit in a *jukung.* The boats must cross the edge of a fringing reef about 75 meters offshore. This will give you a thorough soaking, the skills of your boatmen notwithstanding. When the tide is low, you might even have to get out of the *jukung* to help push it over the reef flat. Once across the reef, you are 10–15 minutes from Mimpang or Tepekong.

Tepekong has the best diving. It is also the coldest—occasionally a bone-chilling 19° C—and most difficult. Tiny Tepekong is just 100 meters long and 50 meters wide. There are no beaches. The sides of the island plunge straight into the sea.

Diving the Canyon

With Wally Siagian as my dive buddy and guide, we twice tried to dive his favorite spot, the southside Canyon, but the combination of over 4 knot current and undertow from swell and waves crashing into Tepekong's western side defeated our attempts. On the third try, however, it worked.

We dropped in about halfway

AT A GLANCE
Candi Dasa

Geography: Steep coral walls; underwater canyon

Access: 20–30 min by small outboard

Visibility: Variable; poor to very good; 6–20 meters

Current: Can be extremely strong, more than 5 knots

Coral: Excellent coverage and variety

Fish: Literally teeming with fish

Highlights: Tepekong's Canyon, good chance to see pelagics

Other: Very tricky currents, strong surge; uncomfortably cold

along the western side of Tepekong, descending in a slight current to a sloping bottom at 9 meters, near the vertical underwater continuation of Tepekong's above-water cliff. We were just nearing the bottom when a large Napoleon wrasse appeared at the edge of our 10 meter visibility. He drifted out of sight, as did a school of 30-odd roundfaced batfish (*Platax teira*). We followed the slope, dotted with coral knolls, to 24 meters, then dropped down into a canyon. The Canyon was lined with huge boulders, and bottomed out at 32 meters.

A Tip

Don't dive the Canyon if there is a swell from the east or northeast. These produce the strong, swirling downward current that turns the Canyon into the "Toilet."

—*Wally Siagian*

RUDIE KUITER

Above: *This unidentified fairy crab, photographed on a sponge at Tulamben, Bali, is probably a new species.*

almost felt my mask was going to tear off. We hung on to outcrops, watching schools of rainbow runners, bigeye trevally, sleek unicornfish and little packs of Moorish idols. We occasionally shifted our position, disturbing a resident whitetip shark at one point, and a cubefish at another.

Each coral-covered pinnacle hosted firefish, which flicked their long dorsal spines in the current, and clouds of lyretail coralfish (*Pseudanthias squammipinnis*). These were all at our 5-meter decompression stop.

This dive was one of the best I have experienced in Indonesia. But it was far from easy. Conditions could well have postponed this dive until my time in the area had run out. And even for an experienced diver, this is a tricky dive. Wally doesn't call it "The Toilet" for nothing.

The teeming fish life makes it well worth any effort it takes, however. It is particularly easy here to get very close to normally wary fish. You might even see an oceanic sunfish, the strange *Mola mola*. Wally has seen one on three occasions in his more than 60 dives here.

East Tepekong

After one of our aborted attempts on the Canyon, Wally directed our *jukung* to the far eastern end of the island. We dropped into surging, cold water, and shivered as we descended. Visibility was restricted by the water movement to around 8 meters. And the surge was too strong to allow us to peer into the many caves— between 16 and 32 meters—as well as a 10-meter-long passage between several huge boulders that appear to have fallen from the topside cliff.

We spotted a tuna, a fairly big grouper and a cuttlefish after we made our way down the slope to about 25 meters. The coral cover was good, including both stony corals and soft corals, and sever-

Here, visibility increased to close to 20 meters and the amount of fish life increased considerably. So did the current, to 2.5–3 knots. Sometimes the current here swirls around the Canyon with a downward pull, leading to Wally's nickname for the place: "The Toilet."

As soon as we entered the Canyon we saw a huge aggregation of sweetlips, 50 or 60 of them, hovering next to a pinnacle: Goldmann's sweetlips, oriental sweetlips, and yellow ribbon sweetlips. Then we saw a very healthy looking grouper, well over a meter in length. Wally thought the fish we saw was an Australian potato cod (*Epinephelus tukula*), perhaps north for a quick vacation.

Groups of schooling fish hung in the current, which "gusted" occasionally to such speeds that I

al blunt pinnacles sheltered reef fish in shallow pockets. Fish huddled between overlapping layers of table coral, each irregular "shelf" holding several species. All this was fine, but the strong continuing surge, lack of visibility and cold water led us to surface before our air ran out.

Gili Mimpang

These same conditions plagued our dive on Gili Mimpang, a cluster of three little exposed rocks between Tepekong and the coast of Bali. Despite our wet suits, we were freezing. Descending to the 12-meter bottom, we disturbed a small blue-spotted stingray, and a much larger black-spotted ray. We swam against a slight current to the top of a wall around 30 meters, working our way around detached clumps of coral. About 10 minutes into the dive and I was ready to quit, due mainly to the cold, but also because of the increasing current and the restricted visibility. I signalled to Wally and we headed up.

Around 18 meters we hit a thermocline, and life took a very definite turn for the better. Almost instantaneously, the water temperature increased 6° C. Fish life improved considerably as well, beginning with a docile star puffer, three easily spooked (as usual) reef white-tip sharks and several blue-finned trevally. A school of blue-lined snappers buzzed us from above.

As we stopped on top of a pinnacle at around 7–8 meters, a school of bignose unicornfish parted just enough to afford us a glimpse of a Napoleon wrasse on one side and several bumphead parrotfish on the other. A small school of longfin bannerfish accompanied us, from a safe distance, almost to the surface.

Back in the *jukung,* Wally said that had we not turned back, we would have seen lots of large pelagics ahead. But I was well satisfied, and happy to be warm.

WOLFGANG BRESIGK
Seasoned Dive Operator

Wolfgang Bresigk, who heads the diving department of Baruna Water Sports in Bali, has tucked 6,000 dives under his experienced weight belt. He is a tall German with a serious demeanor but a ready smile. Since he landed a job there in 1986, he has turned the Baruna scuba operation, by far the biggest in Indonesia, into a a tight, efficient organization. As this is written, he is putting the finishing touches on the first privately-owned decompression chamber in Bali.

Bresigk, 52, started diving in 1964 in Sardinia, using the primitive equipment available then. He is a self-taught diver. At times of financial strain, he dove to 100-meter depths in the Mediterranean to gather red *Corallium* for jewelry, facing decompression times of 2.5 hours. In 1970 he began leading dive safaris to the Red Sea.

From the mid-70s on, Bresigk became a diving globe trotter, covering the Maldives before local operations started, the Caribbean (then not so overcrowded), the Sea of Cortes, the Galapagos, Taiwan, and the four principal dive locations in Micronesia—Palau, Truk, Ponape and Saipan. Along the way, he realized his job prospects were being limited by his lack of formal certification, so he became an instructor and joined a dive school in the Canary Islands.

Bresigk dove Bali as an ordinary tourist in 1984. The following year, he received a work invitation from Baruna, which he accepted in 1986. Bali has been his home ever since. At the time, Baruna was handling some 500–600 diving guests a year, a figure that under Bresigk's supervision has increased six-fold.

He has doubled the number of Baruna's dive guides—there are now 26—and upgraded their skills. He brought in new dive equipment, as well as the very best compressors. Baruna now has more boats, equipment, guides and counters than any other operator in Bali.

The new decompression chamber is designed for four, although it can hold six in an emergency. Bresigk is building the chamber because the few available in Indonesia are all on Navy bases.

Bresigk still refuses to be tied to a desk. He made a series of exploratory dives around Komodo and the north coast of Flores, pioneered 15 great spots, and organized dive cruises to the area in 1988. He still regularly scouts new, pristine dive locations.

— *Kal Muller*

Outstanding Variety of Fishes and Corals

Cemeluk

Below: *A dog-faced puffer,* Arothron nigropunctatus, *has found the perfect resting place in the leather coral* Sarcophyton trocheliophorum. *Bali.*

Divers on a tight schedule could dive Cemeluk in the morning, and the Tulamben wreck—just a few kilometers away—in the afternoon. But these are both excellent dive spots, so why rush? Cemeluk—often called Amed—offers the best variety of fish life we have seen in all of Bali. In this regard it matches even the teeming reefs of Manado and eastern Indonesia.

Cemeluk is just off Bali's main east coast highway. From the resort areas of the south, the highway passes through Klungkung, then Candi Dasa, then

HELMUT DEBELIUS / IKAN

swings inland past Karangasem, skirting 1,175-meter Mt. Seraya, Bali's easternmost mountain. Just before it reaches the coast again, about 10 kilometers before Tulamben, a paved side road from the little town of Culik drops directly to the coast at Amed, 3 kilometers away.

From Amed, the paved road turns right and passes a long stretch of traditional salt works. Two kilometers from Amed, you're in Cemeluk, a fairly small bay with a beach of black, volcanic sand, crowded with about a hundred colorful *jukung,* local outrigger fishing canoes powered by sails or small outboards.

Diving Cemeluk

The reef off Cemeluk curves around a rock outcropping just east of town. We took a *jukung* out into the bay, and dropped into a very slight current pushing us southeast along the reef. At about 8 meters we came down on an extensive spread of staghorn *Acropora* teeming with damselfishes and cardinalfishes. A short slope led to a coral wall, where we dropped to 43 meters, hanging there about 8–10 meters above the sandy bottom. The wall was magic.

Schools of fish of several species cascaded down the wall or took the electric stairs back up in orderly, two-way traffic. The numbers were staggering, the best we have seen in Bali and only rarely matched or surpassed to the east. The schools included black triggerfish, lots of bannerfish, black snappers, humpback snappers, pyramid butterflies, and countless others. Further off from the wall, the usual school of

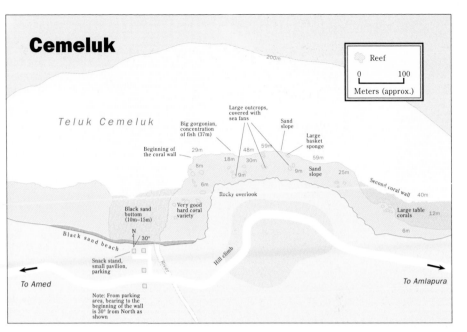

Cemeluk

Teluk Cemeluk

Reef

0   100

Meters (approx.)

200m

Large outcrops, covered with sea fans

Big gorgonian, concentration of fish (37m)

Sand slope

Large basket sponge

Beginning of the coral wall

29m

48m

59m

59m

8m

18m

30m

9m

Sand slope

6m

9m

25m

Second coral wall

40m

Rocky overlook

Large table corals

12m

Black sand bottom (10m–15m)

Very good hard coral variety

6m

Black sand beach

N

30°

River

Hill climb

Snack stand, small pavilion, parking

To Amed

To Amlapura

Note: From parking area, bearing to the beginning of the wall is 30° from North as shown

yellowtail fusiliers kept an eye on proceedings.

According to Wally Siagian, my stellar dive guide, by beginning our dive towards the southeast part of Cemeluk Bay we left the best coral formations behind, although there were still impressive outcrops along our 200-odd-meter journey, covered with sponges, sea fans and crinoids. One sponge sheltered a small lionfish, and in another a well-camouflaged tassled scorpionfish would have passed unnoticed except for Wally's sharp eyes.

Towards the end of the dive, the dense growth of sponges and gorgonians created a tunnel between two of the outcrops. Inside, it was wall-to-wall with life. Large barrel sponges poked out from clearings in this forest. A couple of mean-looking Titan triggerfish eyed us with undisguised hate, but refrained from charging. A clown triggerfish approached, then fled. On a small sandy patch next to an outcrop, a little juvenile blue ribbon eel (the juveniles are black) stood his ground bravely.

The larger fish included a longnose emperor, a patrolling giant trevally, and several blue-fin trevallys. Two very large tuna, both over a meter and in the 30–40 kilo range, shot by quickly. As we finished the dive, we saw a mismatched pair of Napoleon wrasse: a very large adult and a very small juvenile. Wally often sees reef white-tip sharks here, although we saw none on this day. Our visibility was around 10 meters, but can double under the right conditions. The area is calm year around with only very occa-

AT A GLANCE
Cemeluk

Reef type: Coastal reef; flats, slope and wall

Access: Beach; 5 min by small boat

Visibility: Fair to good, 10–20 meters.

Current: Mild

Coral: Excellent; best hard coral variety in Bali

Fish: Excellent numbers, superb variety

Highlights: Density of fish on the deep wall; coral species just off beach

sional surge and high current conditions.

A Dive from the Beach

A dive directly from the black sand and pebble beach at Cemeluk gave a very different perspective: smaller fish, but a great number and variety of corals. We had barely donned our fins and dropped to the less than two-meter depth when we saw a scattered group of orange-band surgeonfish (*Acanthurus olivaceous*), some 15 strong. Their bright orange marks are distinctive, and we had seen very few in previous dives.

Neon blue devils, darted around, two parrotfish paddled furiously, and a graceful pair of Moorish idols swam into view. Two yellow-margined triggerfish were doing headstands while furiously blowing at the sand hoping to uncover some worm or spiny thing to eat. A dozen striped convict tangs (*Acanthurus triostegus*), which we had not seen in Bali before, swam across our path. All this within 15 meters of shore!

Just a bit further out (we were heading due north) all life stopped, the sloping grey sand offering nothing until we saw crate-like enclosures holding bits of coral, an experiment conducted to determine coral growth in this environment. A few dozen meters beyond the crates, several scattered coral outcrops jutted up from the sand, little oases in the sandy desert.

From the outcrops we headed east at about 20 meters, crossing a stretch of grey sand bottom until we came to the reef wall, which follows the coast from this point. About 10 meters from the surface, the irregular wall started sprouting fan gorgonians and pastel trees of *Dendronephthya*. Tube sponges were numerous.

The reef here is topped by a relatively flat area, just 2–5 meters deep and 30 or more meters from the rocky shore.

The relatively small area between here and the sandy beach holds the greatest variety of corals we have seen in Bali, and they are swarming with fish.

Perhaps the area's stable conditions and clear waters are responsible for this abundance.

Below: *An undulate or orange-striped triggerfish,* Balistapus undulatus, *takes shelter in a sponge. This specimen is a male. Bali.*

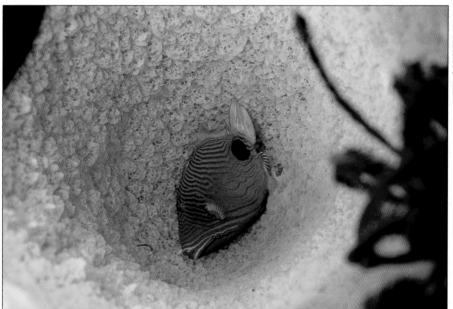

The Liberty Wreck, Bali's Most-visited Site

At first sight, the little village of Tulamben is rather uninviting. Its beach is a rough spread of black sand, small boulders and rubble cast here by nearby Gunung Agung's 1963 eruption. In the dry season, the country-side here assumes a nondescript shade of brown.

Like all the north coast villages, there are no lush rice fields here—Gunung Agung and the other mountains steal the rain, which comes from moisture-laden air that blows in from the south. Thus South Bali is the island's rice bowl.

What brings people to Tulamben is not visible from above water, however. People wake up early, fight the snarled traffic from the tourist centers of the south and emerge from their *bemos,* groggy and cross, for only one reason: to dive the Liberty ship at Tulamben.

The Liberty Ship

Just 30 meters from the beach at Tulamben is a World War II ship of the Liberty class, broken up but impressively large, stretching along more than 100 meters of steeply sloping sand. The top of the wreck is just 3 meters underwater; the bottom is at 29 meters. (See map page 110.)

On January 11, 1942, this ship was hit by torpedoes from a Japanese submarine while crossing the Lombok Strait. The damage was critical, but two destroyers hitched up to the ship and tried to tow it to the port at Singaraja. The wounded cargo ship was taking on too much water, however, and her crew ran the vessel up on the beach at Tulamben. There she stayed there until

1963. Local entrepreneurs stripped the boat of its cargo—one source says raw rubber and railroad parts—and were in the process of cutting her up for scrap when Gunung Agung exploded in 1963. The explosion was disasterous, killing thousands and destroying vast tracts of fertile riceland to the south. It

---

AT A GLANCE
Tulamben

Reef type: Liberty ship wreck; wall

Access: Beach; ship is 30 meters offshore

Visibility: Fair to good, 12–15 meters

Current: None

Coral: Good growth of encrusting animals on wreck; fine coral on wall

Fish: Superb variety, excellent numbers

Highlights: Full moon night dive on wreck

Other: Fish on wreck are regularly fed and quite tame; during midday, wreck can be crowded

---

also pushed the Liberty ship off the beach to its present location, in the process splitting the hull into two pieces.

Welcoming Committee

Divers simply walk out from the beach, spit in their masks, and go. Sometimes the waves are up, churning up the sand and turning a suited-up diver into an ungainly creature. And the rough volcanic rock is always hard on the feet—bring diving boots! Never mind these small indignities, however. This dive is most decidedly worth it. Wave action is strongest during the southeast monsoon, late June through August and again—but somewhat less—from late November through January.

As soon as you dump the air out of your BC and drop to the black sandy bottom, you know that you've made the right move. What at first looks like a bed of seagrass turns out to be spotted garden eels (*Heteroconger hassi*), heads and bodies swaying in the current like plants in a breeze. Their tails remain in the sand as they snap plankton from the current. As you get closer the eels shoot back into their burrows, disappearing into the sand like an illusion. At this disturbance, goatfishes hit the sand, searching for juicy tidbits.

You look up and here comes the welcoming committee: several species of snubnose chubs, sweetlips, parrotfishes and a small army of fearless sergeant-majors, not so numerous elsewhere in Bali. These plucky little damselfishes swim right up to your face, to the point where you can even touch them. If you've brought a camera, excercise restraint. If you don't watch out, you'll shoot your whole roll before even reaching the wreck.

Electric blue neon damsels, darting around with a seeming inexhaustible store of energy, stand out vividly against the black sand and rocks. As I watched, their happy antics were interrupted. A hawkfish pounced,

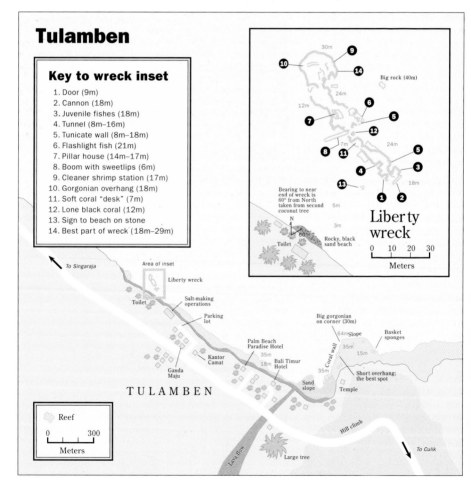

Tulamben

Key to wreck inset

1. Door (9m)
2. Cannon (18m)
3. Juvenile fishes (18m)
4. Tunnel (8m–16m)
5. Tunicate wall (8m–18m)
6. Flashlight fish (21m)
7. Pillar house (14m–17m)
8. Boom with sweetlips (6m)
9. Cleaner shrimp station (17m)
10. Gorgonian overhang (18m)
11. Soft coral "desk" (7m)
12. Lone black coral (12m)
13. Sign to beach on stone
14. Best part of wreck (18m–29m)

snatching a small damsel in a flash. A sudden jerk, the damsel's head disappeared, and the hawkfish resumed its motionless posture, looking for his next meal. Small groupers, cornetfish and trumpetfish, the odd parrotfish and a few morays inhabited patches of coral along our route.

The black sand bottom around the wreck makes an excellent background for fish photos—but be careful with autoexposure cameras, as the meter will want to overexpose your shots. On and around the ship, carefully monitor your buoyancy. Bumping the wreck could lead to a nasty burn from a stinging hydroid, or even a more serious sting from a lionfish or scorpionfish. More likely, however, you will just damage the fragile organisms encrusting the ship. Move slowly and carefully. This is also the best way to get close to the fish.

On to the Wreck

The wreck of the Liberty ship lies parallel to shore on a steep sand slope. Part of the superstructure is within snorkeling distance from the surface. The hulk is broken into large chunks, and there are lots of big holes in the hull, making it easy to explore the vessel's innards. Don't expect to find any interesting mementoes inside, however. Remember, this ship was stripped while still on the beach.

The treasures of Tulamben are swimming in and around the wreck: hundreds of species of fish in good numbers, most having become semi-tame and used to divers. We saw several fairly large—a meter or so—specimens, but it is the huge numbers of medium-sized fish—30–80 centimeters—that make the wreck such an interesting dive. If you planned just one or two dives here, we guarantee you will regret not having more time.

Unfortunately, not everything

is perfect in Tulamben. When we dove there in late June, visibility was just 12–15 meters, and this seldom improves much.

Expert underwater photographers and marine biologists, men like Rudie Kuiter, John E. Randall and Roger Steene, dive Tulamben over and over, coming up with great shots and even new species. Australian Rudie Kuiter, author of the definitive guide to Indonesian fishes, estimates that some 400 species of reef fishes live on the wreck, which is also visited by perhaps 100 species of pelagics. These are remarkable numbers for an area just 100 meters long.

On our dives we never saw any sharks or other really big fish at Tulamben. There were a few good sized tuna, bonito, several 80-centimeter plus emperors, and jacks, Napoleon wrass-

Above: *A school of lunar fusiliers,* Caesio lunaris, *at the Tulamben wreck. Tulamben, Bali.*

es pushing the meter mark, and one huge 80-centimeter scribbled filefish. On the sandy bottom next to the wreck, where I thought rays would abound, I saw only one small eagle ray, and a very large blue-spotted stingray. Both ducked for cover before I could say "Glenfiddich." We also saw a meter-long barracuda, but one of my dive partners, Wolfgang Bresigk of Baruna Water Sports, says a 1.5 meter barracuda regularly forages on the wreck.

Another dive buddy, Wally Siagian, saw a huge oceanic sunfish (*Mola mola*) close to the wreck, four times in a one-week span. On one of these occasions, he saw this most unusual fish being cleaned by several singular bannerfish (*Heniochus singularis*). Off to one side of the wreck Wally took us to visit a colorful black-spotted moray eel (*Gymnothorax melanospilos*), a beautifully marked animal with a yellow body and black markings. The eel lives at the base of a barrel sponge at about 40 meters.

A Swarm of Beggars

Arriving at the wreck, we stayed shallow and settled near the upper edge of one of the ship's large holds. The top of the open hold lies at around 5 meters, with its bottom at around 14 meters. The superstructure reaches to couple of meters of the surface.

It took a good ten minutes before the swarms of sergeant-majors, a couple of insistent crescent wrasses, and a dozen large bignose unicornfish all understood that we had no food for them and stopped bothering us. Fish here are often fed by divers or their guides, which is why they allow divers to get so close. Bananas, strange as this may seem, are their standard fare. Clearly nonplussed that we had not brought any food, the fish finally left us alone—but not before the sergeant-majors gave us a few nips.

Once the beggars left us alone, we were able to look over the swarms of fishes living on and around the wreck. Schools of several dozen golden and lined rabbitfishes hung almost motionless in 6–7 meters of water. Standing out like a sore thumb in this group, was an occasional bigeye emperor, or large red snapper. Below this group were bright pairs of coral and foxface rabbitfishes. These beauties were a bit nervous, and it took patience to get within good camera range.

Lone snappers and mixed schools of sweetlips also inhabited the shallow areas near the northeast corner of the wreck. We identified five species of sweetlips: clown sweetlips, Sulawesi sweetlips, striped sweetlips, Goldman's sweetlips, and, most numerous of all, the oriental sweetlips. These fish allowed us to approach to one meter.

Surgeonfishes were common, and inhabited various depths. We frequently saw yellowfin surgeonfish, orangeband surgeonfish, Thompson's surgeonfish, and clown surgeonfish. We saw a few orangespine unicornfish, with their curious mandrill-like faces, and a few male spotted unicornfish. Bignose unicornfish wandered the wreck in large schools, mostly consisting of drab females, but with an occasional bright blue courting male, his magnificent tail filaments undulating with each flip. These fish allowed us to get very close, and we saw them on every dive.

A variety of fairly large parrotfishes (40–75 centimeters) added color and even sound to every dive. With a bit of patience we could get to within a meter of the blue-barred parrotfishes, but the others—mostly palenose parrotfish and bullethead parrotfish—were more shy.

Small damsels were common,

in particular golden damselfish. These bold little animals frequently nipped us if we got too close to their home turf.

Butterflyfishes are not present here in overwhelming numbers. Perhaps the dearth of hard corals is responsible for this, as many butterflyfishes are polyp feeders, some relying completely on this source of nutrition. The vaguaries of memory have reduced the list to six: lined butterflyfish, raccoon butterflyfish, threadfin butterflyfish, Bennett's butterflyfish, spotnose butterflyfish and the Pinocchio-like longnose butterflyfish.

I had seen Titan triggerfish—a nasty, downright ugly animal with a distinctive "mustache" and loopy eyes—on many previous dives in eastern Indonesia, sometimes as many as a half-dozen in a single dive. They had always been very wary, never allowing me to get close. On the wreck, however, they were much more relaxed, allowing me to get within 3 meters. These were also among the largest I had seen, doing justice to the name "Titan."

Angelfishes were not particularly abundant on the wreck, but those that I saw here were among the largest specimens I have seen. We spotted blue-faced angels, blue-girdled angels, emperor angels and regal angels. None of these fellows shamelessly coddled up to divers to beg for food or out of curiosity, but kept a healthy distance from the human visitors. Moorish idols here shared the same trait; none was as bold as the similarly marked longfin bannerfish.

Groupers prowled around on every dive, including red-mouth groupers and white-lined groupers, although the real stars were the aptly named peacock grouper, and its even more colorful relatives: the coral grouper, the flagtail grouper, and the black-tipped grouper. The largest groupers we saw were the blotchy grouper, and the saddleback grouper, sometimes called the giant coral trout.

Sea Fans and Sponges

The encrusted wreck is mostly a community of opportunists: soft corals, sponges, gorgonians, hydroids, bryozoans, tunicates,

Above: *An emperor angelfish,* Pomacanthus imperator, *on the wreck at Tulamben. Although the steel structure has not yet been much colonized by hard corals, it is heavily encrusted with soft corals, gorgonians and hydrozoans.*

Enoplometopus debelius: A Reef Lobster of One's Own

It was night, and 15 meters down I glided along the sloping reef in pitch black water. I could hear the noise of my bubbles much more clearly than during the day. A pair of cardinalfish swam into the beam from my lamp and, startled, fled at high speed. I had learned to find my way around this beautiful reef off Tulamben during the afternoon, and I was now looking for reef lobsters and other big crustacea as I always do on night dives.

I shone my light into every crevice and cave. Here it fell on dancing shrimps, and there on a marbled shrimp. I saw the brightly colored common reef lobster, *Enoplometopus occidentalis,* and snapped two pictures before it could hide. Suddenly the beam of my light came to rest on a patch of violet. I looked again, and made out the shape of a reef lobster, crouching in the coral rubble.

I could scarcely breathe as I adjusted the focus of the camera, for this species looked completely new to me. The entire

Above: *A gravid female* Enoplometopus debelius. *Author and photographer Helmut Debelius is a skilled aquarist, and has succeeded in spawning the lobsters in captivity.*

body of the little 10-centimeter lobster was sprinkled with small violet dots, an enchanting sight in the bright light. I snapped off three shots as the animal slowly backed up.

Quickly, I laid my camera aside and took a small net from my wetsuit and placed it behind the lobster. With my free hand I gently touched its pincers and, as I had expected, the animal dashed backwards into the net. "A shame for you," I muttered to the lobster, but when it comes to scientific aims, I have no mercy.

Later, my suspicions were confirmed: Dutch crustacean expert Prof. L.B. Holthius examined the animal and said that it was a new species. He named it after me: *Enoplometopus debelius.*

The Reef Lobsters

Reef lobsters are beautiful, but rarely seen inhabitants of the holes and crevices of Indonesian reefs. In size and shape they resemble freshwater crayfish more than the common spiny lobsters of Indo-Pacific reefs. These omnivorous creatures emerge only at night, to feed on carrion, worms and anything else they can catch—even a sleeping fish.

—Helmut Debelius

Left: Enoplometopus debelius *in one of the author's tanks in Germany.*

bivalves and crinoids. It is still much too soon for a really large accumulation of hard corals. In less than 30 years, however, great sections of the wreck's iron hull have been smothered in a bright encrustation of life. Great sea fans, gorgonians up to 2 meters across, jut from the bow section. Several large trees of black coral (*Antipathes* sp.) grow here safe from the jeweler. Sponges, tunicates and hydroids crowd each other for a holdfast. In places, there are great aggregations of thorny oysters, their bright "lips" visible through parted shells. Crinoids cling to every stable growth—a sponge, a gorgonian—and unfurl their arms to the current. In one of the the shallower spots, a growth of hard plate coral has already reached over 3 meters.

The many "cleaner stations" around the wreck offer a great show. Fish line up to be cleaned by one of the small cleaner wrasses (*Labroides* sp.). We saw both bluestreak and bicolor cleaner wrasses at work here. Some divers have actually succeeded in having the fish pick bits of food out from between their teeth—although this requires holding your breath for a minute or so.

Night Dive on the Wreck

Daytime dives are extraordinary on the wreck, but a night dive, especially around full moon, will be among the most memorable dives you will make.

As we walked along the beach to the entry point, three local fishing outriggers sailed silently by in the moonlight. We waded out, took our bearings, and headed toward the wreck. As we approached the ship, we extinguished our lights. The large hulk loomed above us, a massive ghostly presence with the bright moon a distant pinpoint of light.

We kept our lights off for a bit. Each fin-stroke stirred up a twinkling trail of bioluminescence. Peering into the dark hold of the wreck, we saw a magical show of zigzagging lights. These were the curious flashlight fishes, each possessed of a bioluminescent organ behind its eye.

Many sections of the wreck provide the overhangs preferred by the large, bright orange polyps of *Tubastraea* and *Dendrophyllia*. These corals are best appreciated at night. At night one can also see crinoids crawling about in search of a new holdfast, or perhaps even swimming, their feathery legs opening and closing in the manner of a octopus. Sometimes when we trained our lights on the wreck, hundreds of red shrimp eyes stared back.

Here again, however, the fish are the real stars of the show. We saw a couple of unconcerned common lionfish, and a stunning spotfin lionfish. A large red parrotfish slept, secure in its mucous cocoon, under a shallow overhang. We approached a big map puffer, and several groggy unicornfish.

The most interesting fish we came upon was an absolutely huge barred filefish (*Cantherhines dumerilii*). I spotted the big fella at least 10 meters above me, sleeping under a large lacy plate of coral growing horizontally from the wreck. My computer screamed its warning just as I made for this animal, but I paid it no heed. My subject was sleep-

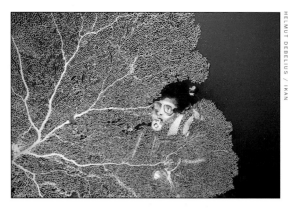

Above: *A huge fan coral gorgonian. Tulamben, Bali.*

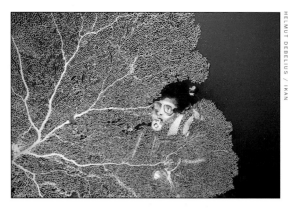HELMUT DEBELIUS / IKAN

ing in a tilted position. After a few shots, I poked him a bit to correct his posture. He didn't particularly appreciate this, but obliged me anyway. I moved him into the open water. A few more shots, and he had had enough, charging straight for me. Swimming backwards, I accidentally caught him on the chin with a stroke of my fin, and he headed off into the night. We photographers really are a pain.

A Popular Site

Tulamben is probably the most popular dive spot in Indonesia (and justifiably so), and during the daily rush, from about 11:30 a.m. to 4 p.m., an average of three or four groups of about a dozen divers each visit the wreck. The ship is big, however, and most of the groups just zip by. But serious divers seldom appreciate crowds, and novice divers, not having mastered buoyancy control, have the unfortunate habit of thrashing up clouds of sand with their fins.

Some of our best dives on Tulamben were in the early morning and late afternoon, before and after the crowds. The only way to do this is to overnight in Tulamben (see "Bali Practicalities" page 129).

Staying overnight also takes a lot of the logistical headaches out of night dives, but be sure to stash a towel on the beach. The 10-minute walk back can be chilly. For day trippers, there's a shower at the toilet block on the beach, next to the dive site, but sometimes there is no water, and there can be long lines.

The Tulamben Wall

Should you want to take a break from wreck diving, there is a good coral wall beginning just off the eastern end of the beach. The rocky knoll southeast of town plunges straight down into the sea, and coral grows along its face. Be careful who you dive with—or what group you follow—as the fine gray sediment here is easily stirred up.

Just as we began our dive, heading down over sloping grey sand, a good sized barracuda cruised by—but that was the only big fish we saw during the dive. We soon found our wall: it has a nice overhang around the 18 meter mark, and drops to a sand bottom at just over 60 meters. We explored only to the 30 meter mark, following the ridge to its furthest extension. This wall does not host huge numbers of fish, but like the wreck has a tremendous variety.

At one point along the dive, Wally stopped at a shrimp cleaning station, manned by the candy-striped cleaner shrimp *Lysmata amboinensis*. Taking out his regulator and opening his mouth wide, he soon had two of the fellows working on the remains of his lunch. Others were eager for leftovers, but there are limits to Wally's breath-holding capabilities.

Lots of large barrel sponges (*Xestospongia* sp.) sprouted from the slope, and sponges in general were abundant here—tube sponges, vase sponges, and encrusting sponges. Once we left the wall, the coral grew only in small knolls. The final part of the dive was a short, boring ride over featureless grey sand.

This area is known for unusual species, including the comet (*Calloplesiops altivelis*), a beautiful fish with elaborate finnage and a false eye-spot. The posture and coloration of the comet mimics the spotted moray eel (*Gymnothorax meleagris*).

As few predators wish to tangle with the eel, the fish is protected. For the really keen-eyed observer, new species are waiting here to be discovered. Just a few years ago science added a new fairy basslet to its list, *Pseudoanthias bimaculeatus,* first discovered here.

Clear Water off Bali's Distant 'Deer' Island

Menjangan Island—the name means "deer"—hangs just offshore of the mountainous point in far northwestern Bali. Because the island is in a protected position, currents and wind-generate waves are rarely a bother, and the reefs here offer fine diving, particularly for beginning and intermediate divers. Occasionally, the water can be crystal clear—a snorkel, distinct, 50 meters above you—and the rest of the time visibility seldom drops to less than 25 meters.

The island is part of Bali Barat national park, a protected reserve area that encompasses much of Bali's little-populated western end. (See map page 119.) The drive from the resort areas of the south is at least three hours, the first hour through the thick traffic that envelops Denpasar like a fog.

Craggy Walls

The coral walls around Menjangan are vertical down to 30–60 meters, and then slope outward. The reef surface is particularly rugged: caves, grottoes, crevasses and funnel-like splits break up the coral wall, and the surface is textured with little nooks and crannies. Gorgonians of many kinds reach large sizes here, and huge barrel sponges are abundant. Soft corals blanket the colorful walls all the way down.

We found the variety of fish here to be somewhat inferior to other dive sites—we ask for a lot!—but the numbers are good and some of the fish are quite bold, as guides feed them regularly. We were blessed with a curious pack of half a dozen fully grown roundfaced batfish, and

two aggregations of bignose unicornfish. A few individuals from a large school of longfin bannerfish approached us, but the majority kept a discreet distance, as did the yellowback fusiliers, which accompany almost every dive in Indonesia.

Small boats ferry divers from the Nature Reserve dock at

AT A GLANCE
Menjangan

Reef type: Walls, particularly rugged; wreck

Access: 30 min by boat from Labuan Lalang post

Visibility: Very good to superb, 25–50 meters

Current: Very slight

Coral: Very good numbers and variety; abundant soft corals

Fish: Good number, only average variety

Highlights: "Anker" wreck

Other: Particularly large variety of parrotfishes

Labuhan Lalang to Menjangan's small beach, where gearing up takes place in the sandy-bottomed shallows. The edge of the reef terrace is at 1–5 meters, and a V-shaped delta of sand points the way out to the edge.

Guides usually take their groups to the east (left) on their first dive—keep an eye out for a huge gorgonian at 18 meters—and down to 15–30 meters, and then back through the shallows (5–10 meters) on the way back. After a lunch on the beach, the group goes west (right). Here the wall has much more relief, and the guides send a boat to pick up divers at the end of their dive, returning them directly to the Nature Reserve dock at Labuhan Lalang.

On the second dive, we saw a couple of names carved into sponges. Please don't join the ranks of the morons.

The Anchor Wreck

Menjangan's western tip holds a deeper, but more interesting dive on an old wreck. The so-called "Anker" wreck is just off the coast, near a small dock and guardpost maintained by the Park Service (PHPA). (See map opposite.) The guardpost—"Pos II"—is about a 30-minute boat ride; our craft anchored about 75 meters from the beach at a point designated by our guide. (Note: few guides know the location of this wreck.)

We entered the water near the reef edge, and dropped some 5 meters through very clear water (more than 20 meters visibility) right onto the large coral-encrusted anchor of our sunken ship. Dropping over the reef edge, we followed a fairly steep slope with bits and pieces of

wreckage and anchor chain down to 30 meters where the ship was resting, prow shoreward. Along the way, we saw a reef white-tip shark (sharks and rays are common here) and a few lizardfishes.

It seems obvious that the craft, probably a copper-sheathed sailor from the last century, tried to anchor just off the reef, broke the anchor chain, sunk and slid back to its resting place on the sloping sand bottom. It's a small ship, just 25 meters long, and its stern sits in 45 meters of water.

Flat rectangular sheets, perhaps copper sheathing material, lay in what had been the hold, which also contains an assortment of ceramic and glass bottles. These perhaps had contained *arak,* a powerful local booze distilled from palm wine that had been a major trade item of the last century. Miraculously, previous divers have not stolen the bottles—yet.

There were fewer fish on the wreck than usual, according to my guide, but this was because a group of divers had just passed through. We saw several snap-

Below: *A dive boat off Menjangan Island.*

Menjangan Island

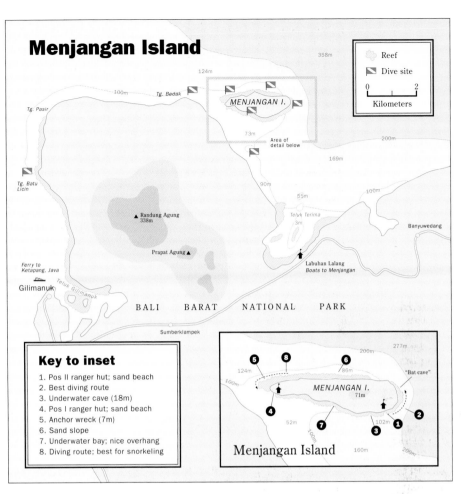

Legend:
- Reef
- Dive site

0 ——————— 2
Kilometers

358m
124m
100m
Tg. Bedak
MENJANGAN I.
73m
Area of detail below
169m
200m
Tg. Pasir
Tg. Batu Licin
90m
55m
100m
▲ Randung Agung 338m
Teluk Terima
3m
Banyuwedang
Prapat Agung ▲
Ferry to Ketapang, Java
Gilimanuk
Teluk Gilimanuk
Labuhan Lalang
Boats to Menjangan

BALI BARAT NATIONAL PARK
Sumberklampek

Key to inset

1. Pos II ranger hut; sand beach
2. Best diving route
3. Underwater cave (18m)
4. Pos I ranger hut; sand beach
5. Anchor wreck (7m)
6. Sand slope
7. Underwater bay; nice overhang
8. Diving route; best for snorkeling

277m
200m
124m
100m
5
8
6
86m
"Bat cave"
MENJANGAN I.
71m
4
52m
100m
7
3
102m
1
2
160m
200m

Menjangan Island

pers, sweetlips, goatfishes, wrasses and Moorish idols. In the vicinity of the wreck, visibility dropped to just 10 meters, again perhaps because of the last group. Large gorgonians grow on the wreck as well as on the slope leading to it. The wreck and the area around it was dominated by soft corals. The sandy slope beyond the wreck was largely bare.

After less than 10 minutes, we decided to ascend a bit, partially because of the depth, but mostly because my guide had said earlier that the reef life was most abundant above, and a bit south of the wreck. He was certainly right. On our slow upward progress, diagonally to the slope, we crossed a slow, orderly cascade of surgeonfish, broken up by two bright, terminal male filament-finned parrotfish, chasing each other at top speed.

Here, and in the shallows above, were more species of parrotfish than we have ever seen on a single dive. There were also many unicornfish, with the blue-spine unicornfish being the most numerous. Several large and colorful bignose unicornfish tried hard to keep their harems under control, but on our approach, the ladies beat a hasty retreat into nearby minicaves. A large, spread-out school of longfin bannerfish was much less concerned with our presence.

The butterflyfishes were well

represented, especially the masked bannerfish (*Heniochus monoceros*). We saw a large pinnate batfish, and several small roundfaced batfish. Rabbitfishes, fairy basslets and damselfish were abundant. Perched on coral knobs and gorgonians were two species of hawkfishes, tiny falco hawkfish, and curious longnose hawkfish. From 20 meters on up, stretches of the coral face were cut with caves and narrow, vertical funnels. These offered refuge to soldierfishes and medium-sized groupers, including a couple of clownish polkadot groupers (*Cromileptes altivelis*). A pair of longnose emperors appeared against the dark blue sea background.

Back in the shallows—5–7 meters—our visibility returned to its original 20+ meters. Here we saw two red snappers, and a small school of blackspotted snappers. A pair of Clark's anemonefish, living in a beautiful green-tentacled anemone, challenged us to a brawl. The tentacles of this anemone (*Entactmaea quadricolor*) have strange, bulbous tips. Nearby, a tassled

scorpionfish did not defy anyone, secure with the power of its venom. Moorish idols were unusually abundant, but shy.

Colorful Picasso triggerfish played hide and seek amidst the coral, and a large scribbled file-fish seemed unconcerned as we closed in on him to within a half a meter for a photo. Two Titan triggerfish, intent on each other, took little notice of us, nor did a small patrol of bumphead parrotfish, following their meter-plus leader. But a school of black triggerfish seemed almost to wish us Godspeed. We reluctantly left our fantasy playground, out of film and almost out of air.

Getting to Menjangan

Most of the people who dive Menjangan sleep in the Kuta–Nusa Dua–Sanur tourist triangle. They are picked up around 7:30 a.m. by one of the dive operators, with filled tanks, weights, any rented gear and box lunches already packed in the minivan. For the first hour or so of the three-hour ride, you might as well catch up on your sleep as the driver maneuvers out of the

Below: *A squad of bumphead parrotfish,* Bolbometopon muricatum. *Although such stories may just be folklore, it has been said that the bumphead parrotfishes use the hump as a ram to break up coral heads into more manageable pieces.*

KAL MULLER

heavy traffic surrounding Denpasar and continuing past the town of Tabanan. The next hour and a half are worth opening your eyes for, with wide spreads of terraced rice fields reaching to the sea on the left.

The road is a good one (it's the main Java–Bali highway) and the drivers really turn it on—if you get nervous at such things, stay out of the front seat. As you approach the town of Negara, the land becomes drier, and there are lots of coconut plantations producing copra. Past Negara, it's a half hour to Cekek, the headquarters of the Bali Barat (West) National Park, just 3 kilometers short of Gilimanuk, the ferry crossing to Java. Macaques, looking for handouts, line the road a bit before Cekik, and after the turnoff for the 12-kilometer stretch to Labuhan Lalang. Labuhan Lalang is a total of 125 kilometers from Denpasar.

At the boat landing, while you register with the park service—name, nationality, passport number—all your gear is unloaded from the minivan into a boat, big enough for six divers and all

their accompanying gear.

While driving through west Bali, keep your eyes out for an unusual bird, endemic to this area. The Bali starling, or Rothschild's myna, (*Leucopsar rothschildi*) is a crested, snow-white bird with black on its wing-points and the tip of its tail, and a bright blue patch of skin around its eyes. Unfortunately, you will almost certainly not see one, as fewer than 100 are thought to remain here.

As a cage bird, Rothschild's myna fetches a very high price; there are many more now in captivity than in the wild. Do not be fooled if you see a white, crested myna with a black tail and wings. This is the black-winged starling (*Sturnus melanopterus*). It has much more black on it than the Bali starling, and the skin patch around its eyes is yellow.

It's just short of a half-hour ride to Menjangan, and on the way you can see three of Java's eastern-most volcanoes. As you approach Menjangan, keep a lookout for dolphins. Menjangan island is uninhabited—except, of course, by deer.

Below: *A pack of grey reef sharks,* Carcharhinus amblyrhynchos. *Although they look ominous here, cruising over a bed of coral rubble, they are not known to be dangerous in Indonesia. Manado, Sulawesi.*

ED ROBINSON / IKAN

Exploratory Dives on Islands North of Bali

We left the port of Benoa, in Bali, at 2 o'clock in the afternoon, after a long wait for port clearance. We had chartered a boat and were bound for the Kangean archipelago, a cluster of small islands that lies 130 kilometers due north of Bali. These were to be exploratory dives, as there is no organized diving in the Kangean group. Our air was to be provided by an on-board compressor.

Beneath the Kangean islands are huge reservoirs of natural gas that are expected to supply the energy needs of Surabaya, Indonesia's second-largest city.

Although north of Bali, the islands are part of the province of Madura, Java. Construction on the 130-kilometer pipeline has started, but the Kangean islands are still undeveloped, and as such, an idyllic destination for a small group of divers.

Leaving from eastern Bali, our course took us through the Lombok Strait, a particularly fickle stretch of water. We knew the strait was subject to strong currents, but we weren't prepared for the persistent monster our craft had to battle the first night—at sunrise, we were still within sight of Bali. Soon, however, our speed improved, and in another few hours we could see the islands ahead.

Arriving at Sepankur

Three waving men, balancing on what looked from our still distant position like a log, welcomed us to Sepankur island, right in the middle of the group. (see map opposite.) As they paddled closer, we realized they were in a small canoe. The men were hunting sea turtles, and one of the divers still wore his goggles.

Below: *A swarm of purple queens,* Pseudanthias tuka, *hovers over a very healthy section of Indonesian reef.*

These were homemade: disks of glass cut from the bottom of soda bottles fitted with pitch into sections of bamboo. The strap came from an old inner-tube.

We dropped anchor in a sheltered bay on the north of Sepankur. There were holding nets here filled with thousands of live sea bass, awaiting their fortnightly shipment to Hongkong. This was an unexpected bonus, as dinner was only a matter of swimming over to the nets, and choosing a fish from the keeper.

This was only one of many beautiful anchorages we discovered in the next four days as we sailed from island to island in this shallow sea. The dozens of small islands are inhabited by Muslim fishermen and their families, and in the evenings we would invite them aboard for conversation. The first night we found out about the crocodiles.

Apparently, a fellow villager who was poaching teak logs from the nearby Kangean Reserve had recently been attacked by a very large saltwater crocodile and severely mauled, dying of blood loss before proper medical attention could be found. We were also told that during the rainy season the crocodiles have been known to swim across to Sepankur and enter the holding nets, helping themselves to the Hongkong delicacies.

(Back in Bali a few months later, we heard that the crocodiles had been particularly active since our visit—there were reports of 10 deaths.)

Diving Sepankur

Our first dive at the southwest point of Sepankur was understandably a nervous one. Unfortunately, however, it was disappointingly uneventful. The greater part of the sea here is shallow, no deeper than 25 meters. On our first dive we explored a shallow (8.5 meter) sandy bottom with coral outcrops

around which we found bluespotted stingrays, angelfish, goatfish and butterflyfish.

On our way back to the boat on the Zodiac, we met a fishing boat with more divers. These men were rigged in hookah outfits, with the air delivered by a hand pump on deck. They had had a successful day fishing for trepang and lobster, which they would sell on Kangean, the largest island of the group.

After this uninspiring beginning to our diving trip, we decided to snorkel any potential diving spots first. We headed for Saebus, a green, palm-fringed island surrounded by white sand beaches and inhabited by more friendly fishermen.

We took the Zodiac to the southwest "corner" of this elongated island and jumped in to snorkel the sandy slopes only 20–30 meters off the shore, immediately coming face to face with a group of four bumphead parrotfish, and a turtle.

We rushed back to the Zodiac, geared up, and descended. As we entered the channel between Saebus and Saur, the sandy bottom gave way to a fine white clay which, owing to the half-knot current, produced poor visibility—at times only five meters.

Huge coral knolls, each with dozens of different types of corals, and terraces of table corals were abundant. Again we saw many rays, angelfish, butterflyfish, parrotfish and wrasse. We gently drifted through the canyons made by the coral bommies. Our maximum depth was 20 meters and the gentle current made for an effortless drift back to the yacht.

Diving a Submerged Reef

We dived early the next day before the swell picked up and disturbed the sediment. We had gone back to the submerged reef we had navigated around the day before, on our way to Saebus, between Sepankur and Saur.

This bank reef was approximately 140 meters by 40 meters, and the local fishermen called it a "taka." At low tide it was only a meter below the surface, and extended down to a sandy bottom, ten meters below.

Coral cover was quite good, although we saw some evidence of bombing by the fishermen. As we descended, we frightened away a reef whitetip shark, and saw a large school of snappers. The variety and numbers of fish were amazing—butterflyfish, angelfish, surgeonfish and more.

Pangerang Island

On our navigational maps, the north coast of Pangerang Island was the next spot that had looked like potential diving. The visibility was great—25–30 meters. A sandy bottom at 18 meters rose to coral slopes alive with fish: firefish, blackspot snapper, fusiliers, bream, humphead bannerfish, six-banded angelfish and emperor angelfish. We swam close to a school of large bumphead parrotfish, came across numerous blue-spotted rays nestled under the edges of coral outcrops, and found a medium-sized turtle.

Sakala Island

Our time was running out, but we had just enough left to dive off the island of Sakala, the most easterly of the Kangean group.

Here we were on the edge of the Sunda shelf, and our dive site was once again on a bank, but much deeper than the others. Its top was at 16 meters, and its sandy slopes descended out of sight. This dive was quite different from our previous dives.

Visibility was 20 meters or more, and we saw many pelagic fish, particularly sharks—at least a dozen reef whitetip sharks, reef black-tips, and even a couple of gray whalers. Schools of mackerel and trevally patrolled the area. The reef was flat with few pinnacles, and very little live coral, other than a few gorgonians. We surmised that it was unprotected, and swept clean by currents.

Coming back from Sakala we hugged the coast of Sepanjang, hoping for another quick dive, but we could only manage an exploratory snorkel as the water was too rough to take the loaded Zodiac out. We discovered a sight not unlike our first dives, only much deeper, perhaps 20 meters. The bottom formation was a flat sand terrace gently sloping out of sight, interspersed with low coral knolls at intervals of 20–30 meters. The knolls were alive with myriad reef fish, and we sighted an enormous spotted eagle ray, and two reef whitetip sharks. The visibility here was very good—25 to 30 meters.

A Wild Storm

We left the Kangean islands and headed back to Bali. Our trip was smooth and uneventful until sunset, when we sighted Bali. Then, a strong wind blew up. We didn't reach land until dawn the following morning, 20 kilometers off course and drenched through by the waves that continually swamped our decks. It wasn't until we were well and truly out of the rough water that Eric, our captain, admitted it was the worst storm he had ever experienced in the Lombok Strait.

—*Cody Shwaiko*

Bali Scuba Tour Operators

Note: All prices in U.S.$; telephone code 0361 unless otherwise noted.

Diving tour operators in Bali are concentrated in the tourist triangle—Kuta, Nusa Dua and Sanur—and in two places close to good dive spots—Candi Dasa on the east coast and Lovina, between the Tulamben wreck and Menjangan Island, in the north. The bigger outfits maintain desks at the major hotels, or at least keep brochures at the desk.

Prices are fairly standard: $40–$85 (depending on location) inclusive of guides, transportation, and lunch, for a two-dive visit and $30–$40 for a one-tank night dive. Operators have some equipment for rent for casual divers (BC and regulator, $10–$20 a day).

Almost all the local dive guides speak some English (and/or Japanese) and dive very well. Where many fall short, however, is in dive planning—particularly tailoring a dive for your specific needs—and emergency assistance.

Most outfits, chiefly for financial reasons, offer "initial" introductory course dives to non-divers (we highly discourage this). They also offer 4–5 day "resort courses" with CMAS (French), PADI (U.S.), PAUI (Australian), or POSSI (Indonesian) certification ($240–$400).

A resort course will give you some of the basics, but definitely *does not* make you at ease in currents, caves or at night. A graduate of a resort course is not an experienced diver. We suggest that you accumulate at least some 20–30 dives before diving at some of the potentially more difficult sites. And always stay above the 25 meter mark, plan your dives and follow your plan. Experienced divers should request that, if at all possible, their group does not include beginners. All outfits require a minimum of two passengers per trip (you need a buddy anyway). Some offer the possibility of a third day dive or one at night. All offer snorkeling for non-divers. The better outfits have their own dive boats, long outriggers powered by twin 40 hp engines.

Of all the operators, we recommend Baruna Water Sports.

Kuta

Baruna Water Sports. Head office: Jl. By Pass Ngurah Rai 300B, Kuta. Mailing address: P.O. Box 419 Denpasar 80001, Bali. Tel: 53809, 53820, 53831, 53884, or 51223 (8 lines); fax: 52779; Telex: 35257 NDBT IA. With sales counters at the following hotels:
Bali Beach Hotel, Tel: 88511 ext. 1764.
Bali Hyatt Hotel, Tel: 88271 ext. 93.
Kartika Plaza Beach Hotel, Tel: 52471.
Melia Bali Sol Hotel, Tel: 71350.
Mirage Bali Hotel and Resort, Tel: 72147.
Nusa Dua Beach Hotel, Tel: 71210.
Nusa Indah Hotel, Tel: 71566.
Puri Bagus Beach Hotel, Tel: 35666.
Putri Bali Hotel, Tel: 71020 ext. 7737.
Sanur Beach Hotel, Tel: 88011.
On Lombok Island:
Senggigi Beach Hotel, Tel: (0364) 23430.

Where no extension is listed, just ask for "Baruna." For Candi Dasa, see below. Baruna will have a counter at the Senggigi Sheraton when that hotel is completed and will begin operations in Labuhanbajo, Flores once the airport extension has been completed.

Baruna, named after the Balinese water deity, is Bali's oldest, largest and best scuba diving operator. As of this writing, they were putting the finishing touches on their own decompression chamber. Using it will be expensive—several hundred dollars per hour—so carry insurance. They operate 4 outriggered speedboats and a larger diesel-powered boat.

Dive tours. Baruna organizes tours for divers, individuals or groups, to all of Bali's dive sites, and anywhere else in Indonesia. This includes obtaining airplane reservations and tickets, quite difficult to places like Manado, Sulawesi and Maumere, Flores in July and August. They also run special-interest diving tours, fixed program tours and can arrange yacht charters (with compressor) for groups of two to six.

Standard Bali dives are all-inclusive (tanks, weights, lunch, land and sea transport, guide, insurance) day trips, minimum two people, two dives: Sanur/Nusa Dua ($42), Nusa Penida ($68); Padang Bai ($52), Tepekong/Mimpang/Biaha ($58), Cemeluk ($56), Tulamben ($56), Menjangan ($68), and Manta Point/Batu Abah ($78). A night dive at Sanur or Nusa Dua, ($32); at Tulamben or Padang Bai ($38). Extra day dive ($15).

Baruna's all-inclusive dive packages range from 3 days/2 nights to 14 days/13 nights. A typical 8 day/7 night package for a group of 4–6 costs $429–$502 for divers, $323-396 for non-divers, based on double occupancy. These are 2 dive per day deals with $30 extra for a night dive. Baruna's normal dive tours have a $10 nightly surcharge for rooms during the two high seasons July1–Aug 31 and Dec. 15–Jan 10. Add $10/day if you need to rent a BC and regulator.

The 12 cabin—24 passenger *Baruna Explorer* operates dive cruises to Komodo and eastern Indonesia, usually 8–10 days, $150/day, all-inclusive. Each AC cabin has its own bathroom with hot shower. The *Baruna Explorer* is a spacious, 3-deck ship with a length of 37m and 7m beam. Cruising speed of 11–12 knots. Everything you need for diving.

Wally's Special Tours. Dive guide Wally Siagian (see profile page 98) offers a special 10 day/9 night tour of all of Bali's best dive spots. Wally caters to small groups (2 to 6 clients) whose special interest includes: marine life or photography. He will also take spear fishermen, although this is very controlled and pelagics only (no spear-fishing gear is available for rent locally). Wally arranges his groups according to diving ability: novice, intermediate and expert. For the last group, there are night dives, deep dives, and dives in up to 3-knot currents.

Wally gives a briefing before every dive, a short de-briefing afterwards, and nights are spent going over the day's dives and talking about the client's special interests over cold beer. We cannot recommend these tours highly enough—but give yourself plenty of time. Optionals include shopping (Wally takes no commission, and even helps you bargain for the lowest possible prices), sightseeing, and even bar- or disco-hopping. It's up to you—Wally's schedule is flexible and interests wide-ranging.

Depending on the class of accommodations desired, Wally's Special Tour, 10 days/9 nights for two, costs $655–$755/person, not including evening meals and night dives ($35 ea.). The price drops slightly as the number of clients increases. Contact Baruna well ahead of time for these tours.

Dive tours with accommodations. Starting at $78 and on up, depending on dive location and hotel/*losmen* chosen. Overnight diving in the Nusa Penida area ($78) includes accommodations on board their Baruna boat (Basic: sleep on mattresses, no cabins, but sit-

down toilet).

Baruna owns a very attractive 50-room, bungalows-style hotel, the Puri Bagus Beach beachside and at the extreme eastern end of Candi Dasa. Their dive operations for eastern Bali are run from here (although you can make bookings from elsewhere).

The architecture, grounds and pool are all in good taste and well maintained. It is best to stay here if you are diving in the area, especially if you are on one of Baruna's package tours. Two-dive all-inclusive tours, including accommodations but not supper, ($85).

Normally, the hotel costs $55S, $60D. Breakfast ($6), lunch ($10), dinner ($12) available. Travel agency on premises, car rental/taxi service available. American Express, Mastercard, Visa and Diners' Club credit cards are all accepted. (Note: Add 15.5% tax to all hotel prices.)

Diving lessons. One day introductory course, SSI ($78) or PADI ($88); 4-day course with certification, CMAS/POSSI ($248), SSI ($278), PADI ($298). Advanced open water courses: normal 3-day PADI advanced course ($260); 5-day PADI "advanced plus"—includes deep, night and navigation dives and 6 student-selected dives ($360).

Bali Dolfin. At the Bali Garden Hotel, Jl. Kartika, Kuta, Tel: 52725 ext. 139. Head office, Jl. Brigjen Ngurah Rai Bypass, Tohpati, Denpasar, Bali, Tel: 72078. Caters chiefly to Japanese divers, but can handle others as well. They have four local guides. Two dives, inclusive: Nusa Dua/Sanur ($42), Nusa Penida ($70), Padang Bai ($55), Tepekong ($58), Tulamben/Cemeluk ($58), Menjangan ($58). Night dive ($38). Introductory dive ($80). Dive gear rental ($10) plus, if desired, 3mm or 5mm suit ($5). Four-day NAUI certification course ($330 plus teaching materials). The instructor is Japanese-speaking with one of the local dive

guides translating into English.
Gloria Maris. Jl. Raya Kuta Airport Ngurah Rai km 10 (Banjar Jaba), Tel: 51730, 51853, fax: 51403. This is the central office, with the operations office just west of Candi Dasa. You can buy vouchers here for diving, all-inclusive—accommodations, meals, diving—for $50 (tanks and weights) or $65 (all equipment). Inexpensive, but not too well organized. Rental equipment is sub-standard, and guides not the best.

Indonesia Diving Adventure. At the Bali Mandira Hotel, P.O. Box 272, Denpasar Tel: 51381 ext. 332. One very good dive guide; others so-so. Good rental equipment and organization. 5-day dive course with NAUI certification ($350). Inclusive, 2-dive trips (min. two): Nusa Dua ($60), Padang Bai ($65), Tepekong ($70), Tulamben ($75), Menjangan ($85). Prices include transportation, tanks, weights, boats and lunch. BC and regulator ($15). Night dives ($35).

Pineapple Divers. Legian Beach Hotel, P.O. Box 308, Jl. Melasti, Kuta. Tel: 51313, telex 35324 LBHTL. A reputable outfit, specializing in Japanese clients. One-day open water class ($150), 4-day scuba course ($400), both taught in English or Japanese. Camera rental, UW light rental ($10). Private charters available. Excellent equipment and guides. Normal prices.

Nusa Dua

There are two dive centers here, located right next to each other about halfway between the Club Med and the northern tip of the Tanjung Benoa Peninsula, in the Benoa Bahari Beach area.

Bali Adventures. P.O. Box 17, Nusa Dua 80363. Tel: 71767. Dive guides/instructors include two Americans, an Australians and a Japanese, a big plus. They own a Balinese *jukung* with two 60 hp outboards, 1.5 hrs to Nusa Penida, up to 15 divers. Excellent rental equipment ($10). Basic and advanced dive courses. Featuring a beginner's "fun dive" direct to open water ($50). The usual prices for the dive spots around Bali. **Bali Divers**. P.O. Box 68, Nusa Dua, 80363. Tel: 72134, fax: 71659. Owned and run by an Indonesian with instructor certification from both CMAS and PAUI; good equipment and guides. Their office keeps diving books and magazines.

Sanur

Oceana Dive Center. Jl. Bypass Ngurah Rai 78XX, Tel: 88652, 88922, fax: 88652. In Jakarta: Jl. Panglima Polim X/19, Jakarta 12160, Tel: (021) 7391747, fax: (021) 3805195. This large, efficient outfit is the only one in Bali to sell scuba gear, expensive but guaranteed: BCs—US Divers Aqualung $370, Mares EDV, $400; regulators—Dacor 360 XLB $217, Sherwood Brut $306; dive suits $95–$190 (the latter, SSA). Rental: basic mask, snorkel, fins ($3); basic plus boots, gloves, BC, regulator, wet suit, ($15). Also: knife ($2), UW light ($7), computer ($7), Motor-marine camera ($15). The rental equipment is well-maintained.

In addition to the usual basic dive course, Japanese and European instructors offer 2-day advanced open water (CMAS and PADI, $250); 2–3 day rescue course ($250); 5-day dive master course ($400). They will pick you up in Ubud for dive trips for $5 extra. Australian, Indonesian and Japanese dive masters. A well-run, serious outfit. **Bali Marine Sports**. Jl. Bypass Ngurah Rai, Blanjong, Sanur, Tel: 87872, 88776, fax: 87872. Good organization, equipment and guides. Basic and advanced dive courses. Regulator with BC ($12), wet suit ($7). Normal dive prices. **Barrakuda**. Jl. Cemara Beach (very close to the Sanur Beach Hotel), at the Semawang Beach Hotel, P.O. Box 252, Denpasar 80001, Tel: 88619, 88761,

fax: 87535. One western guide-instructor, and the rest Indonesians, some of whom speak Japanese. Rooms at the hotel, $27 AC, $20 fan-cooled, S or D. Also located at the Bali Lovina Beach Hotel near Singaraja, Tel: (0362) 41385, and at the 102-room Candi Dasa Beach Bungalow II, Tel: 35536, fax: 35537. **Bali Diving Adventure**. close to the Bali Hyatt, Jl. Duyung South Side Bali Hyatt, Tel: 88871, 87104, 88977. Run by a very experienced and affable Balinese man who speaks English and Japanese. Regulator/ BC ($10). Reasonable prices. **Bali Dive Sports Club**. near the Bali Diving Adventure, Jl. Srikesari 38, next to the Banjar Restaurant, south side of Bali Hyatt Hotel. Beach Tel: 88582, office Tel: 87692, fax: 88743. A very small, new outfit. Regulator/BC ($10), wet suit ($10). Normal prices.

Candi Dasa

Balina Diving. About 4 km west of Candi Dasa, just off the main road, in the hotel by the same name. Could use better organization. Their outriggered dive boat has a 25 hp engine. Single dive, minimum two clients, including dive master, transportation and equipment: Nusa Penida ($50), Tepekong ($35), Cemeluk ($40), Tulamben ($40), Menjangan ($65). Minimum of two clients. Second dive at same location, $15 extra—this also includes lunch. Night dive at same location, including underwater light rental ($15). Introductory course, theory plus one dive ($50). Three-day all-inclusive package (meals, accommodations, diving) with 5 dives at Cemeluk, Tulamben and Menjangan ($210). **Sea Lion Diving Club**. Bali Samudra Indah Hotel, Tel: 35542, fax: 35542. Just opened in 1991. Inclusive, two-dive tours (all gear included): Nusa Penida ($80), Padang Bai ($50), Tepekong ($60), Cemeluk ($55), Tulamben

($55), Lovina Beach ($70), Menjangan ($75). Night dive and beer ($35). Two dives at any location, with accommodation ($90). Five-day course, with CMAS certification ($250). Introductory dive ($85). **Stingray**. Puri Bali Homestay, P.O. Box 24, Amlapura, Candi Dasa. Tel/fax: 35540. This outfit could use better guides and equipment. Two dives, all-inclusive: Nusa Penida ($65 ea. for two people, $60 ea. for three, $110 ea. for one), Padang Bai ($50, $45, $55), Tepekong/ Biaha ($55, $50, $45), Cemeluk ($50, $45, $55), Tulamben ($55, $50, $60), Lovina ($65, $60, $110), Mejangan ($65, $60, $110). Night dive ($35, $30, $40). Two dives, all inclusive, with accommodations (twin share): $65–$70, $60, $75–$125. For BC and regulator rental ($10). Dive course with CMAS certification ($250, $230, $255). **Barrakuda**. Candi Dasa Beach Bungalow II. Tel: 35536, 35537. Western dive instructors. PADI Staff instructor Charlie Snow can give courses up to and including the assistant-instructor level. He can also videotape your dives. Day trips, 2 dives, inclusive: Sanur/Nusa Dua ($40), Nusa Penida ($80), Padang Bai ($50), Tepekong ($60), Cemeluk ($50), Tulamben ($55), Lovina ($50), Menjangan ($75). Night dive ($35). Introduction to diving, including open water dive ($85). Certification course, CMAS ($250) and PADI ($270).

Tulamben

Dive Paradise Tulamben. attached to the Paradise Palm Beach Hotel. Their dive guide, Nanga Putuh, holds an "advanced diver" rating. One wreck dive with instructor-guide ($30), two dives ($50). The dive shop also organizes dives at other spots around Bali. Prices include transportation from Tulamben, dive guide, two dives, and all equipment. Nusa Penida ($85), Padang Bai ($60), Tepekong ($65),

Cemeluk ($55), Menjangan ($75). Night dive off Tulamben or Cemeluk ($35). If you are in Candi Dasa, contact the Friendship Shop for current information and reservations. For snorkelers at Tulamben, the Dive Paradise has 10 sets of fins, masks and snorkels, $1.50 per day.

Lovina

There are three dive operators in Lovina, one of the newest (and most peaceful) coastal-strip tourist developments in Bali. Located on the north coast, about 8 km west of Singaraja, Lovina has a few good hotels in the $30–$50 range, and many inexpensive accommodations, some as low as $4/night.

The Lovina resort stretches for several kilometers along a black-sand beach and through four villages. The seas are usually very calm, and outriggered fishing canoes with colorful sails will take snorkelers to the reef, several hundred meters offshore.

This is a very good spot for beginning divers, with shallow depths and often excellent visibility (15–30 meters). The reef has a good variety of hard corals, sponges, crinoids and anemones, and abundant small reef fish: damsels, butterfly-fish, wrasses and even a few angelfish. But this is not a dive for experienced divers. The outfits take serious divers to Menjangan Island and to Tulamben, each a bit over an hour's drive away, the first to the west, the second to the east.

Spice Dive. On the south side of the main coastal road. Contact through the pleasant Ansoka Home Stay—21 rms, $8–$10/night, Tel: 41841. Dive instructor Iin, a friendly young man, heads up this small, well-run operation. Introductory dives available. 4–5 day courses with POSSI or CMAS certification, ($250). Two dives, all-inclusive, including all gear: Tulamben ($55), Lovina ($45), Menjangan ($60).

Knock off 10% if you bring your own gear. Menjangan package requires a minimum of two clients. You can also arrange day dives at Nusa Penida, Padang Bai and Tepekong (Because of distance, just one dive, however).

Barrakuda. At Bali Lovina Beach Cottages, in Singaraja (34 rms, $30–$50). Tel/fax: 41385 or 21836. In Sanur, Tel/fax: 33386 or 87694. This dive operator is a branch of a large outfit in Sanur (see Sanur, above). Prices and conditions similar to those at Spice Dive.

Denpasar

Aquanaut. Jl. W.R. Supratman, Br. Abiankapas Kaja, Denpasar 80235; P.O. Box 310, Denpasar 80001; Tel: 28562, 28563, 27968, telex 35230 TEDJOD 1A, fax: 32872. Keeps a counter at the Grand Hyatt Hotel in Nusa Dua, Tel: 71188, 71080. Three certified dive masters. Rather expensive. Their dive boat is anchored at Padang Bai for diving in the vicinity as well as further north. Aquanaut offers all-inclusive packages—one dive a day or two dives a day—for one to three days to all the main dive spots. Strange as it may sound, groups of more than four divers sometimes pay more, because of more expensive transportation requirements.

Some sample fares: One dive at Tulamben ($68 for one, $60 per for 2–4, $68 per for 5–7); one dive at Menjangan ($95 for one, $88 for 4–6, $82 for 5–7); two dives at Tulamben and Menjangan ($144 for one, $117 for 2–4, $134 for 5–7); two dives at Padang Bai and Tepekong ($150 for one, $125 for 4–6, $142 for 5–7); three dives at Tulamben, Menjangan or Tepekong ($208 for one, $178 for 2–4, $186 for 5–7). No dives to Nusa Penida.

Equator. At the Safira Hotel, Jl. Seruni 17, Denpasar 80239. Tel: 31338 and 35182, fax: 35182. This outfit gets most of

its clients through agent bookings in Germany and Japan, although they do accept walk ins. They dive the Bali spots, as well as Maumere and Manado with plans to start the Komodo area sometime in 1991.

They operate two ships: the *Moby Dick I,* for 8 divers, day trips only; the *Moby Dick II,* with 2 cabins for four passengers (basic cost, $300/day plus food, guide and equipment if required). Four-day courses POSSI ($300) or CMAS ($350). They use the Oongan Public Pool for training prior to the open-water dives.

Yacht charters

For a unique dive experience, you can charter a boat with compressor and tanks, and head off to explore. A Bauer compressor ($25/day) and tanks ($5/day) can be arranged.

Yachts range from $290/day plus $15/day for meals, to $1,500/ day. Up to 15 people can be accommodated.

Aman Cruises, Tel: 89018. The nautical arm of the Aman Resort group, a chain of elegant resorts. Their cruiser, *Amanpuri I,* is a sleek, 17-meter Italian design with MAN V10 diesel engines capable of 16 knots. Gourmet meals.

Rasa Yacht Charters, Tel: 71571. 5 yachts, the finest being the 14-meter steel-hulled ketches *Rasa III* and *Rasa V.* These boats have state-of-the-art electronics, and twin, 100-hp Volvo engines.

Grand Komodo Tours. P.O. Box 477, Denpasar Bali 80001. Tel: 87166, Fax: 87165. Runs *Wyeema* (14m, 6 per for short trips) for $290/day; *Electric Lamb* (18m, 6 per) for $350/ day. Captained by owner David Plant (English).

Tourdevco, Bali Benoa Port. Tel: 31591, Fax: 31592. Their Jakarta office is at Jl. Johar Menteng 2A, Menteng, Jakarta 10340, Tel: (021) 380 5011, fax: (021) 720 0756. Eight boats, various sizes and prices. Currently the biggest operator.

Bali Practicalities

All prices in $U.S.; telephone code 0361 unless otherwise noted

Arriving by Air. The best way to arrive in Bali is at the Ngurah Rai International Airport which, despite its often being referred to as "Denpasar" is actually on the isthmus connecting the Bukit Badung peninsula to Bali, much nearer to Kuta Beach than Bali's capital city. Daily Garuda flights from Jakarta, Yogyakarta, and many other Indonesian cities connect to Ngurah Rai, and a growing number of international flights—including those from Australia, Hong Kong, Japan, the Netherlands, Singapore and the United States—land here as well.

Flights from the Soekarno-Hatta International Airport in Jakarta are frequent, and if you land in Jakarta before 5:00 pm you can usually get a connection to Bali. (Although in peak season, these 90-min flights are almost always full. Book your flight all the way to Bali.) From the airport, hire a taxi to the place you intend to stay. Domestic airline offices:
Bouraq. Jl. Kamboja 45, Denpasar, Tel: 22255.
Garuda. Jl. Melati 6, Denpasar, Tel: 22028, 24235.
Merpati. Jl. Melati, Denpasar, Tel: 22159, 24457.

The following international airlines have offices in the Hotel Bali Beach in Sanur, Tel: 88511—Cathay Pacific, Japan Airlines, KLM, Qantas, Singapore Airlines, Thai International.
By train. One can also take a train from Jakarta (slow, and a nightmare with scuba gear) which connects to Surabaya (14 hrs, $33 1st class), then a train to Bayuwangi (4 hrs, $4 2d class), then a bus to and across the Ketapang, Java–Gilimanuk, Bali ferry ($2) and on to Denpasar (4 hrs, $1).
By bus. Taking a night bus the entire way is probably a better option (20 hrs, Jakarta–Denpasar, $20.) From Ubung Terminal outside Denpasar, where you are dropped off, a minibus to the tourist triangle of Kuta–Sanur–Nusa Dua runs $3–$5. All in all, best to arrive by plane.

Local transportation

Airport taxis. One-way fares from Ngurah Rai airport to the tourist centers are fixed. You pay a cashier inside, and receive a coupon which you surrender to your driver. (Of course, there will be plenty of touts and free-lancers offering you their services. These are never a better deal.) Fares range from $4 to nearby Kuta Beach to $12 to Ubud, far inland.

Minibuses. All hotels have *bemos* for hire with a driver, or with an English-speaking driver/guide. Rates run $3–$5/hr, with a 2-hr minimum. Day rates run $30–$40, perhaps more for an air-conditioned vehicle.

Bemos. Public minibuses in Bali are called "bemos," a compression of *becak* (bicycle-like pedicabs) and *mobil*. This is the way the Balinese travel, and the cheapest way to get around the island. Fares are very inexpensive, and you could probably get all the way across the island for less than $2. But you will need to know some Indonesian or be very good at charades to make sense of the routes and drop-off points. Public bemos can be rented for the day, usually for $20–$30. Still, it's probably better to get one through your hotel.

For a diving visitor to Bali, *bemos* are most useful for short day trips around the area, or to hop locally around town. Get one of your diving guides or someone at the hotel to explain the ins and outs of the local routes.

Vehicle rental. In almost all cases, it is best to leave the driving in Bali to someone who knows what he is doing. The roads are narrow, twisting, and full of hazards: unmarked construction sites, chickens, dogs, children, Vespas as wide as cars due to huge baskets of produce, and tough, unflinching truck drivers, to name just a few. You can rent a small (100–125cc) motorcycle for $4–$7/day if you have an international motorcycle driver's license, but you better know how to ride.

Renting a car—particularly since you will want to carry diving gear—is perhaps a more practical solution, and these run $25–$35/day for little Suzuki Jimny Jeeps, more for larger, more comfortable Toyotas and a bit less for old VW Safaris. You can rent through an agency (even Avis has an office in Denpasar) or a private party. The best thing to do is to let your intentions be known at your hotel.

Medical care

Emergency. Call the Bali Hyatt for emergency evacuation services—Tel: 88271 (Bali Hyatt), 81127 (house clinic). The affiliated Dr. Saruna clinic is an SOS member of the international evacuation service and on 24-hr standby. Hotel guests are free of charge, others paya set fee for services rendered. The clinic is associated with Dr. Darmianti & Associates, which has clinics in the Nusa Dua Beach and Sanur Beach hotels. It is only open for two hrs in the morning and two hrs in the afternoon.

The two largest hospitals (*rumah sakit*) in Bali are in Denpasar:
General Hospital Sanglah. Jl. Kesehatan Selatan 1, Tel: 27911.
General Hospital Wangaya. Jl. Kartini 109, Tel: 22141.
Both have emergency units with English-speaking doctors on duty 24 hrs, but they are not terribly well equipped.
Doctor. Dr. Handris Prasetya

and Dr. Minarti have a private practice on Jl. Sumatra in Denpasar, open Mon–Sat 5–8 pm. They both speak English well and are accustomed to treating foreigners.

Dentist. For dental treatment, Dr. Indra Guizot's private practice is on Jl. Pattimura 19, Tel: 22445, Mon–Fri 10 am–8 pm.

Photographic Supplies

P.T. Modern Foto. This outfit is the local Fuji agent, with a huge showroom in Kuta just opposite the gas station and Gelael supermarket. They have the best E-6 processing in Bali and the freshest film. For prints, there are many instant mini-labs in all the larger towns and tourist centers offering while-you-wait service. You cannot buy Kodachrome film in Bali.

The biggest range of photographic equipment and supplies can be found in Denpasar at **Tati Photo** on Jl. Sumatra, Tel: 26912, 24578 and **Prima Photo** on Jl. Gajah Mada 42, Tel: 25031, 25038.

Accommodations by area

Bali has a very wide range of accommodations, from 5-star hotels to modest *losmen*. (The word, used all over Indonesia to refer to a small hotel, comes from the French *lodgement*.) You can spend $1,200/night in a lavish suite at Nusa Dua, or $3/night at a friendly little *losmen* in Candi Dasa. It's your choice.

Bali, the land of 10,000 temples, has more than that number of hotel rooms, and it would be impossible for us to list all the available lodgings here. We keep the list short in popular areas, such as the Kuta–Sanur–Nusa Dua triangle, and concentrate on those places divers might have a special interest in staying, particularly Candi Dasa and Lovina.

All the more up-market hotels charge 15.5% VAT on top of the listed prices.

Kuta

A town has grown up around the beach here that has become the tourist center of Bali. Robert and Louise Koke, surfers from southern California, first built their Kuta Beach Hotel here in 1936. Still, it wasn't until the late '60s and early '70s, when a generation of hippies and other western drop-outs discovered Bali, that that Kuta exploded.

Today the town bustles with activity, its streets and tiny gangs (alleyways) lined with shops, restaurants, discos and *losmen*. It is even an international fashion center, with a distinct, colorful style falling somewhere between So-Cal neon sporting wear and a Grateful Dead T-shirt.

Although it is currently fashionable to malign Kuta, the place has an irrepressible, youthful charm.

Bali Oberoi. Jl. Kayu Aya, Petitenget. Tel: 51061, tlx: 35125, fax: 52791. 75 rms. Tucked between ricefields and the sea at the northern end of the beach; bungalows of coral rock scattered tastefully about landscaped grounds. Beds are handcarved 4-posters, and the baths have open-air gardens. $120 up to $650 for a beachside villa with private pool.

Bali Intan Cottages. Jl. Melasti 1, Legian. Tel: 51770, tlx: 35200, fax: 51891. 150 rms. Newer hotel across the road from the beach in Legian. $55S, $60D a night for a standard room, $60S, $65D for a cozy cottage with open-air shower.

Intan Beach Bungalows. Jl. Petitenget. Tel: 52191, 52192, tlx: 35532, fax: 52193. 52 cottages. Past the Oberoi at the quiet, northern end of the beach. Soothing views from the beachfront lobby bar. The hotel is adding a four-level complex with 200 rms, and will have more extensive facilities, including a gym. $65S, $70D, up to $950 for the presidential suite.

Kuta Beach Hotel. Jl. Pantai Kuta. Tel. 51361, 51362, tlx: 35166. 50 rms. Cottage-style hotel by the beach. $58S, $69D; $92 suite.

Kuta Palace Hotel. Jl. Pura Bagus Teruna, Legian. Tel: 51433, tlx: 35234, fax: 52074. 100 rms. Right on the beach; rooms are in large, two-story blocks. Standard $45S, $55D, up to $125 for a suite.

Pertamina Cottages. Jl. Kuta Beach, Kuta. Tel: 51161, tlx: 35131. 225 rms. Just five minutes from the airport, on the beach at the southern end of Kuta. Tennis courts, 3-hole golf course, badminton and watersports. $90S, $95D up to $800 for a suite.

Pesona Bali. Jl. Kayu Aya, Petitenget. Tel: 53914, 53915. 160 rms, 7 2-room bungalows. Near the beach. Kitchenettes in every 2-story bungalow. $180 a night (sleeps 4). Extremely quiet and remote.

Asana Santhi Willy. Jl. Tegalwangi 18, Kuta. Tel: 51281, 52641. 12 rms. In the heart of Kuta. Pleasant, with antique furnishings and semi-open bathrooms. $25.

Bali Mandira. Jl. Padma, Legian. Tel: 51381, tlx: 35215, fax: 52377. 96 rms. Rows of cottages clustering around tidy courtyards. Tennis and squash. $35S, $40D; suites for $70.

Bali Niksoma Beach Cottages. Jl. Padma, Legian. Tel: 51946, tlx: 35537. 52 rms. A quiet beachfront place in Legian. Rooms with fan $15S, $18D; standard AC rms $35S, $40D; suites $45S, $50D.

Garden View Cottages. Jl. Padma Utara 4, Legian. Tel: 51559, tlx: 35218 attn GVC, fax: 52777. 60 rms. $30S, $34D. Secluded, on a Legian backlane. Brief walk to beach.

Kuta Beach Club. Jl. Bakung Sari, Kuta. Tel: 51261, 51262, tlx: 35138, fax: 71896. 120 rms. A tranquil setting with garden and bungalows, right in the center of Kuta. Mini tennis, badminton. $38S, $40D.

Poppies Cottages. Poppies Lane, Kuta (behind Jl. Pantai Kuta). Tel: 51059, tlx: 35516, fax: 52364. 24 rms. Well-designed cottages in a beautiful garden. Refrigerator in every room. 300 metres from the

beach and always filled to capacity; reservations a must. $47S, $48D.
Poppies Cottages II. Poppies Lane II, Kuta. Tel: 51059, tlx: 35516, fax: 52364. 4 rms with fans and fridges. $21S, $22D; $5 extra for a private kitchen.
Sandi Phala. Jl. Kartika Plaza, Kuta. Tel: 53042, tlx: 35308, fax: 53333. 12 rms. Two-story bungalows overlooking the beach in a big compound with pool and beachfront restaurant. $30S, $35D.
Bruna Beach Inn. Jl. Pantai Kuta, Tel: 51565. 28 rms. Across the road from Kuta beach. Attached or bungalow style, AC and non-AC rms. $12S, $17D to $20S, $25D. Family room for $65 sleeps 5.
Made Beach Inn. At the end of Jl. Pura Bagus Taruna, north of the Kuta Palace in Legian. 6 rms. Near beach. $4.
Pelasa Cottage. Jl. Pelasa, Legian. Well-kept and clean. 7 rms. $8S, $10D a night.
Sorga Beach Inn. On a small lane between Jl. Melasti and Jl. Padma in Legian. Tel: 51609. 11 rms. Walk to the beach. $3.50S, $4.50D.
Yulia Beach Inn. Jl. Pantai Kuta 43. Tel: 51055. 48 rms. One of the original Kuta places near the beach, where you have an ample choice of rooms. $3 without private bath, up to $20 for AC.

Nusa Dua

This resort offers luxury, and isolation from touts, peddlers, stray dogs, cold-water showers and other indignities. It's also quite antiseptic. Preferred by the international jet set. There are no cheap lodgings here.
Nusa Dua Beach Hotel. P.O. Box 1028, Denpasar. Tel: 71210, tlx: 35206 NDBH IA, fax: 71229. 450 rms. The spectacular Balinese *candi bentar* gate at the entrance is a Nusa Dua landmark. Elaborately decorated with stone carvings in the manner of a Klungkung palace or *puri*. Where then-U.S. President Ronald Reagan and his wife stayed.

Gym and squash courts. $90S, $100D for a standard room. $1,200 for a suite with private pool and entrance.
Melia Bali Sol. P.O. Box 1048, Tuban. Tel: 71510, tlx: 35237, fax: 71360. 500 rms. Managed by the Spanish Sol chain, the Bali Sol reflects a certain Spanish ambience, including a replica of the Alhambra fountain at the entrance. Popular with Japanese tourists. Indoor pool and spa, outdoor pool with sunken bar. $99S, $105D up to $670 for the deluxe suite.
Club Mediterranée Nusa Dua. P.O. Box 7, Denpasar. Tel: 71521, 71522, 71523, tlx: 35216 BHVCM, fax: 71831. 350 rms. The Bali Club Med looks more like a traditional luxury hotel than other Club Meds around the world. The only noticeable Balinese touches are the palm trunks in the lobby and a few Balinese sculptures. A fun place, where you mingle with an attractive international staff. No room service, TVs or telephones. Packages including airfare, meals and entertainment through your travel agent.
Putri Bali. P.O. Box 1, Denpasar. Tel: 71020, 71420, tlx: 35247 HPB DPR IA, fax: 71139. 378 rms. Managed by the Hotel Indonesia chain, and offering the lowest rates of any major hotel in Nusa Dua. Book the cottages for more privacy. $80S, $90D up to $400 for the suite. Cottages $110–$150.
Hotel Club Bualu. P.O. Box 6, Denpasar. Tel: 71310, tlx: 35231 BUALU IA, fax: 71313. 50 rms. Sports activities are free, and the hotel has a PADI-certified diving instructor. The beach is five minutes away by foot or horsecart. $55S, $60D; $90 for a suite. High season, $15 surcharge.

Tanjung Benoa

This is a recently established resort just north of Nusa Dua. The beach hotels here are small and cozy, although there are some newly opened larger hotels. The nice, white-sand beach here is popular for water

sports: parasailing, windsurfing, waterskiing and, of course snorkeling and diving. All the accommodations are intermediate or budget, and provide a nice complement to nearby Nusa Dua's deluxe digs. All lodgings are on Jl. Pratama.
Chez Agung. 6 rms. The 4-room bungalow is great for a family. Includes pleasant living room with a beach view, a kitchen, a car, a cook and a room boy to serve you. $30S, $40D; bungalows $130.
Puri Joma Bungalows. 10 rms. For people who like staying in a small hotel away from the crowds. Very relaxing beach-front pool. $42S, $52D.
Pondok Tanjung Mekar. 10 rms. Almost like staying with an Indonesian friend who happens to have spare rooms. $17 a night including breakfast.
Hasan Homestay. 10 rms. $7.50 a night. Cheaper during the low season. Simple breakfast is included.
Rasa Dua. Tel: 71751. 4 rms. $9 to $12 a night. Two-story bungalows with thatched roof and semi-open bath. Run by a company that owns yachts and a glass bottom boat that can be rented for island trips.

Sanur

Sanur was Bali's first resort town, and is in a sense the grey eminence of the tourist triangle. Compared to Kuta, it is quiet and dignified (or just dull, depending on your point of view and, inescapably, your age) and compares to Nusa Dua as old wealth does to new. The town is very quiet at night, and the beach here, protected by the reef flat, is very calm. People who intend to spend a long time on Bali often stay in Sanur.
Hotel Bali Beach. Jl. Hang Tuah. Tel: 88511–7, tlx: 35133, fax: 87917. The first large luxury hotel in Bali. Offers the most complete hotel facilities in Bali. One of its restaurants is a rooftop supper club with panoramic views. The 6-hole golf course may be the

reason why lots of Japanese groups stay here. Bowling alleys, tennis courts, local banks, American Express, and airline offices. Rooms: $70–$90. Suites: $105–$270. **Bali Hyatt.** Jl. Hyatt. Tel: 88271–2, 88361; tlx: 35127, 35527; fax: 87693. 387 rms. A blend of traditional Balinese ambience and efficient Hyatt hospitality. On the beach, sprawling across 36 acres of elegantly-landscaped orchids, hibiscus, frangipani and bougainvillea. Several indoor and outdoor restaurants. The Spice Islander restaurant features a "Dutch colonial" rijsttafel buffet — fit for royalty and served in the classic Rajalaya style, one dish at a time presented by women in traditional costumes. Complete sports facilities. One pool has a replica of the famous Goa Gajah — with added waterfall, jacuzzi and cold dip. $105–$130. Suites: $220–$495. $20 high season surcharge.
La Taverna Bali. Jl. Tanjung Sari. Tel: 88387, 88497, tlx: 35163, fax: 87126. 40 rms. The romance of thatched roofs and stucco! Tasteful antique-furnished rooms in a tropical garden. The excellent beachside restaurant serves a variety of Italian and Indonesian specialities. Standard rms: $60S, $68D; family units: $85S, $105D; suites: $150.
Sanur Beach Hotel. Sanur, Tel: 88011, 71793, tlx: 35135, fax: 87566. 428 rms. This 4-story block is one of the older beachfront hotels in Sanur. Known for its friendly service. Super-deluxe bungalow with marbled bathroom and private swimming pool $750. Standard rms: $75S, $85D. Suites: $125–$300. Deluxe bungalow: $450S, $750D.
Segara Village Hotel. Jl. Segara. Tel: 88407–8, 88231, tlx: 35143, fax: 87242. 150 rms. Private bungalows, "rustic Balinese" (some look like traditional rice granaries, *lumbung*), set as mini-villages by the sea. A very good staff, along with amenities such as

Balinese dance classes, a children's recreation room, gym, sauna, etc. Rooms: $38S, $45D; bungalows: $55S, $60D to $65S, $70D; suites: $100S, $110D.
Tandjung Sari Hotel. Jl. Tanjung Sari. Tel: 88441, tlx: 35157, fax: 87930. 30 rms. Tranquil and elegant, with exclusive Balinese-style bungalows and lovely gardens. Managed as a small family business, and catering to a celebrity clientele. Service and food are highly recommended. $96–$200.
Baruna Beach Inn. Jl. Sindhu. Tel: 88546. 7 rms. Pleasant old bungalows on the beach with lots of character, furnished with antiques and opening onto a courtyard bordering the sea. Room with fridge $35S, $40D. Breakfast, tax and service included.
Bali Sanur Besakih Beach Bungalows. Jl. Tanjung Sari. Tel: 88421–2, tlx: 35178, fax: 88426. 50 rms, each set amidst a garden leading to the sea. $40S, $45D.
Puri Kelapa Garden Cottages. Jl. Segara Ayu. Tel: 88999, tlx: 35519, fax: 25708. 15 cottages with 25 more rooms opening in 1990. New place, very quiet and private, set back from the road and away from the beach. Bungalows are set in a spacious garden around a pool. $40S, $45D.
Sindhu Beach Hotel. Jl. Sindhu. Tel: 88351–2, tlx: 35523. 189 rooms in beachside bungalows. $45S, $55D to $50S, $60D; suites $60S, $70D.
Sanur Plaza. Jl. Bypass Ngurah Rai. Tel: 88808. 22 rms. Spacious bungalows with thatched roof and hot water, $12S, $20D; $25S, $30D w/ AC. Breakfast included. A pool is available. Good for the money if you travel with few friends. They have family rooms for 4 persons ($45) and one room for 7 persons ($8/person, breakfast excluded).
Taman Agung Beach Inn. Jl. Tanjung Sari. Tel: 88549, 88006. 20 rms. One of the best budget losmen in Sanur.

Pleasant atmosphere. Five minutes from the beach. $8; $15 w/ AC, breakfast included.
Tourist Beach Inn. Jl. Segara. Tel: 88418, tlx: 35318. 10 rms. Older, *losmen*-style rooms with a central garden. Close to the beach. $8S, $12D, including breakfast.

Candi Dasa

This town is quiet, and relatively uncrowded compared to Kuta and Sanur to the south. There are at least 50 hotels, *losmen*, and homestays, and plenty of restaurants. The availability of services and Its location—between Nusa Penida and Padang Bai to the south, and Cemeluk and Tulamben to the north—make it probably the best place for serious divers to set up base camp.

Accommodations

There is a wide range of prices and quality of accommodations here, from small, practically windowless cement block cells to large suites overlooking the ocean. Prices vary accordingly.
Puri Bagus Beach Hotel. 50 rms. Beachside, and at the extreme eastern end of Candi Dasa. Run by Baruna Water Sports. Attractive, well-maintained place, very convenient if you are diving with Baruna. Breakfast ($6), lunch ($10), dinner ($12) available. Two-dive tours, including accommodations here, run $85/day. Travel agency on premises, car rental/taxi service available. American Express, Master, Visa and Diners' Club credit cards are accepted. $55S, $60D.
Candi Dasa Beach Bungalows II. 37 rms. Consists of a large two-story block rather than individual bungalows. The rooms are spacious and overlook the sea. Swimming pool and an open-air bar. All rooms with AC and hot water; some refrigerators and TVs are also available. $23S, $28D for standard; superior $35D.
Rama Ocean View Bungalows. 44 rms. One km before Candi Dasa, away from the noise and

bustle. A beachside enclave with a pool and restaurant. Hot water, western baths, AC, mini bar, and hair dryers. Group rates. Fitness center. Conference room, game room, video. $44–$50S, $49–$55D; $12 for an extra bed.

The Water Garden. 12 rms. This new hotel venture of TJ's Restaurant in Kuta has been designed with their usual attention to detail and quality. Gorgeous bungalows set in a network of cascading streams, pools and elegant gardens. Mountain bikes, hiking maps and current information about local events and places of interest available. Swimming pool. $23–$30.

Homestay Pelangi. 12 rms. West of town in a quiet oceanside setting. Garden privacy, good-sized rooms of bamboo; bathrooms with open-air garden. The owner, Pak Gelgel, is particularly friendly. Often a pair of bamboo gamelans with flute lull one to sleep. $4–$5S, $5–$9D.

Bayu Paneeda Beach Inn. 14 rms. Also west of town, has medium-sized twin huts in a huge tract of land. A large, grassy lawn makes this a favorite spot for families with kids. Blankets, reading lights and towels are supplied. Some hot water units, with fans and screens. $4S, $5D; $6S, $9D w/hot water.

Candi Dasa Beach Bungalows. 20 rms. A cozy, classy place near the center of town on the beach. The staff is friendly and efficient. The bamboo bungalows are very attractive and nicely set in a garden. All rooms have fan; 5 rooms have hot water. Most of the baths are western style with open-air gardens. One night a week a gamelan orchestra plays for the guests. $12S, $15D, $3 less for Balinese bathrooms.

Ida Homestay. 6 rms. One of the nicest settings in town. East of town on the beach, Ida offers private thatch and bamboo bungalows in a large, grassy coconut grove. Two-story houses provide upstairs bed-

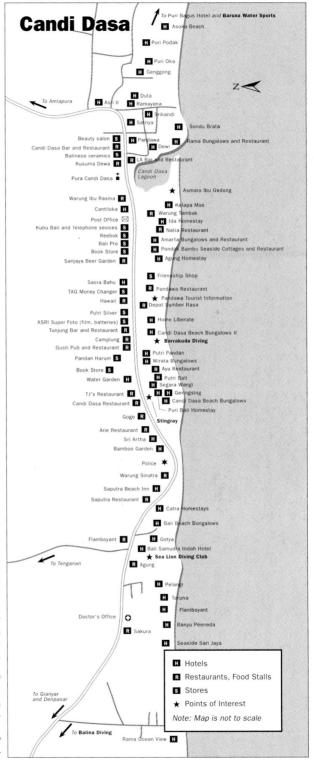

rooms with wide ocean views. Beautiful open-air bathrooms. Carved furniture in some units. No hot water. $12–$20.

Puri Pudak. 13 rms. In the banana groves east of town, home of local fisherman. Rooms are medium to large and some are furnished. Western bathrooms, some with tubs. Overlooks the bay. $4–$5S, $5–$6D.

Losman Geringsing. 11 rms. The best bargain in town. This friendly place offers small bamboo and brick bungalows in a banana grove on the beach. One of the few places to have any beach left, though only at low tide. Renovations are planned and rates may go up. $3–$4S, $4–$6D.

Dining

There are lots of restaurants in Candi Dasa, and the typical menu will contain salads, Indonesian and Chinese standards, and a few basic western dishes. Prices are very reasonable, averaging $4–$5 a head with drinks. Seafood, though delicious, can be considerably more expensive. Most restaurants close up by 10 pm. Breakfast and lunch are available everywhere.

TJ's Cafe. (22 tables.) The best grilled fish, stuffed baked potatoes, and salads around. Elegant open pavilions overlook a carp pond. Popular western music and the delicious desserts.

Pandan Restaurant. (30 tables.) By the beach, well-known for its Balinese buffet of *babi guling* (roast pork), chicken, fish, vegetables, noodles and salads. Many other local and Chinese dishes.

Arie Bar and Restaurant. (8 tables.) A down-to-earth, family-run establishment with a good selection of Balinese, Chinese and Western dishes. Good quality and hard-to-beat prices.

Kubu Bali. (36 tables.) A bit of everything but excels in seafood — grilled, steamed or fried. Their open kitchen is fun to watch. Finish up with Peach

Melba, chilled fruit or a cognac.

Warung Ibu Rasmini. The best *nasi campur* (mixed vegetables, *tempe,* and chicken over rice) in town for under $1. Few other simple Indonesian dishes.

Gusti Pub and Restaurant. (10 tables.) Fish and chips, club sandwiches, French toast, chocolate milk, pina coladas and other fare.

Rama Bungalow and Restaurant. (4 tables.) Swiss dishes such as Roschti, Kartoffel and Puffer Mitgemuse in addition to an already good, typical Candi Dasa menu.

Tulamben

Most divers travel to Tulamben on a package tour from Kuta, Sanur, Nusa Dua or Candi Dasa, but independent-minded divers can make their way by rented car or, if not carrying gear, by motorcycle. It's about 4 hrs from Kuta or Nusa Dua, 30 min less from Sanur. The traffic through Candi Dasa will likely be heavy, and only the last hour of the trip—from Candi Dasa onward—could be called pleasant From Tulamben to Menjangan, about 3.5 hrs.

There is one good *losmen* in Tulamben, offering all scuba gear rental and tank fills, plus two small ones with another one perhaps coming on line in early 1992. We recommend the Paradise.

Paradise Palm Beach. P.O. Box 31, Amlapura 80811 Bali, Indonesia. 20 nice thatched bungalows, each with two beds and toilet. Inexpensive ($1-$3) meals, although not great and the service can be excruciatingly slow. Cold beer and some booze available. Pleasant complex, no mosquitos. Some mice in rooms (the case elsewhere also). Electricity from 6 pm–10 pm, but power lines close and there should be 24-hr juice soon. Usually booked up in July, Aug., Dec. and Jan. For reservations, write to the address above and send one night's room cost. $6–$7S, $7–$9D. Two 2-bdrm, 1-bath bungalows, $23. (Prices

include tax and breakfast.)

From the Paradise, it's about 300m to the entry point on the pebble beach. You can hire someone to carry your gear for about $1 ($1.75 at night.)

Ganda Mayu. ("Fragrant Flower") 5 rms. Closer to the entry point than the Paradise (about 100m). Much smaller rooms than at the Paradise. Attached restaurant serves inexpensive meals. Minibuses of day-divers park next to this *losmen.* Fan-cooled rms, $6–$8, S or D, including tax and breakfast.

Bali Timor. Next to the Sunrise restaurant. 3 rms, inexpensive. Further out from the Bali Timor, another 3-rm *losmen* was under construction in 1991, but operating license had not yet been issued.

Dining

Sunrise. Next to the Paradise, away from the wreck, on the beach. Chicken or fish ($2), also—less expensive—vegetables, *gado-gado,* and sandwiches. Soft drinks and beer.

Equipment rental

Dive Paradise Tulamben. Attached to the Paradise Palm Beach. This outfit maintains a good Bauer compressor. Tank fills $4, full tank and weight belt rental, $10/day. They have 19 tanks for rent as well as 9 well-maintained BCs and regulators, and 10 sets of snorkeling equipment ($1.50).

Lovina

Telephone code 0362
Lovina is the generic name for a cluster of three villages spread along Bali's north coast. They are, east to west: Tukad Munggah, Anturan, Kalibukbuk (Lovina), and Temukus. The beach is shiny black sand, and the surf is calm. It is a quiet town.

Lovina is a good place to stay if you are going to dive at Menjangan; the compressors here are the closest to that island. (See "Bali Scuba Operators," page 125 for more on dive tours from Lovina.)

Accommodations

Most lodgings here are simple intermediate or budget *losmen*. Prices are something of a bargain compared to the tourist towns in southern Bali. There are at least 30 places to stay in Lovina. **Bali Taman Beach Hotel.** On the main road in Tukad Mungga, P.O. Box 99. 24 rms. Newly built bungalow-style rooms. Fridge is available. Non-AC rooms, equally pleasant, are half the price. Breakfast not included. $30S, $40D w/AC. **Bali Lovina Beach Cottage.** On the main road in Lovina (Kalibukbuk). 30 rms. Bungalow-style rooms around a pool. Rates include a generous breakfast, with bacon eggs and toast. $30S, $35D, $35S, $40D w/AC. **Jati Reef Bungalows.** P.O. Box 52, Tukad Mungga. Tel: 21952. 16 rms. Rooms in four separate bungalows, with a brief walk through the ricefields to get there. $6S, $12D. **Yuda Seaside Cottage.** Tukad Mungga. Tel: 41183. Four two-story bungalows. 8 rms. Clean and roomy. The upper rooms are great, with verandas in front and back overlooking the beach and the ricefields. $15 for the lower rooms; $20 for upper. **Banyualit Beach Inn.** P.O. Box 17, Kalibukbuk. Tel: 81101. 20 rms. Offering several options, from simple rooms up to AC'd ones. Friendly and helpful staff. Ask for a room close to the beach. $15S, $18D fan-cooled rooms; $25S, $30D w/AC. **Kalibukbuk Beach Inn.** Kalibukbuk. Tel: 21701. 25 rms. Located at the end of the Banyualit lane, the place is only a few steps from the beach. Their fan-cooled rooms at $15 are quite pleasant. $23 w/AC overlooking the beach. $9 for a budget room. **Nirwana.** Kalibukbuk. Tel: 41288. 37 rms. Right on the beach; rooms are spacious and clean. The biggest can sleep four. Two-story bungalows with bamboo trim, spread around a lush garden. $25 for the biggest room; $14 for twin-bed rooms. **Aditya.** P.O. Box 35, Lovina. Tel: 41059. 52 rms. Some new suites are available—spacious w/ AC, hot water, tub, and a phone to call for a room service. $3.50 for the older and smaller rooms; $23 for suite. **Samudra Beach Cottage.** P.O. Box 15, Temukus. 10 rms. At the western end of the beach. Very quiet. Sea-view rooms w/AC are $16; $8.50 for more simple ones. **Baruna Beach Inn.** P.O. Box 50, Tukad Munggah. Tel: 41252. Has several cottages overlooking the beach. 24 rms. All rooms with private bath. $8 for standard, $9 for cottage, $11 for "suite." **Homestay Agung.** P.O. Box 25, Anturan. 10 rms. One of the first hotels opened in Lovina, the building uses bamboo throughout. Very friendly atmosphere. No private bath. $5–$6 for a seaview bungalow. **Sri Home Stay.** Anturan. 14 rms. Located by the beach, all rooms of bamboo bedeg. Bathrooms are not the cleanest around, but where else can you see ricefields while taking a shower? The owner, Sri, is helpful and friendly. $3S, $4D for a room with no bath; $4S, $6D for a bigger room with private bathroom. **Perama.** Anturan. Tel: 21161. 11 rms. Rooms are very close to one another. Right on the main road, so it can be rather noisy. $6 for rooms with and without private shower. **Awangga.** Tukad Munggah. 6 rms. Newly opened. Rooms are clean and spacious. Located near the beach. $7 a night. **Janur's Dive Inn.** Tukad Mungga. 6 rms. Friendly family place run by Janur and Rose and little Gede, who live in the same compound. Very simple accommodations, but special and cozy. Ask Janur to guide you around. $3S, $4D for room with no private bath; $4S, $4.50D with private bath. **Ayodya.** Kalibukbuk. 6 rms. Despite its location on the main road, pleasantly calm atmosphere with bamboo-walled rooms in a well-kept old house. No private bathrooms. $4S, $5D. **Rini.** Kalibukbuk. 14 rms. New, clean and all rooms with private bath. No breakfast. $7. **Astina.** Kalibukbuk. 12 rms. Right on the beach. Rooms with the bamboo wall around a nice garden. $9 with private bath. **Angsoka.** Kalibukbuk. 21 rms. Their two-story bungalows are quite comfortable. $9 for the upper rooms; $7 for the lower ones. **Puri Tasik Madu/Tama.** 10 rms. This was one of the first hotels in the area. Rooms are newly-renovated. Pleasant staff, and a very friendly atmosphere. $9.

Dining

Nearly all hotels in the area have restaurants. The one at **Janur's Dive Inn** has a very pleasant atmosphere, and serves favorites like *cap cay* (mixed vegetables) for under $1. Try the prawns in garlic butter, $2. **Banyualit Hotel** has a restaurant specializing in seafood.

Chinese dishes and seafood are available at **Khi Khi** (Kalibukbuk), the most prominent restaurant around. Grilled fish and fried prawns are the favorites here — with a selection of 10 different sauces to go with them. More budget-conscious travelers can try their sister restaurant, **Shi Shi**, located right next door.

Menjangan

Boats from Labuhan Lalang to Menjangan, carrying up to 10 passengers (perhaps 6 divers with full gear); $20 for the first 4 hrs, $3 extra for each additional hr. (Note: If you come on a package tour, the boat fare is included.) Leave your valuables with your driver or locked in your car. **Pulau Menjangan Inn.** 3 km from the boat landing. 8 rms, strictly basic accommodation. Simple meals ($1.25–$2). $5 S or D.

Introducing Nusa Tenggara

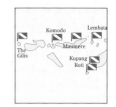

The islands east of Bali, running from Lombok in the west to Timor in the east, are called Nusa Tenggara, the "Southeastern Islands." These rough, dry and sometimes volcanic islands support a culturally diverse population of 10 million people.

Stretching 1,300 kilometers east to west, the islands lie just a few degrees south of the equator. One count yielded 566 islands, 246 of which were named and 42 inhabited. (See map page 140.)

The region is divided into three provinces: Nusa Tenggara Barat ("West"), including Lombok and Sumbawa, Nusa Tenggara Timur ("East"), including Sumba, Flores and West Timor, and Timor Timur (East Timor), which is a special province all by itself. The three provinces together cover 82,161 square kilometers, a little over 4 percent of Indonesia's total land area

Diversity of Cultures

Nusa Tenggara remained for the most part outside the great historical changes that swept through Indonesia, including the period of Indianization, from the 8th through the 15th centuries, and the later spread of Islam and European colonialism.

Only Timor had a trade product of interest: fragrant white sandalwood. For hundreds of years, the wood of the sandalwood tree (*Santalum album*) has been used in China, India and the Middle East for incense. The Portuguese were the first Europeans to reach Timor in 1515, but a century later the Dutch took over control of the trade.

Languages in at least 50 distinct groups are spoken by the people of Nusa Tenggara. The populations of Lombok and Sumbawa are Muslim, and because of a relatively long history of Portuguese colonial involvement in eastern Flores and Timor, the people of these areas are Roman Catholics. But in much of the rest of the region—and even in the areas where one of the modern religions holds sway—community religious life takes the form of animism and ancestral spirit worship.

The most spectacular cultural event in the region is the yearly Pasola in Sumba. In this dangerous celebration, the seasonal spawning of sea worms augers a ceremonial spear fight between hundreds of mounted horsemen.

Volcanoes and Chalk Cliffs

Two geologically distinct island arcs make up Nusa Tenggara. The northern islands—Lombok through Flores and Alor—are volcanic, with jagged coastlines and rich soil. The southern islands—Sumba, Savu, Roti and Timor—were formed from uplifted coral limestone and sediment, and are dry and relatively barren.

Some 40 volcanoes have been identified in Nusa Tenggara, 25 of which are still active. The greatest eruption in modern history took place when Mt. Tambora, on Sumbawa Island, exploded on April 5, 1815. The blast produced 150 cubic kilometers of ash, far greater than that produced by the better-known explosion of Krakatau in 1883 (See "West Java" page 77).

The largest volcano in the islands is Mt. Rinjani in Lombok, which stands 3,726 meters, the highest point in Indonesia after

Overleaf: *An anemone shrimp,* Periclemenes holthusi, *in the anemone* Heteractis magnifica. *Ambon, Maluku. Photograph by Jan Post, IKAN.*

Opposite: *A snorkeler with a whale shark,* Rhincodon typus. *These harmless, krill-feeding giants can be found seasonally at some sites in Indonesia. Indonesian fisherman call the whale shark ikan hiu bodoh, literally "stupid shark," because the animal has so little fight in it. Maumere, Flores. Photograph by Lionel Pozzoli, IKAN.*

Puncak Jaya in Irian Jaya. Perhaps the most beautiful of Nusa Tenggara's volcanoes is Keli Mutu in south-central Flores, a trio of craters, each containing a differently colored lake.

The southern islands have no dramatic volcanoes, and are covered in dry scrub. The terrain of parts of Timor looks like Australian savannah. Limestone cliffs and beautiful white beaches ring some of these islands.

Most of the people of Nusa Tenggara, particularly in the western islands, subsist on rice, which is grown in wet "paddies" or *sawah*. But in the drier areas, corn, manioc and various tuber crops are grown. On Roti and Savu, among the driest parts of Indonesia, islanders depend on the drought-resistant *lontar* palm to give them nourishment through the dry season.

Rainfall patterns in Nusa Tenggara are quite complicated, and determined as much by local geographical conditions as by the seasonal monsoon winds. In general, southeast winds from May to July tend to bring rain to the south coasts of islands, and northwest winds from December to March bring rain to the north coasts. Heavy prolonged rainfall is rare in the region.

Plant and Animal Life

The islands of Nusa Tenggara form a biogeographical transition zone between the animals of Asia and those of Australia. This region is called Wallacea, in honor of Alfred Russel Wallace, a British naturalist who discovered the transition in types of wildlife here when he explored the islands in 1854–1862.

These dry islands are less rich in plant and animal life than the more densely forested islands of Borneo, Java and Sumatra to the west. Offshore, however, the islands teem with life, supporting some of the archipelago's richest reefs.

The region's most famous endemic species is the Komodo dragon (*Varanus komodoensis*), a huge monitor lizard found only on the tiny islands of Komodo, Rinca and perhaps a bit of west Flores. These fierce predators are the size of crocodiles.

—*David Pickell*

Islands of Beaches, Dragons and Volcanoes

Nusa Tenggara is one of the most fascinating parts of Indonesia. The island landscapes possess a rugged charm, quite different from the lush green of Bali and Java, and many of the people here maintain unique cultural and religious practices.

Travel in the region requires some patience and planning, as it is not yet part of the tourist circuit. All of the sites where organized diving is available are, however, on regular ferry lines or near airports.

Lombok: Mt. Rinjani

Most foreign visitors to Lombok settle at the west coast beach resort of Senggigi, or on the Gili Islands. Although we recommend that divers stay on the islands themselves, which offer diving, sunbathing and some limited watersports, visitors may want to wander over to the mainland to do some exploration.

Lombok's most famous site is Mt. Rinjani, a 3,726-meter volcano filled with a crater lake. The view from the top can be spectacular. The climb is not difficult, but requires a three-day hike, and two nights camping out in the cool mountain air. You can visit on your own, but it is best to organize this trip through an agency. (See "Nusa Tenggara Dive Practicalities" page 179.)

There are plenty of other things to see in Lombok, including Balinese temples, weaving and pottery making.Because the island has a good system of paved roads, operators run day minibus tours to the sites.

Labuhanbajo: Dragons

Visiting Komodo Island to watch the "dragons" eat is becoming

Above: *A Bajo pearl shell diver stows his gear aboard the* Mustika Jaya II *after emptying his twin tanks looking for pearl oysters. Although by local standards the occupation pays well, it is extremely dangerous. On any given day one or two of the divers—who use no gauges and take only the most rudimentary safety precautions—are recovering from the bends. Lewoleba, Lembata.*

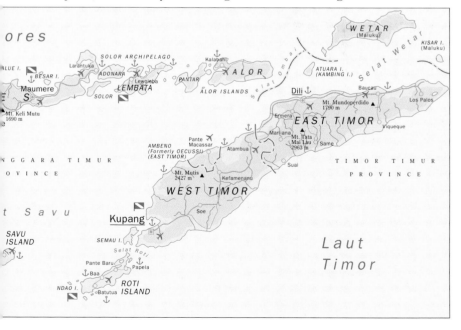

Above: *A group of Komodo dragons disembowel a goat. These lizards, the largest extant, are very efficient predators and scavengers.* Varanus komodoensis, *which can reach 2.5 meters in length and 125 kilograms, has strong claws and a mouth full of large teeth with serrated edges. The dragons are endemic to Komodo and Rinca Islands, with perhaps a small population in Western Flores.*

The scene above was arranged by park rangers on Komodo Island. A goat carcass is hung, and after the smell has attracted several of the giant lizards, it is lowered into a dry culvert. Visitors watch the gruesome show from an embankment.

very popular with tourists. Park service personnel hang goats in designated spots to attract the dragons, and one can watch them feed from close range.

The Labuhanbajo, Flores to Sape, Sumbawa ferry stops at Komodo island, and the fare is very reasonable. One can also charter a boat from Labuhanbajo. Although it is possible to go out, see the dragons, and return in a day, spending two or three days on the island is more rewarding. Komodo Island is managed by the Park Service, and lodgings there consist of 80 beds in comfortable cabins.

One can visit at any time, but during high tourist season—June–August—it is very hard to get a room. Also, this is the big lizards' mating season and they make themselves scarce.

Labuhanbajo itself, which is where one would stay unless traveling to the region on a chartered live-aboard, is basically a sleepy little fishing town. The Bajo Beach Diving Club is (at the time of this writing) the only dive operator in the area.

Pak Hendrik Candra, the Club's founder, offers land tours to an impressive nearby cave, Batu Cermin, and to a hillside outside of town that is littered with petrified wood. He can also take you to Kaper village, 5 kilometers north of Labuhanbajo, where the traditional ritual sport of whip fighting has been

revived. The performances are well worth seeing.

Maumere: Colored Lakes

One of the most famous sites in Flores is Mt. Keli Mutu, a volcano about 40 kilometers south of Maumere. The mountain has three water-filled craters, each a strikingly different color—deep blue, turquoise, green, even black, depending on the light and the mineral concentration. Surrounded by bare, scarred slopes, the sight is like no other.

Because the craters fog in early, seeing Keli Mutu requires starting from the dive clubs in Maumere at an ungodly hour. The staff and drivers are used to this, however, and you can just sleep in the van for the three hours it takes to get there. You reach the vantage point at 5:30 a.m., and really smart travelers bring sweaters, blankets and a thermos of coffee to ward off the early morning chill.

It is still believed by some that the souls of the deceased find their eternal resting places in these lakes, and it was only 50 years ago that the Roman Catholic church succeeded in stopping the regular ceremonies in which water buffalo and pigs were sacrificed to the lakes.

Another nice trip from Maumere is to Wuring, a Bugis village just 4 kilometers away. The ancestors of these fishermen settled here from South Sulawesi. All of the houses sit on stilts in the traditional style, just over the high tide line.

Kupang: Bustling Market

Kupang, a lively town of 125,000 people, has a bustling daily seaside market, Pasar Kampung Solor. The market, partially covered, stretches along the seaside, and the center swells inland to Jalan Siliwangi, the main coastal street. Get there before 6:30 a.m., when the first rays of sunlight hit the market.

Diving on Lombok's Three Islands Resort

The Gilis

The three Gilis—Trawangan, Meno and Air—just off the west coast of Lombok, are beautiful little sandy islands that have become a favorite destination for sun-bathing, frisbee tossing and other low-impact seashore sports. The Gilis are close to Bali, and are particularly popular with young, European tourists.

Although all three islands are ringed by coral, the diving here is not exactly world class. The reef slope peters out into sand at a maximum of 25 meters, and the visibility hovers around 15 meters, just fair by Indonesian standards. Still, we saw a quite good assortment of fish life, including large trevally and sharks. Mantas are said to make an appearance here as well, albeit not often.

The coral is generally quite healthy around the Gilis, but unfortunately the authorities have not yet been able to put a complete stop to fish bombing. Still, the practice—which has literally destroyed some Indonesian reefs—is now quite uncommon here.

The Gili sites are excellent for less experienced divers: most dives were in very calm water, no deeper than 18 meters. During two of our dives the current was slight, and in one it approached 2 knots, a little unsettling perhaps for a novice.

Much of the credit for the good diving here should go to Albatross diving, which pioneered five sites off Gili Trawangan, and Baronang Divers, which takes divers to sites north of Gili Air. Other operators take divers to the Gilis as well, but we recommend these two, which are

headquartered on the islands themselves. In 1990 we had a series of really awful dives here arranged by other companies.

The best time to dive the Gilis is from late April to late August. We dove in late September, when the mid-day and late afternoon winds created some fairly choppy conditions—however the water was always smooth during

AT A GLANCE
Gili Islands

Reef type: Coral slopes and sandy bottom, some wall

Access: 15 min by boat

Visibility: Fair, 15 meters

Current: Gentle, occasionally to 2 knots

Coral: Good variety and fair amount, some bombing damage

Fish: Fair to good variety and numbers

Highlights: Reef whitetip sharks and giant trevally at Takat Malang

the morning hours. Visibility averaged 15 meters. At the height of the northwest monsoon, late December–late February, big waves discourage all but the most fanatic divers.

Gili Trawangan

Trawangan is the furthest west, and at 3.5 square kilometers, the largest of the three islands. Some 700 people live here, and the island is very popular with tourists. We found the best diving off the west coast, at two contiguous sites called, by Albatross, Andy's Reef and Giant Clam. (See map page 144.) While there were neither the absolute num-

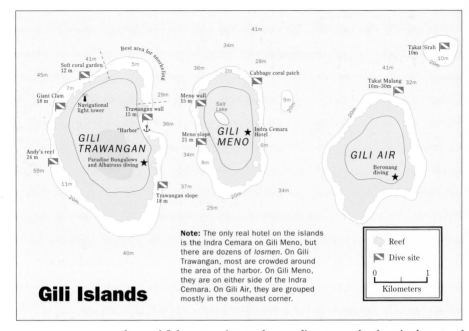

Gili Islands

Note: The only real hotel on the islands is the Indra Cemara on Gili Meno, but there are dozens of *losmen*. On Gili Trawangan, most are crowded around the area of the harbor. On Gili Meno, they are on either side of the Indra Cemara. On Gili Air, they are grouped mostly in the southeast corner.

Reef

Dive site

0 — 1
Kilometers

bers of fish or species we have seen elsewhere in Indonesia, the marine life here was quite enough to make for interesting dives. And we can substantiate Albatross' claim of (almost) guaranteeing sharks in this area. We saw three reef whitetip sharks in one dive and five in another, with remoras in attendance. We were able to approach them to within 4–5 meters before our bubbles sent them off in a lazy retreat.

Andy's Reef and Giant Clam required just a 15-minute boat ride. We entered at some 100 meters from shore, dropped some 6–7 meters to spreads of staghorn coral, checked out the slope to 24 meters where flat sand began, then spent the bulk of the dive between 18 and 20 meters. Visibility was 15 meters. The hard coral cover was decent, with tables, small domes and occasional pinnacles. One stretch showed heavy dynamite damage but elsewhere we saw only a few small bombed out spots. There was a very slight current, less than half a knot. Small channels of low coral and sand, cut parallel to the shore-line, were the favorite haunts of reef whitetip sharks. One dive ended conveniently on a coral pinnacle swarming with fish, just 5 meters from the surface. Another offered us a view of dead coral for our usual 3-minutes-at-5-meters stop before surfacing.

At Giant Clam, our guide took us to see the site's namesake, a *Tridacna gigas* more than a meter long. Such a large specimen is very unusual in this part of Indonesia. Our guide said that he has seen manta rays at this site on two occasions. We had to be satisfied with the mundane blue-spotted lagoon stingrays, plus a fair variety of reef fish.

We saw two quite impressive schools of fish: a packed mass of at least 200 blue-lined snappers (*Lutjanus kasmira)* in the shallows, and a bit deeper, a loose gathering of some 15 Goldman's sweetlips. We also saw schools of ringtail surgeonfish (*Acanthurus blochii*), a graceful cascade of pyramid butterflyfish, a colorful patrol of Moorish idols, and several small groups of bronze soldiers (*Myripristis adusta*). In addition to the common reef fish, we saw a friendly cuttlefish who allowed us several photos before growing weary of our attentions.

Soft Coral Garden

This site is a drift dive along the north coast of Trawangan. The reef slopes to 25 meters where the coral gives way to grayish sand. We saw a lone tuna cruising this depth. During our dive, the current swept us along at a very healthy 1.5–2 knot clip.

There is little hard coral growth here, but the many gorgonians, sea fans and lacy soft corals well justify the area's underwater name.

We saw fair numbers of fish, particularly parrotfish, goatfish, anthias and small groupers. We found a blue-spotted stingray, and a hawksbill turtle allowed us to approach to within 2 meters. We saw a beautiful sharpnose puffer (*Canthigaster solandri*), an outrageous scribble of green and orange, and a lovely wirenet filefish (*Cantherhines pardalis*).

While we drifted swiftly along, a yellow-margined triggerfish showed us what real swimming was all about: with a sudden jerk of his body, he headed straight into the current, making 4 knots against the 2-knot flow. No chance of catching that chap!

Trawangan Slope

We sampled the east coast of Trawangan at night, drifting along the Trawangan Slope in a moderate current. This was definitely not a dive for beginners. At both entry and exit points we had to make our way from the beach over a low, wide, coral ledge. Boots are essential, and a steadying hand from a member of the Albatross staff was much appreciated. Albatross staffers, who had previously checked the strength and direction of the current, followed our progress from shore, and were helpfully on hand at our exit point.

The reef slope became flat sand at 20 meters, and the fish life—whether asleep, somnambulent or alert—was best at about 15 meters. The usual shallow water *Acropora* coral fringe soon gave way to an assortment of knolls, and the in-between terrain was partially covered by cabbage, brain and leaf hard corals.

Groggy Moorish idols, wearing their inconspicuous gray sleepwear, bumped into us several times. The pennant bannerfish were more alert.

The most wide awake animal we saw was a small reef whitetip shark, its eyes looking malevolent and bloodshot red in our lights. A yellow-margined moray, another evil-looking character, was also wide awake.

Scattered soldierfish, out of their daytime lairs, flickered away at our approach as did a number of unicornfish. Emperor

Below: *A young clown triggerfish,* Balistoides conspicillum. *This plucky species is among the most wildly patterned fishes on the reef.*

FIONA NICHOLS

angels, while not as quick as in daytime, were still fast enough to remain out of camera range. But with stealth, we approached longfin batfish, a cube trunkfish and a porcupinefish.

Gili Meno Wall

Gili Meno, the middle island, is home to about 350 people, and has the only real hotel of the three, the Indra Cemara. There is no fresh water here, and drinking water must be shipped in from Lombok.

The Gili Meno Wall is on the west coast, and is quite a nice reef, marred only by more than occasional fish bomb craters. The variety of reef fishes justified this site's claim as a good destination for beginning divers—easy and plenty to see.

From a shallow spread of staghorn *Acropora*, the terrain sloped to sand at 20–23 meters. A few isolated coral knolls rose from the slope, each harboring a mini-world of fish and invertebrate life. As one descended along the slope, more massive and thick-fingered hard coral gave way to carpets of soft corals, sponges and gorgonians. Two short sections of the wall were pocked with ledges and overhangs sheltering fish.

We saw an unusual concentration of a dozen harlequin sweetlips, a good-sized yellow-margined moray, and a cute little blue-spotted stingray. One of the deeper caves held two cowering lobsters, and a milling army of soldierfish. We saw several three-spotted angels (*Apolemichthys trimaculatus*), which wore their species' characteristic poorly applied blue lipstick.

Gili Air

This island is the closest to Lombok, and the most populous, with 1,000 inhabitants. The beach circles the entire island, as does the coral, but the west coast in particular is quite barren. Just north of the island, however, at a site called Takat Malang, we had our best dive in the Gilis, better even than the West Trawangan dives. We counted 9 reef whitetip sharks, and 3 absolutely huge giant trevally (*Caranx ignobilis*).

This trip, organized by Baronang Divers, started inauspi-

Below: *A diver examines an unidentified sea pen and the giant starfish* Choriaster granulatus. *Sea pens are not really coral reef dwellers, but are found in sandy bottomed habitats like this. Maumere, Flores.*

ciously. Our boat anchored at the beginning of the reef slope in a 2-knot surface current. Climbing hand over hand down the line, we encountered a flat, featureless bottom at 9 meters. The current, however, slowed at this depth, and practically stopped by the time we dropped over a small wall to 16 meters. We spotted our first reef whitetip here, in a narrow sand-bottomed channel. From this channel we explored similar cuts, which became wider valleys. Each had its own resident shark. Other fish life was rather limited, except for schools of fusiliers and a lone stingray.

About 20 minutes into our dive, at 30 meters depth, we reached a large, irregular sandy bottomed oval surrounded by oddly-shaped coral-encrusted ridges. It was a natural amphitheater. Two sharks had plenty of room to maneuver. While trying to snap a photo of these two, an enormous silvery trevally swam up to me from behind, distracting me enough that I missed both shots.

Takat Sirah, our second dive, was anticlimactic. Some 15 minutes from Takat Malang, we dropped anchor and descended about 10 meters onto a dome-like bank of coral. Staghorn *Acropora* forms large thickets on this coral bank that rises from the 20–25 meter sandy bottom. We saw anthias and hordes of damsels, but except for one Titan triggerfish, nothing bigger.

Dive Operators

Albatross, on Gili Trawangan, is the best outfit for dives off that island and nearby Meno. While not too well "legally" qualified, we found the guides reliable, knowledgeable and familiar with local conditions. Albatross's Bauer compressor is well-maintained, and while the guides do not use computers, they know their tables. Six regulator and BC sets are available for rent, along with the basic sets of snorkeling equipment.

Prior to dives, tanks and all gear are taken by cart the 500 meters or so to the dive boat's anchorage, so you have nothing to lug. Depending on the water conditions and the number of clients, Albatross uses one of three boats—a small speedboat, a long outriggered canoe, and a wide-hulled fiberglass.

All have 40hp outboards and plenty of space to suit up. A metal ladder provides easy water exits. Boats and engines are well-maintained, and the helmsmen are capable.

During the short rides to the dive sites, if you like, the crew will assemble your gear for you. While there was no first-aid kit aboard (it will probably be provided, on our advice), two-way radios keep the boats in touch with the office on Trawangan and, from there, Lombok. The guide uses a buoy on all drift dives. Our boat was always close-by when we surfaced.

Our dives off Gili Air were arranged by Baronang Divers, named after the locally common lined rabbitfish (*Siganus lineatus*). Baronang is essentially a one-man show, run by Pak Sjahral Nasution. Nasution, a Batak from Sumatra, is a strong, well-trained diver who inspires confidence. Nasution spent 11 years in France, and speaks fluent French. He has a Bauer compressor, 30 tanks and 6 regulator and BC sets.

Baronang does not yet own its own dive boat, and uses small outboard-powered outriggers to reach the dive sites. Water entry requires stepping over a wooden beam, and the exit was a muscle-up over the low rear gunwale. Pak Nasution promised a ladder in the near future, however.

He says diving is year-round off Gili Air, with visibility dropping only temporarily after a heavy rain.

Komodo

Little-Explored Reefs around Dragon Island

The seas west of Flores, containing rocky Komodo Island, Rinca island, and literally speckled with tiny islands and outcrops, offer hundreds of potentially excellent dive sites, most of them unexplored. A few spots we have dived would be fine for snorkeling and beginning divers, but most are only for very experienced divers, able to contend with sudden surges of current and comfortable at 40–50 meters.

AT A GLANCE
Labuhanbajo and Komodo

Reef type:	Sloping reef and some wall
Access:	Up to 2.5 hrs from Labuhanbajo by boat
Visibility:	Variable, 2–50 meters; usually quite good
Current:	From gentle to wicked (8+ knots), often around 2 knots
Coral:	Quite good at most sites
Fish:	Variable, from poor to very good
Highlights:	Many fish and huge Napoleon wrasse off Tatawa Island

Underwater photographers and authors Ron and Valerie Taylor first dove here in 1973, and were so impressed they have returned every year since. Wolfgang Bresigk, who heads the dive operations of Baruna Water Sports in Bali, takes special scuba groups to these waters as well as to sites he has pioneered along the north coast of Flores. These expeditions draw raves from jaded divers with thousands of dives worldwide. Should you be so lucky as to dive with the Taylors or Wolfgang!

For the run-of-the-mill mortal who likes to dive, myself included, there's hope yet. The Bajo Beach Diving Club, in Labuhanbajo, was just getting underway at the time the research for this section was taking place. By the time you read this, Hendrik Candra, the founder of the club, will be able to arrange any of the dives discussed below.

Also, once the landing field at Labuhanbajo is lengthened, Baruna Water Sports plans to set up shop here. Diving out of Labuhanbajo is in its infancy, so don't expect well-oiled tours and state of the art dive boats. On the plus side, there are no crowds either. If you can put up with less than perfect facilities and organization, the underwater rewards will make it all worthwhile.

Dragons and Fierce Currents

Komodo island is most famous as the habitat of the Komodo dragon, the largest lizard extant. *Varanus komodoensis* is a varanid or monitor lizard—what the Australians call a "goanna"—an alert and agile predator and scavenger that can reach 2.5 meters in length and 125 kilos. Locally called *ora*, about 2,000 of the dragons inhabit Komodo and about 600 live on Rinca island. There are reports of a small population on Flores.

Komodo village is a stop-over on the ferry from Sape, Sumbawa to Labuhanbajo, Flores, and has become a very popular tourist destination. People come to this dry, rocky island to watch the great beasts tear apart goats that have been hung at carefully monitored sites by the Indonesian Parks service. The animals are quite impressive, and if you are

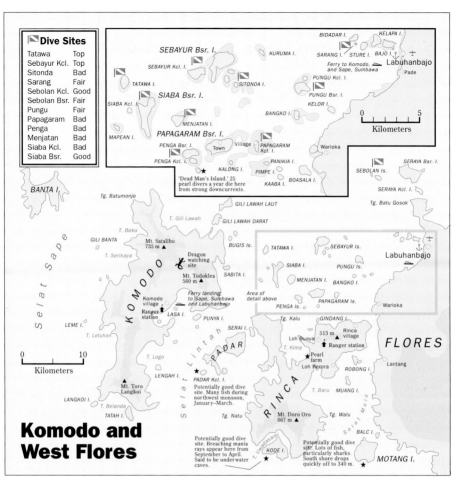

Dive Sites

Tatawa	Top
Sebayur Kcl.	Top
Sitonda	Bad
Sarang	Fair
Sebolan Kcl.	Good
Sebolan Bsr.	Fair
Pungu	Fair
Papagaram	Bad
Penga	Bad
Menjatan	Bad
Siaba Kcl.	Bad
Siaba Bsr.	Good

'Dead Man's Island.' 25 pearl divers a year die here from strong downcurrents.

Potentially good dive site. Many fish during northwest monsoon, January–March.

Potentially good dive site. Breaching manta rays appear here from September to April. Said to be under water caves.

Potentially good dive site. Lots of fish, particularly sharks. South shore drops quickly off to 340 m.

Komodo and West Flores

in the area to dive, you might want to see the show (see "Nusa Tenggara Dive Practicalities," page 179.)

Labuhanbajo is a quiet little Muslim fishing village of about 3,000 people on a beautiful harbor in northwest Flores. Because of tourist interest in Komodo's dragons, Labuhanbajo has enjoyed something of a boom of late, with more *losmen* being built and, of course, the new Bajo Beach diving operation.

Geologically, Komodo and Rinca are part of Flores, separated from Sumbawa to the west by the Sape Strait. In the middle of the strait, the bottom drops to almost 300 meters. The many islands and relatively shallow

seas between Flores and Komodo's west coast mean very fast currents at tidal changes. By "fast" we mean more than 8 knots, which is a problem no matter how experienced a diver you are.

Early Dives

The first dive I made in the area, some years ago, was off Komodo's Pantai Merah, literally "Red Beach." The current was like a raging river. Out of the dozen divers in my group, half came right out and into the Zodiac. My partner and I headed straight down, where the current was a bit less strong and we could grab coral outcrops. By the time we had the situation more or less under control and could take a look around, we were surrounded by thousands of fish of every color and shape, against a beautiful background of corals, gorgonians and sponges. Although worth the struggle, this was not a dive for someone who has just completed a resort course.

My second dive, off the coast of Rinca about a kilometer north of the Loh Buaya conservation department post, was a hell of a lot easier. We dubbed this reef "Staghorn Mile" because of the abundance of branched *Acropora* coral. Staghorn Mile provided a perfect nursery for the young of every imaginable reef fish, the labyrinth of spikes keeping out large groupers and other predators. There were no large fish here, but the abundance of anthias, damselfish, clownfish, wrasses, butterflyfish and angels was excellent. This dive was one of the easiest I have ever made in the area: the reef top was at 2 meters, and the coral covered a moderate slope down to the sandy bottom at just 10 meters.

The waters were rich in plankton, judging from the great concentration of soft corals and other filter-feeding animals. On one large tube sponge, we counted an astounding two dozen crinoids—black, grey and red.

Diving Komodo

In mid-1991 I returned to the area for a somewhat more thorough survey. I made 12 dives, two at locations supplied by Wolfgang Bresigk. For the rest I relied upon the advice of local divers, who make their living gathering pearl oysters. These hardy souls collect the oysters for sale in Labuhanbajo to the Japanese, who manage pearl farms in Rinca's Kima Bay and in nearby Rangko Bay on Flores' northwest coast.

My dive trips through the area were organized by the newly established Bajo Beach Diving Club, using boats that normally carry pearl oyster divers. We had our own gear, but had to borrow tanks and weights from the pros. The weights were assorted bits of rusty steel. The oyster divers attach them to their tanks, but we tucked them into the pockets of our buoyancy compensators. Lumpy but good enough. Since the on-board compressors use motor oil as a lubricant, the air tasted a bit oily, but it was either that or no diving.

Hendrik Candra, the head of Bajo Beach, said he planned to buy a new compressor (which will use proper oil) and some rental equipment. Until this happens, and until a real dive guide settles here, it's pioneer diving, not for the faint hearted. The club provides you with an English-speaking above-water guide who comes along to interpret with the crews.

The local divers and crew had never seen all the cushy gear westerners dive in. (They don't even use pressure gauges on their tanks.) They felt our wet suits, fiddled with our octopus regulators, and—most of all—were fascinated watching the numbers and hearing the beeps of my dive computer. In the early '70s, when scuba gear was first introduced to Labuhanbajo, many of the divers died of the bends. They simply emptied tank after tank looking for the oysters. They are more careful today, but occasional deaths still occur, as they have no depth gauges or watches, not to mention the tables to use them with.

During five days of diving, we checked out 12 different locations, descending to just over 50 meters in several spots. We had two great dives, four very good ones, and six that ranked between so-so and lousy. But remember, these were exploratory dives. Also, water clarity and fish life changes dramatically in this region, and a site that was great

one day could be lousy the next. And visa versa.

We dove in August, but the best weather for diving should be around late March through early May, and again from late September to early November.

Tatawa Island

Our best dive was off Tatawa Island's west coast, starting north of a large underwater coral block locally called Batu Besar, literally "Big Stone." (See map page 149.) We headed south, in no current, and descended a slope populated by dozens of juvenile black triggerfish, which popped into little holes in the reef at our approach. The visibility was fair, and at first we saw nothing special. Then, just below 40 meters—Oh my God!—the biggest Napoleon wrasse I have ever seen, perhaps more than 2 meters long. This behemoth drifted off, accompanied by an escort of two fellows of less than a meter.

As the Napoleons lazed out of sight, a large school of longfin bannerfish appeared, approaching us to less than a meter. Then

a school of a couple of dozen adult roundfaced batfish (*Platax teira*), wonderful, curious animals, obviously fascinated by us and swimming up to within a meter of our masks. As we ascended we saw a couple of clown triggerfish, two skittish Titan triggers, and several groupers. In the shallows, we came across a good half-dozen species of parrotfishes, and a 2-knot current, which came out of nowhere to whisk us back—and almost past—our anchored boat.

Sebayur Kecil

We had another top rated dive off the north coast of Sebayur Kecil Island. Our entry point was 25 meters off a white sand beach. The beach is marked by a clump of three trees, and is next to the highest point on the island. The reef top was just 4–5 meters from the surface, and from here a nice wall, covered with corals and sponges, dropped to a sandy bottom at 25–30 meters. A small Napoleon greeted our entry, followed in a few minutes by a mini-school of five heftier members of the species. A final large

Above: *The scribbled filefish, Aluterus scriptus. This large (to 71 cm.) and weirdly marked fish can occasionally be seen on reefs throughout Indonesia.*

Napoleon saw us off when we started our ascent.

Underwater we headed east, then followed the reef as it curved south. Visibility was excellent, 40–50 meters. We were greeted by a platoon of 5 Napoleon wrasse as we began our descent, and during the dive saw schools of striped bristletooth tangs (*Ctenochaetus striatus*), a clown trigger, two small meetings of harlequin sweetlips, a gossiping group of a half-dozen fat puffers, and a ragged school of pennant bannerfish. We also spotted a very large giant grouper, but quickly hid in a deep cave.

At one point we surprised an absolutely beautiful juvenile pinnate batfish, fringed with bright orange. This bright coloration is thought to mimic a toxic flatworm, affording the young fish some protection from predators. This one was not very confident, however, and peered out at us from a coral niche.

We had no complaints after this dive. The crew of another boat suggested that an even better site would have been a nearby rock outcrop called Barusa Saha. Unfortunately, we didn't have time to check out this contention—let us know if you do.

Sebolan Islands

Our first two dives, on Sebolan Besar and Kecil north of Labuhanbajo, were closer to the norm for our survey of the area. We hit the water off the eastern end of the beach on Sebolan Kecil, where the sandy bottom sloped down to about 40 meters. About 60–70 meters out from shore, several underwater hills of coral rise to about 20 meters of the surface. Visibility was excellent, but not many fish greeted us. The only notable fish life we saw was a large school of striped surgeonfish (The knolls were, however, covered with huge fan corals, gorgonians and a wide variety of soft corals. A couple of

schools of striped bristletooth tangs. After the dive, we were told that usually there were lots of sharks here, and earlier in the day (we dove around 11 a.m.) we probably would have seen more fish life.

Our second dive was off the west coast of Sebolan Besar, heading south underwater. Here, on a coral slope from 7 meters to a sand bottom at 30–35 meters, we encountered a fair variety of soft corals and an interesting selection of stony corals. We saw more fish here, including titan triggers, more striped bristletooth tangs and some sweetlips.

There was also some fish bomb damage here, something we didn't see on "Little Sebolan," but spotting a large turtle put us back in a good mood.

Pungu Island

A dive off the southwest corner of Pungu Besar Island started off well enough. Just as we passed the edge of the 4- to 7-meter-deep reef flat, a bumphead parrotfish drifted into view. But that was the only fish we were to see for the next 20 minutes as we angled down a gentle slope to 50 meters, amidst a forest of whip corals. After 40 meters, the bottom profile started dropping in step-like ridges, ending in a long, narrow valley at 55 meters.

The area was strangely deserted, so we headed up to the top of the coral bed for a decompression stop, whence to return to our anchored boat. Fish life picked up a bit here. There was extensive bomb damage, mostly covered by new growth of soft coral. Some of the damaged stony coral was blackened, and we speculated that this might be the result of cyanide poisoning.

Two years ago Madurese boats started coming into the area by the dozen to collect marine ornamentals for aquariums. Unfortunately, they use cyanide to stun the fish so they can be easily collected. This process is disastrous for the reef, and for the fish—cyanide weakened fish have a very short life in the aquarium. Major U.S. wholesalers test for cyanide, and poisoned fish now only very rarely make it into the U.S. market. The same, however, is not true of Singapore and other Asian markets.

A long period of education has helped stop cyanide capture in the Philippines, and perhaps a similar program needs to be adopted in Indonesia. Until then, however, the Madurese are armed with legal permits issued by the government fishery department in Labuhanbajo.

In the shallows, I saw a giant clam, and a few smaller *Tridacna* species. Just before getting into the boat, I poked my nose under a table coral where I discovered a reef whitetip shark, just about a meter long, keeping a wary eye on me. He categorically refused to come out for a photograph.

Sitonda Island

After on-board lunch and a bit of a rest, we motored to the west, anchoring off tiny Sitonda Island, close to the southern tip of Sebayur Besar. As there was a healthy current (1.5–2 knots), we asked our boatman to follow us for the pickup. Two of the divers who had accompanied us followed us into the drink. Sitonda's reef sloped down to some 25 meters. Right off the bat we disturbed a school of seven bumphead parrotfish, but these were the only fish of note other than a very friendly guineafowl puffer (*Arothron meleagris*). This fellow was willing enough to pose for pictures, but he could handle the swift current better than the photographer could.

While I was struggling to photograph my puffer, the pros found four pearl oysters, which made them happy. We drifted a bit more with the current, but

then visibility dropped and we cut the dive short and surfaced. Our boat had been drifting as well, and was nearby.

Siaba Islands

Two dives off the twin Siaba Islands well illustrate the contrasts we found in the area: the first dive was nothing special, the second one quite interesting. We started off the north coast of Siaba Kecil, where we found a

Below: *The spotfin lionfish,* Pterois antennata, *displaying the eponymous spots on its pectoral fins. Bali.*

HELMUT DEBELIUS / IKAN

HELMUT DEBELIUS / IKAN

good variety of hard corals in the shallows, then a boring slope to 20 meters. Unwilling to waste precious underwater time, we came up to the shallows where we saw some striped bristletooth tangs (we saw these on almost every dive in the area), lots of regal angelfish, an unusually large school of Moorish idols, a large star puffer (*Arothron stellatus*) and, trying to make itself inconspicuous, a nurse shark

Above: *A pair of firefish,* Nemateleotris magnifica. *Firefish are skittish plankton-feeders that hover in pairs or small groups near the reef bottom. Flores.*

(*Nebrius concolor*), which eventually fled in panic. There was no real reason to use tanks on this dive—we would have seen just as much snorkeling.

The southern tip of Siaba Besar was quite different, and we encountered a good variety of fish. Things started with a boring slope from the reef flat at 3–5 meters. The dreary landscape was relieved at first only by juvenile black triggers scurrying into their little holes. We descended to 52 meters, and were rewarded by three fair-sized Napoleon wrasse, but at that depth we had no time to dawdle with our big friends.

We headed up slowly, passing the inevitable school of striped bristletooth surgeons, a school of bluespine unicornfish (*Naso unicornis*) and a half dozen Goldman's sweetlips.

Around 20–25 meters, we crossed a turtle, a bumphead parrotfish, and two reef whitetip sharks. A couple of clown triggers provided a touch of color. In the shallows on the way back to the boat we spotted two groups—with a half-dozen individuals in each—of the spectacular palette or flag-tail surgeonfish (*Paracanthurus hepatus*). This was the largest aggregation of this brilliant blue species we had seen in Indonesia.

Other Sites

Four other dives in the Labuhanbajo–Komodo area were rather ordinary. Off the north coast of Menjatan Island, we followed the gentle coral slope to 20 meters, a rather unexceptional dive except for a good number of parrotfishes. Off the east tip of Penga, we encountered an easy slope buy really lousy visibility. In the shallows we saw a friendly map puffer, a saddleback grouper (*Plectropomus laevis*) and a good-sized school of lined rabbitfish (*Siganus lineatus*).

In front of Papagaram Kecil (the name means "salty cheek" in Bajo), awful visibility combined with a strong current hid whatever was lurking out there. We quickly ascended from the boring scene at 30 meters, and in the shallows saw a huge school of silvery halfbeaks (*Hemiramphus sp.*) hovering in the current.

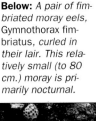

Below: *A pair of fimbriated moray eels,* Gymnothorax fimbriatus, *curled in their lair. This relatively small (to 80 cm.) moray is primarily nocturnal.*

In years past I had snorkeled off tiny Sarang Island, close to Labuhanbajo, and we decided to check the site out with tanks. We started off on the south side of this large, craggy rock, and encountered absolutely zilch visibility—1–2 meters. The rock bottomed out to flat sand at 14 meters, the deepest spot around. Visibility improved somewhat as we swam clockwise around Sarang, the haze parting to show a plethora of blue and yellow *Polycarpa* sp. tunicates and, towards the west, lots of bright red soft corals in just 2–3 meters of water. Around to the east, in 1–3 meter depths, large coral heads were covered with encrusted thorny oysters (*Spondylus* sp.) with brightly patterned lips. A number of small Picasso triggerfish swam around a growth of table corals.

This, however, is snorkeling country. One fun exercise is to cross the island through a channel provided by a narrow cleft that splits the rock. Another passage requires diving 4 meters to a small cave, which leads to daylight about 6 meters away.

Potentially Good Sites

Once the captains and crews of our boats understood what we were looking for—good spreads of coral, clear water, and lots of fish, especially big ones—they came up with a number of suggestions for dive sites. Some proved excellent, others less so. Some we couldn't check out because of the season.

In particular, they suggested we return in March through May, the season of northeast winds (we were there in August, during the southeast monsoon) to check out three sites in the far south of the region: Gili Motang, Kode Island, and Padar Kecil.

Gili Motang Island (the name means "wild boar" in the Manggarai language) is said to have lots of sharks and big fish. Consulting a Dutch marine chart of the area (the only one available, drawn in 1904-1908), the spot seemed logical. A sounding just off the southeast coast of this island yields 135 meters, and just a little further out, 340 meters. We were also told that sites north of the island in the Molo Strait would be a good spot for lots of fish, but because the strait necks down dramatically between Rinca and Flores, the current gets very strong.

Off Kode Island, tucked against the southern edge of Rinca, massive, isolated rocks provide a backdrop for breaching manta rays. This behavior is seen, according to the fishermen, from September to April. The underwater coast of southwest Rinca is said to be lined with caves. Another site for manta rays, during the same season, is Logo Bay, off southeastern Komodo island.

Padar Kecil, between Rinca and Komodo, is said to harbor many fish during the northwest monsoon, January through March. Whales are spotted year-round in many locations but mostly October–January.

In 1991, Valerie Taylor described some of her experiences diving off Komodo in an article in the Australian *Underwater Geographic*. In particular, she noted the fierce water conditions in the Sape Strait, in which 7–8 knot currents are common, and even whirlpools form.

"The water is dangerous and deceptive," she writes. "It can be still one minute and a rushing, uncontrollable swirling mass the next…. A diver has no more control over his or her body than a loose leaf in the wind."

In one dive off Langkoi Island on the southwest tip of Komodo, in just 6 meters of water, Taylor was caught by a sudden current and hurled against a sea urchin encrusted pinnacle, then plunged to 37 meters before being spit back up again to the top. The force of the water was irresistible, and she came dangerously close to rupturing her sinuses or lungs.

The Bajo Villages

During five days of diving in the Labuhanbajo–Komodo area, we employed the services of two different pearl oyster fishing boats and their crews: the *Ismaya,*

ED ROBINSON / IKAN

Above: *A spotted eagle ray,* Aetobatis narinari. *Unlike other reef-dwelling rays, these large animals—the wingspan can reach 2.3 meters—swim well above the bottom, and do not bury themselves in the sand.*

owned by Captain Kahar, and the *Seripati,* owned and captained by Haji Idris. Since the rides to the dive sites were quite long, up to 2.5 hours, we had lots of time to chat with the captains and crews. This conversation, of course, was in Indonesian.

Labuhanbajo means "the Bay of the Bajo," a linguistic/ethnic group famous as fisherman. The Bajo (sometimes Bajau) are still called "sea nomads" although the lifestyle has died out. In the past, they were born, married and died on their boats, keeping no houses on land. Today the Bajo are settled in scattered fishing villages, most in Indonesia.

The area around Labuhanbajo, true to its name, has perhaps the largest population of Bajo anywhere. The town's people are equally divided between Bajo, Manggarai (from inland western Flores), and Bugis (from South Sulawesi). But on the islands in the area from Komodo to Labuhanbajo, very nearly all the inhabitants are Bajo.

There are Bajo villages on Seraya, Rinca, Papagaram Kecil, Papagaram Besar and Pasir Putih. The 1,100 or so inhabitants of Komodo village are a special case, speaking a language that is a real mixture, with elements of Bimanese (from East Sumbawa) and Manggarai dominating. The Bajo, and the Komodo villagers, are Muslims.

All the Bajo villages are on islands that were formerly deserted for a good reason: no freshwater. Rinca and Seraya are the only islands that have sufficient groundwater to supply the populations. The other villages must bring drinking water from Labuhanbajo. The dry islands have few trees, scattered coconut trees are the only useful ones, and no agriculture whatever. The Bajo have retained the one basic element of their former life-style: earning a living from the sea. They fish to feed their families, and sell the excess in the market.

Haji Idris and the crew of the *Seripati* are from Pasir Putih, and they invited us to visit their village. A white sand beach encircles most of the small, elongated island. All the flat space is covered with houses.

I noticed one important change since I last visited (in 1977): now three-quarters of the children attend primary school.

MAUMERE
The Rich Waters off Flores' North Coast

Diving in the Bay of Maumere can be as good as anywhere in Indonesia. In some areas, under the right circumstances, the numbers and varieties of fish are just short of incredible. The reefs range from steep walls, sometimes with strong currents, to offshore detached reefs and broad, shallow reefs for snorkelers and beginning scuba divers. Visibility at the best sites is 50 meters, as good as can be found anywhere in Indonesia.

Large species commonly seen here include stingrays, eagle rays and manta rays, reef sharks, Napoleon wrasse, turtles and, towards the end of the year, whale sharks. The number of medium and smaller reef animals here is staggering—in fact, it is one of the most species rich pieces of coral reef in the world. You will see unicornfish, barracuda, groupers, sweetlips, parrotfish, snappers, tuna, bluefinned jacks, angelfish, Moorish idols, bannerfish, fusiliers, triggerfish, butterflyfish, scorpionfish, puffers, boxfish, trumpetfish, anemonefish and more. Squid, cuttlefish, lobster, shrimp, crabs and nudibranchs can also always be found. The variety of hard and soft corals and other animals is just about as great, including anemones, soft corals, gorgonians, huge sponges and sea fans, and black coral.

Serious divers should consider spending at least several days in Maumere, and even longer is much better. Invariably there is not enough time. With a two week stay, however, you can check out all of the several—different—"best" spots: Pasir Sari, Pomana Besar Island, Wailiti reef, Besar Island, Babi Island, Cape Darat and a spit of sand called Pangahbatang.

Diving Maumere

There are some two dozen dive sites scattered around the eastern end of Maumere Bay. (See map page 158). The further out one goes—to, say Pomana Island—the clearer the conditions and the more fish life one finds. The inshore sites, on the other hand, generally have easier conditions, and despite reduced visibility and fish life, have good

---

AT A GLANCE
Maumere

Reef type: Mostly steep walls, some vertical

Access: Up to 2 hrs by boat

Visibility: Fair to excellent, 15–50 meters, best at the island sites

Current: Gentle at the coastal sites, can be strong (to several knots) around the islands

Coral: Very good coverage and varieties

Fish: Very good numbers and varieties; at the best sites, excellent

Highlights: Spectacular display of fish at Ray Lagoon; mantas at several sites

---

coral growth and are better sites for beginning divers.

In addition to these sites, the staff of the Sao Resort, the oldest operator in Maumere, were at the time of this publication pioneering new locations. The problem in the past had been access, but with the faster and more comfortable dive boats that went into service in late 1991, plans are to begin exploring Sukun

Island, north of Maumere but well outside of the bay, and Palue Island, west of Maumere Bay. Palue's Rokatenda volcano exploded in 1938 with a force almost as great as Krakatau's better-known eruption.

Although the 40-kilometer mouth of Maumere Bay is almost closed off on the eastern side by Besar and the Pomana Islands, conditions can get choppy. Even though it is advertised to be calm during the March to November diving season, winds do come up during this period (especially in July), sometimes lasting—on and off—for a week or more.

With so many dive spots around the islands, however, there are almost always decent places to dive at distances two hours or less by boat. Getting there is not much fun on a windy day, but this happens only occasionally. The new boats should cut travel time considerably.

Whale sharks are seen in the area in November and December. Although this is after the dive season, the seas are often calm enough in this period to boat out to the islands. January and February almost always bring high waves, and access to the sites is cut off.

South Coast Sites

Some eight sites have been established along the south coast of the bay, starting with Pertamina (near the airport) in the west,

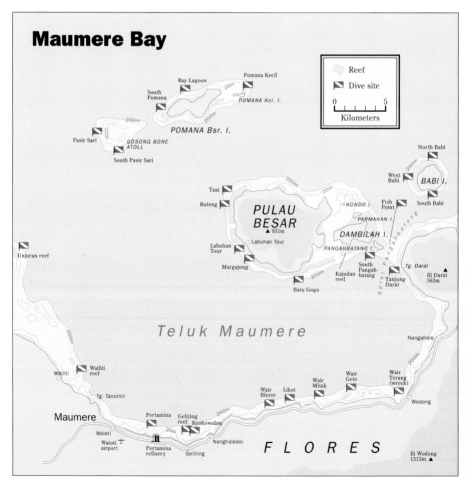

Maumere Bay

and continuing to the Japanese shipwreck at Wair Terang. Many of these site designations include "Wair," which is the local word for an intermittent river. In general, the diving at these sites was quite good, with excellent coverage and variety of soft corals and gorgonians, and good hard coral cover. Fish life, however, was only fair. These dives are quite easy, with little current and maximum depths of 30-40 meters. Visibility was only fair, about 15 meters. There were never any lousy dives, but some were definitely better than others.

Wair Terang

The most interesting of the lot is Wair Terang, a site that includes a Japanese ship sunk during World War II. Nowhere else have we seen so many lionfish (all *Pterois volitans*), in groups of four, six and even up to a dozen, including some huge old fellas. The wreck lies on its side, almost completely turned over, on a slope. Although depths range from 12 to 24 meters, there is no reason to use up your air on the deeper part of the wreck, as there is more than enough to see near the top. The ship is less than 100 meters from the beach.

The substrate here is a fine, gray sand that produces an instant smoke screen as soon as someone gets a fin within two meters of its surface—this is not a dive on which one wants to invite neophytes still struggling with their buoyancy control. On our first visit, we were in a group of a dozen divers who cut the 10–15 meter visibility to zero within five minutes. For our second dive on the wreck, we came as a group of three more seasoned divers, and carefully monitored our movements.

The silty bottom restricts coral growth, and there is none around the wreck. On the hull itself, however, we found small clumps of branching hard coral protecting tiny fish. A few sponges and lots of clams cling to the side of the hull, along with bunches of grassy whip coral. Several fat sea cucumbers crawled along the ship. Juvenile three-spot dascyllus (*Dascyllus trimaculatus*) found protection near the beautiful stinging sacs or acrorhagi of bubble coral, *Plerogyra* sp.

Although far from overwhelming, we found the fish life here quite adequate. In addition to the remarkable number of lionfish, a small cloud of anthias decorated the top of the lower hull and fat goatfish rooted in the silt. A dozen adult pinnate batfish appeared from the wreck, swam off into the haze, and then returned, as if they had forgotten something. We found a beautiful little blue and white juvenile emperor angelfish. Several groupers and wrasses wandered in and out of a large hole in the hull. The silt inside, however, prevented human exploration.

My dive buddies startled a large cuttlefish, and saw two moray eels posturing at each other with open mouths. Was it territorial defense or love?

Wair Likot

This recently discovered spot differs from the others in its underwater geography. Likot, named for a nearby hamlet, features a reef slope with a series of irregular coral pinnacles or bommies near the shore. During our descent, we saw almost no fish, but swam over great spreads of leaf and cabbage coral. Brown and light green tube sponges competed for space with the corals. To give us a bit of excitement, a turtle shot out of its lair.

After reaching the sand bottom at 35 meters, we swam shoreward. The wall had good coral growth, including gorgonians and branching green *Tubastrea* sp., but the visibility dropped to just 8 meters. The fish life was generally poor, but we saw schooling fusiliers and unicornfish, as well as a large moray, who flashed us his fangs. Here and there we could see the evidence of fish bombing.

Once we reached shallower waters, fish life picked up somewhat, with a bright bicolor angel (*Centropyge bicolor*), pairs of foxface rabbitfish (*Siganus volpinus*), and emperor angels. A good-sized grouper shot out from under a table coral, sending the small fish flying to the safety of the branching *Acropora* skeletons. The hard corals here were quite varied in form, including the delicate pink needle coral, *Seriatopora hystrix*.

Pertamina Night Dive

If day dives are not really extraordinary to you, try a night plunge at the Pertamina site. The dive takes place in the shallows (8–12 meters) around the wreck of a large buoy.

You will almost certainly see the interesting little epaulette sharks (*Hemiscyllium ocellatum*) here. During the day these sharks, with two white-fringed "epaulettes" marking their sides, hide under coral. If disturbed in the open during the day, they scurry for shelter, content as long as their head and shoulders are protected. At night, they root in the substrate for worms and crustaceans.

We saw a pair of these sharks, one just under a meter with a smaller 65–70 centimeter partner. Disoriented by our lights, they bumped into chunks of coral, living up to their Australian name: blind shark. Other unusual night prowlers at Pertamina include the tiny (to just 8 centimeters) twinspot lionfish (*Dendrochirus biocellatus*). This fish has a drooping mustache, and two spots on its dorsal fin.

One large common lionfish (*Pterois volitans*) was a nuisance during the entire dive, following

us closely to gobble up little fish blinded by our lights. Dive instructor James Organ of the Sao Resort has been stung several times by these critters, but he says a soaking with hot tea topside relieves most of the pain.

Other South Coast Sites

The other sites off the south-eastern shore of Maumere Bay are basically similar: close to shore, good hard and soft coral spreads in the shallows (2–6 meters), and steep slopes with scattered coral and sand. Although fish life was not as good as the further locations, we saw reef whitetip sharks and hawksbill turtles, as well as a large eagle ray and several stingrays. Other interesting finds included several exquisite juvenile pinnate batfish, and an occasional lobster.

At Wair Mitak, we saw the slender blue and yellow blue ribbon eels (*Rhinomuraena quaesita*) as well as a number of cute little pipefishes. Wair Gete boasts two unusual hot springs pouring water out into the reef-top coral. All the coastal sites are quite close to the resorts, requiring just 30 to 45 minutes in one of the older boats, and less than half that in one of the newer vessels.

Pulau Besar

The diving off the village of Labuhan Tour on Pulau Besar ("Big Island") was considerably better than that off the south coast. We anchored against a dramatic background, steep mountains split by a sloping valley that wound down to a beachside strip of coconut trees. The villagers here have stopped fish bombing, having been successfully convinced that tending seaweed is more profitable. They now look after a maze of bamboo rafts, where sprigs of *Eucheuma* sp. algae are tied to grow out. The seaweed, harvested periodically, is sold for carrageenan, an important ingredient in many

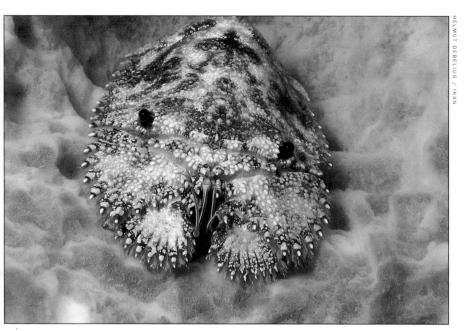

processed foods and cosmetics.

We entered the water about 150 meters from shore, the limit of the reef top, sand and patchy coral 2–5 meters deep. We went over the edge and down a coral wall, reaching a sloping sand bottom at 40 meters. The wall was good and rugged, with many small crevices and caves, and great sloping cracks running down from the reef top.

Coral growth was very good, and there were many sponges—including huge barrel sponges. From around 20 meters, great fan gorgonians spread outward horizontally in a layered terrace.

Fish life and visibility was much better than at the bayshore spots. Schooling fish included surgeonfish, unicornfish and fusiliers. But we did not see any of the pelagics that are often spotted here, particularly tuna and mackerel. Nor did we see a single shark.

On our way back up the wall, we spotted three lionfish, some oriental sweetlips, black-and-white snappers, floral wrasses and a blue-lined sea bream. Near the reef top, male and female whitelined groupers (*Anyperodon leucogrammicus*) drifted around each other.

We saw surprisingly few butterflyfish and angelfish, although there were plenty of damsels, including the plucky sergeant-majors. A group of three very small Moorish idols swam by, miniature bundles of pride. At one point we encountered a beautiful, coordinated cloud of slender fairy basslets (*Luzonichthys waitei*), beautifully shaded in purple and orange.

During our safety stop, over a circle of white sand, we watched the reef fish get on with their lives. Goatfish scrounged in the sand for worms. At the edge of the circle, several parrotfish were busily raking algae from coral chunks with their hard "beaks." A large porcupine fish (*Diodon hystrix*), looking lost, blundered into the scene. An underwater idyll, one of our most pleasant decompression stops. A highlight was a brief, but colorful appearance by a terminal male Java parrotfish (*Scarus hypselopterus*), perhaps the most striking member of the genus.

Above: *A slipper lobster,* Scyllarides *sp., lodged in a small barrel sponge. In these small lobsters, the foremost pair of appendages have evolved into small, flat plates rather than the thorny antennae of the more familiar spiny lobster.*

Another dive off Pulau Besar, further north along the west coast, offered a different mix of fish species, including three reef blacktip sharks and a majestic manta ray.

Tanjung Darat

Tanjung Darat curves around the northeast corner of Maumere Bay, with only a narrow channel separating it from Pangahbatang Island to the west. With the right tides, we were told the current is perfect for drift diving. During our dive there, we had no current whatever.

We descended a steep slope to 40 meters, passing lionfish, blue-spotted stingrays, large sweetlips and several reef whitetip sharks, the latter allowing us to approach to within 1 meter. Near the bottom, we discovered a cuttlefish, who liked human company and collaborated in a photo session. Back in the shallower part of the reef, we saw angelfish, butterflyfish and damselfish in great numbers, trumpetfish, and families of three species of clownfish safe in their anemones.

South Pangahbatang

On the opposite side of the Pangahbatang Strait, we dove off a narrow spit of sand, with a few lonely trees, next to Pangahbatang Island. We saw lots of blue-spotted stingrays, as this was their favorite environment—mixed sand and reef. We also noticed lionfish, a number of batfish, many angelfish, and a huge lobster, more than two kilos, waved its antennae from a cave. The visibility was excellent, perhaps 40 meters. A rarely seen white-and-black-blotched juvenile Titan triggerfish made a brief appearance.

Pulau Babi

Pulau Babi (the name means "Pig Island," and yes, there are wild pigs here) lies just outside of Maumere Bay, to the northeast. The three sites here—north, west and south—all offer caves and underwater passages large enough to swim through. These latter are magic tunnels of bright soft corals, but be careful. Highlights here include manta rays, sharks and very large puffers. If conditions cooperate, the south coast site offers the possibility of a drift dive.

West Babi has a spectacular vertical drop-off, which seems to go on forever. Our chart shows 109 meters, which is well beyond our sphere of competence. The variety of invertebrates was exceptional, with many anemones, soft corals and starfish.

After dropping below the first overhang, we began exploring the caves, finding lionfish—including some very fat ones—groupers and other species that like these hidey-holes. Unusually large triggerfish hung close to the wall. By occasionally paying attention to the open water, we spotted reef whitetip sharks, in the one-meter range, and a gray reef shark bigger than a man. We also spotted a large great barracuda, and a huge eagle ray.

Several deep, canyon-like fissures cut through the vertical wall, reaching down to 40 meters, which was our maximum depth. Relatively few sponges and gorgonians grow here, but the hard coral cover is very good. When we returning to the dive boat, a whale blew less than 100 meters away.

North Babi was a similar dive, with fewer fish but more interesting reef structure. In addition to the caves and tunnels, large horizontal knobs of coral jutted from the wall. The drop-off reached a sandy bottom here at 50 meters.

West Maumere Bay

The west side of Maumere Bay is protected by a shallow reef that extends a considerable distance from the shore, particularly at Cape Nangadelan, its northwestern extremity. We dove here, at a site called Unjuran Reef. The setting was spectacular, with turquoise shallows (2–3 meters) backed by mountains shrouded in clouds. Our dive was on a wall, which reached to 35 meters but had poor fish life and visibility. A second dive, just to the west, was similar, but we were saved from complete disappointment by spotting three large turtles and a huge manta ray. The ray swam just below us as we were swimming back to the boat.

Gosong Bone Atoll

Our best dives in the Maumere area were at sites the furthest north, out of the bay, off Gosong Bone Atoll and Pomana Besar Island. The Gosong Bone dive was at a site called Pasir Sari, the name of a low-lying spit of rock and sand marking the atoll's western end.

The wall here descends vertical as a plumb line to 50 meters, then slopes slightly, eventually reaching bottom at a depth of two kilometers. Dolphins are common in the area—we saw them frolicking from the dive boat—but we didn't see any underwater. However, coral growth was excellent, visibility was 50 meters, and we saw turtles, sharks, groupers, schools of unicornfish, and a solitary Napoleon wrasse.

During a night dive at the same location, our lights revealed an endless procession of gaudy colors, almost too much. We dove to 20 meters, and the caves, nooks and ceilings of overhangs were covered with an almost solid carpet of color. Giant sea stars here reached a half-meter from tip to tip. Lobsters, crabs and shrimp were feeding everywhere.

A big parrotfish slept in his mucous cocoon, and large uni-

RUDIE KUITER
Photographer and Author

Rudie Kuiter's knowledge of Pacific reef fishes and underwater photography is equaled by few others. At first, he comes across as a more handsome Charles Bronson, with a long lion's mane of hair and clear blue eyes. But there is nothing gruff or closed about this man—he is willing to share his endless knowledge of Indonesia's reef animals with peers and beginners alike.

After logging hundreds of dives in Indonesia—mostly in Maumere Bay and Bali—Kuiter authored the country's definitive reef fish guide (in production as of this writing). His interest in this project began in 1985 with an invitation to survey the fishes of Maumere Bay for the Flores Sao Resort. In the process, he catalogued over 1,200 species, including a half dozen new to science. In 1990, Kuiter organized the now yearly underwater photo competition at the Sao Resort.

Kuiter's interest in fishes began in 1948, when at the mature age of five he started catching river fish with cotton and worm lures in his native Holland. His father built him a fish pond where Kuiter raised local species. After training in electronics and a two year stint in the army, he moved to Australia, his home since 1964. Today, he lives with his wife and children in Melbourne.

Within a month of his arrival in Australia, Kuiter was already taking a scuba course. A few years later, he began taking underwater photographs, using a housed Nikon F with a 55 macro. Kuiter's knowlege of electronics, with which he supported himself until 1979 (and on a self-employment basis since) has served him well in putting together his underwater gear and keeping it in working shape in the field.

Today, Kuiter works with 60 mm and 105 mm macro lenses mounted in an F4. The whole is housed in a Hugyfot housing which he has modified. He also tore apart two Nikon SB24 flashes—sophisticated units with active links to the camera's built-in computer and light meter—and rebuilt them according to his requirements. It is a one-off, state-of-the-art setup.

According to Alison, Kuiter's wife and the mother of red-haired Hendrik and blond Steven, Kuiter's success is due to his unbelievable powers of observation and endless patience as much as his technical skill. Alison Kuiter was already a keen diver and underwater photographer when she met Rudy in 1976.

— Kal Muller

corns slumbered in small caves. A big moray stuck its fanged mouth out of a cave. An 80-centimeter puffer swam by, as did a small whitetip shark. Shifting currents occasionally came up, but lasted only a couple of minutes. A fine dive indeed.

Ray Lagoon

Our best dive in the area was at Ray Lagoon, off the northwest coast of Pomana Besar Island.

This is not a dive for beginners: the current was strong, and we went deep.

The dive began easily enough, as we dropped into a lagoon and descended to its sand and patchy coral bottom at 27 meters. We quickly spotted a reef white-tip sleeping under a canopy of table coral, and then three spotted eagle rays, from which the site takes its name.

Exiting the lagoon, through a

U-shaped "door," required some strong finning against the current. But the exertion, and extra air consumption, was worth it. Visibility at the mouth was excellent—50 meters or more—and we gazed in awe at uncountable numbers of fish drifting up and down the sheer coral walls.

The number of fish was incredible, as were the numbers of species—it was like a huge aquarium stocked with every known Indonesian fish. After a quick calculation as to our remaining air, we dropped to 45 meters to gaze up at the show. A couple more large eagle rays swam by, and we spotted two more reef whitetips and a large nurse shark. Fantastic!

When we got back aboard our boat, one of the divers in our group—the first out of the lagoon, said he was greeted at the exit by a whale shark! (This was in July). We joked good-naturedly about what kind of air mixture he had been breathing, but we knew he was not the type for fish stories.

Don't expect Ray Lagoon always to be this good. Two weeks later, I brought a lady diver friend here to impress her. The visibility had dropped, we only saw two rays, and the fish patrols up and down the wall had been significantly reduced.

Sea World

Diving in Maumere began in the early 1970s, when an Italian couple began operating Sea World. The original owners gave up the business, which was taken over by a local Roman Catholic foundation. Sea World still runs dive tours, but only about 15 percent of their clients dive.

Sea World owns a well-maintained Bauer compressor, but the operation has frequent troubles with their dive boat, and their rental equipment could stand to be upgraded. The man who runs the dive operations,

Julianus Ali, does not have dive master certification—he has a certificate at the NAUI open water level. His English is far from fluent.

The accommodations at Sea World are being upgraded, and 16 new rooms are coming on line in mid-1991. Unfortunately, these are rather unattractive, motel-style buildings. The existing beach side cottages are pleasant, although they certainly need some fixing up.

My sleep in one was disturbed by a scampering rat (I can handle that) and a huge spider by the light switch (not handleable, absolutely horrible). The food and service at the restaurant was excellent, however, and the staff helpful and friendly.

Flores Sao Resort

The best place in Maumere for divers is the Flores Sao Resort. While not exclusively a dive operation, almost half of their guests are divers. The Sao Resort is an example of the new breed of Indonesian dive resorts.

As the country becomes a more popular destination, dive operators are upgrading their businesses, hiring experienced westerners to train their staffs and professionalize their operations. Local attitudes have in the past been rather lackadaisical from a visitor's point of view, particularly regarding safety, training and equipment maintenance.

The Sao Resort is being turned into a very professional operation with the help of some outside capital. The newly hired dive master, James Organ, is a very qualified NAUI instructor who was brought in from Australia. To upgrade the resort side of things, Sao brought in Michael MacKaay, an experienced Hollander. Marty Hubbard, another Australian, will be brought in to supervise a planned program of water sports: game fishing, windsurfing and parasailing.

Their boats are reliable, are equipped with two-way radios, and are staffed by a crew well trained in assisting divers. All carry oxygen and first aid kits. There is new scuba rental equipment in the pipeline—BCs, regulators, wet suits and dive computers—plus the expertise to service them properly. A fast dive boat, a 25-knot catamaran large enough for 20 divers, was sched-

KAL MULLER

uled to begin operating in late 1991. A live-aboard is being readied for 1992. At press time, construction started on a new cottage style, four-star hotel.

Dive master Organ has begun a series of exploratory dives, supplementing the current locations, which were scouted by the early owners of Sea World and Andre Pribadi, who was in charge of the Sao Resort until the mid 1980s.

Above: *One of the Sao Resort's dive boats, out on the water in Maumere Bay, Flores.*

Diving with the Pros for Pearl Oysters

The scuba divers of Lewoleba Village, Lembata are real professionals. They do their work at 40 meters, scouring the bottom for pearl oysters. No buoyancy compensators, no pressure gauges, no depth gauges, and no weight belts. And they never dive on Fridays (all the divers are Muslim). Each day five or six members of a 10-man team will be underwater. All are Bugis or Bajo men from Lembata, a small island east of Flores.

Pearl shell gathering is a dangerous occupation. The men have never heard of dive tables, and on any given day two or more team members are recovering from the bends, resting up until they can rejoin the team.

Some have been permanently crippled from the disease, and dozens have died since diving started here in the early 1970s.

The team is staked by a local ethnic Chinese businessman, who supplies a boat, double tanks, regulators, masks and fins. The divers make a good living on a poor island, earning an average of $5 a day for the two species of oysters they collect in

the area. The oysters are sold to one of the Japanese pearl farms, where, in a highly secret process, an irritant is inserted so the oyster will secrete a pearl.

The divers do follow one safety rule, which they said was the advice of a visiting German diver: come up slowly and stay at three meters until you run out of air. This is the only effort at decompression they make after emptying twin tanks at up to 40 meters.

The divers' day begins around 7 or 8 a.m., when the captain, a cook and the divers motor out on the ancient, but sound, *Mustika Jaya II*. The divers trail fishing lines along the way, sometimes hooking tuna and red snapper.

The men breakfast on rice and fish, then prepare large twine baskets for the shells, each of which is connected by a long rope to two empty plastic jerrycans which serve as floats. As we approach the site, regulators are screwed onto the double tanks, masks rubbed with spittle, pants, shirts, and fins donned. One man jumps overboard while the *Mustika* is still moving full speed ahead. He goes straight to the bottom and starts working. The others soon do the same.

Forty Meters Down

We go straight down to 35–40 meters without even slowing to clear our ears. This is no sport dive, and every minute is precious. The visibility here is lousy, maybe 10–15 meters, and the bottom is flat, with small hard and soft corals. There are few fish here, although I found a friendly puffer. I started tickling him to get him to inflate, but my "partner," Askar, motioned impa-

Map

Lembata

Laut Flores

Occasional boats to Kalabahi, Alor

Lamagute
Mawa
Aulesa
Wairiang
Bunga Muda
Sagu
Wawala
Be Ape 1450 m
Tokosaeng
Balauring
Aliuroba
Atanila
ADONARA
Waipukang
Jontona
Lewolein Tapolangu
Kayang
Teluk Walenga
Be Beleng 1659 m
Lewoleba
Hadakewa
Lodoblolong
MARISA I.
Walwerang
LEMBATA
Lamatuka
RUSA I.
Balurebong
SOLOR
Bata
Belang
Karangora
KAMBING I.
Kalikasa
Lamalewa
Loang
Boto
Puor
Lebala
Be Pangora 1121 m
Laut Savu
Mingar
Imolong
Lamalera

0   10   20
Kilometers

★ Whaling village and site of pearl shell diving operation

tiently to move on. There was no time for foolishness.

We swam along with a strong current, Askar staying a couple of meters off the bottom and continuously scanning the sea floor. So it went for the better part of an hour. Unused to diving without weights, I had to struggle to stay down, sometimes hanging onto the bottom for a few seconds.

This was not a pleasant dive.

Then Askar found a shell, and showed just the slightest hint of emotion. I could almost hear him think—"Well, that's one, anyway. At least the day is not wasted." Soon thereafter, thank the spirits, he signaled it was time to go up. Without weights, I struggled to maintain a controlled ascent. Askar drifted up slowly.

We stopped 3 meters from the surface, but I had trouble holding that depth, and finally gave up and popped to the surface. Askar soon joined me and we each grabbed a plastic jerrycan until the boat comes.

One diver was already on board. He also got one shell. We picked up the others, each at least a couple of hundred meters apart. The last diver was the first one in the water. A short, tough, chap, he was also the oldest—probably in his early 40's (he didn't know himself). He had three shells, but wasn't gloating.

We napped on the hot topside roof while the *Mustika*'s two compressors refilled the tanks. An hour or so later, with everyone awake, the crew decided against a second dive: the wind was coming up. We headed back to Lewoleba.

Sonny The Nalley

After the dive, I went to meet the boat's owner, Sonny The Nalley. (His middle name is pronounced *Tay.*) Yes, he says, today was not ideal. June–August brings rough water, as does December–February, along with rain.

Sonny sells the oysters for $2.50–$10.00 each, depending on their size and quality. To simplify accounting, he pays his divers a flat $2.50 for every shell. He provides all the equipment, but hasn't heard of hydrostatic testing or regulator maintenance.

Would he be willing to take other foreigners diving? Yes, as long as they pay, like I did, $15 for the day. One or two dives, according to conditions. Would

KAL MULLER

he charter the boat by the day? He pulls out a plastic-covered calculator. Yup, $200 a day. Does he know any good wall dive areas? Sure. Big fish? Batu Tara island, north of Larantuka.

For longer trips, Nalley suggests the 30-ton *Karya Mandiri,* 25 meters and a compressor on board. His calculator shows $275 a day, plus equipment.

Now *that's* a thought.

Above: *A pearl shell diver displays a pearl oyster. The oyster will be sold to one of the Japanese-run pearl farms where—in a secret, closely guarded process—the animal is induced to form a pearl. Komodo Island.*

Kupang

KUPANG
Big Fish, Good Coral, and Limited Visibility

If visibility weren't so limited, diving around Kupang could be absolutely superb. On all of our dives in the area we saw healthy growths of hard and soft corals, and on almost all our dives, some big animals: mantas, sharks, turtles, rays, Napoleon wrasse, large groupers or bumphead parrot-

year-round, but visibility reaches its peak from August to September. We dove in October. Visibility of 12 meters may seem like paradise to divers from Darwin, Australia (a short plane ride from Kupang), but it is just not up to snuff by Indonesian standards. We swam through a fog of plankton and suspended matter, and sometimes huge clouds of minuscule, tadpole-like fish. Photography was limited to macro work, or at least at subject distances of less than half a meter.

Yet there are some mitigating factors. The diving operation is professionally run by experienced people, who are nice chaps to boot. The equipment is properly maintained, and the dive boat is reliable and well designed. The rates are very reasonable. Two Australians, divemaster Graeme Whitford and his son Donovan, run the show. The operation is organized in conjunction with Pitoby, the largest travel agency in Kupang.

One of the Whitfords accompanies every dive. They will prepare a dive plan with you, in English, based on a great deal of experience with each site. You will be told what kinds of unusual fish or coral formations to expect. If there are caves, the guide will bring an underwater light to illuminate the animals lurking within. Or you can borrow one of their spare lights.

Diving in Kupang

The Whitfords had developed 10 dive sites when we visited in 1991, some of which are worth several repeats. Plans were to check out other spots, including sites where there are Japanese

---

AT A GLANCE
Kupang

Reef type: Mostly walls, some nicely pocked with caves

Access: 45 min by boat from Kupang

Visibility: Poor, 7–10 meters; sometimes worse, rarely to 12 meters

Current: Gentle or none; occasionally to 1.5 knots

Coral: Generally good coverage and varieties

Fish: Generally good numbers and varieties, particularly big fish

Highlights: Stingrays at some sites; rich invertebrate life observed on a night dive at Donovan's Delight

---

fish. The medium-sized reef fishes were also well-represented here, including sweetlips, batfish, angelfish, triggerfish and parrotfish. Butterflyfish and damselfish, by Indonesian standards, were scarce, as were schooling fish, other than the ubiquitous fusiliers, and occasionally, surgeonfish. Invertebrates—particularly nudibranchs, worms, crustaceans and echinoderms—were always plentiful.

But visibility never exceeded 12 meters, and averaged 7–10 meters. Occasionally, it dropped to just 2–3 meters. Diving is good

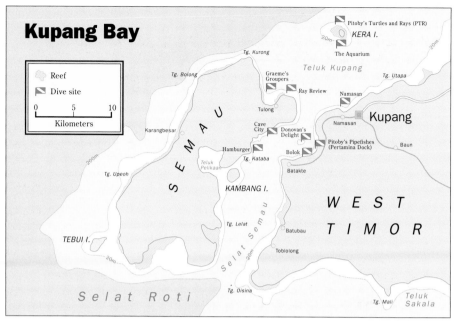

Kupang Bay

Legend:
- Reef
- Dive site

0 — 5 — 10
Kilometers

Map labels:
- Pitoby's Turtles and Rays (PTR)
- KERA I.
- The Aquarium
- Tg. Kurong
- Tg. Bolong
- Teluk Kupang
- Tg. Utapa
- Graeme's Groupers
- Ray Review
- Namasan
- Tulong
- Cave City
- Donovan's Delight
- Namasan
- Kupang
- Karangbesar
- Hamburger
- Tg. Kataba
- Bolok
- Pitoby's Pipefishes (Pertamina Dock)
- Baun
- Teluk Pelikaan
- Batakte
- Tg. Upeoh
- KAMBANG I.
- S E M A U
- W E S T
- T I M O R
- Tg. Lelat
- Selat Semau
- Batubau
- TEBUI I.
- Tobiolong
- Selat Roti
- Tg. Oisina
- Tg. Mali
- Teluk Sakala

ships sunk by the Allies during World War II. At least one of these wrecks lies just off the Japanese built pier on Semau Island, and some of its super-structure extends above the water. Snorkeling here reveals that lionfish have claimed the more shallow parts of this ship as their home.

For a variety of practical reasons, dives from Kupang are restricted to the area around the harbor, the northeast coast of Semau Island, and Kera Island, a low-lying, sand fringed island north of Kupang (see map page 169). It takes about 45 minutes to reach any of the locations on the *Pitoby Sport,* a beamy 13-meter wooden craft powered by a 40hp outboard. The boat has a high tarp roof, and tanks are stored in an out-of-the-way spot. The boat draws very little water, so there could be a bit of spray bouncing around, depending on the wind.

The *Pitoby Sport* picks up clients at the beach near the microbus terminal and Teddy's Bar. There is no pier, and you have to wade into almost waist-high water before climbing aboard. The crew will get your dive bag aboard. On the way to the dive site, divers can either sit in the shade under the awning, or work on their tans out in the bow area. Fishing gear is usually available, if you want to troll on the way to the dive site.

Kera Island

Pulau Kera ("Monkey Island"), circled by a brilliant white sand beach, lies at the entrance of Kupang Bay. Pitoby's has a long-term lease on this little piece of paradise, and plans on building cottages here, and making it the base of their water sports operations, which include, in addition to snorkeling and diving, wind-surfing, waterskiing, surfing, fishing and sailing.

The Aquarium, a site off Kera's south coast, offers good diving, particularly for beginning divers. A shallow (2 meters) off-shore sandbank ends at a coral wall that extends to about 12 meters before becoming a gently sloping sand bottom. Visibility varies considerably, but there are fair numbers and varieties of reef fish here.

NOTE
Potentially Good Freshwater Caves

We brought lights and our snorkeling gear to four large freshwater caves just behind the ferry terminal at Bolok. The water was crystal clear, and passages led off in various directions, to depths way beyond the capabilities of a snorkeler. These places are unexplored and will remain so until divers with the interest and cave diving skills show up in Kupang.

—*Kal Muller*

"PTR," short for Pitoby's Turtles and Rays, is a site on the far side of Kera, and offers just what its name suggests. With the boat anchored offshore, we dropped some 20 meters and landed at the edge of the scattered coral formations that slope up to the island. We were right where the sandy bottom began in earnest, and it sloped gently into infinity. As soon as I neared the bottom, a startled blue-spotted stingray flew off, the first of at least a half dozen we spotted during the dive. We also discovered a very large black-spotted stingray, (*Taeniura melanospilos*), wedged under a maze of hard coral.

Some four or five turtles shot out of our way as we worked along at 20 meters. Then, just off our flight path, we caught another turtle, this one napping, with two striped remoras firmly attached to its back.

About halfway through the dive, a school of perhaps a dozen bumphead parrotfish rumbled in formation at the very edge of visibility. Our safety stop took place along a colorful spread of corals dense with small reef fish, right at the 5-meter level.

Semau Island

Graeme's Groupers lies about 100 meters off the beach at Semau where Teddy's and the Flobamor's cottages are located. The name comes from the unusual number of varieties of groupers (cod to the Aussies) that inhabit this reef. The reef extends from the shore in a very gradual slope, reaching 4–9 meters before the edge of a coral wall, which drops sharply to a sandy bottom at 30 meters. Much of the hard corals has been destroyed by extensive fish bombing here, but soft corals are present in fair numbers. The wall is pocked with shallow depressions and caves reaching back a meter or two.

True to the site's name, we identified a half-dozen species of groupers: blotchy, coral, flagtail, polkadot, saddleback and whitelined. These were all 20–30 centimeters, with an occasional fat 40-centimeter specimen. Cleaner wrasses worked their stations along the wall, servicing the groupers as well as longnose emperors, black-and-white snappers, sweetlips, dogface puffers and roundfaced batfish. We saw several large emperor and six-banded angelfish. Visibility never exceeded 10 meters.

Ray Review is a short distance east of Graeme's Groupers. The reef here is also wide and flat, dropping unevenly to a slightly sloping sandy bottom at 22 meters. Several detached coral pinnacles jut upward. Close to the sand bottom, we saw a half-dozen blue-spotted stingrays, which appear first as a pair of eyes, the rest of their bodies covered with fine sand.

Few fish inhabited the area, except for schools of black triggerfish. We also swam over a small forest of garden eels (*Heteroconger* sp.) which disappeared at our approach.

"Cave City" is on the east coast of Semau, around the northeast tip and past the skeleton of the Japanese pier. The site is a coral wall more than a kilometer long, with at least a dozen good sites. The caves are the distinguishing feature here, some reaching back more than 5 meters. The reeftop, covered by 2–5 meters of water, drops off very close to shore to a sandy bottom, 20–40 meters below.

Hard coral growth is good, and we saw lots of gorgonians, some of them reaching several meters across. Soft corals grew in white tufts like wind-blown snow. On the very deepests sections of wall, we encountered bushy growths of antipatharian black corals.

In one cave we saw a school of yellow ribbon sweetlips, in

another a large hawksbill turtle, and in others several species of groupers. Some of the animals swam back to the far dark corners of their homes before we could make an identification. Smaller caves were guarded by detachments of soldierfish.

We spotted two large, but skittish Napoleon wrasse (they are frequently sighted here). The waters near the wall were dominated by schools of black triggerfish, and we also spotted several gaudy clown triggerfish and small Picasso triggers. The six-banded angelfish we saw here were among the largest and fattest we had ever seen. As we ascended, we crossed paths with a school of tank-like bumphead parrotfish.

Visibility in the shallower waters was reduced to almost zero by hazy clouds of tiny fish. Below 20 meters, it was about average for this area.

Donovan's Delight

While flying into Kupang a while back, Graeme Whitford noticed a large, relatively shallow area in the Semau channel, fairly close to the main port. This looked promising to his trained eyes. His son Donovan embarked on a series of exploratory dives here, and was delighted after each one. The site, marked by a navigational buoy, is now featured in all of Pitoby's dive series, and makes an especially good night dive. This is fine, fascinating diving indeed—with the usual caveat of poor to fair visibility. In our five dives here, it never surpassed 8 meters, and once it dropped to a really miserable 2–3 meters.

Donovan's Delight covers an irregular, oval shaped rise, more than 200 meters along its long axis. The reef top is 3–9 meters below the surface, and a vertical coral wall partially encircles the rise, dropping to a sandy bottom at 25–40 meters. A fair variety and number of hard corals cover the top of the dome (there is some fish bomb damage, but it is not extensive) and soft corals are plentiful. The wall features several shallow caves.

During several dives here we saw sharks, both reef whitetips and reef blacktips, a number of

Below: *A common lionfish,* Pterois volitans, *taking refuge in a sponge. Note that at least eight differently colored crinoids,* Himerometra *sp., grip the edge of the sponge.*

KAL MULLER

Above: *A crown-of-thorns starfish,* Acanthaster plancii. *Outbreaks of this large, voracious coral-eating animal have occasionally proved ruinous for entire reefs. Do not handle these starfish, as their thorns can cause a toxic reaction.*

large hawksbill turtles, and groupers up to 90 centimeters. Blue-spotted lagoon rays hide under table coral in the shallows or in the sandy bottom. Towards the ragged bottom of the wall, we saw clusters of sweetlips, emperor fish and puffers. Groups of 10 to 20 roundfaced batfish patrolled the walls, and pairs of very large six-banded and blue-girdled angelfish wandered the reef face. Lionfish hovered near the top of the wall, including black morphs of *Pterois volitans.*

The wide, relatively flat reef top was ideal for safety stops. Several times we saw cuttlefish that would allow us to handle them gently. Large clusters of bright red anemones held their aggressive little guests. There was, however, a strange absence of butterflyfish and damselfish here. In several areas we found small (5–8 cm.) bright yellow feather sea cucumbers (*Cucumaria miniata*), spread in a carpet over several square meters.

One afternoon dive, thanks to Donovan's keen eyes, we spotted more than a dozen species of nudibranchs.

Night Dive at Donovan's

A night dive at Donovan's Delight was one of the most fascinating hours of my life. I had hardly reached the shallow reef top and Donovan was already playing with an indignant puffer. Then he spotted three Spanish

dancer nudibranchs (*Hexabranchus* sp.), one of them with a silvery diamond pattern on its back. The crinoids were hard at work, waving their feathery tentacles through the water. Following us around was the longest trumpetfish I have ever seen. This fellow was so intent in participating in our fun that he kept bumping into me.

Sea urchins ambled around, some looking like World War II mines, others fuzzy balls, and still others with long, banded spines. Basket stars, creeping little bushes with agitated branches, clung to the high ground on coral and sponges, wherever there was a bit of room.

Ever alert Donovan spotted a large hawksbill turtle, tugged the sleepy giant out of its lair and tried to go for a joyride—but by then our turtle was wide awake and shot away at breakneck speed. In contrast, several cuttlefish and a squid were in a playful mood, allowing us to gently pet them. Our attentions caused one to change colors unbelievably fast, from a brownish red to barely spotted white and back again.

A fimbriated moray eel (*Gymnothorax fimbriatus*) nestled in the crack of a spread of red sponge, and the lionfish were out in force.

A great non-stop show all around—the only things we missed were the slipper lobsters and large bailer shells often seen on night dives here. Topside, a couple of swigs of Glenfiddich capped my best night dive ever.

Pitoby's Pipefishes

Just 10–15 minutes by boat from Donovan's Delight is Pitoby's Pipefishes, a shallow dive off the Pertamina dock. The very irregular coral slope drops to 12–14 meters, but most of the action is above 10 meters. In addition to the pipefishes, we saw a good variety of small reef fish. A fine dive for beginners.

Manta Rays and still Little-Explored Diving

The western tip of Roti offers a fine underwater show. Walls of bright soft corals grow amid the rugged limestone formations of the island's coast. Fish life, particularly large and medium-sized species, is very good. Only the restricted visibility we encountered (8–10 meters) keeps the site from being world-class.

Roti is a small, dry island just off Timor's southwestern tip. In some areas dramatic white cliffs line the rugged coastline. Perhaps 100,000 people live here, tending small farms and fishing. The staple food of Roti—and Savu, further west—is the rich sap of the draught-resistant *lontar* palm, which is made into syrup, sugar and even a mild toddy.

The island capital is Ba'a, a town of 3,000 midway along the island's northern coast. (See map page 174.) Here, passable accommodations are available for visitors. We hired Graeme and Donovan Whitford of Pitoby Water Sports in Kupang to take us to Roti.

Batu Termanu

Batu ("Stone") Termanu is just a half-hour northeast of Ba'a. We puttered along coastline of mixed beaches and rugged chunks of raised coral in an open fishing boat, 8 meters long and powered by a 25 hp outboard. There are two sites at Batu Termanu, each marked by differently shaped stone pinnacle.

The closest and largest one, with a tip of sculpted limestone with two holes cut through it, is locally dubbed Batu Termanu Mai, the "female." Some 15 minutes further east, Batu Termanu Jantan, the "male," is less impres-sive: a low, rounded rock with a detached, oval pinnacle. At high tide, only the pinnacle shows.

The vertical rock face of "Lady" Termanu continues a few meters underwater, and then a flat reef begins that slopes gently to a wall just 100 meters offshore. This wall drops vertically to 25–27 meters. It is almost completely covered with bright and pastel soft corals, yielding at the deeper end to green soft corals and stands of black coral.

As we began to explore the small caves in the wall, we were distracted by a large school of surgeonfish, followed by a quite large shark, heading down the wall. Just as the big fellow disappeared, a smaller reef whitetip appeared out of the gloom. He would not allow us to get within four meters, but he stuck around for at least 10 minutes.

Fish cascaded down and up the wall: schools of surgeonfish and unicornfish, groups of pinnate batfish, and big parrotfish.

AT A GLANCE

Roti

Reef type:	Slopes and drop-offs, often amid rocky outcrops
Access:	30 min to 4 hrs from Ba'a
Visibility:	Poor, 8–10 meters
Current:	Generally mild
Coral:	Good growth and variety, particularly soft corals
Fish:	Variable; sharks and rays relatively common
Highlights:	Manta rays and good wall at Batu Termanu

Yellowtail fusiliers flashed by traveling horizontally. Below, sweetlips hung in small groups, and a large barracuda shot off into the darkness. Prides of lionfish—including a group of nine!—patrolled the reef wall. We drifted along the slight current, one-half to one knot, until our air was finished.

The seaward dive path from Batu Termanu Jantan—Christened "The Cathedral" by the Whitfords—leads through narrow passages between rocky outcrops. The bottom deepened gradually to 25–30 meters, the limit of our journey.

A reef whitetip shark monitored out our progress, but the highlight of the dive was a school of blackfin barracuda (*Sphyraena genie*). Discovered in the shallows, these 50–75 centimeter fish were almost friendly. During the deeper part of the dive, we saw two schools of jacks. We barely noticed the groupers, lobster and rainbow-hued parrotfish.

Termanu beach

The Whitfords have also pioneered another dive in the area

of Termanu Mai, beginning from the beach. The reef starts close to shore, and soon one encounters a series of craters, 2–4 meters across, and 5–6 meters into the rock. The current turns these into swirling funnels, which are sometimes full of fish trapped by the outgoing tide. Further out from shore, great chunks of rock covered with soft corals lead to the near side of Termanu.

In this channel, at around 12 meters, I saw the grand spectacle of two manta rays, at least two meters across, gliding overhead. Later, at similar depth, a single manta cruised by overhead. Gently flapping his wings, he banked directly overhead. As he reached the limit of visibility, around 8–10 meters, he turned sharply and made another overhead passage, just two meters away. Two little remoras stuck to his smooth, wide belly. Donovan Whitford, who has dived here in April, May and August, has seen mantas every time.

Ndao Island

On a special arrangement basis, Pitoby's offers a two-day, one-

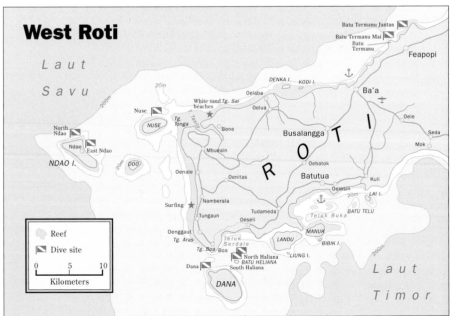

night trip from Ba'a to Ndao Island, a tiny island off the tip of Roti about 4 hours by boat from Ba'a. This is neither for fanatical divers, nor for tourists hungry for cultural events. It is a casual mix of interesting diving and contact with friendly people who seldom see foreigners in their midst. Ndao Island is a dry, poor island that is the home of itinerant silver and goldsmiths. These men spend from March to November in Roti, Sumba, Flores and Timor, making jewelry out of old coins with simple tools.

We made the trip in August, but we recommend that you do so between September and May, as the June–August period has the strongest winds and worst waves. It was unseasonably calm when we went, but we were still drenched with spray on several occasions. We followed Roti's coast, past Nuse Island, and then out to the pristine beaches of Ndao. We checked in with the local authorities and walked around the village of thatch- and tin-roofed huts, all laid out on neatly swept sand.

Diving Ndao

Our marine chart showed a contour line at 50 meters just off Ndao's deserted northwest coast, so we decided to try a pioneer dive there. Despite the chart, the underwater profile turned out to be quite different. We descended to about 8 meters, then swam far out on a strong current over a very slight slope. The bottom reached only 25 meters, with detached outcroppings of coral rock covered with hard and soft corals, and the usual complement of reef fish. A couple of small reef whitetip sharks vanished as soon as we saw them, and a school of ringtail surgeonfish (*Acanthurus blochii*) drifted by. A large group of longnose emperors followed us for much of the dive. Visibility was poor, just 7–8 meters.

Our marine chart proved wrong again on our second dive, just in front of Ndao village. Instead of an 8 meter bottom, dropping very gradually to 16 meters, we went right down on a steep sand slope to 35 meters. The slope just kept going into the gloom. After a few patches of seagrass, the bottom was bare sand. Scattered here and there we saw cerianthids and strange-looking sea urchins sheltering tiny fish in their spines. In the shallows, we saw sea pens and several fat, long worms. Neither I nor my buddy had ever experienced such a dive—almost pure sand below, and menacing gloom ahead and on either side.

An Evening on Ndao

As dusk settled on Ndao, we bucket-bathed in the back of our host's house, then settled in to enjoy our home-stay. A supper of rice, vegetables and salted fish was followed by singing and dancing in the living room. An elderly gentleman played the *sasando,* a Rotinese string instrument made from bamboo and folded *lontar* palm leaves. While we were drinking *tuak,* the juice of the *lontar* palm, three little girls danced for us, decked out in beautiful wrappings of locally woven *ikat* cloth.

Although the people of Ndao originally came from Sawu, much of their culture—weaving styles, the *sasando*—has been borrowed from their near neighbors, the Rotinese. Very little of original Ndao culture is left, except gold and silver smithery. After a night in very comfortable beds, complete with (unnecessary) mosquito netting, we woke to hot coffee, followed by a breakfast of rice, vegetables and chicken curry. We left early on the outgoing tide.

Nuse Island

Our boat cruised past Doo Island, deserted, and lined with

Above: *A terminal phase pale-nose parrotfish,* Scarus psittacus, *asleep in its mucous cocoon. This covering, which is secreted from the skin, is thought to block the parrotfish's scent from night predators. Mapia atoll, Irian Jaya.*

white beaches. We decided against a dive there. Continuing to Nuse Island, we motored past a small hamlet of Ndao fishermen and anchored off the north coast to try a dive. Just then we saw a manta ray breaching. Our crew said the large rays are often hooked by local fishermen.

Things didn't look too promising at first, however, as we dropped to scattered patches of coral. We went along a slope to 40 meters, where all life ceased. Returning to shallower depths, and more life, we spotted a large, light brown stingray keeping a wary eye on us. We approached carefully, however, and got to within an arm's length before it slowly drifted away.

Just about then my buddy grabbed me and pointed up. Holy cow! A huge manta ray hovered over us, turned slowly, and, with exquisite grace, flew out of our range of visibility. We came up in ecstasy, ready for the long tanning haul back to Ba'a.

Batu Heliana

The Whitfords have also pioneered some dive sites off southwest Roti, the southernmost extremity of Indonesia. We dove off both sides of Batu Heliana, a jagged pinnacle rearing up from the sea a short (15–20 minute) boat ride from Oeseli village. The sheer sides of the rock unfortunately do not continue underwater. There is no wall, only sloping bottom, well-covered by soft corals. Here and there, detached coral blocks—at 10–15 meters—support good populations of reef fish and invertebrates. We saw two small reef sharks, a turtle and a stingray.

Off the southwest face of the rock, the only large fish we saw was a single golden trevally. We descended to 20 meters, but saw nothing of interest. The visibility was lousy, less than 8 meters. In the shallows, we discovered a good number of *Tridacna* clams, and the largest spreads of carpet anemones we had ever seen.

As we motored away, the engine's racket flushed out hundreds of flying foxes. These large fruit-eating bats are the only permanent inhabitants of the "island." Birds nest here as well, but only seasonally.

Large Dana Island has an inviting beach, but no one lives here. Its inhabitants were massacred several centuries ago, and their spirits keep out everyone except occasional deer hunters (the island teems with deer.) We worked our way around the island's northwest tip to a spot beyond the big waves, which broke in perfect tubes, enough to make any surfer drool.

We dropped 8 meters to the reef top, which was cut through with narrow surge channels. The reef sloped to 12 meters, then dropped sharply to 25 meters. Visibility was about 10 meters. We saw a spotted grouper, a hawksbill turtle and a 1.5 meter reef whitetip shark. Along the wall we saw a school of a dozen or more pinnate batfish, and a couple of large schools of fusiliers. A shadowy mass of surgeonfish, distinguishable only by the silhouette they cast, passed by at the limit of visibility. On other occasions, the Whitfords have seen huge specimens of almost every kind of tropical fish here, all in excellent visibility. On this day I was not so lucky.

Luxury Live-Aboard for Fine, Genteel Diving

The two vessels operated by P&O Spice Island Cruises, the 41-meter *Island Explorer* and the 37-meter *Spice Islander,* present the most luxurious dive option available in Indonesia. These are not purpose-built dive boats, but instead were built to take small groups of well-heeled travelers through the islands of Nusa Tenggara. They feature large cabins for two and five-star meals.

Passengers can dive during the normal one-week cruises between Benoa, Bali and Kupang, West Timor along the northern route, or the one-week return from Kupang to Bali along the southern route. One can also book a two-week round-trip from either port.

Don't expect three dives a day, however. Diving is only one activity in an overall program of sight-seeing and watersports, including snorkeling, waterskiing, sailing, windsurfing, and glass-bottomed boat exploration. There is only a dive coordinator/guide to handle clients.

Serious divers should sign on for one of the special two-week dive charters. These are held three or four times a year, and almost always include Kupang, Banda and Ambon. On these trips, internationally certified dive masters run the show, and three dives a day are scheduled, with night dives thrown in here and there. Dive sites include "secret" locations, considered among the best in Indonesia, including Penyu Island way out in the middle of the Banda Sea.

Lecturers on these dive charters have included Ron and Valerie Taylor, Dr. Eugene Clark (world famous deep sea scientist), and the late Peter Scott (renowned ichthyologist and son of the polar explorer). These are very well-run charters, and space on them evaporates quickly. Contact P&O for scheduling and availability (see "Nusa Tenggara Dive Practicalities," page 179).

We were not fortunate enough to participate in one of the special dive charters, but still experienced plenty of good diving on one of the *Island Explorer*'s regularly scheduled cruises.

Island Explorer

There is no question that it is great to bask in the lap of luxury between dives. And the ship is quite well equipped from a diver's point of view. Zodiacs zip divers from the mother ship to the dive sites, which are always nearby. The *Island Explorer* has good compressors, plenty of tanks and weight belts, and some spare BCs. The suiting up area is large, and includes a big freshwater barrel for cameras and other sensitive gear, and a place for a quick post-dive shower.

The dive coordinator and crew are most helpful with dive preparations and exits. The boatmen in the Zodiacs are alert, and ready to pick up divers within a minute of surfacing.

A few improvements could be made, however. (Note: We dove with P&O in 1989.) The water level platform, used for getting into and out of the Zodiacs, was right next to one of the exhaust ports. A dose of fumes is not an ideal way to start a dive. And, perhaps most importantly, the dive coordinator did not have a good command of English, and seldom announced a dive plan. It

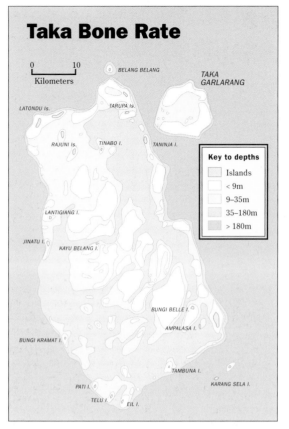

Taka Bone Rate

0   10
Kilometers

BELANG BELANG

TAKA GARLARANG

LATONDU Is.

TARUPA Is.

RAJUNI Is.

TINABO I.

TANINJA I.

Key to depths

	Islands
	< 9m
	9–35m
	35–180m
	> 180m

LANTIGIANG I.

JINATU I.

KAYU BELANG I.

BUNGI BELLE I.

AMPALASA I.

BUNGI KRAMAT I.

TAMBUNA I.

PATI I.

KARANG SELA I.

TELU I.

EIL I.

dives (2,240 sq. km.) are larger. The 21 small islands of Taka Bone Rate offer nesting areas for sea turtles, which thrive here on the huge meadows of seagrass.

The atoll rises sharply from the side of a submerged ridge, 2,000 meters down. Once a huge volcano, it has since subsided, leaving a wide ring of coral. The waters inside the atoll are magnificent turquoise, surrounded by the deepest blue imaginable. And they are rich: a survey found 158 species of coral growing here.

Our dive started at 2–3 meters over the reef top, and then we swam out over the outer wall of the atoll. Visibility was well over 30 meters, and the wall seemed to extend downward forever. The growth of coral and gorgonians was excellent, and schools of jacks cruised the wall. In the huge cuts and crevasses in the wall, we saw three giant groupers, Napoleon wrasse, turtles, lionfish and moray eels. World class diving.

Haiding Bay

Although our dive in Haiding Bay off northeast Flores was in shallow water, it had some of the richest coral growth I have ever seen, including soft corals, tube sponges and tunicates. Since we were in just 12–15 meters of water, really big fish were scarce, but smaller, colorful reef fish were present in abundance, including a beautiful dwarf angelfish and a twinspot lionfish.

Moyo Island

This large island, blocking the mouth of Saleh Bay north of Sumbawa Besar, is surrounded by a beautiful wall that starts at 12 meters and descends to infinity. The wall was cut through by some of the largest crevasses I have ever seen. We saw sharks, giant groupers, moray eels, stingrays, puffers, Moorish idols and large schools of foraging surgeonfish.

was the follow-me-if-you-want school of leadership. In his defense, he was very good underwater at finding and pointing out unusual animals.

The great advantage of a liveaboard is that it gives you access to isolated dive sites. Some of the places I dove off the *Island Explorer* can be reached by other means, and they have been described elsewhere in this book. Others, however, can at the time of this writing be reached no other way.

Taka Bone Rate

Spread over 2,220 square kilometers in the Flores Sea south of Sulawesi, Taka Bone Rate is the largest atoll in Indonesia, and the third-largest in the world. (See map above.) Only Kwajalein in the Marshall Islands (2,850 sq. km.) and Suvadiva in the Mal-

Nusa Tenggara Dive Practicalities

Most of Nusa Tenggara is not yet part of the standard Indonesian tourist circuit, although the places where organized diving is available are among the easiest in the region to reach. Also, if you schedule ahead of time, many dive operators will meet you at the airport.

Gili Islands

Lombok, Nusa Tenggara Barat (NTB); Telephone code for Mataram, Lombok is 0364

These islands, because they are so close to Bali, have become a very popular destination. The simplest way to get here is to take the ferry from Padangbai, Bali (3.5 hrs), which leaves at 9 am, 2 pm and 5 pm. The strait can be rough, and schedules change, so check. Fare: $2 economy, $3 VIP. The ferry reaches Lombok at Labuhan Lembar. From Lembar, minibuses head to any of a number of destinations, including Mataram (the island's capital and largest city) and Senggigi Beach.

You can also fly from Bali to Lombok's Selaparang airport. Five flights a day are scheduled ($25, 25 min).

The jump off point for the Gili Islands is Bangsal, north of Senggigi. You can take a public minibus to Pemenang ($1.10), and then hire a *cidomo*, a horse-drawn cart, for the short remaining trip to Bangsal harbor (15¢). Or you can just charter a minibus to take you directly to Bangsal (maybe $8–$10).

At the harbor, book your passage at the official ticket booth on one of the regular 20-seat boats to Gili Air (30¢), Gili Meno (40¢), or Gili Trawangan (60¢). These leave regularly in the early morning and late afternoon, and at other times when they fill up. You can also buy a one-way charter to Gilis Air (20 min, $6); Meno (30 min, $7); or Trawangan (45 min, $9).

Dive Operators

Albatross. Book through BIDY Tours, Jl. Ragigenap 17, Mataram, Lombok, Tel: 22127, Tel/fax: 21821, Telex: 35304 BDY MTR IA. Located in a two-story *lumbung* or traditional rice barn–shaped building within the Paradise bungalows *losmen* on Gili Trawangan. 11 bungalows; three communal bathrooms. Restaurant serves inexpensive sandwiches, rice and noodle dishes, fruit juices and cold beer. Foreign currency and travelers' checks changed for only about 1% less than in Bali or Mataram. Owned by Andy Chan. Rooms, $4.50S, $6D.

All-inclusive 3-day, 2-night dive package: $175 (extra $10/day for BC/regulator rental). Minimum 2 clients. Includes 5 boat dives, one night dive and unlimited beach dives. Airport pickup and drop-off. Accompanying non-divers, $75, including snorkeling. Extra days (2 dives) $60; add $10 for night dive. Non-divers, $25 extra per day. Simple accommodations in bungalow-style beachside cottages with enclosed facilities, plus three meals. Optional one-day land tour of traditional Lombok, $24/person for 2, $18/person for 3, $15 for 4–6 people. Extra $75, split among clients, for traditional dances and rattan stick and shield fighting.

Single day of diving from Senggigi or Mataram hotels: $55 (plus $10 for BC/regulator) for 2 boat dives, lunch and unlimited beach dives.

Single day of diving, for walk-ins on Gili Trawangan: $35 (plus $10 for BC/regulator) for 2 boat dives. lunch and unlimited beach dives. Less $10 for just 1 boat dive. Plus $25 for night dive. Add $5 for weekend introductory dive.

Baronang Divers. Pak Sjahrul Nasution, P.O. Box 24, Mataram, Lombok. This operation caters only to walk-in clients on Gili Air. For 2 boat dives (min. 2 clients) $48. Price drops to $43 for group of 3–6 clients. Take off 20% if you bring your BC/regulator. Beach night dive $28 with rental gear, $20 with your equipment.

Baruna. A branch of this large, Bali-based diving operator is located at the Senggigi Beach Hotel. Tel. 23430, ext. 8412.

For 2 boat dives in the Gilis, $65 (add $10 for BC/regulator). Minimum 2 clients. Single dive off Senggigi Beach (strictly for beginners), all equipment provided, $35. "Fun dive" for beginners off dive boat, $50. Introduction to diving (in pool, plus one open-water dive) $75.

Rinjani Divers. At Senggigi's Lombok Intan Laguna Hotel. Tel: 23659 or 21402, ext. 131; Fax: 23253. In-town office, Jl. Banteng 9, Mataram, Tel: 21402. Single day of diving off Gili Trawangan or Tanjung Bonita, $60. Includes tanks, weights and lunch. Add $3/day for BC. 2 dives, 2 client minimum. Same to Gili Petangan (a small island off the east coast of Lombok) $65. Diving in Senggigi area, $35/person, minimum of two. Pool training for beginners, $35; pool plus one open water dive, $60.

Climbing Mt. Rinjani

Wisma Triguna. Jl. Adi Sucipto 76, Ampenan, Tel: 21705. Pak Eddy has organized climbs for thousands of foreigners. His rate is $125/person for the 3-day, 2-night jaunt. (The price goes down as the number of people in the group increases, to a maximum of 5.) Book at the address above or through Nazaret Tours, Senggigi Beach.

Labuhanbajo

Flores, NTT

The easiest way to dive this relatively unexplored region is to join one of the occasional dive cruises out of Bali. Check with Wolfgang Bresigk of Baruna Water Sports, or P&O's *Spice*

Islander. Or charter your own dive boat in Bali from one of the operators. (See "Bali Scuba Tour Operators" page 125.) Otherwise, you have to make your own way to Labuhanbajo, and dive with the Bajo Beach Diving Club.

Theoretically, you can fly from Bali to Labuhanbajo, via Bima (eastern Sumbawa), twice a week, Friday and Sunday mornings at 7:15 am ($78). The airplane is a small, 20-passenger Twin Otter. Reserve early and reconfirm often. The landing field at Labuhanbajo is being extended so larger planes can land here, and this should improve the situation. Chartering a taxi from the airport (a couple of km out of town) should cost $3.

Bajo Beach Diving Club. At the Losmen Bajo Beach, on the main road along the coast near the post office. It is best to contact owner Pak Hendrik Chandra to set things up for you ahead of time. As there is no telephone yet, write: Pak Hendrik Chandra, Bajo Beach Diving Club, Labuhanbajo, Flores, NTT, Indonesia.

You can also just show up, but it might take a day or two to get things organized with one of the pearl diving boats. Once the Bajo Beach Dive Club gets a boat, compressor, tanks and weights, divers will have an easier time.

Bring your own equipment, and count on spending $65–$90 a day for room, board and two dives. The price difference reflects the type of room you get, the higher cost applying to rooms in the almost completed Peda Flower Beach Hotel.

Should you want to take a break from diving, Pak Hendrik has land-based tour packages. One includes a cave (Batu Cermin), a whip fight and an area where there is petrified wood. This tour runs $125/person for a party of two, $50/person for a party of six.

Komodo dragons

A ferry runs from Labuhanbajo to Komodo (and then to Sape, Sumbawa) on Tuesdays, Thursdays and Sundays. You can catch the return on Mondays, Wednesdays and Saturdays. Passage to Komodo costs $2. The ferry anchors off the beach at Komodo Village, and local boats will take you to the beach for a minimal fee.

You can charter a boat from Labuhanbajo as well. The 50 km crossing takes several hours, and depending on the boat and your skills at bargaining, costs $35–$75.

The park service maintains cottages at the Loh Liang ranger station, $3/person each night. Inexpensive meals and tea and coffee are available. Food is very basic, so bring fruit and a few canned goods.

You must hire a guide to walk around the island, and prices are reasonable, e.g. $1.50 per group to see the dragons being fed.

Note: At last notice, the lizards were being fed only on Sundays and Wednesdays.

Maumere
Flores, NTT

Maumere is the visitor's center of Flores, offering the best accommodations and infrastructure for tourists. Both of the dive clubs are close to each other, 12 km east of Maumere town and 10 km east of the airport. At the airport you can buy taxi coupons (approx. $4.50 to the resorts) while you wait for your luggage. The Sao Resort usually has transportation for guests with reservations.

Merpati schedules daily flights between Maumere and Bali ($97); Bima, Sumbawa ($52); Kupang ($33); and Ujung Pandang, Sulawesi ($60). There are connections to Surabaya and Jakarta.

Merpati. Jl. Don Tomas, Tel: 342.

Dive Operators

Flores Sao Resort (Sao Wisata). Maumere office at Jl. Don Tomas 18. Resort phone 342. For bookings and arrangements, contact their Jakarta office: Sao Wisata, Room 6B, 2nd Floor, Hotel Borobudur Inter-Continental, Jl. Lapangan Banteng Selatan, Jakarta 10710. Tel. (62-21) 370 333 or 380 5555, ext. 78222 or 78223. Fax: (62-21) 359741, Telex: 46139 BDOOFC IA.

This resort is a two-star hotel with a well-run dive operation. All inclusive (including accommodations) 4 night/3 day (6 dives) packages, $260. (For non-divers, $160.) Day diving for guests: $55 (2 dives), $35 (1 dive). For walk-ins: $65 (2 dives), $40 (1 dive). Night dive, $30 ($35 for non-guests). Complete equipment rental, $15/day.

NAUI Entry Scuba Experience course. This course runs a day and a half and includes instruction in theory, pool session, two boat dives, and all equipment. $100.

NAUI Openwater I course. Runs 4 days and includes theory, pool session and boat dives, training materials, and all equipment. Certification at end of course. $350.

Seaworld Club (Waiara Cottages). P.O. Box 3, Maumere, Flores, NTT, Tel: 570. 22 rooms and bungalows. Lunch ($4) and dinner ($5) available. $10–$20S, $15–$25D including breakfast.

All inclusive dive packages (accommodations, meals, boat, two tanks and weights) run $70/person for a minimum of 4 divers. Night dive $45, minimum of three clients. Regulator and BC, $17/day; basic snorkeling equipment, $3/day.

Seaworld's one dive boat was out of order when we checked in 1991, as it was in 1990, so we could not assess their operation.

Keli Mutu

Both dive clubs run tours to the colored lakes of Keli Mutu, which are several hours away just off the trans-Flores highway before Ende. One must leave very early in the morning—late at night, really—to get to the mountain at sunrise. Prices run $40–$60 per person.

Kupang

West Timor, NTT; Tel. code 391

Kupang is a large town, the capital of the Nusa Tenggara Timur province, and has four one-star hotels and a good range of more moderately priced accommodations. English is spoken at most places. Kupang's El Tari airport is 15 km east of downtown Kupang. A taxi from the airport costs $4, and try to get a taxi to yourself or you could end up running all over town while others are dropped off.

Kupang receives daily Merpati flights from Jakarta ($185), Bali ($96), Ujung Pandang ($79), and Maumere ($33) among other cities in the region. **Merpati.** Jl. Sudirman 21, Tel: 21121, 21961, and 22654.

Dive Operators

Kupang Klub. Contact Lance Marshall at the Karang Mas restaurant, Jl. Siliwangi 88, Tel: 22062.

Marshall pioneered diving in the area (he used to fill his tanks in Maumere and take a boat back!). He is a one-man show, a tough, colorful Aussie—just the person you want around if an emergency comes up. He prefers to take out experienced divers.

Marshall has been exploring the area for years and knows all the dive sites. He also knows Kupang history, and starts newcomers with a short boat tour of the seafront and then on to one of the *bagans*, net fishing platforms.

Kupang Klub's rates, based on a group of 4: Full-day (2 dives) tour, $72/person ($50/person if you have your own gear); half-day (1 dive) tours, $40/person; snorkeling, $30; fishing, $20. Children 50% of adult fares. For fewer than 4 in a group, add 50% to above prices. Full equipment rental, $23/day. Hotel transfers not included. **Pitoby Water Sports.** Jl. Sudirman 118, Kupang NTT, Tel. 21443 and 21444; Fax: 31044; Telex: 35461 PITOBY IA. Diving hotline, 24-hr, 32910 or 31634.

This operation is part of Pitoby Travel Agency, an efficient agency and the biggest in this part of Indonesia. Diving operations—"Dive Kupang"—are run by an Australian father and son team, divemaster Graeme Whitford and PADI-certified dive instructor Donovan Whitford. The Whitfords have not been around as long as Lance, but their boat is more comfortable than the Kupang Klub's and their rental gear is newer. They also offer more services for novice divers, and assemble and test the equipment for you and carefully work through dive plans.

Dive Kupang offers three basic all-inclusive packages: diving off Kupang, diving off Roti and a combination of the two. These range from 4 days/3 nights to 11 days/10 nights. Here's a sample:

Kupang Bay. 4 days/3 nights (5 dives), $245; 6 days/5 nights (9 dives) $345; 8 days/7 nights (11 dives) $595. Roti. 5 days/4 nights (3 dives) $375; 7 days/6 nights (7 dives) $575.

Kupang and Roti. 8 days/7 nights (10 dives) $645; 11 days/10 nights (15 dives), $895.

All packages include one night dive. 10% discount for divers who bring their own gear. Accommodations and full board (at the Pitoby Lodge, see below) included, only extra is booze. These prices are based on a group of four divers (add 50% for less), but if you arrive only with your dive buddy Dive Kupang will likely (but it's not guaranteed) find another couple to join you. All tours include a "cultural show," two if you go to Roti. The agency takes care of everything, beginning with picking you up at the airport and ending with seeing you on your plane back home.

Client-booked or "walk-ins" can have two day dives, including transfers and lunch, for $75 ($50 w/ own gear); single day dive, $45 ($30 w/ own gear). Group discounts possible. There are also non-diving tours for snorkelers. **Pitoby Lodge.** Jl. Kosasih 13, Tel: 32910. 12 twin rooms and 3 shared bathrooms. One "suite" has its own bathroom. Downtown location, clean and pleasant atmosphere, lots of nice woven cloths and terrible wood carvings for sale. A good restaurant features seafood, Italian and Indonesian food. Lobster ($12.50/kilo) is available with notice. The western food is excellent, the Indonesian dishes, so-so. Room rates (if you're not on a package): $7.50–$15.00S, $10–$20D.

P&O Spice Island Cruises

This outfit runs a 42-passenger luxury ship, the *Spice Islander,* through the islands of Nusa Tenggara. (The company also runs the *Island Explorer* around Krakatau and West Java). P&O Spice Island Cruises P.O. Box 98/MT, Jakarta Pusat—Indonesia Tel: (62-21) 593401, 593402 Fax: (62-21) 593403 P&O can also be contacted through most travel agents. *United States representative:* Abercrombie and Kent International Inc. 1420 Kensington Road Oak Brook, Illinois 60521-2106 Tel: (708) 954-2944, (800) 323-7308 Fax: (708) 954-3324 The *Spice Islander*'s week-long route "A" begins in Bali, and calls at Lombok, Sumbawa, Komodo, Flores, Lembata and Timor. Route "B," also a week, goes from Timor to Savu, Sumba, Komodo, Satonda, Lombok and Bali. "A" and "B" is the full two-week round-trip.

Sample fares: 7 days/6 nights, $1,989 based on double occupancy; 14 days/13 nights, $3,655. Add 30% for suite. Add 50% for single occupancy. Add 40% for a third person in cabin. All inclusive except bar, laundry and tips for the crew.

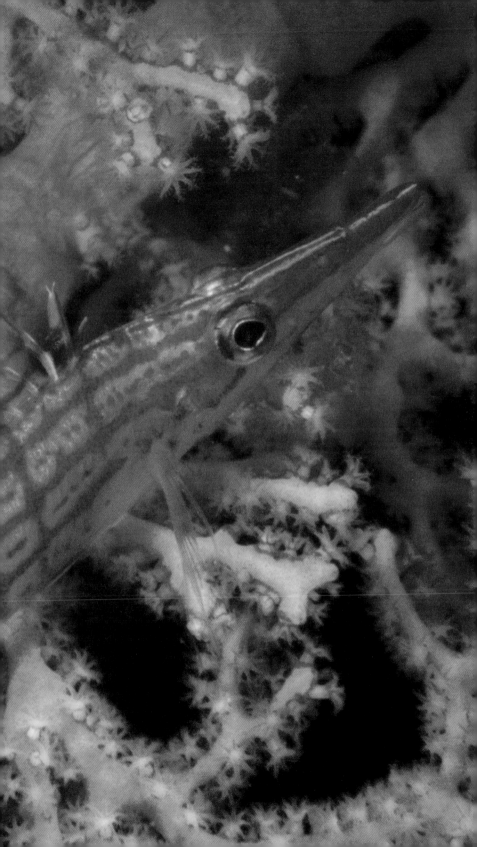

Introducing Sulawesi

The contorted island of Sulawesi lies in the middle of the archipelago's sweep, north of Flores and reaching almost to the Philippines. Formerly—and on some maps, still—called the Celebes, the island offers some of the most stunning scenery in all of Indonesia, both above and below water.

The people of Sulawesi are culturally diverse, ranging from the cosmopolitan Bugis of Ujung Pandang, Sulawesi's largest city and the hub of eastern Indonesia, to the traditional Toraja of the highlands.

Shaped by Fire

The island took its unusual shape about 3 million years ago, when a chunk of land that had split from western New Guinea and drifted eastward (Sulawesi's eastern and southeastern peninsulas) collided with a volcanic island that had formed along a fault line east of Borneo (the south and the northern peninsula). The force of collision spun the two islands and left them joined in the middle.

The great majority of Sulawesi's 227,000 square kilometers is higher than 500 meters. The province has 17 active volcanoes, concentrated in North Sulawesi and in the Sangihe Islands. In the past few years, Lokon near Manado and Siau Island's Karangetang have been the most active.

Exquisite Reefs

Because of its unique shape, no part of the island is more than 100 kilometers from the sea, and Sulawesi has a whopping 6,000 kilometers of coastline. More than 110 small offshore islands are also part of the archipelago.

Most of this coastline is ringed with reef.

Although too disturbed to be of interest to divers, the 16,000 square kilometers of reef off Ujung Pandang supports one of the most productive fisheries in the world. In the north, the near pristine reefs off Manado are famous for their sheer walls and abundance of fish life.

Perhaps the best diving in the island remains inaccessible: the Togian Islands in Tomini Bay, famous for displaying in a very small area every known type of coral reef; Taka Bone Rate, southeast of Selayar Island in the south and the third-largest atoll in the world (see map page 178); and the Tukang Besi Islands off southeast Sulawesi, rumored to have moved Jacques Cousteau—who recently passed through Indonesia—to declare them the finest diving site in the world.

Because it straddles the Asian and Australian biogeographical zones and offers a wide range of habitats, Sulawesi has a great number of endemic species. Discounting bats, fully 98 percent of the island's mammals are found nowhere else. Among the most unusual of these are the babirusa—literally "pig deer"—a wild pig with huge, curving tusks; the rare anoa, a water buffalo the size of a dog; and the tiny tarsier, a big-eyed primate little larger than an insect. Some 34 percent of the non-migratory birds—88 species—are endemic.

Famous Entrepôt

Although the Bugis and Gowanese developed their own writing systems, adapted from an Indian alphabet, the early texts

Overleaf: *A long-nosed hawkfish,* Oxycirrhites typus, *in a gorgonian. This little predator keeps a lookout from its perch, and then swoops down and 'hawks' small crustaceans. 34 meters, Manado, Sulawesi. Photograph by Mike Severns.*

Opposite: *A colubrine sea snake,* Laticauda colubrina, *pokes its head (lower right) behind a sponge in search of food. Too slow to snatch a swimming fish, these snakes must corner their prey in tight crevices or feed on spawn. This species, with leather much smoother than its terrestrial brethren, is heavily collected in the Philippines, where it supports a very large snakeskin industry. Though not in the least aggressive, the colubrine sea snake is quite venomous and should not be harassed. 25 meters, Manado, Sulawesi. Photograph by Mike Severns.*

are concerned chiefly with myths of origin and royal genealogies. Until the Europeans arrived in the 16th century, little is known of the island's history.

The Portuguese pioneered the European trade route to the spice islands, and Makassar (now Ujung Pandang) was a regular stop on the route from Malacca to the nutmeg and clove islands of Maluku. At the time, the Gowanese and Bugis sailed the monsoon winds as far as Australia in search of trepang and other sea products.

The king of Gowa petitioned the Portuguese for missionaries, but these never arrived. The proselytizers of Islam were more responsive, however, and by the early 17th century South Sulawesi—both the Gowanese and the Bugis—had become a Muslim stronghold.

The Dutch arrived at this time, and quickly muscled the Portuguese out of the spice trade. Although Holland used force of arms to insist that sellers accept low prices, spices continued to "escape" to Makassar, where sellers got a fair return. To save their monopoly, the Dutch fought the famous "Battle of Makassar," defeating Gowa by allying with the Bugis.

The People of Sulawesi

Among the 11.5 million people living on Sulawesi are dozens of ethnic groups, of which the Bugis, Makassarese and Mandarese of the south, the Minahasans of the north, and the Torajans of the interior are the best known.

The Muslim Bugis have always been famous seafarers, and their distinctive wooden *pinisi*—schooner-shaped boats now fitted with diesel engines—still serve as the vehicles for much of the inter-island cargo carried around the archipelago.

The people of Manado and the Minahasa region in the north are predominantly Christians, having converted early during the period of Dutch colonial control. Good relations with the Dutch led to the region being blessed with schools and other perquisites of colonial favor.

The most famous of Sulawesi's ethnic groups among visitors are the Toraja, who live in the beautiful highlands north of Makale. The Torajans' tall, swaybacked *tongkonan,* or origin houses, graced by huge stacks of water buffalo horns, are the archipelago's most distinctive architectural feature.

Even Torajans working in the big cities of western Indonesia return home for an important funeral of one of their kinsmen. At these grand events, in which the entire community participates, hundreds of very valuable water buffalo are slaughtered.

Volcanoes, Old Graves and Spicy Chili Rat

Although the underwater charms of Manado Bay will probably not wear off, after a week or so of steady diving you might be ready for a land tour. There are lots of things to see in the hill country of Minahasa, as the area of north Sulawesi around Manado is known, while you rid your tissues of residual nitrogen.

A History of Change

The Minahasans, a loose association of groups speaking the same language and practicing the same traditional culture, were largely successful at resisting domination by the Portuguese, Spanish and the Sultan of Ternate. The foreign powers established outposts, but exercised no control beyond their fortified walls. Nor could the Iberians establish Catholicism, or the Ternateans establish Islam.

The Dutch were more persistent. They built Fort Amsterdam in 1673 at what is now Manado, supplanting the Spanish. It was only in the early 19th century, however, after the colonial soldiers began winning tough battles in the Tondano area, that the Dutch came to control the north.

The transformation of Minahasan society was then swift. Mass conversion to the Dutch Reformed Church took place, and the colonial government introduced forced coffee cultivation (later brought to Java) and a system of schools. By the turn of the century, educational opportunity in Minahasa was the best in the archipelago, with a school for every 1,000 people.

Minahasans adopted western culture with a vengeance, and were represented in the colonial administration and army in numbers vastly out of proportion to the population of the region. Minahasa became known as Holland's 12th province. Many immigrated to Holland after independence, but those who remained continue to integrate western ways into their culture.

Thanks to the colonial schools, and particularly to the rich volcanic soil of the region, Minahasa's statistics for education and economy rank among the highest in Indonesia. The efficient farming of copra, vegetables, rice and, especially, cloves have brought a high standard of living to the region.

Manado Town

The dive clubs are outside of town, but sooner or later you will have to thread your way through the city of Manado. This city of 250,000 people bustles, but has few attractions for visitors. Aside from the gleaming new banks and a few stores, the downtown looks rather drab. The number of satellite dishes on the roofs attests to the residents' wealth, however.

Most of the business, like elsewhere in Indonesia, is concentrated in the hands of ethnic Chinese. The Ban Hing Kiong *klenteng,* or temple, the oldest in eastern Indonesia, is worth a short visit: here is a colorful effervescence of gods and dragons, and two old Dutch cannon, which point to the rusting roofs lining Jalan Panjaitan.

Manado's Chinese community is wealthy and integrated enough to be the only one in Indonesia allowed to hold the annual Cap Go Mei celebration,

Above: *This larger than life sculpture, rendered in a heroic style, stands in front of the Nusantara Diving Centre (NDC) in Molas Beach north of Manado. The center, founded by Loky Herlambang in 1975, pioneered diving on the reefs of the Bunaken Island group.*

with its dragon dancing in the streets. Cap Go Mei takes place two weeks after the beginning of Chinese New Year, around mid-February. It marks the end of the new year celebrations.

For sight-seeing, Manado's ocean drive is nice, especially at sunset. If you are up early, visit the dawn fish auction near the harbor, and walk through the adjacent Pasar Bersehati market. This is the town's largest, and features a chaos of people and "distinctive" smells. Dog meat—referred to by a euphemism, "RW" (pronounced "airway")—is a great delicacy in the distinctive, very spicy Minahasan cuisine. The animals are sold in a special part of the market.

Tomohon Village

More fun than Manado is a trip to the scenic hills east of town. We suggest the mountain town of Tomohon, and then—if you are up for a bit of a workout—a climb up Mahawu volcano.

If you get an early start, stop near Tinoor, about halfway to Tomohon, for a coffee with a good view of Manado and the

harbor. On the way back, stop for lunch: specialties are rat, covered in a thick paste of very hot chilies, fruit bat wings in coconut gravy, and "RW," chopped dog cooked in a dry, *rendang* style. Believe it or not it is all quite good, but blistering hot.

On the approach to Tomohon, you can see 1,579-meter Mt. Lokon, which held a crater lake until a recent small eruption boiled it off. The best view of Mt. Lokon is from Bukit Inspirasi, a hill at the edge of town where the Christian University is located.

Tomohon is a busy and attractive little mountain town. Nurseries here supply flowers to Manado, and the plots of croton are particularly colorful. The pleasant little wooden houses here are crowned with rusting steel roofs, rather charmless to foreign eyes. The local market features dogs, rats and bats for the pot, on Tuesdays, Thursdays and Saturdays.

Everywhere in the highlands you will see cloves drying on burlap bags by the side of the road. Freshly picked, they are light green, and when they reach a deep red color they are ready

Below: *The smoking crater lake at Mt. Mahawu, due south of Manado. The lip of the crater reaches 1,311 meters. The climb makes a nice day trip if you want to take a break from diving.*

for sale, the current rate being $2 a kilo. The tall, well-shaped trees are visible everywhere. Cloves, along with copra, form the basis of the region's wealth. Although Indonesia is one of the world's largest clove producers, thanks to the nation's appetite for *kretek,* clove cigarets, it is also the world's largest clove importer.

Mahawu Volcano

About 5 kilometers out of Tomohon, on the steep and narrow (but well-paved) road to Rurukan, a side path leads to the crater rim of Mt. Mahawu, a 1,311-meter-high volcano. The path is a good one (although you need a guide) and it takes 30 minutes to an hour to reach the top, depending on your physical shape and how many rest and photo stops you make on the way up.

The path first cuts through vegetable gardens, and then forest. You get a view of the volcano only once on the way up. On the way, you might meet men out hunting with their dogs, or men leading a bullock cart loaded with firewood. The cart trail stops about three-quarters of the way to the top. The last bit is steep, and you have to push through thick pampas grass. When you smell sulphur, you know you are almost there.

The view from the top can be stunning. The crater is filled with a steaming emerald lake, its shoreline stained yellow by sulfur-encrusted fumaroles belching fumes. The steep-sided caldera is 400 meters wide at the top, and the oval lake below measures 150 meters by 70 meters. It would be possible to climb down, if one was skilled and careful.

Looking westward, the of the lake, with even taller Mt. Lokon in the background spewing smoke, makes a spectacular sight. If the weather is right, Manado and Bitung are both visible, and you can see two seas. Unfortunately, even if it is clear enough to see, it is usually too hazy for photography.

Temboan, just beyond Rurukan and part of the same village complex, offers a fine panorama of the Manado area. Albert Bickmore, an American who traveled the East Indies in the 1870s, called the view here the "finest in the archipelago." In fact, there are better in Indonesia, but the trip here is still worth it. From Temboan you can see majestic, 1,995-meter Mt. Klabat, the Bitung area and Lake Tondano.

Lake and Gravestones

Another recommended trip is to continue past Tomohon to Tondano, drive around the west shore of this large lake, and then continue on to see the famous decorated tombstones at Sawangan. Tondano lake is 27 kilometers long, and 3–10 kilometers wide. Offshore, fishermen live on stilted villages, and fish from their small canoes. The surface of the lake is more than 600 meters above sea level.

A good road leads from Tondano down to the plains to Sawangan village. The very special cemetery has 144 ancient tombs, dating from the 14th or 15th century to the 19th. The rectangular, upright stone sarcophagi, called *waruga,* are topped by steep two-sided roofs which often bear carvings relating to some characteristic of the deceased. All the area's tombs were gathered here in 1977.

Grave robbers mostly cleaned out the fine jewelry and valuables the graves contained, but some have been recovered and are in a small museum at the site.

Sawangan's *waruga* were already famous when Bickmore visited. A missionary told him the graves had originally been decorated with "obscene ornaments," but a puritanical Dutch official ordered them broken off. There are still plenty of interesting carvings left, however.

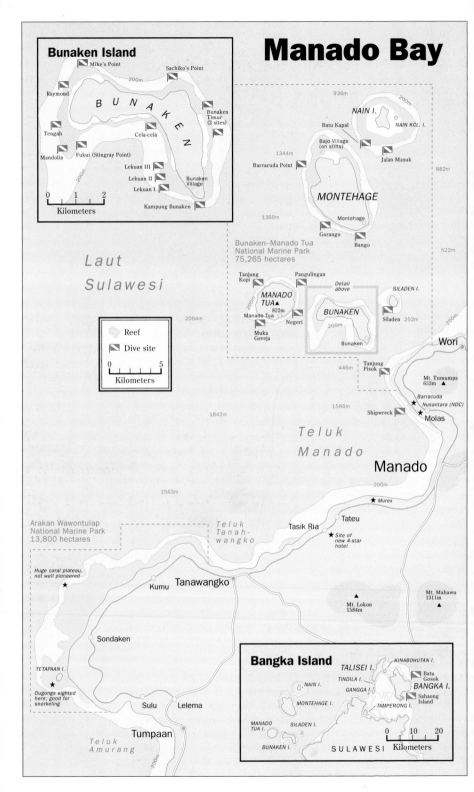

Manado Bay

Bunaken Island

- Mike's Point
- Sachiko's Point
- Raymond
- B U N A K E N
- 200m
- Tengah
- Cela-cela
- Mandolin
- Fukui (Stingray Point)
- Bunaken Timur (2 sites)
- Lekuan III
- Lekuan II
- Lekuan I
- Bunaken Village
- Kampung Bunaken
- 200m

0 1 2
Kilometers

Laut Sulawesi

936m

NAIN I.
200m
Batu Kapal
NAIN KCL. I.
Bajo Village (on stilts)
Jalan Masuk
882m
Barracuda Point
1344m

MONTEHAGE

1360m
Montehage
Gorango
Bango
522m

Bunaken–Manado Tua
National Marine Park
75,265 hectares

Tanjung Kopi
Pangulingan
Detail above
SILADEN I.
MANADO TUA ▲
822m
Manado Tua
BUNAKEN
Siladen
252m
Negeri
Muka Gereja
200m
200m
Bunaken

2064m

Reef
Dive site

0 5
Kilometers

1843m

446m
Tanjung Pisok
200m
Wori

1566m
Shipwreck
Mt. Tumumpa 653m ▲
★ Barracuda
Nusantara (NDC)
★ Molas

Teluk Manado

Manado

200m
★ Murex

1563m
Tateu
★ Site of new 4-star hotel
Tasik Ria

Teluk Tanah-wangko

Arakan Wawontulap
National Marine Park
13,800 hectares

Huge coral plateau, not well pioneered
★
Kumu
Tanawangko
Mt. Lokon 1584m ▲
Mt. Mahawu 1311m ▲

Sondaken

TETAPAAN I.
★
Dugongs sighted here; good for snorkeling
Sulu
Lelema

Tumpaan

Teluk Amurang
200m

Bangka Island

TALISEI I.
KINABOHUTAN I.
Batu Gosok
BANGKA I.
NAIN I.
TINDILA I.
GANGGA I.
Sahaong Island
MONTEHAGE I.
TAMPERONG I.
MANADO TUA I.
SILADEN I.
BUNAKEN I.
SULAWESI

0 10 20
Kilometers

World-Class Walls and Outstanding Fish Life

Divers, from neophytes to those who have dived all the world-famous spots, have nothing but praise for the reefs surrounding the small islands in Manado Bay. These are very steep, pristine coral walls, covered with a particularly incredible amount and variety of soft coral. Visibility here is a bit less than the tropical ideal, usually 12–25 meters, but this is due to plankton, which sustains the area's rich fish and invertebrate life.

The reefs here are basically untouched. Little damage from fish bombing is visible, in part because the reefs are steep, and drop off so near the shore. Nor have there been enough divers here to tear up the sites. In 1989, thanks to the efforts of Loky Herlambang, founder of Nusantara Diving Club and the pioneering dive operator here, 75,265 hectares of underwater area around Bunaken, Manado Tua, Siladen, Montehage and Nain islands became a national marine reserve: Taman Nasional Laut Bunaken–Manado Tua.

North Sulawesi and the islands in the Bunaken group face the Sulawesi Sea, which reaches more than 6 kilometers. Even on the short boat rides to the dive sites, one passes over more than a kilometer of water covering a trench that separates the islands from the mainland. Nutrient-rich water from these depths sweeps across the islands' reefs.

The variety of marine life here is excellent; the surfaces of the walls are crowded with hard and soft corals, whip corals, sponges, and clinging filter-feeders like crinoids and basket stars. Huge schools of pyramid butterflyfish (*Hemitaurichthys polylepsis*) and black triggerfish (*Odonus niger*), and clouds of anthias swarm around the reef edge and the upper part of the wall. Sharks, schools of barracuda, rays, moray eels and sea snakes—particularly the black-and-grey–banded colubrine sea snake (*Laticauda colubrina*)—are relatively common here.

Beginners like the ease of the conditions. There is usually very little current, and the boats anchor right on the edge of the

AT A GLANCE
Manado

Reef type:	Steep coral walls
Access:	45 min to 1.5 hr by boat
Visibility:	Fair to very good; 12–25 meters
Current:	Usually gentle; at some sites to 2 knots or more
Coral:	Excellent condition and variety, particularly soft corals
Fish:	Good numbers and excellent variety
Highlights:	Pristine walls; sheer number of species; interesting wreck

walls. Even experts appreciate the operators' skilled handling of their gear, and the fact that groups are kept small: four to seven people.

The Bunaken–Manado Tua reserve features some dozen-and-a-half dive sites. Most are concentrated off the south and west coasts of Bunaken, a low, crescent-shaped coral island completely surrounded by a steep fringing reef. Adjacent

Manado Tua—"Old Manado"—is a volcano, a well-shaped cone reaching 822 meters. Three other islands complete the group: tiny Siladen, a stone's throw northeast of Bunaken; Montehage, the largest of the islands, north of Bunaken; and Nain, a tiny island north of Montehage surrounded by a large barrier reef. (See map page 190.)

Bunaken Island

The reef is good all the way around Bunaken, and the 6-kilometer-long island features no less than 13 dive sites. Bunaken is the centerpiece of the reserve, and with careful observation, on this one island you could probably see the majority of coral reef fishes found in Indonesia.

All the sites are similar in that they feature steep walls of coral, pocked with small caves, and buzzing with small and medium-sized reef fish. Good coral growth usually extends down to 40–50 meters, and in the deeper parts of the wall one can see sharks, large rays and Napoleon wrasse. The current is usually gentle, perfect for a slow drift along the face of the wall, although it can occasionally come up in the afternoon.

Lekuan I, II and III. The most frequented site on Bunaken is a three-pronged coral wall in front of Lekuan Beach. Here your chances are very good of seeing Napoleon wrasse, turtles, bumphead parrotfish, scorpionfish and lionfish, and on the reef edge, swarms of anthias.

The Lekuan sites offer little current and clear water, and are perfect for beginners. They are popular for night dives as well.

Here—and everywhere else in the Manado Bay area—watch out for the stinging hydroid *Aglaophenia*. This "sea nettle" looks like a pinkish or brownish fern, and when brushed by unprotected skin causes a burning sensation.

Kampung Bunaken. This site, in front of Kampung ("Village") Bunaken on the island's southeastern tip, offers much the same underwater scenery as the Lekuan sites. However, the shallow reef flat here has suffered the most damage of any around the island, thanks to its proximity to the village.

Bunaken Timur. The two sites called "East Bunaken," barely separated from each other, feature a more sloping profile than the sites on the south and west of the island. Here we discovered turtles, Napoleon wrasse, and some sleeping reef whitetip sharks.

Sachiko's Point. Named after a Japanese tour leader, this steep wall is prowled by big fish, including large tuna, and turtles. The soft coral growth here is particularly good, and there are nice caves around 30 meters. The current is often quite strong at Sachiko's Point.

Mike's Point. Named for photographer Mike Severns (whose work appears in these pages), the profile here features wall and a pinnacle. The coral growth—including large, showy gorgonians—is very good. This site is particularly rewarding at depths of 30 meters or more. The point is sometimes swept by strong currents, and one can occasionally see sharks, and large schools of jacks. Pelagic visitors such as yellowtail tuna also call on Mike's Point.

Raymond. This is a wall, with good hard and soft coral growth and some nice whip corals. Fish life is good, including Napoleon wrasse. Colubrine sea snakes are particularly common here, both on the reef flats and in the reef itself. *Laticauda colubrina* is sometimes called the amphibious sea snake, and it spends more time ashore than most of its brethren. Although not aggressive, the snakes are poisonous and should not be

harassed, although the guides and crew members often round one or two up for photographs. Strong "gusts" of current can sometimes be felt here, both horizontal and vertical. Don't panic, just hang onto the coral rock if necessary until it passes.

Tengah. This site, which means "middle" or "midway," is about in the middle of Bunaken's western reef face. This spot and nearby Mandolin are known for large schools of yellowtail fusiliers. One can also see an occasional turtle or shark here.

Mandolin. Just south of Tengah, this site also offers schooling fusiliers, and good coral growth. The wall here is best at depths of 30–35 meters.

Fukui Point. This site, also called Stingray Point, has a stepped profile: the reef top is at 2–4 meters, and then slopes down with several short, but steep, drops. It is known for its rays, of course, as well as turtles, barracuda and a couple of good-sized *Tridacna* clams.

Cela-Cela. This site, in the crook of the reef along the south face, offers many of the same charms as the popular Lekuan sites. Good coral growth and fish, and mild currents.

Siladen. There is one regular site off the small island of Siladen, just 2 kilometers northeast of Bunaken. The wall is steep down to about 35 meters, and coral growth—particularly soft corals—is good. Siladen is a good place to see big pelagic fish, and the largest stingrays in the reserve.

Manado Tua

"Old Manado" is a dormant volcano jutting up just west of Bunaken. The two best sites are wall dives, on the west coast.

Muka Gereja. This site, in front of the church, is a steep wall with vertical canyons cut into it. Coral growth is good, and there is a nice cave at 20 meters. Sharks, barracuda and Napoleon wrasse are common.

Tanjung Kopi. "Coffee Cape" is also a wall, and offers sharks—usually reef whitetips, but with an occasional hammerhead—and barracuda. The cape is often swept by strong currents.

Negeri. A decent wall, with

Above: *A school of blackfin barracuda,* Sphyraena genie. *Groups of these swift predators can be seen at several locations around the Bunaken group.*

caves and good soft corals.

Pangulingan. This site, on the northeast of the island, has a sloping profile. There are nice shelf corals here, but the current can be very strong and there are few fish. It is best at 35 meters.

Montehage and Nain

Montehage is a large, flat island north of Bunaken. A community of Bajo fishermen has built a village on stilts in the shallow estuarial back reef area north of the island. The dive sites are off the west and south, which is fringed with a wide, shallow reef flat, much of it exposed at low tide.

Bango. The profile here is slope, then wall. Soft coral growth is good, and there are some caves. Scorpionfish are easy to find here, and Napoleon wrasse and sharks are common.

Gorango. The name of this site means "shark" in the local dialect, and these can usually be seen here. The reef profile is a steep wall to about 40 meters.

Barracuda Point. This is a steep slope from 5 meters to about 20 meters, then a sheer wall to more than 30 meters. Schools of barracuda can be seen here, as well as sharks—at a shallower depth than at most sites—Napoleon wrasse, and bumphead parrotfish. Occasionally, huge tuna appear here.

Nain is a tiny island, but is surrounded by a wide lagoon filled with patches of reef, and a barrier reef. The people living on the island have cut a path through the reef just wide enough for their canoes. The island features two dive sites, both on the outer edge of the barrier reef. We didn't dive Jalan Masuk ("Enter"), but were told the scenery was the same as Batu Kapal, which we dove twice.

Batu Kapal. This site, literally "Stone Boat," is a slope down to 42 meters to a coral outcrop shaped like a boat (hence the name). A narrow canyon begins

here that plunges way, way down. A couple of European dive instructors in our group went down to 90 meters (on a single tank) into the canyon to look at some big jacks under an overhang. A light and a depth gauge exploded. (This is not recommended for beginners. These two were used to diving in the Mediterranean, where dives to 60 meters are common.)

There is some bomb damage on the reef flat, but the rest of the coral is pristine. We saw sharks, big tuna and Napoleon wrasse. We also saw large groups of parrotfish, and at the reef top one of the guides found a couple of the strange crocodile fish (*Cymbacephalus beauforti*).

Tanjung Pisok

The dive at Cape Pisok is just off the mainland, some 15 minutes motoring from Molas Beach. The profile begins with a gentle slope, and then becomes a wall. Tanjung Pisok is one of the best places to see blue ribbon eels (*Rhinomuraena quaesita*), slender and gaudy relatives of the morays. The animals are quite shy, and guides and a great deal of tact are required to see them. One can also see blue ribbon eels in relatively shallow depths at some of the Bunaken sites. There are barracuda at Pisok, including an occasional big one, and—particularly in the afternoon—squid and sharks.

The Manado Wreck

A steel-hulled Dutch merchant ship lies in the mud just 5 minutes from Molas beach, and makes a fine break from wall diving. It might take the crew a few minutes to find it, as there is no buoy—if the local fishermen knew its exact location, they would soon catch all its fish.

Loky Herlambang of NDC found the wreck in 1980 while diving for trepang to try to make ends meet at his fledgling diving

Opposite: A pair of candy-striped cleaner shrimp, Lysmata amboinensis, *have set up a cleaning station on a* Porites sp. *coral head. The presence of long, white antennae seems to be almost universal among cleaner shrimps.*

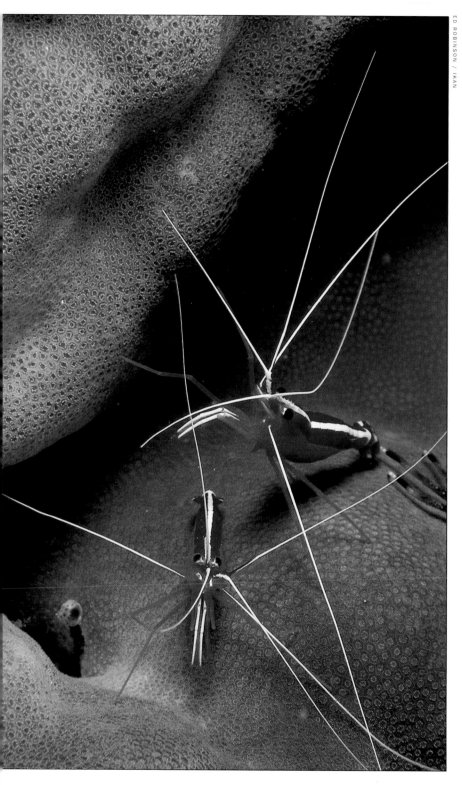

club. The harbormaster's office has no records of the ship. It is assumed to be Dutch, because of a few porcelain plates found on board. She probably sank during World War II, as when Loky first found it there was a machine gun and belts of ammunition on the foredeck. (Long gone now.)

Once the wreck is found, the crew drops anchor and you follow the line down, as visibility is usually lousy here. The wreck

narrow passage, you must remove your BC and tank. The engines and pistons are in good shape, as is one of the two electrical gauges. Move very slowly: perhaps a half-meter of fine sand and mud fill the compartment. A few careless strokes of your fins and you won't be able to see your hand in front of your face.

Because of the depth and the generally murky water (8–10 meters at best), there is little hard coral growth here. But there are plenty of giant black coral bushes, and some gorgonians and feather stars. Fish are not normally abundant. We saw a reef whitetip shark, a bright yellow trumpetfish, a large puffer, angelfish, some butterflyfish, Moorish idols, and small schools of sweetlips and snappers.

Our favorites were a beautiful and shy juvenile pinnate batfish (*Platax pinnatus*), and an adult roundfaced batfish (*P. tiera*) that seemed to be living in the wheelhouse. If you ask your guides ahead of time, they might find and point out to you two unusual species in the wreck: banded pipefish (*Doryrhamphus dactyliophorus*) and the longsnout flathead (*Platycephalus chiltonae*).

As this is a fairly deep dive, be aware of your depth times or check your computer, and keep a close watch on your air supply to allow for a decompression stop. Usually the crew will hang a spare tank and regulator at 5 meters, but this is really a precaution, and you shouldn't count on it. If you want to have a look inside the ship, we suggest you make two dives: one to get acquainted with the wreck, and one to explore inside.

Nusantara Diving Club

North Sulawesi's reefs are becoming internationally famous, and credit can only go to one man: Loky Herlambang. Loky was studying biology at Bandung, Java when he read Jules

Below: *Sea pens. Rooted in the substrate, these animals strain the water for plankton.*

Above: *Spiral whip coral,* Cirripathes *sp. Manado.*

lies on a sandy slope, at 25–40 meters. The twin screws of the 60-meter ship are still intact.

The hull is largely undamaged, but you can enter the wreck through several openings on the deck. Bring good underwater lights! Most of the cargo space is easily accessible, but the engine room is tricky. Following the ladder (towards the stern) down the first couple of meters is easy, but to get through the

Verne's *20,000 Leagues Under the Sea*. Thus began his fascination with the underwater world. After being certified as a diver, he looked all over Indonesia for a good dive site to develop. He finally picked Manado.

He formed the Nusantara Diving Club (NDC) in 1975 at age 36, and in 1977 his choice was confirmed by a visit from John E. (Jack) Randall, Curator of Ichthyology at the Bernice P. Bishop Museum in Hawaii. Randall encouraged Loky's efforts.

Loky started a program of conservation among the local fishermen. In 1982, the local government declared the Bunaken–Manado Tua area a protected zone (as well as the Arakan–Wawontulap area southwest of Manado), and the federal government made them both marine parks in 1989. In recognition of his conservation efforts, President Soeharto awarded Loky the prestigious Kalpataru Environmental Award in 1985.

But in our opinion Loky's greatest accomplishment has been his program of involving local Manado youth in NDC. He provides them with a job, pays for their education, and trains them to dive and be guides.

He now has 25 guides, each with thousands of dives, three Scuba Schools International (SSI) certified instructors, and drivers and other land-support personnel. All these are local people who he has taught to operate a dive resort. He has helped them build their homes, celebrated their marriages, and in general shared their joys and pains. Those who work long enough receive shares in NDC.

As you might expect, service at NDC is friendly and efficient—from pickup to drop off at the airport. The club is at Molas Beach, north of Manado and about 30 minutes from the airport. The club doesn't always have enough BCs and regulators, so it is best to bring your own equipment, although more rental gear is in the pipeline.

Diving with NDC

Divers are grouped according to ability and/or affinity, and dive sites are selected the night before. The first few dives are in little or no current, off Bunaken's walls. After the morning dive, everyone breaks for lunch, car-

ried along from NDC, on the beach. After a hour's siesta, you head for the day's second dive.

Departures are around 9 a.m. You bring your gear to the staging patio next to the open dining room—but usually before you get there someone will grab your dive bag and carry it for you. If you brought a camera, ask to have a tub of fresh water on the boat for soaking after dives. At

Above: *A half-grown pinnate batfish,* Platax pinnatus, *in the wreck just off Molas Beach. The ship, which appears to have sunk during World War II, lies on a soft bottom, 25–40 meters underwater.*

low tide, the boats anchor some 100 meters offshore. You have to walk through muck to get there, so wear dive boots or go barefoot—watch the mangrove roots and bits of coral, however.

NDC operates 11 boats, usually running two 40hp kerosene outboards. The 7-meter boats are quite comfortable, with enough space for six divers and their gear. An awning provides some protection against the sun, but there is enough space on the foredeck for several people to turn lobster red.

Rides last 45 minutes to an hour-and-a-half. The only kerosene available is of low quality, so it is not unusual for a motor to die once or twice on the way to the site. It's soon repaired, primed and jerked back to life. Loky was going to switch to gasoline engines, but in deference to the crew's constant smoking, decided against it.

At the dive site, an oval concrete anchor (to minimize damage to the coral) is dropped on the reef top. While you suit up, crewmembers assemble your tanks and turn on the air. There's

not much of a dive plan as the guides are shy about using English. In general, you go with the current, if there is any.

You can either follow one of the two guides—their outfits do not include redundant second stages, but this will be remedied in the future—or go off with your buddy. The guides are excellent at pointing out big fish or any unusual marine life.

Night dives are well-organized and carried out efficiently. Just remind the crew to bring a pressure lamp, as this very handy item for the boat was forgotten on one of my night dives. Following the afternoon dive, you have coffee, fried bananas and a rest stop on Bunaken. Shortly before dark you get on board, and the boat anchors before darkness falls, giving you time to organize odds of gear.

The boat is right there when you come up at the end of the dive. Hot supper, kept for you, awaits when you get back to NDC. We found the meals at NDC invariably good. Tops are the sashimi, and baked or grilled red snapper and tuna.

Below: *A red-spotted blenny,* Istiblennius chrysospilos, *pokes its clownish face out of a hidey hole. This fish is relatively common in quite shallow water, but only the sharp-eyed will see it, as the red-spotted blenny grows to just 10 centimeters and rarely shows more than its head.*

A Private Paradise on Tiny Mahoro Island

The night's problems are quickly forgotten during the dawn approach to Siau Island. Standing on the boat's roof, you take in the magnificent scenery, including Karangetang—"The Highest"—volcano, 1,827 meters and still smoking. The other passengers, seeing nothing extraordinary, stare only at you.

As the ferry enters the passage between Siau and Buhias islands, the pitch ceases, as the boat is now crossing what was once an enclosed lake, the carter of a huge, ancient volcano. Central soundings here are in the 500 meter range. The verdant slopes of Buhias glide by on the right, with Siau's six, ever higher peaks on the left, culminating with the northernmost Karangetang, furiously spewing out a stream of sulfurous gas.

By Ferry to Siau

Our party of four had borrowed tanks from Nusantara Diving Club in Manado, and headed north by ferry. Our destination: Mahoro, a tiny island southeast of Siau, rumored to be an earthly paradise of white sand and coral-filled water. (See map page 201.)

The boat trip was not pleasant: the cabins were hot, and the passageways on the boat were paved solid with belongings and sleeping bodies. Access to the toilets, far away, was impossible. Uninhibited men peed over the rail; others suffered their full bladders. As the boat tied up to the jetty and two gangplanks were lowered, bedlam broke out as porters try to come on board and everyone struggled to get off as fast as possible.

. We opted to wait out the rush hour, since our cabin was stuffed with dive gear and eight tanks of compressed air. But we did take turns guarding our gear to allow the others to use the toilet facilities in the "canteen," a little restaurant in the harbor area.

We met with the still sleepy harbormaster of Siau Ulu, and he produced an old Dutch marine map of the area, which we traced for reference. We were anxious to head out to Mahoro. Fortunately, the harbormaster had a small covered boat which he was willing to rent for $30/day, including wages for Albert and Damas, two tough, experienced longshoremen who were to serve as our crew.

It took a couple of hours to organize our little expedition. Albert went to buy provisions, rice, instant noodles, vegetables, fish, salt, sugar, coffee ($16 for 6 people for 3 days). Damas went to get fuel for the 25hp kerosene outboard, and to borrow a portable stove, and pots and plates from the harbormaster.

While the two men were busy with their chores, we relaxed in the canteen, drinking iced beer and cokes, and snacking on tidbits of dough stuffed with spicy meat. When everything was ready, including the transfer of gear from the large boat to the small craft, we hopped aboard and motored away.

On to Mahoro

After just 30 minutes from Siau Ulu, we rounded Bunaken Village, which sits under a 280-meter forested cliff at the northeast tip of Bunaken Island. As we rounded the point, we motored past a panorama of jagged peaks jutting from the ocean, interspersed with white sand beaches and a few tiny settlements.

An hour after leaving Siau, we reached the wide sand beach of Mahoro. Inland from the sand was a grove of coconut trees, then steep grassy slopes, and finally rocky peaks. This paradise is uninhabited—for good reason. The only well on the island, a few meters back of the sand, draws brackish water good only for washing dishes or rinsing off after a swim. We knew this beforehand, and had brought plenty of drinking water in big plastic jerrycans.

The beach faced clear water that shaded from pale green to light blue to cerulean before becoming deep blue. The rugged green coastline of Buhias lay less than a kilometer away. Visible over Siau's lesser peaks was one of Siau's lesser peaks, and Karangetang, partially shrouded in clouds, asserted itself to the north. The little village of Tapile was directly west of our beach, and we could see Laweang Island in the hazy distance to the south.

While we gazed at the scenery, Albert and Damas unloaded the food, cooking gear and our bags, then climbed the coconut trees to present us with refreshing young coconuts. The clear, sweet juice is followed by the soft meat, eaten with a spoon hacked right from the green shell with a swift blow of the *parang.* As the afternoon wore on, we set up camp: our large plastic sheet (in case of rain) on the sand, topped by a large mosquito net (there were few of the critters) hung from a half-toppled coconut tree. Watch where you rest under these trees—one thudded down just over a meter from where I sat.

Spear-fishing for Dinner

Albert spear-fished with his homemade goggles and spear powered by a rubber thong, and Damas started supper. We swam off the beach and chased sand-colored crabs, scrambling sideways across the beach. We also picked shells from the tide line. Albert came back with an assortment of reef fish, including some beautiful Picasso triggerfish, which unceremoniously ended up in the pot. After dinner, we sat by a bonfire built from the abundant driftwood.

A good breeze kept things fresh at night, just cool enough that a sheet or light blanket comes in handy. (And don't forget a flashlight to answer the call of nature.) At night, the sky was crowded with stars, and a few fishing lanterns twinkled in the distance. Karangetang rumbled twice, which gave us a touch of apprehension. It last erupted just two years ago. The peak glowed red in the darkness.

First thing in the morning, the volcano's peak was clear, but in a few hours it was once more shrouded. The rest of the sky was sparkling blue, so we went snorkeling off our private beach.

The hard coral was abundant and healthy, mostly various branched forms of *Acropora.* We saw some sponges, and a number of large sea anemones. One tuna cruised by, but the rest of the fish were reef species. We saw several more of the Picasso triggers we had for supper, and an unusual number of the brilliant blue-and-black hepatus tangs. We saw schools of sergeant-majors, pyramidal butterflyfish, regal and blue-faced angelfish, and a few sweetlips, the largest fish around. Here and there, we surprised a lobster, which we snatched for dinner.

An Idyllic Routine

For three days we fell into an idyllic routine in our little private paradise: beachcombing, snorkeling, scuba diving and lots of just scenery gazing. Two of Siau's former rajas must also have thought

Sangihe–Talaud Islands

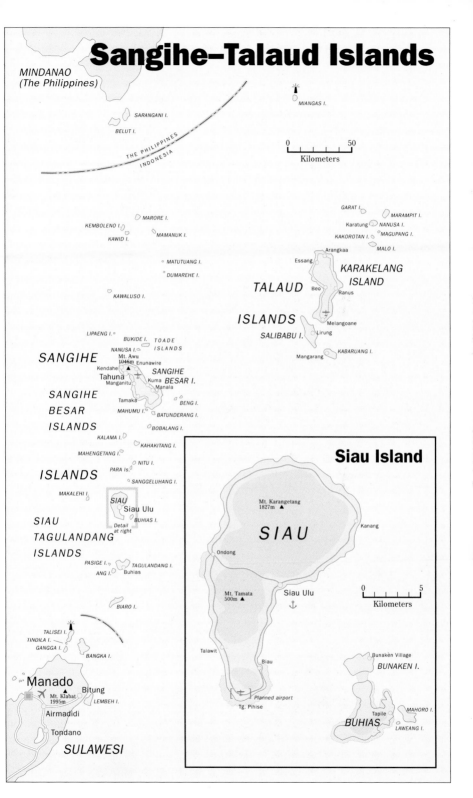

MINDANAO
(The Philippines)

SARANGANI I.

BELUT I.

THE PHILIPPINES
INDONESIA

MIANGAS I.

0   50
Kilometers

MARORE I.

KEMBOLENO I.

KAWID I.

MAMANUK I.

GARAT I.   MARAMPIT I.

Karatung   NANUSA I.

KAKOROTAN I.   MAGUPANG I.

MALO I.

Arangkaa

MATUTUANG I.

DUMAREHE I.

Essang

KARAKELANG
ISLAND

TALAUD

Beo

Ranus

KAWALUSO I.

ISLANDS

Melangoane

SALIBABU I.   Lirung

KABARUANG I.

LIPAENG I.

BUKIDE I.   TOADE

Mangarang

NANUSA I.   ISLANDS

SANGIHE

Mt. Awu
1046m Enunawire

Kendahe

SANGIHE

Tahuna   Kuma BESAR I.

Manganitu   Manala

SANGIHE

Tamaka

BENG I.

BESAR

MAHUMU I.   BATUNDERANG I.

ISLANDS

BOBALANG I.

KALAMA I.

KAHAKITANG I.

MAHENGETANG I.

ISLANDS

NITU I.

PARA Is.

SANGGELUHANG I.

MAKALEHI I.

SIAU

Siau Ulu

SIAU

BUHIAS I.

TAGULANDANG

Detail
at right

ISLANDS

PASIGE I.   TAGULANDANG I.

ANG I.   Buhias

BIARO I.

TALISEI I.

TINDILA I.

GANGGA I.

BANGKA I.

Manado   Bitung

Mt. Klabat

1995m   LEMBEH I.

Airmadidi

Tondano

SULAWESI

Siau Island

Mt. Karangetang
1827m

Kanang

SIAU

Ondong

Mt. Tamata
500m

Siau Ulu

0   5
Kilometers

Talawit

Biau

Bunakèn Village

BUNAKEN I.

Planned airport

Tg. Pihise

Tapile   MAHORO I.

BUHIAS

LAWEANG I.

that Mahoro's scenery was outstanding, as they chose a slight elevation at either end of the beach for their graves. One of these was an old style, rectangular masonry block tomb with a steeply pitched roof. The other was so modern and general in design that had it been surmounted by a cross rather than a crown, it could easily be taken for a Christian tomb.

MIKE SEVERNS

Above: *jacks (Caranx sp.) sweeping past a gorgonian. Bunaken Island.*

One morning a little outriggered canoe sailed to our beach from one of the hamlets on Buhias' east coast. An elderly man and his wife, both short and rotund, made an unusual plea. Several weeks previous the holding pin on their outboard had snapped, and the precious Yamaha sank just in front of the village. They had heard we were using scuba gear. Could we

please try to find and bring up the lost motor?

Jochem, a superb diver and instructor with many hundreds of dives under his weight belt, was skeptical of our chances. Bringing up the motor with our BCs or a rope was no problem, but finding it would be. Seldom, he said, can people remember exactly where something sank. But, of course, we would try. The old couple were delighted, and anxiously asked right away how much we would charge for the attempt. They were relieved when our "bill" amounted to a few fish for our next meal.

We set off a couple of hours later, at low tide, and reached the village in a few minutes. The old couple were there, indicating the "exact" spot. The entire village came along in a flotilla of little outriggers to see the show. In order to conserve our precious supply of air, only Jochem and Sabena, who hardly breathe underwater, attempted to find the motor.

The flat, sandy bottom was 50 meters from the surface. But even though visibility was very good, there was no motor in sight. Even for people who hardly use any air, bottom time at 50 meters is extremely limited, so they soon had to give up. We still received our "pay" of fish on the spot, and another installment was delivered to our beach the following morning.

Diving off Mahoro

We tried our first dive off a steep mini-island, Laweang, between Mahoro and the southern tip of Buhias. Damas told us that two kinds of birds are Laweang's only inhabitants, one of them a large species of pigeon which feeds exclusively on nutmeg, eating the fruit but excreting the still-fertile nut, thus propagating the tree. We saw nothing interesting underwater, and soon popped back up to the surface.

For another dive, we motored around the north point of Mahoro to a cave Albert and Damas knew of. We snorkeled up to the entrance, grabbing a good-sized lobster on the way. The cave's opening fronted a huge chamber, filled with bats and edible nest swiftlets (*Aerodramus* sp.).

Twice a year, in August and January, the swiflets' nests are gathered for export to the markets of Asia, where they fetch up to $1,200/kilo wholesale. Gathering the nests is a very risky occupation, and requires erecting elaborate scaffolding of bamboo and climbing way up into the tall, narrow caves. The only light is usually provided by torches.

Payment for the privilege to collect the nests must be made to the family of Siau's last Raja, as they retain hereditary rights to Mahoro.

Just past the cave, an offshore outcrop of rock showed good dive potential, but to conserve our precious air we first snorkeled around it to see if strapping on tanks would be worthwhile. From the surface round-trip, we saw a couple of good-sized Napoleon wrasse, then, rounding the last edge, a school of four huge bumphead parrotfish wandering around in 25 meters depth. We went back for the tanks.

We found our two Napoleons right away, but the huge parrotfish had left. The underwater profile, huge, connected boulders, held a three-meter-deep cave, just crowded with lobsters. We also saw a few weird, and very poisonous stonefish.

At around 20 meters, we came upon the largest school of sweetlips we had ever seen. Most of the attractive fish were large, around a half-meter. They allowed us to approach them to within two or three meters, and then swam slowly off.

Just a bit further on Mahoro's east coast, under the lighthouse, we dived again. Here, for the first and only time in our dives, we saw a fair variety of hard and soft corals, as well as sponges. A shallow slope turned into a steep wall, which bottomed at 35 meters. The sheer numbers of reef fish were not impressive, but we saw some large lionfish and one big Napoleon wrasse. Jochem teased a good sized

moray eel out of its cave, and it slithered quickly away, straight between my hastily parted legs.

We continued our circumnavigation of Mahoro. On the island's southeast tip, just as we hit the waves generated by the southeast monsoon, we passed a great natural stone archway.

The rock formation continued horizontally under a few meters of water to connect to stone out-

Above: *Soft corals and crinoids on a wall in Maumere Bay, Flores.*

crops some 50 meters from shore. We though it looked like a fine dive site, and kicked around the idea of strapping on our tanks, but eventually decided that the water was too rough.

A Cold Beer and a Bath

Too soon it was time to leave our paradise on Mahoro. We had each saved a bit of air, as we had heard there was an underwater cave just off Siau's harbor. We never found the cave, however, and the silt-covered sloping bottom offered little of interest.

But there was plenty of interest in the creature comforts of Siau after are three days playing Robinson Crusoe. The Mohede family, who own a three-story house, rent out a couple of their rooms—the only decent accommodations for visitors in this town of several thousand.

First we had a beer, then a delicious ladle-bath to wash off various dubious smells and crusts. Supper was lobster, five kinds of fish, chicken and vegetables. The comfortable bed was also welcome, with no sand whatever, and no worries about coconut bombs. The house's flat roof also gives a sweeping panorama of town and Karangetang volcano, always spectacular in dawn's first light.

Karangetang was where my partners headed in the early morning, led by our new friends, Albert and Damas. I decided to check out the town a bit.

Siau Island

Siau is part of North Sulawesi's Sangihe–Talaud district (sometimes it is written Sangir-Talud), which stretches from just north of Bangka and Talise islands to within 150 kilometers of the Philippines. Some 77 islands make up the archipelago; 47 of them are populated. The district population is 260,000.

You can fly from Manado to Naha, on Sangihe Besar Island, or to Melangoane, on Karakelang in the Talaud group. But until a planned airport in south Siau is completed, you have to get here by overnight ferry.

Siau Ulu is an irregular urban spread hugging the coast, with a main street separated from the sea by a narrow row of shops and houses. The town gives every appearance of being prosperous, due largely to its exports: nutmeg and mace, followed by cloves, copra, a bit of salted fish and, just recently, lobsters for Bali's tourist hordes.

Along the main street, spices are spread on burlap to dry in the sun. Like most places, one can tell who the wealthy people are by their houses. Here, what passes for ostentation are three-story homes covered with white tile and topped by parabolic television dishes.

Lively Market

A lively market covers a maze of tiny shops and stalls, constructed of concrete block with earthen floors, stretching 100 meters in back of the government offices and ending at the site of the local raja's grave. At the small beach where the market begins, local boats bring fish for sale at dawn. The catch is displayed on banana leaves for inspection by local housewives.

We saw mostly mackerel, along with a few red snappers, parrotfish and sweetlips. Octopus and squid was heaped into piles. Some of the octopus was smoked, as were several bunches of fish. Coconut crabs are occasionally offered at the market, making for an absolutely delicious dish.

In the rest of the market, various vegetables were displayed along with clothing and dry goods. A grinding machine produced a steady stream of fine-smelling coffee. At the far end of the market, a goldsmith and a couple of barbers had set up

shop. In several places there were little *warungs*, small places to get a coffee, snack or even a simple meal.

Government officials told me of Karangetang's 1976 eruption, which caused considerable material damage but claimed just one life, that of a man who got curious and went up to the volcano for a closer look. Far worse than this explosion were the earthquakes that struck two years before. For two weeks the island shook at ten minute intervals. With houses crumbling and roads disintegrating, many Siau Islanders fled to Manado.

The road system has been rebuilt and extended since then, with asphalt covering most of Siau's 50-odd kilometer circumference. Only one 12-kilometer stretch along the north coast still needs paving. The circle road allows the villages access to Siau Ulu town, and an 8-kilometer paved road cuts across the island to Ondong on the west coast.

From Ondong, it's a 12-nautical-mile, two-hour boat ride to Makalehi Island, which the local government would like to devel-

op as a tourist destination. This paradise—with a freshwater lake in the middle—is inhabited by just a few very traditional-minded folks. The Makalehi islanders make plaited leaf baskets and follow ancient customs. There is said to be a cave full of ancestral skulls here. Unfortunately, we had no time to check out this highly touted island.

I was also told that the people of Siau still perform old dances in traditional costume. Although dances can be arranged for visitors, the best time to see them is during the Taude festival, which takes place on January 31 every year. It is sort of a thanksgiving ritual, and is celebrated throughout the Sangihe Islands. There is one "central" festival site, which shifts every year. The local officials say the site is always listed with the regional office of tourism in Manado, but so far no tourist has yet shown up.

Trek to the Volcano

My friends arrived back at our lodgings shortly after I returned. They were hot, sweaty and tired, but elated with what they had

Above: *A leopard shark,* Stegastoma varium. *This animal is quite sedentary during the day, preferring to forage for molluscs and crustaceans at night. Although the sluggish creatures can reach more than two meters, they are not dangerous. Juvenile leopard sharks— which are born fully formed—have an attractive striped pattern.*

seen. Beer-over-ice was the perfect accompaniment to their stories of steep, slippery trails and magnificent vistas of seas dotted with islands, including "our" Mahoro.

Their trek started off easily enough, with a quarter hour of paved road followed by a good path, fitted with steps of sorts for the first hour of walking. In this stretch, my friends passed coconut trees, and groves of nutmeg and clove trees, the fruit of which were drying everywhere.

Neat tin-roofed houses showed off scrupulously clean, flower-filled yards, each a well-maintained botanical garden. The houses were rigged with clever networks of bamboo, which directed rainwater into concrete cisterns. Several pigs grunted around each house, a sure sign of wealth.

The altitude and high humidity provided the perfect conditions for ferns and mosses, which covered everything. And the hikers saw lots of thick, long, venomous millipedes.

The people of Siau's hill country were very friendly. As the little expedition approached a settlement, Albert and Damas whistled, setting the dogs barking and bringing out whomever was home. Coconuts—young and full of refreshing liquid—were quickly brought when requested. No payment was expected, but the cash offered was appreciated. The same went for some delicious tree-ripened papayas, which grew near the houses in a small plantations.

Just about at the end of the good, step-cut path, our team noticed a small masonry schoolhouse and lots of little kids, all dressed in red and white (the Indonesian primary school uniform, the same color as the flag), each carrying a *parang* which was about half as big as they were. Two kids fondled a tiny baby cuscus whose mother had just died.

Just beyond the school, the good trail stopped and the going got rough: steep and slippery. The guides, who had already proved their worth by picking the right path in a labyrinth of trails, became essential—one of the party was wearing grossly inadequate, smooth-soled canvas shoes. A rock steady hand prevented more than a couple of ego-bruising sprawls. Everyone fell a few times, in spite of stout walking sticks.

But the final half hour's sweaty effort was rewarded by several stunning overviews from the penultimate peak. Because of the thick vegetation, one has to reach this crest to see anything. Although the summit itself was still ahead—following a long drop into a valley and then back up a long, steep stretch—the party thought of turning back. Karangetang was still a good four to five hours away. A few drops of rain did not help morale any, and sealed the decision to return.

But not they didn't leave before finding an impressive old lava flow, a river of jagged rock. This was perhaps from the 1989 eruption, which reached the sea at Siau Ulu, cutting across the main street.

Back to Manado

We pulled out of Siau early in the evening under a myriad of stars, leaving Karangetang in our wake with its summit emanating a red glow. Our boat was as crowded as on the trip out, with the added bonus of being awakened in the hot night by cockroaches. Again, the woes of the night were forgotten at dawn as we approached Manado, watching the sun's first rays illuminate Mt. Klabat.

Soon after we pulled into the harbor and the mad disembarking began, an ambulance pulled up to our boat. During the night, one of the women on board had given birth to a little girl!

Sulawesi Dive Practicalities

Manado telephone code 0431

Manado is a large city, and is well-connected by air to the rest of Indonesia. The Dr. Sam Ratulangi airport Airport is 7 km outside of town, and taxi coupons to just about anywhere in town cost $3. If you reserve ahead with one of the dive operators, they will meet you at the airport. Airport information, Tel: 52117 or 60865.

Merpati. Jl. Sam Ratulangi 138, Tel: 64027 and 64028. Open 8 am to 4 pm; Sat. 7:30 am to 12:30 pm; Sun. 8 am–noon. Merpati runs a good number of flights to Manado, including: **Ambon**, daily, $94; **Biak**, twice weekly (via Sorong or Manokwari), $125; Bandung, daily (via Ujung Pandang and Surabaya), $200; **Bali**, daily (via Ujung Pandang), $155; Gorontalo, daily, $40; **Jakarta,** daily (via Ujung Pandang), $210; Jayapura, weekly, $160.

Garuda. Jl. Diponegoro 15, Tel: 52154 and 51544. Hours same as Merpati. All of Garuda's domestic routes are slowly being switched over to Merpati. Prices and schedules as above, and the flights can be booked through Merpati. At the time of this writing, Garuda was operating the flights to Ujung Pandang and Jakarta, using Airbus jets. If Garuda's computer system works (a miracle), you can reconfirm international flight reservations through their Manado office.

Bouraq. Jl. Sarapung 27B, Tel: 62757 and 62675. Runs a number of frequent flights to Kalimantan, as well as some flights around Sulawesi and other nearby islands. Approximately the same prices as Merpati and Garuda.

Sempati. At the Kawanua City Hotel, open 8 am–6 pm, Sun. 9 am–4 pm. Four weekly flights on Fokker 100 to Surabaya, $180 economy,

$200 first class; to Jakarta $190/$235. The Jakarta flight continues to Singapore for an extra $88/$188.

Local Transportation

Any of the dive resorts will be able to arrange some kind of transportation for you if you want to sightsee or travel anywhere. There are also several forms of public transportation around Manado.

Oplet. Travel around the city is by *oplet,* tiny minivans one enters by the rear. They run regular routes, and the destination is displayed on a sign in the front. The driver will stop for you anywhere along the route, just flag them down as you would a taxi. When you get to your stop, pull the cord inside (or bang on the window behind the driver if the cord is broken, as it often is) and the vehicle will stop sharply. The fare is Rp 150 (less than 10¢). Larger minibuses (*mikrolet*) also run regular routes. These cost the same, but carry more people and one enters on the side.

The problem with this form of transportation (in addition to the fact that they are cramped) is making sure you get in the right one. If you are confident you have gotten past this hurdle, don't be overly alarmed if the little truck veers off the main road and starts heading down a tiny back alley somewhere. Passengers often make special requests to be dropped off at their doorsteps.

Taxis. Two types of *taksi* operate in Manado. One is unmarked, with no meter, and you must negotiate a price to your particular destination. The other type, recently introduced, consists of white sedans with signs on their roofs. These run meters. Rp 600 (35¢) for the first kilometer, Rp 300 (17¢) for subsequent kilometers. You can also call either of two taxi

companies: **Indra Kelana Taxi Company,** Tel: 52033; and **Dian Taksi,** Tel: 62421.

Charters. One can charter any of the above forms of transport. Empty *oplets* can be chartered for around $1.60/hr (no minimum), and *mikrolets* for a bit more. Taxis can be hired by the hour, around $2.75/hr (3-hr minimum around town, 5-hr minimum out of town).

Dive Operators

There are currently three dive operators taking divers to the Bunaken group. For serious diving, we suggest booking a package—including accommodations and board—with one of the dive clubs.

Barracuda. Located in Molas, just beyond NDC, office in Manado: Jl. Sam Ratulangi 61 (Babe Palar), Tel: 62033 and 66249, Fax: 64848. European representative: Michael Smith, Geibelstr. 43, 3000 Hannover 1, Germany. Tel: (0511) 888-8836 and 647-6129, Fax: 647-6120.

This dive center was established in 1989, and sits on a seaside hill, offering the best views of the resorts. 12 double rooms, more under construction. Good seafood restaurant. Room rates: $20S, $25D. Food, $2.50 for breakfast, $3.50 lunch, and $4 supper.

Day rate—(2 dives, tanks, weights, boat, lunch)—$60, min. 2 persons. Sightseeing, $20; snorkeling, $30. Package rate, including full room and board and two dives, $70/day. Night dive, $10 extra. One dive master and three guides (no dive instructor). 56 tanks, 30 BCs ($10/day), 25 regulators ($5/day), and 8 UW lights ($2.50/day).

One glass-bottom sight-seeing and dive boat—carries up to 28—with two 80hp engines, three large dive boats, and 6 outriggered dive boats, one 40hp engine each. Barracuda offers dives off Bangka Island, at no extra charge. They take you there by catamaran (2.5 hrs) and bring you back overland from Likupang (1.5 hrs).

Murex. Jl. Sudirman 28, (or P.O. Box 236), Manado 95123. Tel: 66280, Fax/phone: 52116. About 25 min. drive south of Manado, with 14 rooms in both old-fashioned and modern cottages. The premises are very nicely landscaped with lots of flowers and trees, and the lotus ponds keep the area cool. A few early evening mosquitoes, but no more than anywhere else around Manado. $18–$25S, $24–$30D, $12/day for board.

Day rate—(2 dives, tanks, weights, boat, lunch)—$60/head, minimum 3 in group. Package rate—double occupancy room, meals, diving—$80/person. Dives to the Bitung area or Bangka Island, $20 extra, as it's a lot further from this site. 60 tanks, 6 BCs ($5–$15/day), 12 regulators ($10/day). Medical doctor and NAUI instructor Hanny Batuna offers a 40 hour dive course leading to NAUI certification ($250). Three other dive guides in addition to Hanny.

Quite good, wide diving boats. The ride from here to Bunaken is a bit longer than that from the Molas-based clubs, and the boats cut through more open waves (thus waves and spray). Good use of space on boats for tank and equipment storage and suiting up. Murex plans to have a 16-berth live-aboard dive boat operating by late 1991. Our dive guide had a safe second stage and a computer, the first time we saw this in Manado.

Nusantara Diving Centre (NDC). P.O. Box 15, Molas Beach, Manado 95001. Tel: 63988 and 60638, Fax: 60368 and 63688, Telex: 74293 Sutras and 74100 BCA. Located close to the sea, but the beach is mangrove and mud. With 25 fan-cooled rooms in several cottages. Rooms $7.50–$25S, $10–$30D. Meals $10/day.

Day rate—(2 dives, tanks, weights, boat, lunch)—min. two persons, $60. Package rates— 2 dives, room, meals— run $70–$80, depending on room.

NDC has 11 boats, 12 outboards (40hp), 25 guides, 140 tanks, 6 BCs ($5/day), 6 regulators ($5/day) and a very friendly atmosphere. Night dive (after two day dives) $15 extra. Snorkeling or sightseeing (land or sea) available.

Dive courses $250 for those who can already snorkel, no pool, all beginning underwater instruction takes place a shallow reef. 100 meter jetty is planned. Until the souvenir shop is set up, the staff will run errands to town for you (ticket confirmation, cigarettes, film processing). E6 slide processing (no mounting) taken to town for you takes one to three days, $3.50/roll of 36. Beer $1.50/bottle, 80¢/can. Best ambiance of all the clubs with young staff singing, playing guitar or xylophones during supper and afterwards.

Reservations recommended, especially for July and August. Major travelers' checks accepted as well as Mastercard, Visa and American express, with at least one day's notice before checkout.

A new dive center was scheduled to open in late 1991 on the coast about 10 km north of Bitung. The operation, we were told, is being financed by Americans and run by Billy Matindas, who owns the Tarsius restaurant in Manado (Tel: 65165 and 65164). There is apparently little coral in the immediate area of the new center, but some deep caves and lots of sharks.

Communications

Post office. (Kantor Pos.) Jl. Sam Ratulangi 23, 5 minutes walk south of Kawanua City Hotel. 8 am–8 pm, Mon.–Fr.; to 6 pm, Sat. and Sun.

Perumtel. (Telephone office.) Jl Sam Ratulangi between the Kawanua Hotel and the Post office (on the opposite side of the street). Open 24 hrs.

Photo processing

There are many shops in Manado, and the dive outfits can take your film in for you. If you are taking care of this yourself, we we recommend these two outfits:

P.T. Modern Photo Film Co. Fuji Color Plaza, Jl. M.T. Haryono, between Jumbo Supermarket and the central square. Tel: 51556.

Angkasa Color Photo Service. Jl. Yos Sudarso 20, Tel: 62467. One-day slide service.

Bookstores

The **Toko Buku Borobudur** is the best for English language materials. We saw English, German and French/Indonesian dictionaries, English language Indonesia travel books, and a good selection of postcards. **President,** located in the shopping complex, has dictionaries and a few books in English, children's stories based on Indonesian myths, postcards. An unattractive place.

English language journals. The Jumbo Supermarket gets *Time* magazine and the *Jakarta Post,* a daily English language newspaper. The Kawanua City Hotel receives *Time* magazine, although a bit late.

Tours and Guides

These can be arranged through the dive clubs, or at a travel agency or some of the hotesl. Tours available include the popular day trip through the Minahasa area ($25), Tomohon and the crater lake of the Mahawu volcano ($15), and the much less frequent jaunt, with 4-wheel-drive vehicle, through a section of the Tangkoko–Batuangus–Dua Saudara Nature Reserve ($45). Prices based on a minimum of two clients.

North Sulawesi Tourism Office. Hard to find, on a side street justt off Jl. 17 Augustus, Tel: 64299. Open Mon.–Thurs. 7 am–2 pm, Fri. to 11 am, Sat. to 12:30 pm.

Sangihe Islands

There are two airports in the Sangihe–Talaud group: Naha, a few kilometers from Tahuna, the largest city on Sangihe

Besar Island; and Melangoane, on the southern tip of Karake-lang Island (see map page 201). Merpati flies small Cassa olanes from Manado to Naha daily, except Sundays ($35), and twice a week the flight continues to Melangoane ($60). Note: these flights are often cancelled.

Tahuna on Sangihe Besar Island has a population 24,000, and a half-dozen good *losmen*; the best are **Victoria Tangaroa** and **Nasional**. There is some carving of souvenir items such as miniature canoes here. To visit Karake-ang Island, head north from the port town of Beo to see crocodiles around the mouth of the Rai River. Nearby Arangkaa is a traditional village, and its ancestral cave is full of old skulls. In this area the local government is setting up a 500-hectare nature reserve: here are said to be lots of birds, and wild cattle and pigs.

Boats to Sangihe–Talaud

To get to Siau Island (until the airport is finished) and other sites in Sangihe–Talaud, one must take the medium-sized wooden passenger boats that leave Manado. These stop at Buhias on Tagulandang Island ($3/8 hrs/110 km), Siau Ulu on **Siau Island ($4.50/10 hrs/150 km)**, Tahuna on Sangihe Besar Island ($7/14 hrs/240 km), Lirung on Salbabu Island, just south of Karakelang Island ($9.50/24 hrs/322 km), and Beo on Karakelang Island ($9.50/24 hrs/366 km). These prices are for passage only, including a small mattress. Several agencies sell tickets, and they are all close to one another, at the harbor entrance.

The passage to and from Siau Ulu and Taruna is mostly at night, with the boats leaving Manado in the early evening, around 7 pm, and arriving in Siau Ulu at 6 am and Taruna a couple of hours later (faster boats on the Taruna run). Return trips depart Tarun in the late afternoon, and Siau Ulu in the evening. The boats are crowded, and uncomfortable. You can rent a bunk in a cabin by negotiating with one of the crewmembers (he will be giving his up). Figure about $4–$6 for the bunk. Go very early if you want a bunk, or they will all be taken.

One can also continue on from Tahuna to the northern-most islands in the group: Nanusa Island (just north of Sangihe Besar), Marore Island, and Miangas Island, the furthest north. Regular and irregular boats leave at least every two weeks from Tahuna to these destinations. The boats handle the seas well, but for those with weak stomachs we suggest traveling from April to late June, when the seas are the calmest. The rainy season—the worst time to travel here—runs from October through March.

Other Boats

Manado's small harbor (Bitung to the north is far larger and more important, as it can handle large tonnage ships) also offers passenger service to ports along Sulawesi's north coast, and down the west side as far as Pantaloan, the port of Palu, the capital of The Central Sulawesi province.

There are two ships a week from Manado to Tolitoli (about 2/3ds of the way to Palu, $12) calling at several points along the way and going on to Pantoloan Harbor, Palu ($18.50). Count on two days and nights to Tolitoli (including stops along the way) and another day and night from there to Pantaloan.

There is also one weekly departure from Manado to Ternate Island in Maluku ($9), but more ships go there from Bitung. The Manado–Ternate ship continues to Mangole and Sanana in the Sula Islands group east of Central Sulawesi, and ends its run at Ambon ($26), taking some three days.

For ships out of Bitung, have an Indonesian friend or your hotel contact the harbormaster there, Tel: (044) 2167.

Also, for the PELNI passenger ships (Indonesia's national passenger line), heading to Ternate, Ambon, Ujung Pandang and many other large ports from Bitung, check in Manado at: PELNI, Jl. Sam Ratulangi, Tel: 62844. In mid-1991 there were rumors of an incipient passenger ship service from Bitung to the Philippines.

Siau and Mahoro

The best accommodations in Siau Ulu are in the two rooms, each with a double bed, offered by the Mohede family. $5/room, or $10/room and three meals. There is also the Penginapapn Serui (no sign), with 4 rooms, each $3, $7.50 w/ 3 meals. Somewhat run-down, but probably okay for budget travelers.

Meals are available at the "kantin" (canteen) at the harbor, the food stalls at the market, or, of course, at where you are staying. Ask about the availability of coconut crab (50¢–75¢ apiece at the market) or lobster ($1.75/kilo).

What to bring. From Manado, bring: sunscreen and a hat; a tent or good plastic sheet in case of rain; a light blanket or sheet; insect repellent and/or a mosquito net (not too many bugs around, but still); fins, mask and snorkel; and a camera and lots of film.

Local boat rental. By the day, you can make arrangements through the harbormaster or the Mohede family. Prices depend on distance.

To Mahoro, $40/day (without scuba gear, up to 8 people would have fit in the boat we had). To the undersea volcano (bubbling top at 5 meters) at Mahenge–Makalehi, about $60–$75/day.

Bargaining may be required, and the results will be better for you if this is conducted in Indonesian. The above prices include wages for two crewmen who can also cook.

Guides. Bring a English-speaking guide from Manado unless your Indonesian is fairly fluent.

Introducing Maluku

The islands of the Moluccas—Maluku in modern Indonesian—were the first in the archipelago to capture the imagination of the Europeans. Not for their beauty, although these thousand-odd islands, with powder-white beaches, swaying coconut palms, and constant, lazy sunshine certainly fit most northerners' definition of paradise. The Europeans came in search of one of the world's most coveted commodities—spices.

The Spice Islands

In the 16th century, cloves, nutmeg and mace were literally worth their weight in gold in Europe. When the 18 men aboard the *Victoria,* the only survivors of Ferdinand Magellan's original expedition of 230 men and five ships, hobbled home with their load of just over a ton of cloves, they were very rich men for life.

From the beginning of the spice trade—Chinese sources make reference to cloves as early as the beginning of the common era—until the Dutch planted cloves on Ambon Island, every clove in the world came from the tiny islands of Ternate and Tidore, just off the west coast of Halmahera (see map page 214). All the world's nutmeg—and the even more precious mace, which comes from the bright red aril that surrounds the nutmeg "nut"—came from the tiny, and isolated, Banda Islands.

Today, Indonesia grows more cloves in Sulawesi than in Ternate or Tidore, and nutmeg and mace is produced in Grenada, in the Caribbean. The early European explorers would no doubt be shocked to find out where most of the world's cloves end up today: in *kretek,* the ubiquitous Indonesian clove cigarets.

The People of Maluku

Maluku no longer attracts much attention. The old Dutch forts sit crumbling, and ancient Portuguese armor and gold pieces have become heirlooms to be passed down by families through the generations. Other than Ambon—a city of 275,000 and the center for communications in the three provinces of Maluku—and Ternate, the islands have only scattered small population centers.

Most Moluccans are fishermen and farmers. Because many of the sandy islands do not support rice, they rely on manioc, taro and sweet potatoes as staples, with fresh fish for protein.

In the interiors of Seram, Halmahera and some of the other large islands, people who trace their genealogies back further even than the arrival of the first Malays live lives relatively untouched by the modern world.

Two Island Arcs

The islands of Central and South Maluku are made up of two parallel, but differently formed, island chains. The outer arc of islands—continuing from Timor through Leti, the Babar Islands, the Tanimbars, the Kei Islands and then around through Seram and Buru—is made of calcareous rock, the remainder of ancient reefs. The inner arc—continuing from Flores and the Alor archipelago to Wetar, the Damar Islands, and ending in the isolated Banda archipelago—is part of Indonesia's "Ring of Fire," a string of volcanic islands that

Overleaf: *The view from Gunung Api in the Banda Islands. Visible here is Banda Neira island and Bandaneira town, and in the background, the curve of Lontar and tiny Sjahrir Island. The Banda Islands once supplied the entire world with nutmeg and mace. Photograph by Kal Muller.*

Opposite: *Pearl oysters hanging from an underwater fence. The oysters are cultivated in this way until they are large enough to form pearls. Then they are shipped off to one of the many Japanese-run pearl farms where they are seeded and left to grow pearls. The secret of inserting a seed pearl is highly guarded by the Japanese, and they defend their farms with private armies. This is Bobale Island, off the east coast of Halmahera's north peninsula. Photograph by Helmut Debelius, IKAN.*

mark the edge of a crustal plate.

North Maluku is quite separate. Halmahera Island, shaped like a miniature Sulawesi, was formed, like its larger neighbor, when two long islands were joined together by the forces of continental drift. The western side of the island, including tiny Ternate and Tidore, is volcanic; the eastern side is a mixture of limestone and other rock.

Underwater Riches

The sea was never low enough to allow land crossings between all the islands of Maluku, and the animal life of the islands reflects this: although there are few mammals, birds and insects have done well on the islands. The birds are varied and beautiful—kingfishers, lories, parrots and, in the Aru Islands, the legendary birds of paradise.

According to 19th century naturalist Alfred Russel Wallace, the fishes of Maluku are "perhaps unrivaled for variety and beauty by those of any one spot on earth."

Unfortunately, diving in the region is currently limited to the Banda Islands and a very new operation in Ambon. One can only dream of what the diving is like in the Gorom and Watubeli Islands, or the small islands in the Kei group, seasonally washed by rich upwellings from the depths of the Banda Sea.

—*David Pickell*

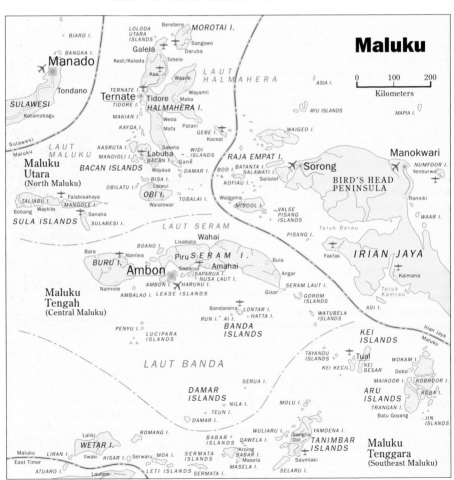

Old Forts, Strange Spirits and Sacred Eels

Ambon is the communications center of Maluku, and all travelers and divers pass through here. Although the city itself offers little of interest to tourists, daytrips around the Ambon and Saparua Islands lead to clove plantations, centers of pottery and craft-making, scenic mountain villages, and the strange sacred eels of Waai.

The 'Queen of the East'

Before the Europeans arrive in the Spice Islands in the 16th century, Hitu on the north coast was Ambon Island's center of trade. The Portuguese were the first Europeans to arrive, in 1512, but it was the Dutch, who arrived almost a century later, who were to dominate the spice trade, enforcing a monopoly on clove production for almost 200 years.

Because the sultanates of Ternate and Tidore were well-established by the time the Dutch arrived in the region, the Europeans moved the center of clove production to Ambon and nearby Seram. They forced clove growers to accept low prices and useless Dutch goods for the spices, and sent armed flotillas of fast local vessels on *hongi* missions to find clove trees growing outside the range of Dutch control. Hundreds of thousands of clove trees were destroyed to hold down supply and maintain the Dutch monopoly.

At the height of Holland's control of the trade, the late 17th century, Ambon was a bustling town of 7,000 people called "The Queen of the East" by travelers there. But even before the Dutch East India company went bankrupt a century later, Ambon had

faded in importance, and coffee, tea and sugar planted in Java soon completely overshadowed Maluku's spices.

Today, Ambon City itself is rather charmless, having been built up quickly and cheaply after being bombed to rubble during World War II. Except for Fort Victoria, which serves as a base for the Indonesian Army, no old colonial buildings or other landmarks survived the war, and the city of 275,000 is a busy, commercial town.

If you have any time to spare in town, we recommend visiting

Above: *Feeding the sacred eels of Waai. These fish are pampered with treats of chicken eggs because they embody deified ancestral spirits and guard the spiritual health of the village.*

Below: *Soft corals and* Tubipora *sp. polyps. Flores, Indonesia.*

KAL MULLER

HELMUT DEBELIUS / IKAN

the Siwalima Museum, located just outside and above the city on the slope of Gunung Nona. The museum displays ancestral woodcarvings from South Maluku, porcelain, and anthropological and natural history displays.

Sacred Eels

If you can arrange a car, definitely go see the sacred eels at Waai, a village about five kilometers north of Tulehu.

Here, a crystal clear stream flows out of an underground cave into a shallow pool, which appears empty except for some carp. Then the keeper flicks his fingers on the surface, and at this signal the large freshwater eels slither out of the cave. He then takes a chicken egg and breaks it underwater, and it is immediately gobbled up by the eels.

The fish—a meter or more long—receive these attentions because they embody ancestral spirits. If the eels ever disappear, it is believed, a disaster will befall the village of Waai.

Hila and the North Coast

A good road cuts north across Ambon Island, then follows the coast to the west. The destination is Hila village. Here stands a lovely church, the Immanuel, built by the Dutch Reformed sect in 1780 and still faithfully attended today. Nearby is the small but attractive Mapauwe Mosque. Built in 1414, it is the oldest mosque in Ambon.

Just a short stroll from the mosque is Fort Amsterdam. The thick, high walls of the Dutch fort were built atop existing Portuguese fortifications. A tree has somehow taken root at the very top of the fort, and is the only current inhabitant of the building. The sea shows through a curtain of vegetation.

Soya Atas

This little village is perched at 400 meters on the flank of 950-meter Gunung Sirimau, just a few kilometers southeast of Ambon city. A pretty little church sits in Soya Atas' clean plaza, and it is faced by the raja's house. His house is filled with mementos from the days of past splendor, when his forebears controlled Ambon Town.

There is something strange

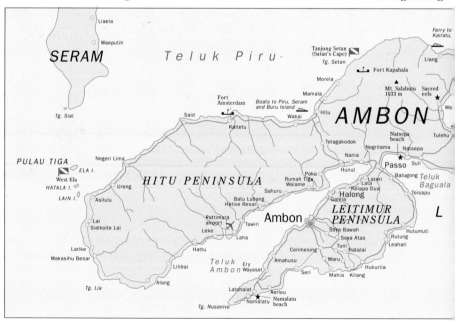

about Soya Atas, however. Lurking here is a female spirit who has a predilection for kidnapping foreign men. After a few days she "releases" them—sometimes dead, sometimes alive. If still alive, the victim is found in a trance, and a drink of sacred water is required to restore the man to his senses.

The best documented case involved the Dutch Governor General of the Indies, kidnapped just before World War II. He vanished without a trace and was found in a trance three days later.

Soya has the best preserved *baileo,* or ritual meeting house, on the island. This includes megaliths, and ancient stone seats for dignitaries. A path next to the *baileo* winds up to about 700 meters, where there is a holy side at the top of the hill. Here a stone throne, encircled by croton bushes, faces a splendid panorama—the Lease Islands, and sometimes, in the faint distance, even Banda's Gunung Api.

The throne holds Tempayan Setan, the "Devil's Urn." This stone vessel never empties of water, even during the dry sea-

son. The water cures illness, brings prosperity, and can even encourage the affections of the person of your choice.

Saparua Island

From your diving base on Saparua, you can take a day off to visit nearby clove and nutmeg plantations or, on Wednesday and Saturday, visit the Saparua Town market. Sellers begin arriving very early, but activities don't peak until late morning.

You will see strange-looking produce, 5–10 kilo cones of sago paste, palm sugar, and a large variety of smoked fish. The herring and tuna were our favorites. Most selling takes place curbside on Saparua's main streets, but a large covered area is much sought-after on rainy days.

Ouw village, 9 kilometers south-east of Saparua town, is the island's pottery-making center. The utilitarian clay pieces are worked by hand into bowls or other simple items of kitchenware. The craftsmen work every day except Wednesdays and Saturdays, when they are at the market with the rest of the island.

AMBON

The Secret is Out on Some Excellent Diving

In the Ambon and Saparua areas, aficionados can find dive sites that are truly world-class. Scuba has just begun here, and the divers who have experienced the area have been trying hard to keep it secret. Sorry chaps, here is the lowdown.

Our two dives off Ameth village on Nusa Laut island rate the very highest marks, particularly for the number of big fish seen there. Divers have asked Tony Tomasoa, currently the only dive operator in the area, not to spread the word. But you can't blame Tony. He is a businessman, and has no objections to more clients.

A Parade of Giants

In just one and one-half hours underwater off Nusa Laut, we saw: three gray reef sharks of 1.5 meters; three large turtles, including one of over a meter; a dozen enormous Napoleon wrasse, including one school of four; two very impressive giant groupers; two large dogtooth

tuna; two black-spotted rays; a barracuda of more than a meter; a dozen longnosed emperors; and two huge reef lobsters.

In addition to the big fellows, we were enveloped at one point by a huge school of fearless longfin bannerfish (*Heniochus diphreutes*). We saw a school of black jacks (*Caranx lugubris*) and a few giant jacks (*C. ignoblis*); several large schools of unicorn-fish; and a school of Thompson's surgeonfish.

The colorful crowd of reef fish were out in force. We counted 12 species of butterflyfish, six species of angelfish, and saw Moorish idols, snappers, rainbow runners, and more. This is really a rich site. Some divers have reported spotting the rare, lumbering dugongs here.

Our dives took place during the June–August southeast monsoon, and visibility was reduced to 10–12 meters, just fair by Indonesian standards. The rest of the year, visibility improves considerably. The seas are also roughest during the southeast monsoon, although we had some unusually calm and sunny weather. The rest of the year, calm seas are the rule, although they come up a bit around the north-west monsoon, around January–February. We were told, however, that diving is usually fine at this time.

Tony Tomasoa

Although we found Ameth village to be the best site, there are several other developed spots around the islands. We didn't have time to visit them all, unfortunately, and more are being pioneered all the time by Tony

---

AT A GLANCE
Ambon and Lease

Reef type: Walls and slopes

Access: 30 min to 1 hr by speedboat

Visibility: Fair, 10–12 meters; usually better, but we dove during the southeast monsoon

Current: Moderate or none

Coral: Some areas quite good

Fish: Excellent at the best site

Highlights: The sheer number and variety of large fish off Ameth village on Nusa Laut

---

Tomasoa's P.T. Daya Patal Tour and Travel. Tony and his capable boatmen and guides know all the spots. Tomasoa has two compressors: a small Bauer unit (which can also be taken on a boat) which he keeps in Ambon, and another at the Mahu Village Resort on Saparua.

For diving in the region, it is best to stay at the Mahu Village Resort, in Mahu on the east shore of Tuhaha Bay north of Saparua Island. Tomasoa runs divers to the various sites by speedboat from Mahu. Powered by twin 40hp outboards, these boats—which can fit six divers with gear—can whisk you to the dive sites in record time. Larger, albeit slower, craft are available for groups of more than six.

Speedboats for diving can also be chartered out of Tulehu, a port town in eastern Ambon Island. From here, it is an hour and a half to Nusa Laut, less than an hour to some of the sites off north Haruku and Saparua. These boats can also take you to locations in Seram Island's Piru Bay—due north of Ambon—or on Ambon's northwest coast.

Ameth Village

Ameth village (see map page 220) faces a small bay filled with sand and coral that is exposed at low tide. Dives begin off the reef edge, which drops vertically to sloping sand at 40–60 meters. The far ends of the site are coral and sand slopes. Corals—both hard and soft—were abundant in areas, but not overall. But sponges of all kinds grew in unusual numbers. The fish life here was tremendous.

The people of Ameth take good care of their reef, and no fish bombs are used. Local permission is required before diving, but this is readily granted. Akon village, just south of Ameth, is also said to have a fine reef, although we had no time to check it out. One should ask the villagers' permission to dive there as well.

Molana Island

We had time only to snorkel off the northwest coast of Molana Island, just south of Saparua's southwest point (See map page 216). We saw a mixed sand and

Above: *Cuttlefish can often be coaxed into allowing a diver to touch them. Although molluscs, they have a very large repertoire of behaviors, and like their relatives, squid and octopus, can be among the most entertaining animals encountered on the reef. The cuttlefish's "cuttlebone" is a porous calcareus structure that helps the animal with buoyancy control. Cuttlebones are hung in bird cages to provide them with dietary calcium.*

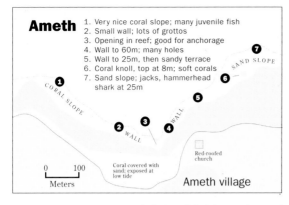

Ameth

1. Very nice coral slope; many juvenile fish
2. Small wall; lots of grottos
3. Opening in reef; good for anchorage
4. Wall to 60m; many holes
5. Wall to 25m, then sandy terrace
6. Coral knoll, top at 8m; soft corals
7. Sand slope; jacks, hammerhead shark at 25m

SAND SLOPE

CORAL SLOPE

WALL

WALL

Red-roofed church

0   100
Meters

Coral covered with sand; exposed at low tide

Ameth village

coral slope with fair numbers of schooling reef fish. Close to the surface, we swam past many small jellyfish, along with a few larger ones. The large jellyfish, 10–12 centimeters, sheltered schools of tiny fish in their tentacles.

Too late, we found out from one of our boatmen that the deep waters off South Molana are full of medium-sized schooling fish and big sharks. The currents here are strong, we were told.

Tanjung Setan

Tanjung Setan, between Morela and Liang on Ambon's north coast, is said to offer the island's best diving. We had time for only one dive here, however, and that was quite disappointing. We dove off a vertical wall, but the hard coral cover was limited and there were few fish. We did see some unusual brown sponges, tubular and connected in root-like spreads.

Two large lionfish kept us occupied briefly, and our spirits received a boost at the sight of some clownfish in a beautiful anemone (*Heteractis magnifica*), its tentacles partially contracted to show off its blue column.

Kasa and Babi Islands

These two islands are in Piru Bay, about 35 kilometers due north of Hitu on Ambon's north coast. Off southwest Kasa, we found a gentle slope covered in rubble and sand, and despite that

the islands are both in a designated marine reserve, we found heavy fish-bombing damage. Visibility was restricted to 8 meters. The dive's only redeeming features were a large school of jacks and a group of some 15 round-faced batfish (*Platax teira*). We snorkeled a couple of sites on the east and west coasts of Kasa, and conditions did not justify putting on scuba gear. Nor did the large submerged reef extending north from Kasa almost to Babi Island.

Diving off western Babi was only marginally better. We saw large formations of cabbage coral, one turtle, a big box fish and two schools of jacks. We spot-checked other areas around the small island with snorkeling gear, but found nothing to warrant putting on tanks.

Nusa Tiga

Things improved considerably the next day. We anchored for the night at Asilulu, on the far western tip of Ambon's Hitu Peninsula, and after obtaining permission from the traditional ruler of the area, headed out for Nusa Tiga, the "Three Islands."

We started both dives off the west coast of Ela Island, following the reef north on the first dive, south on the second one. The reef profile was a slope of 45 degrees, well-covered in diverse species of coral. Several large schools of black triggerfish (*Odonus niger*) checked us out, and moray eels weaved menacingly out of several holes.

We saw fusiliers, a very large aggregation of unicornfish (at least 70 individuals) and a small group of sweetlips. Clown and Titan triggerfish patrolled the reef, and we counted a dozen species of butterflyfish.

At depths of 15 to 25 meters we saw several large bamboo fish traps, belonging to the Butonese fishermen who maintain a few huts and a prayer house on Ela Island.

Blue Water, Nutmegs and Fire Mountain

The tiny Banda Islands rise from the 4,000 meter depths of the Banda Sea, 140 kilometers from Ambon and in the middle of nowhere. They are breezy and verdant, among the real jewels of Maluku. The view, as one descends to Banda Neira Island's airstrip in one of Indoavia's tough little Twin-Otter airplanes, is dominated by Gunung Api's perfect green cone and the crescent-shaped Lontar, or the "Big Island," the surviving rim of a huge caldera.

Bandaneira town

Just 12 vehicles ply the few streets of Bandaneira, the biggest town in the archipelago and the location of the only hotels. It is a quiet and charming place, and it is difficult to picture the bloodshed and intrigue that wracked these islands during the height of the European grab for the Spice Islands.

The little town of Bandaneira is pleasant to stroll around. Make certain to visit the hilltop Fort Belgica, whose foundations were laid in 1611 to enforce Holland's nutmeg monopoly. The mansions of many of the Dutch planters—*perkeniers*—lie about in various states of genteel decay, awaiting funds for renovation. Some have been handsomely rebuilt and can be visited.

The town's old church is paved with the gravestones of the Dutch who did not amass their fortunes in time to return to Holland. There is also an attractive mosque in town. The waterside market offers a fair amount of life, especially when one of the local boats comes in with a catch of several hefty yellowfin tuna which can be converted into deli-

Above: *The fruit of the nutmeg tree,* Myristica fragans. *The nuts, brown and the size of an acorn, provide the powdered spice. The red aril, which forms a lacy network over the nut, is dried and ground into mace. The fruit, hard and slightly fuzzy like an unripe peach, is sliced and preserved to make a spicy snack. Recently, nutmeg prices have dropped dramatically. Ironically, the* kenari *nut trees planted to shade the delicate nutmegs produce an oily nut now worth five times more than nutmeg.*

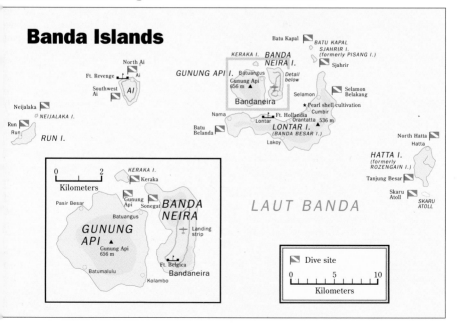

Above: *View of Gunung Api from Fort Belgica, on a small rise in Bandaneira. Api last erupted in 1988, causing considerable damage and forcing residents of the island to be evacuated.*

cious sashimi.

Your hotel can arrange for you to see the spectacular local dance, the *cakalele,* in the past used to whip up enthusiasm for war. The dance includes some very graceful flowing movements, along with lots of shouting and stomping. If you want to see a *cakalele,* we suggest you follow all the preparations, including the prayers over the sacred cloths, helmets and other paraphernalia used in the dances.

Gunung Api

Gunung Api (literally "Fire Mountain") rises 656 meters above the Banda Sea. Although normally quiet, Api is still quite alive. Between 1910 and 1977, 33 tremors of 5.0 or greater on the Richter scale have been recorded, 20 of them in one year, 1975. In May 1988, Api's top blew with great violence, killing three and forcing a mass evacuation of the 2,000 people living on its slopes.

Climbing Api is relatively easy if you take a local guide. Start early in the morning, no later than 5:30 a.m., and bring a hat and plenty of water. It takes just 5 minutes to cross the lagoon from Banda Neira, where the well-marked trail begins with a gentle climb past manioc gardens. Make sure you bring or find a good walking stick—it will make both the climb and the descent a a lot easier.

Wooden steps make the climb relatively easy for well over half the distance. After perhaps an hour, the steps run out, and the footing consists of loose pebbles. Nevertheless, after less than a half hour you should make it to the top of the tree line. From there it's just five minutes to an incredible bird's eye view of the three central Banda Islands—if, that is, you started early enough and clouds haven't socked you in.

The first two craters are shallow, with a few fumaroles edged by yellow sulfur and a white mineral deposits. Test the ground before you pick your next step: it could be too hot for comfort. The path to the main caldera requires another slight climb, but reveals a sight usually reserved for volcanologists: a jagged, vertical-sided hole 250-meters across and equally deep. Hot fumes waft up, and great spreads of sulfur mark the most active vents.

Green moss-like vegetation somehow survives along a section of the crater's upper lip. In the background of the smoldering crater, you can see nutmeg plantations, and the deep blue sea. It's a spectacle worth every effort to see. Be very careful walking around the rim, however, as the ashy rock crumbles easily. You don't want to tumble into the bowels of the earth.

If you feel up to it, you could try to beat the record for climbing the mountain, set by an Englishman in 1987. (43 minutes, no stairs.) A local guide, Nyong Rus, came in second in the race. Don't even try the climb with a heart condition. A Dutchman suffered a fatal stroke during his attempt. If you have your own helicopter, as Jacques Cousteau did, you can fly right down into the crater. But then don't expect the certificate proving that you climbed Gunung Api ($2, U.S. currency), which also makes you an honorary citizen of Banda.

Pristine Reefs and Many Pelagic Fish

Banda

The Banda Islands are one of Indonesia's top destinations for divers. Both experts and beginners will enjoy themselves here, as the diving ranges from the shallow lagoon between Banda Neira and Gunung Api to the vertical walls of Hatta Island, the most easterly in the group.

The variety and numbers of fish are both excellent; the chances here are always good to see several big animals of a meter or more: reef sharks, Napoleon wrasse, turtles, rays and groupers. Schools of medium sized fish, and the usual kaleidoscope of small reef fish in the shallows are all here in abundance. The reefs we saw were pristine, with no signs of fish bombing damage. Currents were negligible at the sites and times we dove.

Banda has two dive seasons—one centered around April, the other in October. The months before and after these are usually quite good also, but any more than that is a matter of luck. The off seasons bring high waves and relatively turbulent seas, usually December/January during the northwest monsoon, and early June through August for the southeast monsoon.

But, with enough time and patience, one can enjoy good diving even off-season, as there are always breaks in the weather. Visibility, however, remains restricted to 10–12 meters off season, reaching 30–40 meters only around the ideal months.

Staying in Banda

Diving is available only to guests staying at one of Des Alwi's hotels, although this is hardly a problem. Des Alwi is Banda's most famous son, and a tireless promoter of his islands. While Mohammed Hatta and Sutan Sjahrir—two of the leaders of Indonesian independence—were exiled in Banda, they became mentors to the young Des Alwi, who later entered the world of Jakarta politics himself.

AT A GLANCE
Banda Islands

Reef type: Vertical walls, and some slopes

Access: 5 min to 1.5 hrs by speedboat

Visibility: Fair to good, 10–20 meters in the off season; up to 40 meters during the best months

Current: None or moderate, to 1.5 knots

Coral: Excellent, undamaged reefs

Fish: Excellent numbers and varieties at the best sites

Highlights: Pristine, sheer walls and great number of fish off Ai and Hatta

---

After a quarter of a century, he returned to his native islands, and there applied himself to building up the infrastructure and the economy, and raising the profile of the little islands in the Indonesian nation and in the world. He is extremely knowledgeable about the history and culture of his islands.

The cost of diving—boat, tanks, weight belts—is quite reasonable, and if there are just two people diving, there are good spots near Banda Neira to keep boat costs down. For trips further out, it's easier on the wallet to form groups of 4 to 6 divers.

Although there are a few BCs and regulators for rent, we suggest, as always, that you bring your own equipment, including lights for night dives. The boatmen know the good dive spots, but there are no dive masters.

Non-divers need not worry about boredom: the snorkeling is good in the lagoon right off Banda Neira, there are tennis courts, and jaunts can easily be arranged to ruined forts and nutmeg plantations. Although the Bandas are not the ideal place for children, attentive hotel staffers will look after them as they jump off seaside diving boards, swim in calm waters, or watch the sharks, fish and turtles in two coral enclosures in the lagoon.

Sonegat

You could start diving the day you get to Banda, as the flight from Ambon arrives in the early morning. The nearest site for a decent dive is just five minutes by boat from the hotels. It is in the *sonegat*—"sea arm"—between Banda Neira and Gunung Api, just offshore from a little seaside house owned by Des Alwi.

The dropoff here is steep, and the wall extends down 25 meters to a grey, sandy bottom. The wall is cut by vertical clefts, and is overgrown with huge patches of cabbage coral. There were few fish around, but a good-sized dogtooth tuna cruised by, and we saw some of the beautiful blue-girdled and emperor angelfish.

Keraka Island

Pulau Keraka—"Crab Island"—is just a few minutes further out, and protects the north entrance of the Neira–Gunung Api sea passage. A nice sandy stretch on the north coast is perfect for a picnic. We started our dive just off the south shore, descending some 18 meters down a mini-wall covered with hundreds of large blue-and-yellow tunicates (*Polycarpa* sp.).

Swimming to the east, we rounded Keraka's tip, where there is a lighthouse, and started along the north face. Just as we turned the corner, we met a huge grouper, who examined us unhurriedly. At 10 meters we encountered a good assortment of reef fish, and a school of half-meter-long barracudas, hanging out like hoodlums deciding on their next move.

Sjahrir and Batu Kapal

Just off the northern tip of Lontar Island is Sjahrir (formerly Pulau Pisang, "Banana Island"), recently renamed for Sutan Sjahrir, one of Des Alwi's childhood mentors and a former Prime Minister of Indonesia. Sjahrir Island, and Batu Kapal—"Boat Stone"—off its northern point, are just 20 minutes by boat from the hotels on Banda Neira. These two sites

Sjahrir Island
(formerly Pisang Island)

BATU KAPAL I.
Batu Kapal

Reef
Dive site

0   100   200
Meters

Tg. Garam

The diving on Sjahrir is off Batu Kapal Island, and off the reef edge of Pisang Bay.
Batu Kapal.
Slope, then sandy bottomed trench at 25 meters. Two large coral outcrops north of the island are dense with fish, including great swarms of butterflyfish.
Pisang Bay.
The reef profile is a coral slope down to about 35 meters. There is the usual array of reef fishes here, as well as a large number of rays.

Rocks

SJAHRIR
10m
▲ 35m   ▲ 15m

Teluk Pisang
Note: Reef flat of Pisang Bay is exposed at daily low tides.

▲ 20m

▲ 10m

Pisang Bay
Rocks

Village
Tg. Mantutu

combine well for a morning dive, a picnic on the beach, and an afternoon dive.

Our first dive was off the south edge of Batu Kapal, and at first we encountered a boring slope leading to a sandy trench at 25 meters. This did not auger well for an interesting dive. But further down the slope a profusion of large barrel sponges, fan coral and a good variety of soft corals cheered us up.

Then a meter-long grouper met us just off the sandy bottom, and we swam into a cloud of bright reef fish, notable for the profusion of butterflyfish. The best was just ahead: two enormous, rounded coral pinnacles, reaching to around 10 meters of the surface. From 30 meters depth, the bottom dropped down out of our range of vision. The variety and number of fish swimming around or lurking in the caves in these towers of coral was overwhelming. This was a superb dive, marred only by restricted visibility, 10–12 meters. (This was early June.)

The afternoon dive, off the south coast of Sjahrir, started well. A steep coral slope dropped us down to a resting black-spotted stingray at 22 meters. He let us approach quite close before trying to hide under a shallow ledge. As we started our ascent, a large spotted eagle ray, well over a meter across, buzzed us, flapping by just two or three meters away. We also saw an unusual number of triggerfishes, including several Titan triggerfish, and at least six species of butterflyfish in good numbers, including schools of pennant bannerfish. Other divers have reported reef sharks in this area.

Gunung Api

The last major explosion, in May 1988, killed of most of the offshore coral formations around Gunung Api, but amazingly spared many sponges. Some corals are beginning to grow back, but by and large the seascape remains bleak. There are no walls off Gunung Api. The bottom slopes gradually to 30–35 meters, where life peters out.

It is startling to see bright reef fishes in such a barren seascape. We saw a fair number of colorful

Above: *The strange crocodile fish,* Cymbacephalus beauforti. *This creature, which here looks a perfect match for the algae-covered coral boulders, lies in wait for any small fish or crustacean to wander within range of its prodigious mouth. Mapia atoll, Irian Jaya.*

individual species, including clown triggerfish, a bright yellow trumpetfish and some sweetlips. Huge schools of fusiliers cruised the area, and we spotted a few small dogtooth tuna. The stars of the show were a fat, 90-centimeter-long grouper, and an eagle ray a meter-and-a-half across.

Lontar Island

The outer edge of Lontar Island, which represents part of the rim of a sunken caldera, offers several good dive sites, of which we visited two.

Selamon Belakang. We dove off Selamon Belakang (*belakang* means behind), so named because it lies across the island from Selamon village. The dive was superb from the start, as we descended down a steep dropoff split by a vertical cleft and covered with coral. The wall extended down to 45 meters.

We stopped at 30 meters, finding an unusual barrel sponge—huge, and with three openings. We encountered gorgonians and black coral trees. The wall held an unusually large concentration of lionfish, including a black-and-white juvenile who seemed very curious about the intruders. Visibility was 20 meters, very good for this time of year.

We swam north through a good variety of reef fish, with unusual numbers of Vlaming's unicornfish and schools of black triggerfish. The wall was interrupted here and there by sand falls. The dive's highlight was a bumphead parrotfish, a crusty old giant of almost a meter.

Batu Belanda. This site—literally "Dutchman's Stone"—is at the opposite end of Lontar Island. Here we found a good wall, this one ending with sloping sand at 30–35 meters. The drop featured many barrel and tube sponges, and small caves and cracks which offered refuge to abundant fish. The fish were varied and plentiful: a school of snappers, large emperor and blue-girdled angelfish, wrasses by the dozen, a large pinnate batfish, and numerous bannerfish.

Hatta Island

We rode in the newest of the Hotel Maulana's 8-meter open fiberglass dive boats—powered by twin 40hp outboards—to Hatta Island, about 25 kilometers by sea from Banda Neira. Because of the calm seas, usual for October and November, the trip took just 50 minutes.

Hatta is a recent name for the island, bestowed in honor of Mohammed Hatta, one of the founding fathers and the first vice-president of Indonesia. History buffs will recall the island's old name, Rosengain, a British possession at the time when control of the Banda spice trade was still disputed.

Skaru Atoll. Our first stop was the Skaru atoll, a barely submerged reef a few hundred meters off the southern point of Hatta. (See map page 227.) The atoll is completely underwater, and is only visible from a distance because of the waves breaking over it.

The sea was milky with a whitish sediment more commonly found here during the *panca roba* season in July and August. The conditions lingered because of an errant weather pattern associated with the El Niño effect, which irregularly every few years brings warmer water temperatures to the East Pacific off the coast of South America. The promised visibility of 30–40 meters usual in October and November has thus eluded us.

We began our first dive at the western end of the north edge of the atoll, as the site provided protection from the southeast swell and took advantage of a slight current running east. We dropped onto a coral slope that quickly became a wall, ending in

Ai, Hatta and Run Islands

Ai Island

5 Tg. Kelip
6 Fort Revenge
Parigi
Ai Village
4
3 Tg. Besar
2
Tg. Batu Udang
1
Tg. Goranga
Tg. Nama
Nama
Tg. Keli
_AI_
136m ▲
Batu Dua

0   1
Kilometers

1. Best wall in Banda, to 70m; caves at 25m and 35m; schools of jacks, sharks
2. Wall to 45m; large gorgonians; terrace at 7m–12m with coral outcrops
3. Wide terrace to edge, wall to 45m; barrel sponges, soft corals
4. Wall continues, terrace narrows; fishermen here
5. Wall to 50m; clefts, cracks, overhang at 35m; huge gorgonians—largest seen in Banda
6. Wall breaks up; spurs and sand falls

Hatta Island
(formerly Rozengain)

3
4 Tg. Kenari
2 Hatta village
1
Tg. Salamasa
Mt. Hari 140m ▲
HATTA
Tg. Pulu
Tg. Pohon Pinang
Batulobang
Tg. Besar
5 **6** **7**
8 **9**
Tg. Buton
10
11
12
SKARU ATOLL

0   1
Kilometers

1. Vertical wall to 60m; many grottoes
2. Wall to 30m–40m; soft corals on 5m shelf
3. Wall to 30m–40m
4. Coral slope; very good hard corals
5. Wall to 40m; distinctive formations, many gorgonians—most anywhere in Banda
6. Very nice overhang at 27m; gorgonians
7. Coral terrace at 10m; coral knolls to 10m; huge schools of fish
8. Wall to 35m
9. Sandy slope with terrace at 20m; pinnacles
10. Wall to 30m–40m
11. Many pelagics at point; current picks up
12. Sandy slope at 12m; coral outcrops to 6m

Banda Islands

BANDA NEIRA I.
BATU KAPAL
SJAHRIR I.
Batuangus
Ai
_AI_
GUNUNG API I.
Lontar
Bandaneira
NEIJALAKA I.
Run
RUN I.
Nama
LONTAR (BANDA BESAR)
Hatta
HATTA I.
LAUT BANDA

0   5   10
Kilometers

Run Island

1. Coral slope to 35m; many coral spurs, clefts and overhangs, all dusted with white sand
2. Sand slope, 45°, with coral knolls; good dive for beginners

2 Tg. Timbal
NEIJALAKA I.
Tg. Tenusan
Sand and coral exposed at low tide
Tg. Robin
Reef exposed at low tide
Tg. Soawor
Tg. Tuledan
Tg. Cincin Seleman
Run Village
1
RUN
Tg. Lenore
Waynero beach
Tg. Sehee
Tg. Nuret
Mt. Tanah Merah ▲
188m ▲
Tg. Gandulang
Reef always submerged
Tg. Waynero
Reef exposed at low tide

0   1
Kilometers

a sandy bottom 35 meters below. During the first part of the dive we encountered many sandy terraces at around 20 meters, and the wall reached 45 meters before ending at the eastern reach of the north edge.

At the point, to current quickened to 1.5 knots, and we encountered. a multitude of schooling fish. We perched on a coral outcrop and watched the passing parade of unicornfish,

Above: *Nudibranchs,* Polycera *sp. (above) and* Chromodoris bullocki. *Polycera was photographed in Bali, and Chromodoris, Flores.*

fusiliers, jacks and rainbow runners for a good ten minutes. In the course of the dive, we also saw some giants: a reef whitetip shark almost two meters long, two dogtooth tuna, a Napoleon wrasse, and a hawksbill turtle.

At this point the wall ended, and we passed over a sloping terrace of fine white sand, here and there broken up by coral knolls. In this area we found colonies of garden eels (*Heteroconger hassi*),

and a prolific assortment of butterflyfish, angelfish (including the blue-faced angel, *Pomacanthus xanthometapon,* which has a very spotty distribution and is not often seen), triggerfish and schools of sergeant-majors.

Tanjung Besar. Our next dive was off the south coast of Hatta itself, east of a point called Tanjung Besar ("Big Cape"). The wall was sheer, and ended in white sand at 40 meters. Its surface was honeycombed with small grottos and overhangs—at times we felt ourselves in a hanging garden, due to the unusual variety of soft coral dangling from the roof of the grottoes. We saw more gorgonians here than anywhere else in Banda.

This was a perfect environment for moray eels, and we found them in abundance. No sooner would we find one, but another would slither out—invariably right next to our faces!

A gentle current bore us east, past large schools of fish riding thermoclines up and down the wall. We decompressed on a coral terrace at 12 meters. This flat was studded with huge coral outcrops, each reaching almost to the surface. The "plain" was swarming with schools of snapper, fusiliers and unicornfish. The colors and variety of forms of the hard and soft corals here were outstanding.

Northeast Hatta. Our third dive was off the island's north coast, near Hatta village. Although the reef formation was virtually the same on every dive, this area is different in that we encountered many coral spurs, interspersed with falls of fine, white sand. The deepest wall here extended down 60 meters.

Halfway through our dive we encountered a very strange sight: a white object that looked like one of the margarine sculptures one finds in the restaurant of a fancy hotel. We descended to a sand terrace at 30 meters to investigate, and what we found was the whitened corpse of a Napoleon wrasse. Closer inspection revealed that a chunk of flesh was missing from behind the cranial hump. We surmised that this individual had been bested in a territorial dispute.

Just then, two enormous Napoleons buzzed us, an unusual display for such normally shy creatures. We were amazed that the corpse was intact, especially as we had seen two sharks earlier in the dive. From its white color, we judged the body had lain here for at least three days. It was fascinating to observe this monster at leisure, and at such close proximity. The strong teeth are intimidating, and combined with the animal's thick lips, one can see how it so easily dispatches the hard-shelled and thorny crustaceans and echinoderms that are its preferred prey.

Later, we told Des Alwi what we saw, and he had another explanation. There is, he said, a small green shrimp capable of poisoning the Napoleon wrasse.

For our second dive, we continued along the same formation, but heading east from the northwest corner of the island. We found a 45 degree coral slope that continued down to 30 meters. Here we spent a few minutes playing with a large stingray, and then explored the reef.

Twenty minutes into the dive, the reef profile once again changed into a wall. We were back into the earlier formation, and found the dive to be much the same. There was an abundance of semi-pelagic predators, including dogtooth tuna, a giant jack and a school of bluefin jacks (*Caranx melampygus*), and kingfish (*Carangoides* sp.).

Ai Island

Together with Hatta, this island offers Banda's best diving. Both the north coast and the southwest of Ai are ringed with flaw-

less coral walls, dropping in one place to 70 meters. The walls are rugged and full of caves, just the kind of habitat that harbors fish. Some of the gorgonians are the biggest we have seen.

The highlights go on and on: a fat grouper, pushing a meter-and-a-half; a school of more than 300 Heller's barracuda; a couple of meter-long chevron barracuda; a lobster with a body the size of a

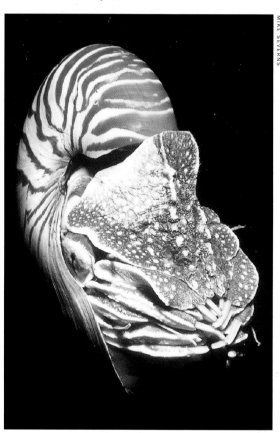

MIKE SEVERNS

Below: *The pearly nautilus,* Nautilus pompilius. *These animals spend the day at near abyssal depths, and only rise to near the surface at night. Ascending some 1,000 meters is a tedious process, and can take several hours. Because*

man's thigh; endless schools of fusiliers; a longnosed emperor close to a meter, the maximum for its species; a group of spotted sweetlips, with one close to its maximum 70 centimeters; many unicornfish; an abundance of clown triggerfishes, and Titan triggerfishes within sight the entire dive; a large school of pyramidal butterflyfish; turtles; and moray eels.

their tentacles are not equipped with suckers, nautilus are poor predators and feed on carrion and the molts of crustaceans. Only rarely—and always at night—are they found in depths divers can reach. Manado, Sulawesi.

BANDA **229**

Above: *A school of lunar fusiliers,* Caesio lunaris. *Fusiliers are among the most common schooling fish seen in Indonesia.*

North Ai. Along the north coast, the wall drops to 50 meters at the northwest point—where there is a large overhang—and then to 30–40 meters until it breaks up near Ai village. At this point, coral ridges alternate with sand filled clefts, and huge swarms of fish congregated. Perhaps it was the shifting warm and cold currents flowing here that attracted the fish.

Southwest Ai. The southwest area features perhaps the best wall in all of Banda, with good growth to 70 meters. Growing on wide terrace on the west coast were tube and barrel sponges, and great quantities of soft coral in red, beige, purple and orange hues.

Run Island

The furthest dives from Banda Neira are off Run Island and tiny Neijalaka off its northern point. In moderately choppy seas, it took an hour-and-a-half to reach Run. The British once claimed Run Island, and it remained a hold-out against the Dutch, who controlled the rest of the archipelago, until 1667. In this year the Dutch and the British tried to consolidate their holdings. Britain gave the Dutch Run, and the Dutch gave the British New Amsterdam—or, as it is now called, Manhattan.

Run. The coral wall on the coast off Run village was somewhat disappointing. While there were shallow caves and clefts in the wall, the coral spreads were poor and covered in a layer of fine white sand. Reef fish were moderately abundant at 15–25 meters, and we spotted one turtle and a couple of fairly large barracuda. The best of the dive came at 3–5 meters, snorkeling depth: two big barracuda, a 90-centimeter Napoleon wrasse, and four huge parrotfish.

Neijalaka. We followed with a dive off the north coast of this tiny island, attached to Run by a wall of coral exposed at low tide. The gently slope had only isolated coral heads, and the fish were notable for their scarcity. Only a pair of barracuda, some 80 centimeters each, saved this dive from total disappointment.

—*Kal Muller and Cody Shwaiko*

Maluku Dive Practicalities

Ambon

Ambon telephone code 0911

Arriving in Ambon. Pattimura Airport is on Ambon Island's Hitu Peninsula across the bay from Ambon City—37 kilometers and 45 minutes by road. A vehicle and passenger ferry runs every few minutes between Poka and Galala, where the bay narrows, which cuts the traveling distance in half. Sometimes a long queue of vehicles waits at the ferry, so it might be faster to take the long way around. In either case, the airport taxis charge $7.50 or $9 (AC cars) for the trip.

Merpati. Jl. A. Yani, Tel: 52481.
Indoavia. Jl. A. Rhebok, Tel: 53866.
Mandala. Jl. A. Y. Pattimura, Tel: 52444.

Local transportation

Ambon Town. Taxis and public minibuses (and *becaks*, three-wheeled bicycle carts) provide transportation in and around Ambon town. Taxis run about $3/hr, sometimes with a two-hour minimum. The main transportation center is in the Mardika market. Private taxis out of town run about $3/hr ($5/hr w/AC). For a round-trip to Hila, including waiting time, a non-AC taxis would cost $20–$25. For a run to Liang, stopping at Natsep and Waai (to see the eels) on the way, figure about $30–$35 w/AC, $18 w/o AC.

Crowded minibuses go everywhere around the island, more often in the early morning and late afternoon. Fares run from 8¢ to nearby Galala (6 km) to 76¢ to Asilulu (70 km). You can charter one of these for about $3/hr.

Dive Operators

P.T. Daya Patal Tour and Travel. Jl. Said Perintah SK II 27 A, Tel: 53529, 53344, 52498, 41136, 41821. Fax: 44709, Telex: 73140 DPAB IA. Contact: Tony Tomasoa. P.T. Daya Patal is at present the only dive operator in Ambon. (See below for their resort on Saparua.) They can arrange boats, tanks, guides, food, and, if needed, a compressor. For rent: Regulators $14/day, BCD's $10/day.

While there are no certified dive guides yet, staff members can show you where the good spots are located. We had superb diving with this outfit, with all arrangements running like clockwork. Try to have Hentje, a pleasant young man and good diver, as your guide. He will look after your gear and be generally quite helpful.

One day, all-inclusive, two-tank tours in Ambon/Saparua area run $125/person (group of 1) to $50/person (group of 4). All-inclusive packages: Ambon 3D/2N $225/head (2–4 persons), $217/head (5–9 persons); Saparua, 5D/4N, $325/head (2–4 persons), $313/head (5–9 persons); to Misool, 12D/11N, $650/head, only groups of 5–9 persons.

Land Tours

The Daya Patal agency also runs non-diving tours to Banda, Tanimbar and Misool, an island off western Irian Jaya. Contact Hans Rijoly or Salomon, they both speak excellent English.
Natrabu Tours and Travel. 53 Jl. Rijail SK 8 No I, Tel: 53537. Contact: Mrs. Tanasaleh.
Sumber Budi Tour and Travel. Jl. Mardika II/16, Tel: 53205, Telex: 73198 TXBTH AB. Contact: Bruce Nanloh (After hours: 52625.)

Accommodations

We recommend the following hotels and *losmen* in Ambon:
Mutiara. Jl. Raya Pattimura, Tel: 53075, 53076. 31 rooms, all with TV and AC. Pleasant staff. Restaurant and bar. Live music nightly. English language *Jakarta Post* available in the lobby for guests. Discount possible if staying more than a couple of days. $29S, $49D.
Cendrawasih. Jl. Tulukabessy, Tel: 52487. 18 rooms with TV. Restaurant. $41S, $45D.
Manise. Jl. W.R. Spratman, Tel: 42905. 56 rooms. This is a businessman's hotel, the newest in Ambon. $25–$40S, $30–$45D. Add 20 percent service charge.
Amboina. Jl. Kapitan Ulupaha, Tel: 41725. 38 rooms. Restaurant, bar, shops, conference room, and TV room. $21S, $32D. New rooms will be coming on line, 20%–30% more expensive.
Game. Jl. A. Yani. 14 rooms. One of the best of the cheaper hotels. $12.
Beta. Jl. Wim Reawaru, Tel: 53463. 26 rooms. One of the best of the cheaper hotels. $5–8S, $8–$10D.
Irama. Jl. St. Babulah, Tel: 53307. 6 rooms w/ inside bath, $8; 14 rooms without, $6.50.
Silalou. Jl. Sedap Malam, Tel: 53197. 15 rooms. $4.50S, $7.50D.

Dining

The traditional cuisine of Ambon is not one of the archipelago's most exciting. The staples — such as sago cakes — are generally bland. The fruit, however, is excellent, and lobsters ($6–$10 each, best at the Hotel Manise) can often be obtained. We recommend the following establishments:
Pondok Asri. Next to the Manise Hotel. Features Chinese and Indonesian dishes as well as Japanese meals ($12–$14), imported US beef ($11–$12) and lots of seafood. Nice decor and quiet setting.
Halim. They claim to serve the best ice-cream in town but we did not find it especially good. Seldom are there small fish and the larger ones are too much for even two hungry divers. But their beer is cold and most dishes well prepared. A bit noisy indoors when the big satellite TV turns on. There is

an outdoor dining patio.

Amboina. Jl. A. Y. Pattimura 63. Best bakery in town, locally-made ice cream. A nice place for a quick meal. Makes a good *roti saucise,* a hot dog in a bun.

New Garden. Jl. P. Revolusi, Tel: 41669. Chinese and Indonesian. Very good.

Banks and Money-changing

There are plenty of banks around Ambon for money-changing, and credit cards are becoming more popular—the best are Visa and the card issued by Bank Central Asia.

Medical

Kantor Kesehatan Wilayah (District Health Office). Tel: 52861 or 52392. Three doctors—Dr. Krisna (clinic telephone: 52715), Dr. Polanunu and Dr. Ristianto (home phone: 53411, 51526)—speak English.

Rumah Sakit Umum (Public Hospital). Tel: 53438 ext. 118 or 348.

Pelita Farma pharmacy. Jl. Setia Budi. Open 24-hours.

Communications

Telephone Office. Jl. Raya Pattimura. In general, phone connections are good, both nationally and internationally. Fax and telex machines are available as well as telephones.

Like everywhere else in the world, hotels in Ambon take a cut on long distance telephone calls, and can charge a bundle for fax and telex services. Ask before making a call.

Photography

Master Photo. Jl. A. Y. Pattimura 41. In-store print processing, $1 for negatives, 15¢ for each print. Kodacolor and Fujicolor negative films; Ektachrome 100 slide film, but no slide processing.

Saparua

Getting there. Regular boats leave from Tulehu on Ambon Island's east coat to the bigger villages on Haruku and Saparua. The regular boat from Tulehu to Pelau, on the north coast of Haruku and the island's largest village, costs $1.50. To Saparua, a regular ferry leaves daily, and stops at Saparua Town ($1.50) and Tuhaha ($1.75) on the east coast of Tuhaha Bay in the north. Another boat goes to Saparua Town ($1.50) and then continues on to Amahai on Seram Island to the north (another $1.50 and 2.5 hrs.).

Regular boats from Saparua Town head to Nusa Laut only on Wednesdays and Saturdays, when they have lots of business ferrying people back and forth to Saparua's market. If you want to go to the little island on another day, you will have to charter a boat.

Chartering speedboats. You can also charter a speedboat—able to carry 3–6 passengers—from Ambon to various villages on Haruku and Saparua. Prices vary, depending on distance, traffic and your bargaining ability. Figure maybe $25–$50.

Land transportation

On the two big islands, buses wait for passengers in the morning at the ferry terminals. Fares range from 6¢ to 40¢ from the ferry terminal on either Haruku or Saparua to anywhere else on the islands. Charters run $3–$5/hour.

Dive Operators

Tony Tomasoa (of P.T. Daya Patal in Ambon, see above) operates a resort on Saparua, the Mahu Village. A compressor and dive gear are kept on the premises. Although you can dive with Daya Patal from a base in one of the hotels in Ambon City, it is much more pleasant out on Saparua.

Mahu Village Resort. Near Kampung Mahu on Saparua's north coast, on the east shore of Tuhaha Bay. Four attractive bungalows face mangrove trees at the sea's edge in a coconut plantation. The resort is locally called "Kelapa Indah" ("Beautiful Coconut"). Dugongs have occasionally seen feeding in the shallow beds of sea grass not far from the resort. The cottages are spacious, airy, thatch-roofed structures with showers and flush toilets. Electricity (220/240 volts) available 24 hours a day. Guaranteed no mosquitoes. $25S, $35D.

The diving just in front of the resort is not good, but the coral on the other side of the bay is fine for snorkeling, in 2–3 meter depths. The resort has "paddle-yourself" outrigger canoes to make the short cross-bay run. Light tackle available, as are fishing trips with boat and pilot/guide. In August and September, black marlin and tuna in the 50–100 kilo range hit regularly.

All diving services available here. (Prices are listed above under P.T. Daya Patal.) The resort also has its own speedboat, which can whisk you over from Ambon in an hour ($42).

Other Accommodations

Losmen Siri Sore. In Siri Sore Saram, on the east shore of Saparua Bay. 12 clean rooms, breakfast included. $12–14S; $13–18D. Breakfast and dinner available, and land and sea excursions can be organized.

On Haruku and Nusa Laut, the traveler must negotiate for a place to stay with a family.

Weather

During the southeast monsoon, June–August, the seas are roughest and underwater visibility is reduced. The rest of the year things are fine, although the seas get a bit rough again during the northwest monsoon, January–February. This does not affect diving, however.

Banda

Getting there: From Ambon by Indoavia on Monday, Wednesday and Saturday, one hour by 18 passenger Twin Otter, $37 (you can also charter a plane from Ambon, $1,200 one-way). Inter-island mixed freighters or large Pelni passenger liners also make the trip about every three weeks (see Travel Advisory, page 253.) You can easily walk from the airstrip to the

Bandaneira hotels, but not with dive gear. Hop in one of the mini-buses that will be waiting.

Dive Operators

Diving is available to guests at either of Des Alwi's three hotels—the Maulana Inn, the Laguna Inn and the Rumah Budaya. For reservations, contact: Hotel Maulana, P.O. Box 3193, Jakarta. Tel: (021) 360372, Fax: 360308. In Banda: Tel: (0910) 21022 or 21023, Fax: 21024.

Maulana Inn. The best rooms in Bandaneira are in the 50-room Maulana Inn, and offer a nice view of Gunung Api across the lagoon. Three meals $16/person +10%. Cold beer $1.75. Bottle of arrak $3. Separate meals: breakfast $3, lunch $5, supper $8. A big plate of sashimi, $4.50 extra (subject to availability, must be ordered one day ahead.) Sea front rooms, $35S, $45D; other rooms, $30S, $40D; bungalows $45. All plus 10% tax.

Laguna Inn. 12 rooms. Three meals $12, all plus 10% tax. $25S, $30D.

Museum Rumah Budaya. Four rooms in the back for budget travelers. $11, including tax and breakfast.

Diving. Daily charges: tank & weights $14, refill $8. BCs ($8) and regulators ($7.50) also available by the day. Also mask and snorkel sets ($2) and fins ($1).

Boat rental. Boats can run divers to Hatta Island ($25) and to Ai and/or Run ($30) with a 5 person minimum. The cost is less for closer spots, such as Sjahrir. You can also rent the boats by the hour, for example for night dives: speedboat (4–6 people) $30/hr; diesel-powered boat (8 people) $25/hr; or a bigger diesel powered boat (12 people) $35/hr. The largest boat, the *Boi Kherang,* can accommodate 20 people and goes for $40/hr. The rental fees for the larger boats include a Zodiac with a small outboard.

For snorkeling off Banda Neira, the near coast of Lontar

and Gunung Api, a boat can drop you off and pick up at pre-determined time for $6/person (6 persons or more). The same arrangement to Sjahrir Island and the far side of the Lontar, $10/person.

For a special trip to Manukang (Suangi) Island or Manuk Island (lots of birds), contact the manager of the Maulana Hotel. Essentially, it is the cost of the boat charter—to Manukang, 4 hours each way by diesel, 1.5 to 2 hours by speedboat; to Manuk, about 11 hours each way (diesel only).

Other watersports. Windsurfing, mid June to September, January to March, $2/hr; waterskiing $30/hr; fishing is included in price of boat rental. May to September, the yellow-tail tuna, sailfish, swordfish, and Spanish mackerel run; from October to June, it's barracuda. Jacks are caught all year round.

Other Accommodations

Aside from these places owned by Des Alwi, there are two simple *losmen*: The **Delfika** with 8 rooms, all enclosed facilities, $9.50/person including tax and three meals; the **Selecta** with 7 rooms, also offering full board, $10 with attached toilet facilities, $8.50 for rooms with shared facilities.

The Rumah Budaya, Selecta and Delfika are all quite close to the main mosque and its blaring loudspeakers. All accomodations on Banda tend to fill during the last two weeks of December as well as most of October. Make sure to reserve ahead during these times.

Dining

Best at the **Maulana** and the **Laguna,** where you usually are served two kinds of fish and a vegetable. There are many little restaurants in Bandaneira town where the simple meals of rice or noodles with chicken cost about 75c. We found the **Selecta II** the most pleasant of these—there is cold beer available here (sometimes) for a $1.40 per can.

Excursions

Sunset cruise. Two-hour cruise around Gunung Api by boat, and a stop at Sambayang to visit a cinnamon plantation, and to snorkel in the sea and in hot water springs. $6 (6 person minimum).

Climbing Gunung Api. It takes one to three hours to climb the 656-meter-high volcano. (See text, page 222.) One day's notice is required. Guide $5.50 per person (whether he carries anything or not) and round-trip boat $5. Upon returning, you obtain a certificate declaring you an honorary citizen of Banda. This document requires a $2 donation to the museum.

Lontar Village. This is a trip to Lontar island to see a nutmeg plantation, sacred wells and Fort Hollandia, this last reached by climbing 360 steps. The tour starts at 4 pm, and takes about two hours. $6/person, minimum of two; if guide needed, extra $5.

Cultural Events

In April and October, 37-man *kora-kora* (war canoe) races are held. The rest of the year, you can commission a demonstration: $150 for one *kora-kora* and crew. A *cakalele* war dance costs $350, and requires 10-day's notice.

Banks and Money-changing

There are no banks on Banda, so bring all the rupiahs you will need from Ambon.

Weather

The very best for sun and calm seas: April, and late September–early November. The southeast monsoon brings wind and rain from late May till around mid-August. It is very difficult during this period to make the crossing to Hatta Island, although Ai and Run can usually be reached.

The northwest monsoon starts in late November and runs until mid-February. During this period it is possible to cross to Hatta, but Ai and Run are hard to reach.

Introducing Irian Jaya

Irian Jaya is one of the last really wild places on earth. Although a few roads have been laid that lead a bit inland from some of the population centers on the coast, parts of the interior of the western half of New Guinea, an almost continent-sized island, are still shrouded in mystery. Even today, the flight maps used by pilots working the highlands for Protestant missions and mineral exploration contain large areas marked: Relief Data Incomplete.

Fewer than 2 million people live in Irian Jaya's 410,660 square kilometers. The largest city and capital of the province is Jayapura, a buzzing town of 170,000 on the north coast near the border with Papua New Guinea, which neatly cuts the island in half. Modern Jayapura boomed after World War II, based on infrastructure laid by U.S. General Douglas MacArthur, who began his famous island-hopping strategy from here.

Irian Jaya was not relinquished by Holland at the same time as the rest of the former Dutch East Indies, and did not formally become part of Indonesia until 1969. The territory was dubbed Irian Jaya—"Victorious Irian"—in the early 1970s.

The transition was far from smooth, and local rebellions by spear-wielding warriors and an independence movement, the Operasi Papua Merdeka (OPM) —"Free Papua Movement"— haunted the changeover. There is little OPM activity today, but the Indonesian government keeps a large military presence in the province, and many areas are still off-limits to tourism.

Linguists do not agree on how many unique languages are spoken in Irian, although most estimates hover around 250. The island's indigenous people, dark-skinned and kinky-haired— hence "Papua," Malay for kinky hair—trace their ancestry back to before the expansion of the Malays through Indonesia.

An Impenetrable Island

The interior of Irian is craggy and mountainous—Puncak Jayakesuma, at 4,884 meters, is the highest point between the Himalayas and the Andes—and to reach it from the coast one must cross thick swamps and forests. The rivers of the north are so full of oxbows that running them doubles or triples the overland distance to the interior. In the south, treacherous tides—changing the water level in rivers even 100 kilometers inland—conspired against explorers.

Until American explorer Richard Archbold flew over the Baliem Valley in 1938, and saw the neat little compounds and sweet potato fields of the Dani, these people had lived in their valley isolated from contact with any outsiders for some 10,000 years. Today, the Dani are Irian's most famous ethnic group. Their numbers have grown to about 70,000, and Wamena, a small town in the Baliem Valley and the de facto capital of Dani country, has been attracting some 100 visitors a month.

Farmers and Artists

Famous warriors in the past, today the Dani are simply farmers, living in thatch and wood huts and raising their staple sweet potatoes and pigs in the

Overleaf: *An undersea ledge, encrusted with cup corals. These corals extend their bright yellow tentacles to snare plankton only at night. Mapia atoll. Photograph by Kal Muller.*

Opposite: *Bigeye jacks,* Caranx sexfasciatus, *at Batu Kapal off Nain Island in the Bunaken group in North Sulawesi. The photographer "called" these jacks using a trick he learned from a Melanesian fisherman. Photograph by Mike Severns.*

salutary climate of the 1,500-meter-high Baliem Valley. Despite 40 years of Protestant missionaries, many Dani are unregenerate in wearing their *kotekas,* or penis gourds.

If the Dani are the most famous of Irian's peoples, the Asmat are the most notorious. Living in the hostile tidal swamps of the south coast, ritual head-hunting had in the past been the centerpiece of Asmat culture.

This fact made international headlines in 1961, when Michael Rockefeller, the young son of then-governor of New York Nelson Rockefeller, disappeared after trying to swim ashore when his boat capsized. Whether or not Rockefeller was actually eaten by the people of Otsjanep has fueled many speculations, but has never been determined.

Rockefeller was visiting the Asmat to collect their art, among the most powerful and respected in the world. Huge war shields, canoe prows and several-meters-long *bisj* poles, decorated with abstract and heavily expressionistic figures, display the kind of raw energy that modernist Euro-pean painters treasured in their collections of "primitive" art.

Rich, Unexplored Waters

The Cenderawasih—"Bird-of-Paradise"—Bay north of Irian Jaya, and the islands off New Guinea's western tip hold some stunning, unexplored reefs. There are reports here of huge "fields" of giant clams. Currently, only the *Tropical Princess,* operating out of Biak Island, offers sport diving in this region, chiefly to the isolated islands at the northernmost reach of the province.

South of Irian is the shallow Arafura Sea, which until perhaps just 18,000 years ago connected New Guinea to Australia. The coast here is silty, and fringed with brackish rivers and stands of mangrove and casuarina.

Bintuni Bay, cut deep into the Bird's Head Peninsula, offers one of the largest and most unmolested mangrove swamps in the world. Athough such habitats are not a paradise for divers, they play an important ecological role in developing the larval stages of fish and crustaceans.

—David Pickell

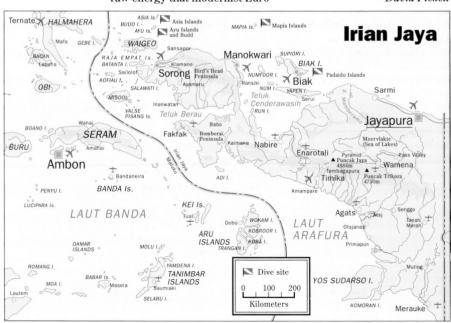

IRIAN JAYA

Our Best Dives Ever off Irian's Live-Aboard

The two-meter shark shot straight out from the blue limit of visibility, some 20 meters off a vertical wall of coral. Before you could say "Jack Daniels" he was at my partner, Easy Ed, who had been banging a knife on his tank in an attempt to attract a smaller shark to within range of my camera. A meter away from Ed, the big grey reef shark twisted up and away, flashing his white belly before disappearing back into the void.

The Clenched Fist

Our human brain waves coincided—*Fantastic!*—before our eyes met and we gave each other the clenched first salute, our private underwater hand signal for any extraordinary happening. Nothing gets the adrenaline pumping as hard as a visit by a big shark.

It was around 8 a.m., and we were just 10 minutes into our first dive of the day, drifting in a 1–2 knot current off a coral wall, under about 20 meters of fairly clear water. Several sharks had come up from the dark to check us out, but they kept too respectful a distance. At each sighting, my partner would bang his knife on the tank, hoping our shy friends would mistake the noise for the dinner bell. None had heretofore paid any attention, but Easy Ed is a persistent hombre.

During our 10 days and 30-odd dives off the *Tropical Princess,* a live-aboard based on Biak Island, in northern Irian Jaya, Easy Ed and I raised the clenched fist salute a couple of dozen times: a swarm of thousands of jacks enveloping us, a bewildering storm of silver; a cruising school of 300 large barracuda; a huge spotted eagle ray flying gracefully by; a big crocodile fish laying on the floor of an open cave; several dozen meter-long bumphead parrot fish lurching back and forth at us in the shallows; an exquisite and profoundly ugly stonefish holding still as death in a shallow cave; a giant turtle staring at us from an overhang; and the constant thrill of swimming through the night plankton, each movement leaving behind a glowing trail of phosphorescence.

AT A GLANCE
Asia, Ayu and Mapia

Reef type:	Vertical walls, lagoon channels
Access:	Zodiac rides from ship just 5 min
Visibility:	Good, 20–25 meters
Current:	Moderate, 1–2 knots, good for drift diving; gets strong during tide changes at lagoon mouth
Coral:	Excellent, undamaged reefs
Fish:	Excellent numbers and varieties
Highlights:	Visit by a large shark; sheer number of fish in channel at Mapia during tide change

---

After a few days, we became blasé—sights that would thrill most divers left us unimpressed. What? another moray eel poking its open mouth out of a cave? Another school of Moorish idols? More big Napoleon wrasses? Yet another formation of barracuda, or another 1.5-meter shark? We were hard to please. But pleased we were. Easy Ed, with thousands of dives worldwide, considered this trip his best ever. And so did I.

Diving North Irian

The home port of the *Tropical Princess* is Biak, a large island north of Irian Jaya's Cender-awasih Bay. Biak town is one of the biggest in the province, and because planes can't make the long flight from the United States to Bali or Jakarta without refueling, it has an international airport. So far—in early 1992—booking a berth on the *Tropical Princess* is the only way to dive in the Irian Jaya province.

The ship's range covers a wide swathe of seas north of Irian: from the Padaido Islands, just off the south coast of Biak, to tiny Budd Island, some 600 kilometers (325 nautical miles) northwest of Biak. All of these islands are within a degree north or south of the equator, and rise from depths of from several hundred to thousands of meters.

Because the islands are so isolated, and are washed by deep currents, the fish—particularly pelagic and schooling species—are plentiful. But there is a price to pay for this rich water: plankton and suspended matter cut the visibility to a good, but not excellent, 20–25 meters.

Superb diving was not the only reason our two-week cruise was such a great experience. Because of last-minute cancellations (this was just in the aftermath of the Gulf War), there were only four of us on board: Harvey and Armand, two businessmen and long-time buddies from Chicago, Easy Ed and myself. Twelve of the ship's bunks went empty.

We thus were the focus of the helpful 10-man crew and Glenn Barrall, the American divemaster. Further, our first two series of dives were pioneering exploratory dives in virgin waters to determine the suitability for future groups. Our unanimous verdict, as the first jury to explore the waters of the Asia and Ayu Islands, was that they are suitable indeed.

Atolls and Steep Walls

The owners of *Tropical Princess* pioneered and charted a number of dive sites beginning in 1989. These include the Padaido Islands, just east of Biak, some

Below: *Two crew-members filet a freshly caught wahoo,* Acanthocybium solandri, *on the* Tropical Princess *'s diving platform.*

sites off Supiori Island, northwest and almost attached to Biak, and those we visited on this trip: the Ayu Islands, Budd Island, the Asia Islands and the Mapia Islands. (See map page 242.)

The Ayu group includes an atoll—a wide ring of coral 30 kilometers north to south and 15 kilometers wide, with some 10 tiny islands—and a separate wide fringing reef that has grown up around the somewhat larger Ayu Island. The atoll's lagoon opens in a narrow channel to the west, an area that during tide changes can be both exciting and difficult to dive, due to strong currents.

Ayu is within sight of large Waigeo Island, perhaps 20 kilometers to the south and just across the Dampier Strait from the tip of Irian Jaya's Bird's Head.

Tiny Budd Island, just half a kilometer from stem to stern, lies 35 kilometers or so west and slightly north of Ayu Island. It is surrounded on all sides by a narrow fringing reef.

The three islands of the Asia group all sit on one chunk of coral, a long apostrophe-shaped outcrop that lies just 40 kilometers north of the Ayu atoll. The fringing reef is narrow, and drops off very steeply.

All of these reefs are drop-offs, steep walls extending down to 200–300 meters. We very occasionally saw some fish-bombing damage (this has become a severe problem at some sites inside Cenderawasih Bay), but 99 percent of the reefs we saw were absolutely unmolested.

Mapia atoll, north and slightly west of Biak, is the climax of the *Tropical Princess's* run. Around Ayu, Asia and Budd Islands, soundings reach 1,000–1,500 meters. Around Mapia, the bottom is four kilometers down. Mapia stands in splendid isolation far north in the province.

The group consists of three islands: Mapia (formerly Penguin, or "Pegun" on some maps),

KAL MULLER

a vertical needle of land marking the south of the atoll, Bras and Paniloso (formerly Fanildo).

Pirates and Ghosts

In the early 20th century Elinor Mordaunt stopped in Mapia on a swing through the islands of the then Dutch Indies, which she recounts in her 1926 *The Further Venture Book*. Mapia, she writes, is "the strangest island I have yet visited."

She repeats a story she heard of David O'Keefe, either a pirate or a "common carpenter put on shore from a whaling boat because he was ill." In the 1860s, it seems O'Keefe stole the island at musketpoint from Van Renesse van Duivenbode, who had obtained the concession from the local rajah.

This O'Keefe, with "flaming red hair," went on to marry the rajah's daughter and subsequently populate the island.

Even Mordaunt, however, figures that the story is probably apocryphal, dismissing the young Dutch copra farmer—the grandson of Van Renesse—who told it to her with the arch: "I feel (he) has sadly mistaken his profession in becoming a planter when he might so greatly distinguish himself as a novelist."

Mordaunt's skepticism of oral history did not, however, extend to the supernatural. Walking through Mapia's forest, she saw her first ghost.

Above: *The 30-meter* Tropical Princess *was originally built to ferry personnel to offshore oil platforms. It has now been converted to a dive boat, and carries two Zodiacs, two compressors and air banks, and even an E-6 film processor.*

Asia, Ayu, Budd and Mapia

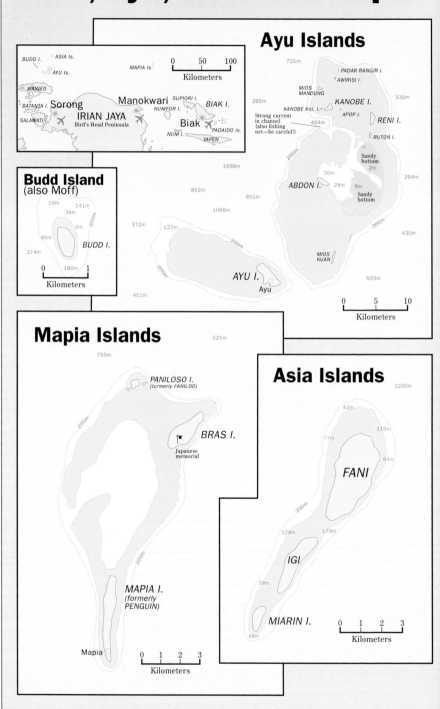

Ayu Islands

721m

PADAR RANGIR I.
AWIRISI I.

MIOS MANDUNG

295m

330m

KANOBE I.

KANOBE Kcl. I.

APOP I.

RENI I.

Strong current in channel (also fishing net—be careful!)

464m

RUTON I.

200m

Sandy bottom 2m

30m

ABDON I.

28m

8m

Sandy bottom

294m

200m

430m

MIOS KUAN

503m

0   5   10
Kilometers

BUDD I.   ASIA Is.

AYU Is.

MAPIA Is.

0   50   100
Kilometers

WAGEO

BATANTA I.   Sorong   Manokwari

SUPIORI I.

BIAK I.

SALAWATI   IRIAN JAYA
Bird's Head Peninsula

NUMFOR I.

Biak

NUM I.

YAPEN

PADAIDO Is.

1698m

852m

951m

1086m

Budd Island
(also Moff)

19m   141m
39m

6m   200m

96m   BUDD I.

274m

0   180m   1
Kilometers

372m

121m

200m

200m

AYU I.

Ayu

451m

Mapia Islands

521m

750m

PANILOSO I.
(formerly FANILDO)

200m

BRAS I.

Japanese memorial

Asia Islands

1200m

42m

119m

77m

84m

FANI

200m

129m

179m

IGI

59m

200m

MAPIA I.
(formerly PENGUIN)

Mapia

0   1   2   3
Kilometers

MIARIN I.

48m

0   1   2   3
Kilometers

"I walked along the shore and cut inland through groves of coco-nut palms, interspersed with some of the largest iron-barks that I have ever seen, and immense fallen trunks of forest monsters, which—looking altogether too big for the little island—were massed with every sort of fern imaginable.

"And it was in one of these glades, moving along a pathway at the edge of the sea, that I saw the first ghost that I have ever seen in my life, or could swear to having seen, if I was not altogether and temporarily mad. A small, square man with very wide white trousers driven sideways by the sea wind, walking with his head covered with a broad brimmed, shiny black hat, bent against the rain, the end of a short pigtail showing beneath it; wearing a coat of thick blue pilot cloth, cut like a boy's Eton coat buttoned tight around him, his cutlass dangling—all alike clear cut out against the white coral path."

Visiting the Islands

All the islands are today inhabited by Melanesians who speak the language of Biak. They claim descent from Gurabesi, a semi-historical cultural hero who established diplomatic relations with clove-producing Tidore Island by marrying a princess.

The Asia and Ayu islands have been inhabited for generations. Hamlets are scattered about, always near a source of fresh water. The 13 families that now live on Mapia moved there only in the last decade (The planters Mordaunt met probably left at the onset of World War II.)

When the *Tropical Princess* anchored off the reefs, the curious residents of the islands would paddle up to offer us fresh coconuts and have a look at our strange outfits. As their sources of supply are quite limited, they invariably asked us for cigarets, and sometimes, anti-malaria pills. They were all pleasant chaps.

The only cash crop produced on the islands is copra, which is processed into cooking oil and soap. The mature coconuts are split, and then the meat is dried over fires made from the husks. Small ships occasionally call to pick up the copra. The islanders also sometimes earn some extra income by collecting trepang or trochus shells.

The staple of the diet is taro, a starchy tuber, and some imported rice. A few vegetables are raised in small plots. There is plenty of fresh fish, of course, which the men spear, using homemade rubber-powered spear guns underwater, or long trident-tipped spears from the shallows or their little outriggers.

One of the *Tropical Princess*'s Zodiacs can take a small party ashore if you want to have a look around one of the hamlets. Bring your dive boots, as there might be a bit of walking over shallow coral. Also, biting flies are for some reason plentiful on the islands, so bring repellent. They also come aboard, uninvited, when the *Tropical Princess* lies close to land.

On the southern tip of Bras Island, in the middle of the Mapia group, the Japanese government has erected a small monument to three soldiers who died manning an observation post here during World War II. Japanese divers respectfully bow to the statue of the Shinto deity and to the spirits of their countrymen. (Their physical remains have been repatriated to the motherland.)

Drifting with the Current

The dives are almost all drift dives off beautiful, vertical walls. On these plankton-swept islands, the variety of soft corals, gorgonians and crinoids is outstanding. Some of the fan corals growing horizontally off the wall at

Mapia had stems 15 centimeters in diameter, and stuck out 3–4 meters. Giant clams were more common here than anywhere else I have dived in Indonesia, some of them real monsters in excess of a meter long.

We saw huge chunks of smooth, brown *Porites* coral sprouting hundreds of Christmas-tree worms (*Spirobranchus* sp.) of every imaginable color.

Reef sharks were common, including the big 2-meter customer described above, and on a couple of occasions we spotted hammerheads.

Although we never saw any underwater, large sea mammals are common in the area. On the way out to the islands, we were treated to a frolicking show by several hundred dolphins. On the way back to Biak from Mapia, a pod of killer whales performed for an hour. A bit later, we crossed paths with a group of sperm whales. When we spotted the whales, the captain of the boat circled slowly so we could watch the big mammals' antics.

Schooling fish are abundant on these reefs, and on several dives we were surrounded by jacks. We always saw small groups of barracuda, but on one dive encountered a school of at least 300 individuals, averaging 60 centimeters in length. On a shallow dive, we encountered a veritable small army of bumphead parrot fish, some of them a meter long, submarine tanks cruising slowly in a ragged file. Fusiliers, various schooling butterflyfish and small groups of batfish were common.

Among the best dives were at the channel openings of the atolls, particularly Mapia. During a tide change, we literally shot along with the current at the mouth of Mapia atoll through huge schools of jacks and barracuda, and over eagle rays and sharks. It was a fantastic experience. The lagoon mouths proved the best place to see large rays—mantas and eagle rays—majestically propelled by slow flips of their wings.

The reefs' caves, nooks and crannies sheltered a bewildering variety of species, including lionfish, scorpionfish and crocodile fish. One tight cave could hold a

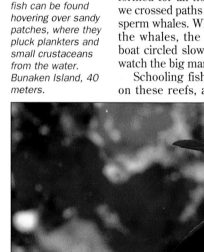

Below: *The decorated dartfish,* Nemateleotris decora. *Pairs of these beautiful little dartfish can be found hovering over sandy patches, where they pluck plankters and small crustaceans from the water. Bunaken Island, 40 meters.*

half-dozen big lobsters, their long tentacles sticking out. We regularly saw large turtles.

Night dives were among our favorite experiences. The water was so rich in phosphorescent plankton that each movement left a glowing wake. A really brusque gesture set off fireworks.

The Tropical Princess

At the time of this writing, the *Tropical Princess* is the only year-round, live-aboard dive boat operating in Indonesia. Bookings are targeted at American (10-day cruises) and Japanese (5-day cruises) divers, booked in groups through overseas agents. (See "Irian Practicalities," page 249.) The boat's schedule is often filled far in advance, so don't expect to find any space without a reservation.

While beginning (but certified) divers may sign aboard, the cruise is really better suited to more advanced divers. We suggest you have at least 100 dives before booking this trip.

The ship was built in Singapore in 1979, and was originally designed for ferrying oil personnel to offshore rigs. It has been fully refitted as a dive boat by Andre Pribadi, an experienced Indonesian diver.

The ship is 30 meters long, has a 6.5-meter beam, and weighs 500 tons. It runs a satellite navigation system. Cruising speeds of 10–11 knots come from twin screws, each powered by an 880 hp engine. Two additional engines serve as backup power and to run the generators.

There are 8 two-passenger cabins, small but serviceable, with enough space for clothes, cameras and odd non-dive gear. Two cabins have their own toilets and the rest each share a toilet between two rooms.

The dining/common area is a bit small, a limitation of the ship's original design. If all the passengers are eating at the same time,

or watching one of the library's many videos, things can get rather crowded. Space is also at a premium in the pre-dive suiting up area. An open top deck, however, is quite large—great for sunrise or sunset watching or checking out the wheelhouse. (Plans are to shade some of this space to make it more usable, a real advantage if there is a full house.) The dining room and cabins are air-conditioned and no smoking is allowed indoors.

There is a good library of feature films and diving documentaries, and the video and sound system is excellent. The video equipment includes Super VHS, Beta, Hi-8, and editing facilities, and can handle a variety of international formats. Lacking, however, is a decent library of books, particularly fish and invertebrate identification books.

The meals are served buffet style, and are excellent and plentiful, with soup, rice and vegetables, two or three main courses (beef, chicken, fish, squid, shrimp), and dessert of fruit and cake. Cold lemonade is always available. Soft drinks and beer ($2/can) are extra, as is liquor ($4/shot), paid for at the end of the cruise. Special dietary requirements can be taken into consideration. Crewmembers fished as we motored from site to site, and we usually had fresh wahoo, jack or tuna on the table.

Competent Staff

The divemaster is the key to any successful cruise, and the owners of the *Tropical Princess* hit the jackpot with Glenn Barrall, a young, red-headed American. Barrall is extremely good-natured, and as experienced as they come.

He plans the dives well, taking into account his clients' levels of ability, and provides plenty of dive opportunities without pushing anyone. He is an accomplished underwater photogra-

Above: *A bluestreak cleaner wrasse,* Labroides dimidiatus, *has set up a station at the base of this wonderfully encrusted coral boulder. Bunaken Island, 25 meters.*

pher, and is quite handy with his Hi-8 underwater video rig.

Our cruise was the first Barrall led as divemaster of the *Tropical Princess,* having just been hired from Saudi Arabia, where he managed a dive shop on the Red Sea. He was still a little unfamiliar with the names of some local fish, but by the time you read this we are certain he will have done his homework in this area. He is extremely knowledgeable about underwater photography, and diving science.

The 10-man, all-Indonesian crew, while speaking very little English, were always helpful without being obtrusive. Lots of smiles and all kinds of attention to the guests made for pleasant, efficient contact despite the language barrier. Wesley, a Batak from Sumatra who is trying hard to improve his English, is the

hardest working man on board. You are always welcome in the wheelhouse to look over the charts or chat with the captain.

Smooth Diving

The diving operation has been well planned and operates smoothly. Two compressors located below the suit-up area in the back of the main deck fill air banks which can fill 22 tanks in 40 minutes. The tanks are refilled to 3000 psi (or close to this) after every dive.

Storage and filling of tanks takes place on the stern dive platform, and they are loaded into the Zodiacs by the crew.

Space provided around the suit-up area holds each diver's basic personal gear (mask, snorkel and fins) along with the weight belt provided. A row of hangers take the wet suits.

After wiggling into suits and boots, and donning weight belts, you hand any camera gear to one of the crew members who carefully places it in the Zodiac tied to the dive platform. Carrying only mask and fins, you walk down four steps to the dive platform.

Steadying hands ease you into the 5-meter Zodiacs (powered by 40hp outboards), where you are helped into your tank and BC rig. Somebody usually turns your air on by the time you are strapped in. A short ride, less than 5 minutes on the average, brings you to the dive site.

Coming up from below, the boatman picks you up quickly and hauls your gear aboard. He will help, if needed, to haul you over the side and remove your flippers. Back to the ship, the crew takes all the gear out of the Zodiac while you get out of your suit and shower on the back deck, drying with fresh towels. A large plastic garbage can of fresh water is available to soak your cameras. You pick your personal gear up, put it in your space, and—Voila!—time for a snack.

Simple Pleasures of a Dive off Ruebas Island

After a hard early morning rain, the landscape was glazed and dazzling. The chickens were the first to come back out. We sat in the open dining room of our hotel on the edge of Biak town, drinking strong, sweet coffee. The bright croton bushes and unkempt banana trees dripped water, and one could almost see them growing.

The air was fresh and felt cool, although not in a sense that a thermometer could confirm. But within an hour, a steady, stifling heat would shroud the island. By then, however, we would be out over the water, headed to one of the nearest islands in the Padaido group.

Biak Island

Everybody who flies on Garuda airlines from the United States stops in Biak, yet few ever see the island. They simply wait until the plane undergoes refueling and crew change, and continue on to Bali. Even those who get off do so simply to catch the flight across to Sentani, whence to the Baliem Valley in the middle of Irian Jaya.

But there is constant talk of developing tourism on Biak. Entrepreneurs plan to take advantage of Biak's international airport, and coax some of the people passing through into staying. A star-rated hotel (with a golf course!) is going up on the shore a half-hour's drive east of Biak town, although construction has been very slow.

Currently, there is no way to dive in the Padaido Islands. We have included this essay only because there is persistent talk of land-based diving here, and

the opportunity may present itself in the near future.

To Ruebas Bawah

Our boatman pointed the *prahu* toward the twin Ruebas Islands, tiny pillars of compacted coral that rise 400 meters from the bottom. Once past the sandbars and fringing reef off the big island of Biak, the water turns from azure blue to inky blue-black. A dark storm was visible in the distance, and scattered clouds appeared, on occasion sweeping the boat with rain.

The island of Ruebas Bawah—"Near Ruebas"—has a small beach in the lee of the prevailing current, but the rest of the island presents a rock face several meters high. Thick vegetation perches on top the rock like a mop of hair. At the waterline, the waves have worked steadily into the soft limestone producing a cleft. Underwater, just a few paces out from this groove, a wall of coral drops almost vertically to the inky depths.

The approaching storm and cloud cover made things a bit dark underwater, but the sun came in and out in sudden flashes. The water here is clear and fresh, welling up from the 400-meter depths that surround Ruebas. A gentle current swept across the reef face.

In a sense, there is nothing particularly spectacular about this site. It is a typical eastern Indonesian wall. I saw no really large fish or huge fan corals. Nevertheless, this is a very healthy reef.

Stony coral of dozens of species grows in branches, plates and shelves along the reef edge

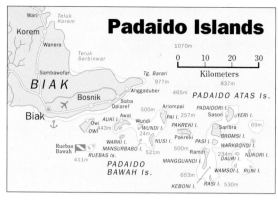

and down the wall. Deeper down, gorgonians spread flat, stiff nets of purple into the current. Here and there sprout colonies of the stinging hydroid *Aglaophenia,* which looks like a fern dipped in thick, pinkish-brown paint.

The cupped oblong plates of mushroom coral were scattered everywhere. These animals seem poorly adapted to life on a drop-off reef and no more than half of those I saw were rightside up. Because it doesn't grow from a holdfast, mushroom coral is at the mercy of surge and currents, particularly on such a steep reef.

Dendronephthya, soft and fluid and downy, grows here in small clumps of fluorescent pink, dark green and even black. Comparing this animal to a flower is unjust; there is nothing stiff about it, it is as liquid as the seas in which it lives. Its beauty is all the more exquisite for its apparent fragility, as if any sudden motion in its vicinity would cause it to dissolve.

Clouds of Fish

Clouds of pyramidal butterfly-fish, with black faces, yellow fins, and pearly white flanks, and schools of black triggerfish, blue-black and shaped like compressed footballs with undulating fins, hovered off the edge of the coral drop-off. In the deeper parts of the reef, coral overhangs and caves, some cut three meters into the wall, were the lairs of fat

emperor and regal angelfish, the elegantly striped species familiar from postcards and coffee-table books.

Near the top of the reef, where the sunlight is strongest, giant anemones squeeze into cracks and breaks in the compacted and overgrown coral. These huge mops of colored tentacles are always tended by a family of clownfish, nestling deep into the tentacles and plucking at bits of food and debris trapped in their midst.

A young spotfin lionfish sat on a lump of coral jutting out from the wall, placid and slightly awkward, his nose pointed into the current. Still a juvenile, perhaps the size of a man's fist, the animal's elaborate finnage seemed still a bit much for him to control, like a puppy whose paws are big out of proportion. He bristled and leaned his poisonous dorsal spines menacingly in my direction, most unusual behavior for such normally mild creatures. Chalk it up to the aggressive vanity of youth, perhaps.

I have always thought that batfish were the real intellectuals of the reef. Perhaps it is their large eyes, or the shape of their faces, which seem to be all forehead. About 20 meters down, three round-faced batfish looped up from the depths to examine the strangers. I tried to get closer to one, which had broken off from the group, kicking in a steady, controlled way so as not to spook him.

To my surprise, he turned and swam straight up to my faceplate, and looked me right in the eyes from about a foot away. We both froze for a few seconds. Did he sense a kindred intelligence? I winked at him, but of course a fish can't return that gesture. He wheeled slowly around, and dropped out of sight, to join his companions in the inscrutable depths below.

—*David Pickell*

Irian Jaya Practicalities

Telephone code for Biak 0961

Currently, 10-day tours on the *Tropical Princess* are being marketed to U.S. divers, and one-week tours to Japanese divers (Japanese usually get less time off than Americans.)

The most efficient way to get to Biak from the United States is on the Garuda flight from Los Angeles (via Hawaii).

The flight lands in Biak quite early in the morning, usually around 5:30 a.m. (Important: The scheduling of this flight is notoriously unreliable. The return flight is supposed to leave in the early evening, but it can sometimes be 6–8 hours late, or even not leave until the next day. Do not plan on making an important meeting the day you get back.)

Crewmembers will pick you up at Biak's small airport, hustle you through the largely perfunctory immigration, and have you on the boat in less than a half hour. By the time you finish breakfast, the boat will be underway to your first dive. On your return, they will perform the same service in reverse.

All the *Tropical Princess'* dive cruises include the Mapia Islands, along with a dive or two off Supiori Island along the way. The longer 10-day trips could also feature the Ayu group, the Asia Islands, or the islands of Padaido Atas.

Dive equipment (Scubapro) is available for rental: mask, snorkel, fins, boots, $11/day ($55/week); regulator with gauges $15/daily ($60/week); BC $12/day ($48/week); underwater flashlight $6/dive; scooter $15/dive. Various sizes of batteries can be purchased, and E-6 film processing is available on board (the unit was not yet up and working on our trip). Processing $7.50/roll; mounting, 10¢/slide.

The boat is being heavily booked, so make your arrangements early. The 10-day cruise runs $2650, and round-trip by Garuda airlines from Los Angeles to Biak costs $1050.

Indonesian Agents

P.T. Prima Marindo Paradise. Jl. Pintu Masuk Pelabuhan, Biak, IRJA, Indonesia. Tel: (961)21008 Fax: 21804

Hotel Borobudur. 3rd flr, shop 34, Jl Lapangan Banteng Selatan 1, Jakarta 10110. Tel: (21)380555 ext 7602 or 7604; Fax: 3803567

U.S. agents

Poseidon Ventures Tours. Tel: 800/854-9334 or 714/644-5344 (Southern California).

Sea Safaris. Tel: 800/821-6670 or 213/546-2464 (Southern California).

Tropical Adventures Travel. Tel: 800/247-3483 or 206/441-3483 (Washington state).

Weather

The *Princess* runs year-round, but the best diving is March to November (July–September is the very best.) Avoid December and January.

Biak Town

You might wish to stick around Biak for a few days after your dive trip. If you do, here are a few suggestions.

Flights

Garuda. District Manager Tel: 21331; Station Manager Tel: 21199.

The Los Angeles flight leaves Biak Tu–W–F–Su. Regular flights to Jayapura ($53), Ujung Pandang ($111), Denpasar ($210), Jakarta ($305) and elsewhere.

Accommodations

Biak town, with a population of 25,000, has a good number of decent and relatively inexpensive hotels. Try the following:

Wisma Titawaka. Jl. Selat Makassar 24, Tel: 21658. 12 rooms, on a little hill near the water. Pretty view, quite pleasant. $27S, $42D, including meals and AC. (There are two additional, equally nice Titawaka hotels. Contact all at P.O. Box 536, Biak, IRJA or Fax: 961/ 22372.)

Hotel Irian. Across from the airport on Jl. Mohammed Yani, P.O. Box 137, Tel: 21939 and 21839. 55 rooms, 31 w/AC. Spacious lobby and dining area. Dutch-built, nice colonial feel. Only good bar in Biak. Two kilometers out of town. $12S, $21D fan-cooled room; $21S, $35D AC rooms; $29S, $41D VIP room. Price includes meals.

Losmen Maju. 19 rooms. $13/person w/AC, $5–$7.50/ person w/o; all w/breakfast.

Local Transportation

Within the town itself, minibus are abundant and make frequent runs (12¢). Chartering must be negotiated, but should cost around $3/hr.

Tour Agencies

P.T. Titawaka Indah Tour & Travel. Jl. Mongonsidi 7, P.O. Box 127 Tel: 21794 Fax: 22372.This outfit runs day tours of Biak Island. Mr. Joop Tetelepta speaks English and Dutch. Smaller vehicles (up to 6 persons) $4/hr; daily guide fee $40. For a visit to the Japanese cave, add $5, and $2 for the bird park. Fire-walking ($100), traditional dances ($90). Biak has some interesting caves where Japanese troops hid out in WWII, a small bird park, a crocodile farm and other interesting sites. One nice trip is to bring your mask to a nice blue-water cave behind the school in Opiaref village.

Banking

The Expor-Impor Bank. Jl. A. Yani. Changes a variety of notes and travelers checks at good rates.

Dining

We recommend: **New Garden, Restaurant 99, Binan Jaya.**

Travel Advisory

In many ways, Indonesia is a very easy place to get around. Indonesians are as a rule hospitable and good-humored, and will always help a lost or confused traveler. The weather is warm, the pace of life is relaxed, and the air is rich with the smells of clove cigarettes, fresh fish in the market, the blessed durian fruit and countless other wonders.

On the other hand, the nation's transportation infrastructure does not move with the kind of speed and efficiency that western travelers expect, which often leads to frustration and irritation.

In most cases, however, the best thing to do is adjust your way of thinking. There is nothing more pathetic than a tourist who has come all the way around the world just to shout at some poor clerk at the airport counter.

The golden rule in Indonesia is: things *will* sort themselves out. Eventually. Be persistent, but relax and keep your sense of humor. Before you explode, have a *kretek* cigaret, a cup of sweet Java coffee, or a cool glass of *kelapa muda* (young coconut water). Things might look different.

Travel

Air travel. Bali and Jakarta have the best air connections in the country. If you are going to be diving elsewhere, you will likely come in through either of these points. [Two exceptions: if you are coming from Australia and going to dive in eastern Indonesia, you could arrive at Kupang's El Tari airport; if you are coming from the United States to dive on the *Tropical Princess*, you arrive in Biak.]

Internal air connections in Indonesia are accomplished by the monopoly carrier, Merpati Nusantara (Garuda is being repositioned as an international

airline, with Merpati taking all the intra-Indonesian flights, although this changeover has not yet been completed).

Although this is already a steady refrain throughout this book, it bears repeating: Merpati is not well-organized or efficient, and you must make aggressive efforts to make sure you are booked and will get a seat.

NOTE: SCHEDULES AND PRICES ARE SUBJECT TO ARBITRARY, UNANNOUNCED AND NERVE-WRACKING CHANGES.

It is frustrating—both for the customer and airline officials—to try to negotiate language difficulties and try to sort things out. It is much better to have someone from your hotel take care of this for you. Show them your return ticket when you arrive, and ask them to confirm your reservations for you. All of the recommended diving clubs noted in this book will provide this service. Use it.

Air connections to all of the places where organized diving is available are relatively unproblematic, except for two. Reaching Labuhanbajo, Flores (to dive the Komodo area) requires taking a flight on a small airplane from Bali, via Bima, Sumbawa. This flight can be cancelled or overbooked, and does not leave every day. Banda is the other troubled destination. To get there, you must catch a flight from Ambon on a small plane that leaves three times a week. Baggage limits are quite low on these planes (although you can usually have it waived) and again, scheduling is not regular. Keep these caveats in mind when planning your trip.

Garuda. Head office: 13 Jl. Merdeka Selatan, Jakarta, Indonesia. Tel: (62) 21/380-1901, 380-6276, 380-6558.

Merpati. Head office: P.O. Box 232/JKT, Jl. Angkasa 2, Jakarta, Indonesia. Tel: (62)

21/413608, 417404. Telex: 49154 MERPATI IA.

Land travel. Bus travel through the larger islands of Indonesia is frequent, quite dependable, and inexpensive. While a nice option for a backpacking tourist, this is not terribly useful for a diver who is lugging around lots of equipment.

If you do decide to take a bus, keep the following hints in mind. Always check if your hotel or *losmen* will book the tickets for you. On many buses, you can reserve a day ahead, which you should do. If you want a good seat—the buses are always crowded—board early, although this will mean a long wait before you leave. (Try to get the seat near the driver, or at least a window seat.)

Sea travel. As an island nation, passenger ferries are an essential part of Indonesia's transportation infrastructure. However, these do not usually provide the kind of romantic experience you might imagine. They are always crowded—literally packed—and toilet facilities are primitive and often so limited in number as to be almost non-existent. There are few ferries that would prove useful to a diver visiting any of the sites in this book, except for the Bali–Lombok ferry (to get to the Gili Islands), which is mercifully short and efficient.

The ferry to the Sangihe Islands north of Manado is described in the Sulawesi section above, and is probably about typical for large passenger ferries in Indonesia.

Indonesia also has a national passenger line, Pelni—Pelayaran Nasional Indonesia—which runs seven large passenger liners around the archipelago. Each of these boats holds 1,000–1,500 pas-

Overleaf: *A swarm of striped eel catfish,* Plotosus lineatus, *on a shallow reef at Manado, Sulawesi. Photograph by Ed Robinson, IKAN.*
Opposite: *A diver over a gorgonian, Manado, Sulawesi. Photo by Ed Robinson, IKAN.*

sengers, and there are five classes, from First Class to Economy.

PELNI. Head office: P.O. Box 115/JKT, Jl. Angkasa 18, Jakarta, Indonesia. Tel: (62) 21/416262, 417136, 417137, 417319. Telex: 44301 PELNI IA. Tickets: Jl. Pintu Air 1, Jakarta, Tel: (62) 21/358398; Jl. Pelabuhan Benoa, Bali, Tel: (62) 361/4387; 50 Telok Blangah Road, 02-02 Citiport Centre, Singapore 0409, Tel: (65)2726811, 2715159, 2718685.

Formalities

Visas

Nationals of the following 30 countries are granted visa-free entry to Indonesia for 60 days. For other nationals, tourist visas are required and can be obtained from any Indonesian embassy or consulate.

Australia	Austria
Belgium	Brunei
Canada	Denmark
Finland	France
Greece	Iceland
Ireland	Italy
Japan	Liechtenstein
Luxembourg	Malaysia
Malta	Netherlands
New Zealand	Norway
Philippines	Singapore
South Korea	Spain
Sweden	Switzerland
Thailand	United Kingdom
United States	West Germany

To avoid any unpleasantness on arrival, check your passport before leaving for Indonesia. You need at least one empty page for your passport to be stamped. Passports must be valid for at least six months upon arrival and you should have valid proof of onward journey, whether return or through tickets. Employment is strictly forbidden on tourist visas or visa-free entry.

Visa-free entry to Indonesia means not staying over 60 days. This is not extendable and is only valid when entering via the following airports: Medan, Batam, Pekanbaru, Padang, Jakarta, Bali, Manado, Ambon, Biak, Kupang, Palembang, Pontianak and Surabaya, or the seaports of Medan, Batam, Banten, Jakarta, Surabaya, Semarang, Riau, Bali, Manado and Ambon.

Customs

Carrying narcotics, arms and ammunition, TV sets, pornographic materials, printed matter in Chinese characters and Chinese medicines is prohibited. Advance approval is necessary to bring transceivers or large movie equipment. All films and video cassettes have to be reviewed by the Indonesian Film Censor Board.

On entry 2 liters of alcoholic beverages, 200 cigarettes, 50 cigars or 100 grams of tobacco are allowed. Perfume in reasonable amounts is also permitted. There is no restriction on import and export of foreign currencies in cash or travelers' checks, but there is a limit on the export of Indonesian rupiah—no more than Rp 50,000.

What a Diver Should Bring

How much of your gear to bring depends on the extent of your diving and location. Always bring the basics—mask, snorkel, fins and boots (if your fins require them)—plus extra straps in case something breaks. While all resorts have these items for rent, the fit, quality and level of comfort varies greatly.

Equipment. There is no sense in bringing your own weights and tanks unless you speak Indonesian, have access to a compressor and plan to do exploratory diving. (and of course airlines do not allow filled tanks on board, which means exposing your tanks to corrosion, etc.).

All the resorts have buoyancy control jackets and regulators, but the quality varies widely. If you are planning on a few dives, say in Bali or Kupang, don't bother to bring BC and regulator. But for anything more serious than this, bring your own, after a thorough maintenance check. You can also save $10–$25 per day by bringing all your own gear.

Most resorts rent underwater lights for night dives, but we suggest bringing your own, or at least a backup. IMPORTANT: only D and AA size dry cells are widely available in Indonesia. Do not bring any equipment which requires C or AAA batteries. All resorts have electricity for recharging batteries, but voltage fluctuates wildly. We suggest disposable alkaline batteries. Don't forget a spare bulb.

Suit. Although these are tropical waters, bring at least a Lycra or 1mm suit, mostly as protection against stinging hydroids. If you plan on more than two dives a day, or night diving, we strongly recommend a 3mm suit. We personally cancelled some night dives due to the cold and having only a good (but inadequate) 1 mm suit.

In some areas (e.g. Nusa Penida) upwellings can make the water very cold. For these sites, even a 1/4 inch farmer john with a hood would not be overkill. Believe us, you will not regret bringing a full 3mm (1/8 in.) suit. Bring gloves too, essential during drift dives or if you want to stop in current.

Spares. Divers traveling in Indonesia are advised to bring a spares kit. There are no dive shops to speak of (except in Jakarta) and spare parts are simply unavailable. Bring: extra O-rings (including tank O-rings), extra straps, silicon lubricant, a weight belt strap. If you are diving in the remote areas—for example with pearl divers—also bring: compressor lubricant, activated carbon.

Spares are especially crucial for photographic equipment. We were unable to find a wide-angle diffuser for a flash even in Singapore. Bring extras of anything you need for your particular equipment.

Health

Indonesia is a tropical country, and with that comes certain health risks for particularly temperate-accustomed visitors. I is a good idea to have a thorough medical (and dental) checkup before leaving. Depending on how careful you want to be, and where you will be going, ask which inoculations your doctor recommends— tetanus, definitely, and the cholera vaccine, although it is painful and doesn't eliminate the risk, can help. A gamma globulin shot, effective for about six months against some strains of hepatitis, may also be worth getting.

Get another medical checkup when you get back home, including blood and stool tests, to see if you picked up any microscopic tropical creatures. Another good idea is to buy most of your basic pharmacy and medical kit before you leave home.

Malaria

Malaria is a problem in parts of Indonesia. This is nothing to be irresponsible about. If you will be diving in Komodo–Labuhanbajo, Maumere, Kupang and Roti, or Irian Jaya, pay particular attention to this section.

Malaria is caused by a protozoan, *Plasmodium,* which affects the blood and liver. The vector for the *Plasmodium* parasite is the *Anopheles* mosquito. After you contract malaria, it takes a minimum of six days—and up to several weeks—before symptoms appear.

If you are visiting any of the above sites you *must* take malaria pills. Do not think that pills offer complete protection, however, as they don't. A very virulent strain of malaria has become dominant particularly in Nusa Tenggara, and malaria is a real risk to be weighed before traveling there. If you are pregnant, have had a splenectomy or have a weak immune system, or suffer from chronic disease, you should probably not go to Nusa Tenggara.

Chloroquine phosphate is the traditional malaria prophylactic, but in the past 10–15 years, the effectiveness of the drug has deteriorated. Deciding

on an appropriate anti-malarial is now more complicated. There are actually two forms of malaria: *Plasmodium vivax,* which is unpleasant, but rarely fatal to healthy adults; and *P. falciparum,* which can be quickly fatal. *P. falciparum* is dominant in parts of Indonesia.

Malaria pills. As a prophylactic for travel in the malarial areas of Indonesia, take two tablets of Chloroquine (both on the same day) once a week, and one tablet of Maloprim (pyrimethamine) once a week. Maloprim is a strong drug, and not everybody can tolerate it. If you are planning on taking Maloprim for more than two months, it is recommended that you take a folic acid supplement, 6 mg a day, to guard against anemia. Note: The anti-malarial drugs only work once the protozoan has emerged from the liver, which can be weeks after your return. You should continue on the above regimen for one month after returning.

Another recent drug that has been shown effective against both forms of the parasite is Mefloquine (Larium), although unpleasant side effects have been demonstrated for it as well. Mefloquine is also very expensive, about $3 a tablet. However, it can be a lifesaver in cases of resistant *falciparum* infection.

These drugs are not available over-the-counter in most western countries (or, indeed, at most pharmacies), and if you visit a doctor, you may have trouble convincing him of what you need. Doctors in the temperate zones are not usually familiar with tropical diseases, and may even downplay the need to guard against them. Do not be persuaded. Try to find a doctor who has had experience in these matters.

You can also buy Chloroquine and Maloprim over-the-counter in Indonesia, for very little (a few dollars for a month's supply). Maloprim, however, may still be difficult to find. [Note: there is a non-

–chloroquine based drug sold in Indonesia called Fansidar. This drug is NOT effective against resistant strains of *P. falciparum.*]

Treatment. Malaria in the early stages is very hard to distinguish from a common cold or flu. A person infected may just suffer from headache and nausea, perhaps accompanied by a slight fever and achiness, for as long as a week until the disease takes hold. When it does, the classic symptoms begin:

1) Feeling of intense cold, sometimes accompanied by shaking. This stage lasts from 30 minutes to two hours.

2) High fever begins, and victim feels hot and dry, and may vomit or even become delirious. This lasts 4–5 hours.

3) Sweating stage begins, during which the victim perspires very heavily, and his body temperature begins to drop.

If you think you have malaria, you should IMMEDIATELY call on professional medical help. A good medical professional is your best first aid. Only if you cannot get help, initiate the following treatment:

1) Take 4 Chloroquine tablets immediately.

2) Six hours later, take 2 more Chloroquine tablets.

3) The next day, take 2 more.

4) The following day, take 2 more.

Note: If the Chloroquine treatment does not cause the fever to break within 24 hours, assume the infection is the very dangerous *P. falciparum* and begin the following treatment immediately:

1) Take 3 tablets (750 mg) of Mefloquine (Larium)

2) Six hours later, take 2 more tablets (500 mg) of Mefloquine.

3) After 12 hours—and only if you weigh 60 kg (130 lbs) or more—take one more tablet (250 mg) of Mefloquine.

Prevention. Malaria is carried by the *Anopheles* mosquito, and if you don't get bit, you don't get the disease.

1) While walking around, use a good quality mosquito repellent, and be very generous with it, particularly around your ankles. Wear light-colored, long-sleeved shirts or blouses and long pants.

2) While eating or relaxing in one spot, burn mosquito coils. These are those green, slightly brittle coils of incense doped with pyrethrin that were banned in the United States some years ago. They are quite effective and you will get used to the smell. (If you are worried about inhaling some of the poison they contain, re-read the classic symptoms of malaria above.) In Indonesia, the ubiquitous coils are called *obat nyamuk bakar*. In some places where there is electricity, there is a repellent with a similar ingredient that is inserted into a unit plugged into the wall.

3) While sleeping, burn *obat nyamuk* and use a mosquito net. Some hotels in Nusa Tenggara have nets, but not many, and you should bring your own. The *obat nyamuk* coils last 6–8 hours and if you set a couple going when you go to sleep you will be protected. Remember that mosquitos like damp bathrooms—where few people bother to light a mosquito coil.

Stomach Problems

While traveling in Indonesia, drink only boiled or bottled liquids. Bottled water—"Aqua"—is widely available, if a bit expensive. Try not even to brush your teeth with tap water. Hotels usually provide boiled water, but ask to be sure.

Diarrhea is a frequent problem, and it does not necessarily come from bad food. Most cases can be traced to a combination of climate, fatigue, change of food and culture shock. Your system has to get used to a new set of bacteria in Indonesia.

This is not widely known, but Indonesians or Mexicans often come down with diarrhea when visiting the United States or Europe. Whatever you do for relief, don't take Enterovioform, as there might be dangerous side effects.

While affected, drink plenty of water with a bit of salt and some sugar, or better yet, bring oral rehydration salts. And keep your diet simple. No meat, spicy foods or milk products. Start with plain boiled rice or dry biscuits, then papayas and bananas.

Remember that you have diarrhea, not dysentery. If you contract the latter, which is much more serious, you must seek medical help. Do this if your stools are mixed with blood and pus, are black, or you are experiencing severe stomach cramps and fever.

For starters, if no medical help is available, try tetracycline and Diatab, effective for bacillary dysentery. If you feel no relief in a day or two, you have the more serious amoebic dysentery which requires additional medication.

To prevent stomach problems, try to eat only thoroughly cooked foods, don't buy already peeled fruit, and stay away from unpasteurized dairy products. If you encounter constipation, eat a lot of fruit.

Cuts and Scrapes

Not every mosquito bite leads to malaria, but in the tropics a scratched bite or small coral abrasion can quickly turn into a festering ulcer. You must pay special attention to these things. Apply Tiger Balm—a widely available camphorated

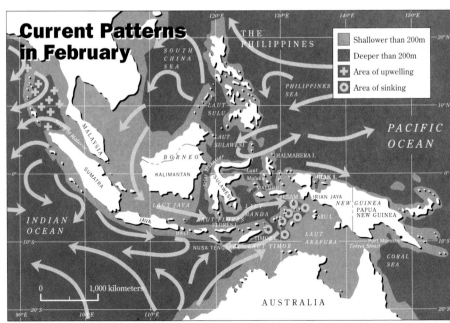

salve—or some imitation thereof to relieve the itching. Treat any broken skin with strong disinfectant—Dettol, Betadine—and/or antibiotic powder (try Trofodermin), and change bandages at least once a day. For light burns, use Aristamide or Bioplacenteron.

Exposure

Visitors insist on instant sun tans, and overexposure to the heat and sun are frequent health problems. Be especially careful on long riverboat rides where the roof gives a good view. The cooling wind created by the boat's motion disguises the fact that you are frying like an egg. Wear a hat, long-sleeved shirt, pants, and use a good-quality sunscreen (bring a supply with you). Tan slowly—don't spoil your trip.

To avoid exposure, drink plenty of fluids and take salt. Wear loose-fitting, light-colored cotton clothes. Do not wear synthetic fibers that do not allow air to circulate.

First Aid Kit

A basic health kit should consist of aspirin and multivitamins, a decongestant, an anti-histamine, disinfectant (such as Betadine), antibiotic powder, fungicide, an antibiotic eye-wash, vinegar (for hydroid stings), Kaopectate or Lomotil, and sunblock. Also good strong soap, perhaps Betadine or other antiseptic soap. Go easy on the oral antibiotics unless you know how to use them. For injuries, make up a little kit containing Band-aids and ectoplast strips, a roll of sterile gauze and treated gauze for burns, surgical tape, and an elastic bandage for sprains. Also very important are Q-tips, tweezers (to remove sea urchin spines, etc.) scissors, needles and safety pins. Keep your pills and liquid medicines in small, unbreakable plastic bottles, clearly labeled.

Bring your kit along on the dive boat, too, since few of them carry one of their own.

Pharmacies—apotik—in the major cities of Nusa Tenggara carry just about everything you might need, but you could run into communications problems. You can readily get malaria pills here, and an excellent anti-bacterial ointment called Bacitran. Tiger Balm is available everywhere in Asia, and it is excellent for itching bites and lots of other things. Mycolog is a brand of fungicide sold in Indonesia. Oral rehydration salts are usually sold in packets to be mixed with 200 ml of (clean) water, a glassful.

Stock up on tampons, as your brand will probably not be available, and bring condoms. Outside the major cities, it's nearly impossible to purchase medicines or first aid supplies.

Doctors and Hospitals

If you should happen to fall sick, your dive club will probably be able to find you doctor who speaks English. Doctors and health care are quite inexpensive by western standards, but the quality leaves much to be desired. (At least they're familiar with the symptoms and treatment of tropical diseases, however, which is something your family doctor might have a real tough time recognizing back home.)

Like everywhere else, the bigger the city, the better the health care resources. In Jakarta, Bali, Manado, Kupang, and Ambon, the availability of health care is quite good. In a place like Banda, or the Sangi-

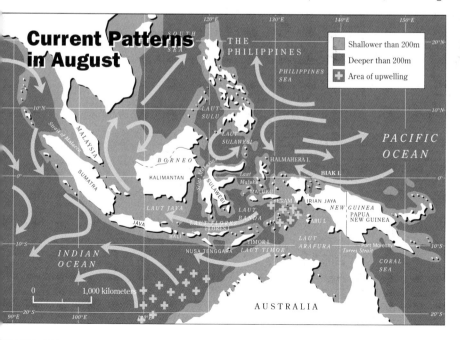

he Islands, you are quite isolated. Keep this in mind when planning a dive there.

Consultations with doctors are very cheap in Indonesia, usually about $2–$5 for general practitioners, $4–$10 for specialists. If you check into a hospital, get a VIP room ($12–$25 for everything—including doctors' fees—but not medicines) or a somewhat cheaper "Klas I" room. If you stay in a cheaper hospital room of a ward, your doctor will be some young, inexperienced kid, fresh out of medical school. Government hospitals, at provincial capital and district level, have improved considerably since the late 1980s.

Dive emergencies. If you have a real disaster, for example with decompression sickness, you probably need to get to Singapore or Australia. The only recompression chambers in Indonesia are at military facilities, with limited—or no—access for civilians or tourists. Wolfgang Bresigk of Baruna Water Sports in Bali should have his recompression chamber up and running by the time you read this, however, and we suggest you contact Baruna for information regarding this resource (see "Bali Scuba Tour Operators," page 125).

Evacuations and hyperbaric medicine are expensive, and we suggest you make sure your insurance is in order before visiting Indonesia.

U.S.-based divers should call Divers Alert Network, which at the time of this writing was organizing an international divers emergency service that would cover Southeast Asia.

Divers Alert Network. Box 3823, Duke University Medical Center, Durham, NC 27710. Membership and information, Tel: 919/684-6002, Fax: 919/684-6002.

The Asia Emergency Assistance is a health emergency network for Southeast Asia. Contact them for services and membership.

Asia Emergency Assistance. 319 Joo Chiat Place #03-03, Singapore 1542. Tel: (65) 3450425, Fax: (65) 3459496, Telex: RS 53522 ASIAAS.

The emergency doctor in Indonesia is Jeffrey Kier:

S.O.S. Medika/Asia Emergency Assistance. Dr. Jeffrey Kier, Jl. Putri Sakti 10, Cipete, Jakarta. Tel: (62) 21/7506000 in Jakarta; (65) 4400445 in Singapore.

Money Exchange

Some of the dive resorts will take U.S. dollars or other western currencies, or even credit cards. But at some point you will have to convert some money into Indonesian rupiahs. The best rates are available at one of the larger banks (e.g. Bank Impor-Expor) in the biggest cities. Rates are good all over Bali. Other than rupiah, the best currency to carry is U.S. dollars, although many banks will convert cash (perfect bills only) from Australia and Singapore, and occasionally from Japan and Western Europe.

The better known travelers checks are also taken at banks, especially American Express, Visa, Barclay's, and Bank of America. You usually get the best exchange rate on U.S. dollars. Moving out of the capitals, most *kabupaten* capitals will also change money, but often just U.S. dollars or U.S. dollar–denominated traveler's checks.

Clothing

Bring wash-and-wear, light cotton clothes. (Synthetic fabrics are really uncomfortable in the tropics.) A sweater (it can get cold at night) and a light rain jacket with a hood are also essential. Tennis shoes and sandals are fine for basic footwear, unless you plan on any volcano-climbing or hiking, in which case you will need sturdy shoes. Also, bring a Raiders cap to keep the sun off during long boat rides or walks. Long-sleeved shirts and long pants are best, although shorts are acceptable in some places.

It's a good idea to bring at least one set of "decent" clothes: leather shoes, and trousers and a batik shirt for men, and a blouse and knee-length dress for women. Foreigners, especially young ones, are the worst-dressed people in these islands, and Indonesians judge by appearances. You will meet more interesting people if you are well-dressed. And "decent" dress is advised at all government offices, even to call on a *camat* way out in the sticks. Or if you want to visit a mosque or a church.

Most dive resorts, hotels and *losmen* have efficient, inexpensive, one-day laundry service. Always make sure everything you sent out is returned: they might have just forgotten, or perhaps figured you won't miss an item or two.

Accommodations

Hotels in Indonesia range from luxurious to very basic. Most of interest to divers, however, fall into the $20–$50 price range. At a hotel of this caliber, one can expect to find comfortable rooms, good service, and a restaurant serving quality meals. Most of the dive operators are associated with good hotels, but for whatever reason you might find yourself negotiating the wealth of lodging possibilities in Indonesia.

"Hotels" in Indonesia go by a variety of names. Theoretically, the organization is the following: "hotel," an upmarket establishment catering to westerners and tourists; "losmen," a medium-priced place, basically a cheaper hotel; "wisma," a small guesthouse; and "peng inapan," very basic lodging, no frills and very cheap. In practice, however, there is often little to distinguish the many medium-range places called "losmen" and "wisma," and sometimes "hotel." Most are called "losmen."

Whatever the name, check the place out before you settle in. Many of the cheaper digs have only squat toilets (no toilet paper) and ladle-type baths (*mandi*). Some of the *losmen* have AC rooms at higher prices, along with toilet/baths attached to your room. Otherwise, the rooms are either fan-cooled or have no fan, and the toilets are shared among the guests, with possible waiting times at critical moments.

We suggest you bring your own towel and soap (although many places provide these for their guests) and a packet of mosquito coils. Mosquito nets are the best protection, but they're a hassle to put up in most hotel rooms. Everywhere, upon request, your room will be sprayed for insects. Be sure that this is done long before you are ready to sleep if you want to avoid the smell.

Where there are no commercial lodgings, you have to rely on local hospitality. In the *kecamatan* centers, either the police or the *camat* could help you find a place to sleep. In the villages, you should find the *kepala desa* (village chief), who will help. Although you will certainly not be treated like one, keep in mind that you are a bother. Villagers in rural Indonesia do not, routinely, maintain guest rooms.

You should insist on paying about $5–$6/day for a place to sleep and the meals to which you will be invited. In many places, there could be shortages of food, especially if you are there just before the harvest. Bring some basics to share with your host. Gifts such as sugar, salt, cigarettes, batteries and clothing are always appreciated.

Food

Western-style meals are usually available only in the best hotels. The price runs $5–$20, and much of this expense comes from imported ingredients like beef. A typical meal in Indonesia, on the other hand, consists of heaps of rice, perhaps garnished with vegetables, fish, or chicken. Fish, at least the way westerners are used to it being served, is not that common, despite that the sea is never far away.

When you eat out, your choices are often limited to Chinese style food—soups, fried vegetables, steamed seafood—and Padang food (named after the region from where it originated in Sumatra), which consists of lots of small dishes served together, with the customer paying only for what he eats. Depending on your location, you might also find local foods. Although Chinese food is often quite mild, Padang food and other local Indonesian cuisines are usually very spicy.

The beers available in Indonesia are Bintang and Anker, both brewed under Dutch supervision and rather hoppy and light (perhaps appropriate for the tropics). With electricity such a precious commodity, however, in many places the only way to quaff it cold is to pour the beer over ice.

Time Zones

Indonesia has three time zones: Western Indonesia Standard Time (Sumatra–Bali), Greenwich Mean Time plus 7 hours; Central Indonesian Standard Time (Lombok–Timor), Greenwich Mean Time plus 8 hours; Eastern Indonesia Standard Time (Maluku and Irian Jaya), Greenwich Mean Time plus 9 hours. The time in Bali is the same as Singapore.

Weather

In general, Indonesia experiences two yearly seasons of monsoon winds: the southeast monsoon, bringing dry weather (*musim panas*—dry season), and the northwest monsoon, bringing rain (*musim hujan*—rainy season). Often the change of seasons can bring the time of high waves (*musim ombak*).

The dry season usually runs from May through September, and the rainy season from November through March. The times of seasonal change are around April, and again around October.

This nice, neat picture is interrupted in Maluku, where local affects alter weather pat-terns, and in areas where the rain shadow of mountains changes seasonal patterns. We have tried to give the best local times for diving in each relevant section.

Tides

Tides in Indonesia average between one and three meters. The only place in the country with really big tidal fluctuations is the south coast of Irian Jaya, where the shallow Arafura Sea rises and falls from 5–8 meters.

Dive Tour Agencies

In addition to the local agencies listed in the relevant sections, Christian Fenie offers specially constructed tours to out of the way places in Indonesia. Using local boats based in Maumere, Manado or Ambon, Fenie takes small groups of divers (fewer than six) to areas he has pioneered and where there are no land-based facilities. This is exciting, pioneering diving.

Working through his Makassar Water Club (under the auspices of the efficient, Ujung Pandang–based Ramayana Tour and Travel agency), Christian specializes in putting together individually tailored land tours to eastern Indonesia, such as cross-Flores, Sumbawa, Sumba and in the vicinity of Maumere and Manado.

His sphere is expanding to the Moluccas where it is likely that Christian will start a school to give proper training to Indonesia dive guides, a much needed endeavor.

Berths on the diving tours are rudimentary (but adequate), but Fenie provides excellent meals. Having dived in Indonesia for over a decade, he combines his knowledge of local culture for contact with the coastal villagers along with dive spots of unusual features.

His tours of 7–10 days average out to an all-inclusive $100 per person per day.

Christian Fenie. P.O. Box 1085, Manado 95001, Fax: (62) 431/60939.

Underwater Hazards

We have all heard far too many shark attack stories. There is a remote possibility of a shark attack of course, but the odds are against it. You are far safer diving in Indonesian waters than riding around Bali on a motorcycle.

The biggest hazards are currents and cold water, and cuts and scrapes on coral. Still, there are a number of danger-

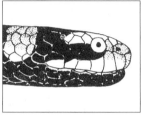

Above: *The colubrine sea snake,* Laticauda colubrina.

ous animals on Indonesia's reefs, and they should not be toyed with. In 1991, a diver died from trying to ride a large reef stingray. He must have thought it was a manta, and climbed on its back.

In almost 300 dives in Indonesia, my problems have been few. I brushed stinging hydroids with my exposed wrists, and small jellyfish stung the area around my throat. And I was once attacked by a Titan triggerfish (*Balistoides viridescens*), although all he got were a few clumps of hair.

My biggest problem in the beginning was cold. I had a 1mm suit, but this left me shivering in some of the cold water off Bali. Later, I added a 3mm shorty on top when we encountered cold water. A few times, I wished I had a hood as well.

Animals that Bite

Sharks. Of the hundreds of species of sharks, only 12 have been known to attack humans, and another 28 are considered capable of such an act. The great white shark (*Carcharodon carcharias*), reaching 6.5 meters, is probably the most fearsome of these. This animal prefers cool waters, and sticks to Australia and the west coast of the United States. We only know of one great white sighting, off Bali. The diver held still, stuck to the coral wall and prayed (he's an atheist) as he watched the monster cruise by. Jacques Cousteau considers the oceanic whitetip (*Carcharhinus longimanus*)—a chiefly pelagic species almost never seen by divers in Indonesia—to be the most unpredictable and dangerous species.

The only really dangerous species one is likely to see diving off Indonesia's reefs is the tiger shark (*Galeocerdo cuvier*), a large deepwater fish that sometimes comes up onto the reefs to feed, particularly in the late afternoon and at night. It is probably not worth tempting fate with this animal, which is occasionally sighted by divers.

The common reef sharks you will see in Indonesia are not considered dangerous, and one never hears of attacks. (In fact, your big problem will be that they're so shy it's hard to get good photos.) But still, don't harass them, and spearfishing always dramatically increases the risk of attack.

Sharks are very highly developed predators, with a very keen sense of smell, and a lateral line sensitive to the vibrations given off by a wounded or distressed fish. Since there is easier prey around—smaller, more familiar and less menacing—sharks very seldom attack humans. When they do, it is more likely to be a territorial defense than an attempt at getting a meal.

Prior to a territory related attack, a sharks will warn divers with a "dance" display: the circling animals shake their heads back and forth, arch their backs, and point their pectoral fins downward. It is very distinctive (much like a big dog defending his territory) and even without this description you would probably get the message.

The classic shark feeding behavior consists of circling the prey, gradually increasing in speed and moving in closer. Sharks are more cautious than you might think they need to be, and the animals often test their potential prey's defenses by brushing against it with their abrasive skin.

Should either of these behaviors develop while you are underwater, it is best to get out of there as soon as possible. Stay calm, stick to your buddy, and back up against the reef wall. Work your way steadily up and get back to the beach or the dive boat. If one or more of the animals comes too close try banging it on its sensitive nose with your camera, a dive light, or your fist—whichever is most handy.

Barracuda. Barracuda are far less dangerous than sharks, but have sharp teeth and the great barracuda (*Sphyraena barracuda*) grows to 2 meters. These fish are sometimes drawn to flashy jewelry (and speared fish). Dive lights occasionally attract them at night, and if temporarily blinded, they could become disoriented and dangerous. For some reason, Atlantic Ocean barracuda are much more likely to attack than their Pacific Ocean brethren.

Sea snakes. Sea snakes carry some of the most deadly poison known (they are the most poisonous of snakes) The species seen in Indonesia however, are not aggressive Sea snakes are sometimes inquisitive, and don't panic i one should explore your face underwater. Remember: they have very short teeth, very rarely bite, and even if they do bite, often they do not inject their venom. It seems that it takes the snakes a day or more to regenerate their venom supply, and they are loath to use it unless faced with a real emergency. Do not make them feel they are facing an emergency.

If bitten (with poison), restrict circulation from the affected limb, and get the victim to a doctor. There is little pain at first, but paralysis and death can follow hours later.

Others. Sea turtles, and even small reef fish, particularly triggers and puffers, have powerful jaws and strong teeth that can do damage. It may seem silly to run from a foot-long fish, but better that than a painful wound.

Stinging Fish

Stingrays. These common animals use their tail stinger when stepped on or startled. They frequent sandy areas, and are sometimes practically invisible. A good habit if walking in the shallows is to shuffle your feet giving them time to get out of your way. When diving, don't try to sneak up on a stingray. Approach slowly, from in front. The sting from a ray is rarely fatal to an adult, although it is extremely painful. (Note: in the example cited above, the stinger literally pierced the victim's heart.)

Scorpionfish. All scorpionfish carry poison in their dorsal, anal and pelvic fins. The pain from most can be excruciating, but only the stonefish (*Synanceia verrucosa*) has been responsible for human fatalities. The stonefish is the world's most venomous fish, and being stung by one is a real disaster—at best you can expect local tissue death and perhaps the loss of your toes; at worst, a painful death. Be careful! Many scorpionfish are masters of camouflage, making it easy to step on or brush one.

Lionfish (*Pterois* spp.) are more conspicuous. They sometimes travel in packs, however, and particularly at night, when they are attracted to the small fish stunned by your lights, you could accidentally bump one.

A sting from a ray or scorpionfish causes excruciating pain, which can bring on unconsciousness. Get the victim topside immediately. Remove any spine still stuck in the skin, and wash and slightly bleed the puncture area. As quickly as possible, immerse the wound in hot water, up to 50°C (use tea if you have some on the boat), or use hot compresses. If attended to quickly enough, good results are likely from this method. Treat for shock, and take the victim to a doctor.

Animals that 'Burn'

The hazard presented by these animals can usually be prevented by even a thin suit. Often it is the areas around the face or the wrist where you can get stung.

Jellyfish. The most dangerous jellyfish is the sea wasp (*Chironex fleckeri*). It is a problem in Australia, and swimming is prohibited in the Darwin area when the mature animals are about. Children and adults with cardio-respiratory problems are the most at risk from this transparent, 20-centimeter creature. A coma and death can result.

Remove the victim from the water, and gently remove any still-adhering tentacles. Vinegar may reduce further discharge of nematocysts, or use local anaesthetic sprays or ointments. Resuscitation may be required. Other jellyfish are more unpleasant than dangerous, but vinegar or creams may help with them as well.

Stinging hydroids. The stinging hydroid *Aglaophenia* is common in Indonesia, looking like a beige or pinkish fern. Fire coral (*Millepora*) grows as smooth, wrinkled sheets (brownish or greenish) or as encrusting forms. Gloves and even Lycra suits offer protection, but a brush against it with bare skin will burn, and leave an itchy, bumpy rash. This is irritating, but not enough to make you abort a dive.

Pricks and Cuts

Sea urchins. The long, black spines of the *Diadema* spp.

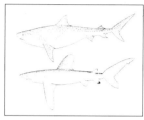

Above: *(Top to bottom)* Grey reef shark, Carcharhinus amblyrhynchos; *reef whitetip shark,* Triaenodon obesus; *tiger shark,* Galeocerdo cuvier; *oceanic whitetip shark,* Carcharhinus longimanus.

sea urchins are not something one would voluntarily bump against. But it happens. These animals are found more often in harbors, lagoons and rather eutrophic back-reef areas than on the fore-reef where divers spend their time. Be careful walking out, particularly through cloudy water! Other urchins are not as dramatic, but can still be a real irritation, and some are venomous.

Try to remove the spines with a tweezers, but if this is impossible, try crushing them: use a shoe or a weight from your belt. This will relieve the pain somewhat, and the spines will eventually be absorbed.

Coral scrapes. Infected coral cuts are the divers' most frequent problems in Indonesia. Do not neglect any broken skin in the tropics. A festering, pus-filled sore will develop, possibly swelling your lymph glands and starting real trouble.

Don't let things get this far. Clean and disinfect the wound as soon as you are finished diving. Keep a loose open bandage on it and change it frequently.

Indonesian Dive Terms
(with English, German and French)

ENGLISH	INDONESIAN	GERMAN	FRENCH
Dive	Selam	Tauchen	Plonger
Flipper/fin	Sepatu bebek (duck shoe)	Flosse	Palmes
Regulator	Regulator	Lungenautohat	Détendeur
Mask	Masker or Kecamata Selam	Maske or Taucherbrille	Masque Combinaison
Snorkel	Snorkel	Schnorchel	Tuba
BC	Pelampung	Tarierweste	Bouée
Weight	Timah or pemberat	Gewicht	Plomb
Weight belt	Ikat pinggang	Bleigurt	Ceinture
Tank	Tenki or tabung	Pressluftflasche	Bouteille
O-ring	Oli sel or karet	Dichtung/O-ring	Joint thorique
Flashlight	Senter	Taschenlampe	Pile
Compressor	Kompresor	Kompressor	Compresseur
Air, wind	Angin	Luft, Wind	Air
Follow	Ikut	Befolgen	Suivre
Bubble	Gelembung udara	Luftblase	Bulle
The air is no good (oily)	Angin kurang bail (rasa oli)	Die Luft ist nicht gut (Oelig)	Mauvais air (huile)
Current	Arus	Ströhmung	Courant
Strong current	Arus kuat	Starke Ströhmung	Courant fort
Fast	Cepat	Schnell	Vite
Slow	Palan-palan	Langsam	Lentement
Danger	Berbahaya	Gefahr	Dangereux
Look out!	Awas!	Pass auf!	Attention!
Careful	Hati-hati	Vorsichtig	Attention
Water	Air	Wasser	Eau
High tide	Air pasang	Flut	Marée haute
Low tide	Air surut	Ebbe	Marée basse
Wave	Ombak	Welle	Vague
Big wave	Ombak besar	Gross Welle	Grosse vague
Little wave	Ombak kecil	Kleine Welle	Petite vague
East	Timur	Osten	Est
West	Barat	Westen	Ouest
North	Utara	Norden	Nord
South	Selatan	Süden	Sud
Full moon	Purnama	Vollmond	Pleine lune
Deep	Dalam	Tief	Profond
How deep?	Berapa dalam?	Wie tief?	Quelle profondeur?
Shallow	Dankal	Seicht	Peu profond
Sand	Pasir	Sand	Sable
Coral	Karang	Koralle	Corail
Sea urchin	Bulu babi (pig bristle)	Seeigel	Oursin
Boat	Kapal	Boot	bateau
Canoe	Prahu	Kanu	Pirogue
Outrigger	Tangah (also ladder)	Ausleger	Echelle
Outboard	Jonson (Johnson)	Aussenborder	Horsbord
Horsepower	P.K.	Pferdestärken, P.S.	Chevaux
How much horsepower?	Berapa P.K.	Wie viele PS?	Quelle puissance?
How long?	Berapa panjang?	Wie lang?	Quelle longueur?
Rent, charter	Carter, sewa	Mieten, chartern	Louer
How much?	Berapa?	Wie viel?	Combien?
Per hour, per day	Per jam, per hari	Pro Stunde, pro Tag	Par heure, par jour
Spark plug	Busi	Zündkerze	Bougie
Cave	Gua	Höhle	Grotte

Rain	Hujan	Regen	Pluie
To swim	Berenang	Schwimmen	Nager
Towel	Handuk	Handtuch	Serviette
Drinking water	Air minum, Aqua	Trinkwasser	Eau potable
I	Saya	Ich	Je
You	Anda	Du	Vous
He, she	Dia	Er, sie, es	Il, elle
We	Kita (including person addressing) Kami (excluding person addressing)	Wir	Nous
They	Mereka	Sie	Ils, elles
One	Satu	Eins	Un
Two	Dua	Zwei	Deux
Three	Tiga	Drei	Trois
Four	Empat	Vier	Quatre
Five	Lima	Fünf	Cinq
Six	Enam	Sechs	Six
Seven	Tujuh	Sieben	Sept
Eight	Delapan	Acht	Huit
Nine	Sembilan	Neun	Neuf
Ten	Sepuluh	Zehn	Dix
Eleven	Sebelas	Elf	Onze
Twelve	Dua belas	Zwölf	Douze
Twenty	Dua puluh	Zwanzig	Vingt
Thirty	Tiga puluh	Dreissig	Treize
One hundred	Seratus	(Ein)hundert	Cent
Three hundred	Tiga ratus	Dreihundert	Trois cents
One thousand	Seribu	(Ein)tausend	Trois mille
Five thousand	Lima ribu	Fünftausend	Cinq mille
Monday	Hari senin	Montag	Lundi
Tuesday	Hari selasa	Dienstag	Mardi
Wednesday	Hari rabu	Mittwoch	Mercredi
Thursday	Hari kamis	Donnerstag	Jeundi
Friday	Hari jumaat	Freitag	Vendredi
Saturday	Hari sabtu	Samstag	Samedi
Sunday	Hari minggu	Sonntag	Dimanche
Day	Hari	Tag	Jour
Week	Minggu	Woche	Semaine
Moon/month	Bulan	Mond/Monat	Lune/Mois
Year	Tahun	Jahr	Année
Tomorrow	Besok	Morgen	Demain
Day after tomorrow	Lusa	Übermorgen	Après-demain
Next week	Minggu depan	Nächste Woche	Semaine prochaine
Last month	Bulan yang lalu	Letzten Monat	Le mois dernier
Today	Hari ini	Heute	Aujourd'hui
Yesterday	Kemarin	Gestern	Hier
Now	Sekarang	Jetzt	Maintenant
Later	Nanti	Später	Plus tard
Good morning	Selamat pagi (till 10 am)	Guten Morgen	Bonjour
Good day	Selamat siang (till 4 pm) Selamat sore (till night)	Guten Tag Guten Tag	Bonjour
Good evening, night	Selamat malam	Guten Abend, Gute Nacht	Bonsoir, bonne nuit
Goodbye	Selamat tinggal (to those staying) Selamat jalan (to	Auf Wiedersehen	Au revoir

	those leaving)		
Welcome	Selamat datang	Willkommen	Bienvenue
What time?	Jam berapa?	Wie spät?	A quelle heure?
Seven o'clock	Jam tujuh	Sieben Uhr	Sept heures
Eleven o'clock	Jalam sebelas	Elf Uhr	Onze heures
Hour	Jam	Stunde	Heure
Eleven thirty	Jam setengah duabelas (half-twelve, literally)	Elf Uhr dreissig	Onze heures trente
Friday night	Malam sabtu (night of Saturday, literally)	Freitag Abend	Vendredi soir
What time do we leave?	Kita berangkat jam berapa?	Wann gehen wir ?	A quelle heure part-on?
What time do we return?	Kita pulang jam berapa?	Wann kommen wir zurück?	A quelle heure revient-on?
Ready?	Siap?	Bereit?	Prêt?
Not (yet) ready	Belum siap	Noch nicht bereit	Pas encore prêt.
Already	Sudah	Schon	Déja
Let's go	Mari (or) mari kita pergi	Gehen wir	Allons
Don't! Not allowed	Jangan! Tidak boleh	Lass das! Verboten	Interdit

Wound, injury	Luka	Verletzung	Blessé
Serious injury	Luka berat	Schlimme Verletzung	Blessé gravement
Toothache	Sakit gigi	Zahnschmerzen	Mal aux dents
Sick, painful	Sakit	Krank, Schmerzhaft	Malade
Hospital	Rumah sakit	Spital, Krankenhaus	Hôpital
Medicine	Obat	Medizin	Médicament
Head	Kepala	Kopf	Tête
Stomach	Perut	Magen	Ventre
Leg	Kaki	Bein	Pied
Eye	Mata	Auge	Oeil
I need medicine	Saya perlu obat	Ich brauche Medizin	J'ai besoin de médicaments

Cold	Dingin	Kalt	Froid
Hot	Panas	Heiss	Chaud
Dark	Gelap	Dunkel	Sombre
Light	Terang	Hell	Clair
Clear (water, air)	Jernih	Klar	Limpide
Clean	Bersih	Sauber	Propre
Dirty	Kotor	Dreckig/schmutzig	Sale
Good	Bagus	Gut	Bien (beau)
Bad	Jelek	Schlecht	Mauvais
White	Putih	Weiss	Blanc
Black	Hitam	Schwarz	Noir
Red	Merah	Rot	Rouge
Blue	Biru	Blau	Bleu
Green	Hijau	Grün	Vert
Yellow	Kuning	Gelb	Jaune

Tired	Cape	Müde	Fatigué
Rest	Beristirahat	Ruhen	Se reposer
Sleep	Tidur	Schlafen	Dormir
Food	Makanan	Essen	Nourriture
Drink	Minuman	Getränk, Trinken	Boisson
Grilled fish	Ikan Bakar	Gebratener Fisch	Poisson grillé
Vegetable	Sayur	Gemüse	Légume
Fruit	Buah-buahan	Früchte	Fruits
Spicy hot	Pedas-pedis	Scharf	Epicé
Meat	Daging	Fleisch	Viande
Delicious	Enak	Wohlschmeckend	Bon
Full (stomach)	Kenyang	Genug	Replet

Indonesian Reef Fishes
(in English, Latin, Indonesian and local languages)

Family name (Latin family name)
English common name (*Genus species*); standard
length (does not include tail)

Indonesian; Bajo (Ba); Bugis (Bu);
Manado dialect (M); Ambon dialect (A)
—Indonesian often includes ikan (*fish*)

Sharks (Rhincodontidae, whale shark; Orectolobidae,
nurse and zebra sharks; Hemigaleidae, reef
whitetip; Carcharhinidae, requiem sharks;
Sphyrnidae, hammerheads; Alopiidae, thresher
sharks)

Cucut (*kiss, suck*), ikan hiu; kareo (Ba);
mengihang (Bu); gorango (M); kalayu
(A); also bengiwang

Whale shark (*Rhincodon typus*); 12m, perhaps more

Cucut gender (*gamelan instrument*),
cucut lintang, ikan hiu bodoh (*stupid*)

Nurse shark (*Nebrius concolor*); 3.2m
Leopard shark (*Stegastoma varium*); 2.3m
Reef whitetip shark (*Triaenodon obesus*); 1.7m
Silvertip shark (*Carcharhinus albimarginatus*); 2.8m
Grey reef shark (*C. amblyrhynchos*); 2.3m
Oceanic whitetip shark (*C. longimanus*); 2.7m

Cucut buta (*blind*); kareo bisu (*deaf*) (Ba)
Cucut kembang (*a flower*), cucut tokek
Cucut sirip putih (*white fin*); kareo batu (Ba)

Cucut sirip putih laut dalem (*deep sea
white fin*); kareo pansa (Ba)

Reef blacktip shark (*C. melanopterus*); 1.8m

Cucut sirip hitam (*black fin*); kareo
mengali (Ba)

Tiger shark (*Galeocerdo cuvier*); 5.5m, perhaps more
Hammerhead shark (*Sphyrna blochii*); perhaps 5m

Cucut macan (*tiger*)
Cucut ronggeng (*Javanese dancer/bar
girl*), cucut rongceng, ikan hiu martel
(*hammer*); kareo bingkoh (Ba);
gorango martelu (M)

Thresher shark (*Alopias pelagicus*); 3.3m

Guitarfishes (Rhinobatidae)
White-spotted guitarfish (*Rhynchobatus djiddensis*); 3m

Cucut biola (*violin*), cucut panrong

Stingrays (Dasyatididae)
Leopard ray (*Himantura uarnak*); 1.8m width
Blue-spotted stingray (*Taenura lymma*); 1m width

Pari, Pareh; Pai (Ba); Pari, Nyoa (*bird*) (Bu)
Pari macan (*tiger*), pari kembang
Pari pasir bintik biru (*blue spotted sand
ray*); pai kiam (Ba); nunang, nyoa
pasir (*sand*) (Bu)

Black-spotted stingray (*T. melanospilos*); 1.7m width

Pari pasir; pai kikir (Ba)

Eagle rays (Myliobatidae)
Spotted eagle ray (*Aetobatis narinari*); 2.3m width

Pari burung (*bird*), pari ayam (*chicken,
for the taste*); pai mano (Ba); pari
mano, nyoa burung (Bu)

Manta rays (Mobulidae)
Manta ray (*Manta alfredi*); 6.7m width; usually to 3m

Pari jurig, pari satan (Sundanese); pai
saranga (Ba); pari pangka (Bu); bele-
lang, bou, moku (Lamalera dialect)

Moray eels (Muraenidae)
Snowflake moray (*Echidna nebulosa*); 75cm
Fimbriated moray (*Gymnothorax fimbriatus*); 80cm
Yellow-margined moray (*G. flavimarginatus*); 1.2m
Giant moray (*G. javanicus*); 2.4m, maybe 3m
Spotted moray (*G. meelagris*); 1.2m
Black-spotted moray (*G. melanospilos*); 1m
Zonipectis moray (*G. zonipectis*); 46cm
Blue ribbon eel (*Rhinomuraena quaesita*); 1.2m

Ladu (*lava*), morea, kerundung (*veil*);
ndoh (Ba); lado (M). [Note: belut,
sidat for "eel" in Indonesian]

Garden eels (Congridae; subfamily Heterocongridae)
Spotted garden eel (*Heteroconger hassi*); 35cm

Snake eels (Ophichthidae)
Banded snake eel (*Myrichthys colubrinus*); 88cm
Spotted snake eel (*M. maculosus*); 1m

Milkfishes (Chanidae)
Milkfish (*Chanos chanos*); 50cm, rarely to 1.8m

Gelondongan (adult), nener (fry) [Note: these are farmed in fishponds]

Eel catfishes (Plotosidae)
Striped eel catfish (*Plotosus lineatus*); 30cm

Sembilang karang (*coral catfish*); titinagan (Ba)

Anchovies (Engraulididae)
Anchovies (*Stolephorus* spp.); 5–10cm

Teri; puri (A); ikan bilis (Malay)

Herrings (Clupeidae)
Sprats (*Dussumieria* spp. and *Spratelloides* spp.); 10cm
Herrings (*Herklotsichthys* spp.); 15cm

Japuh [also terubuk (*Clupes toli*), tembang and lemuru (*Sardinella* sp.)]

Lizardfishes (Synodontidae)
Graceful lizardfish (*Saurida gracilis*); 31cm
Nebulous lizardfish (*S. nebulosa*); 17cm
Twin-spot lizardfish (*Synodus binotatus*); 13cm
Reef lizardfish (*S. englemani*)
Black-blotch lizardfish (*S. jaculum*); 14cm
Variegated lizardfish (*S. variegatus*); 20cm

Beloso, gabus, ikan kepala busok (*fish with depraved expression*); taropatau (Ba); gosi cina (M)

Frogfishes (Antennariidae)
Painted frogfish (*Antennarius pictus*); 16cm
Sargassumfish (*Histrio histrio*); 14cm

Needlefishes (Belonidae)
Keeled needlefish (*Platybelone argalus platyura*); 37cm
Reef needlefish (*Strongylura incisa*); 1m
Crocodile needlefish (*Tylosaurus crocodilis*); 1.3m

Cendro, ikan julung-julung (*unlucky*); timbaloah (Ba); sori (Bu); sako (M)

Halfbeaks (Hemirhamphidae)
Island halfbeack (*Hemiramphus archipelagicus*); 25cm
Spotted halfbeak (*H. far*); 40cm

Ikan kacang-kachang (*beans*), ikan julung-julung (*unlucky*); pipilangan (Ba); cado-cado (Bu); sako (M)

Flashlightfishes (Anomalopidae)
Flashlightfish (*Anomalops katoptron*); 9cm
Flashlightfish (*Photoblepheron palpebratus*); 9cm

Ikan leweri air, ikan leweri bau; oho (Ba)

Soldierfishes and Squirrelfishes (Holocentridae)
Bronze soldierfish (*Myripristis adusta*); 25cm
Bigscale soldierfish (*M. berndti*); 24cm
Red soldierfish (*M. murdjan*); 22cm
Fine-lined squirrelfish (*Sargocentron microstoma*); 16cm

Karoo, kabakok, ikan mata bulan (*moon-eyed*), ikan mata besar (*big-eyed*); karango (Ba); susunu, gora (Bu)

Trumpetfishes (Aulostomidae)
Trumpetfish (*Aulostomus chinensis*); 62cm

Manok, ikan terompet; tarigonoh (Ba)

Cornetfishes (Fistulariidae)
Flutemouth cornetfish (*Fistularia commersonii*); 1m

Ikan terompet; teligonoh (Ba); malo (Bu)

Shrimpfishes (Centriscidae)
Shrimpfish (*Aeoliscus strigatus*); 15cm

Ikan pisau-pisau (*knife*); barbadisamo (Ba)

Ghost pipefishes (Solenostomus)
Ghost pipefish (*Solenostomus cyanopterus*); 16cm
Ornate ghost pipefish (*S. paradoxus*)

Pipefishes and Seahorses (Syngnathidae)

Tangkur, tangkur buaya (*crocodile*), ikan kuda (*horse*); pipilando (Ba)

Thorny seahorse (*Hippocampus histrix*); 15cm   Pipilando samo (Ba)
Common seahorse (*H. kuda*); 30cm   Tangkur kuda; pipilando jarang (Ba)
Crowned seahorse (*H. planifrons*); 15cm
Network pipefish (*Corythoichthys flavofasciatus*); 11cm
Scribbled pipefish (*C. intestinalis*); 16cm
Double-headed pipefish (*Trachyramphus bicoarctata*);
   39cm

Flatheads (Platycephalidae)   Papangao (Ba)
Crocodilefish (*Cymbacephalus beauforti*); 50cm
Longsnout flathead (*Platycephalus chiltonae*); 20cm

Scorpionfishes (Scorpaenidae)   Lepu (*fish with toxic spines*), ikan anjing
Devil scorpionfish (*Scorpaenopsis diabolus*); 19cm   (*dog fish*), pangaten, ikan suanggi
Tassled scorpionfish (*S. oxycephala*); 19cm   (*witch doctor*); kelopo (Ba)
Weedy scorpionfish (*Rhinopias frondosa*); 19cm
Stonefish (*Synanceia verrucosa*); 35cm   Ikan tembaga (*copper*); laroh (Ba)
Devilfish (*Inimicus didactylus*); 15cm
Twinspot lionfish (*Dendrochirus biocellatus*); 8cm   Lepu ayam (*chicken*)—all lionfishes
Shortfin lionfish (*D. brachypterus*); 15cm
Zebra lionfish (*D. zebra*); 25cm
Spotfin lionfish (*Pterois antennata*); 19cm
Tailbar lionfish (*P. radiata*); 20cm
Lionfish (*P. volitans*); 30cm

Fairy Basslets and Groupers (Serranidae)   All fairy basslets: Nona manis (*sweet
Magenta slender basslet (*Luzonichthys waitei*); 5cm   girl*), ikan pisang-pisang (*bananas*);
Peach fairy basslet (*Pseudanthias dispar*); 8cm   dayasuboh (Ba)
Red-cheeked anthias (*P. huchtii*); 8cm   All groupers: kerapu, garupa; kiapu (Ba);
Lyretail coralfish (*P. squammipinnis*); 10cm   suno (Bu)
Purple queen (*P. pascalus*); 12cm
Pink-square anthias (*P. pleurotaenia*); 10cm
Purple queen (*P. tuka*); 8cm
White-lined grouper (*Anyperodon leucogrammicus*); 41cm
Peacock grouper (*Cephalopholis argus*); 42cm
Leopard grouper (*C. leopardus*); 20cm   Kiapu tongko, kiapu geang (Ba)
Coral grouper (*C. miniata*); 30cm   Kiapu mirah (Ba)
Flagtail grouper (*C. urodeta*); 19cm   Kiapu pedi betah (Ba); loong (Bu)
Polkadot grouper, pantherfish (*Cromileptes altivelis*);   Kerapu bebek (*duck*), Geris Keli (*Grace
   70cm   Kelly!*)
Black-tipped grouper (*Ephinephelus fasciatus*); 29cm
Blotchy grouper (*E. fuscogattatus*); 89cm   Kerapu macan (*tiger*)
Honeycomb grouper (*E. merra*); 23cm
Giant grouper (*E. lanceolatus*); 3m total length, 400 kg   Kerapu lumpur; kiapu lohong (Ba)
Saddleback grouper (*Plectropomus laevis*); 1m   Suno Bendera (Bu)
Lyretail grouper (*Variola louti*); 56cm   Suno enro (Bu)

Soapfishes (Grammistidae)   Cantik jelita (*lovely, usually to girls*)
Lined soapfish (*Grammistes sexlineatus*); 27cm

Prettyfins (Plesiopidae)
Comet (*Calloplesiops altivelis*); 11cm
Argus comet (*C. argus*); 11cm

Dottybacks (Pseudochromidae)
Paccagnalle's dottyback (*Pseudochromis
   paccagnallae*); 6cm
Magenta dottyback (*P. porphyreus*); 5cm

Hawkfishes (Cirrhitidae)
Falco hawkfish (*Cirrhitichthys falco*); 5cm
Pixy hawkfish (*C. oxycephalus*); 7cm
Longnose hawkfish (*Oxycirrhites typus*); 8cm

Arc-eye hawkfish (*Paracirrhites arcatus*); 11cm
Forster's hawkfish (*P. forsteri*); 17cm

Cardinalfishes (Apogonidae)
Cardinalfishes (*Apogon* spp.); av. 5–8cm
Pajama cardinalfish (*Sphaeramia nematoptera*); 6cm

Serinding, ikan sang karang; bebeseh (Ba)

Bigeyes (Priacanthidae)
Glasseye (*Heteropriacanthus cruentatus*); 23cm
Goggle-eye (*Priacanthus hamrur*); 26cm

Gora suanggi (*witch doctor*), serinding tembako (*tobacco cardinalfish*)

Remoras (Echeneididae)
Striped sharksucker (*Echeneis naucrates*); 90cm
Remora (*Remora remora*); 40cm

Gemih

Jacks and Trevallies (Carangidae)

Kuwe or kuweh, bubara (jacks), selar (*Selar* sp. scads), ikan layang (scads), tetengkek (hardtail scads); pipili (Ba) (jacks)

Slender scad (*Decapterus macrosoma*); 35cm
Bigeye scad (*Selar crumenophthalmus*); 30cm
Threadfin pompano (*Alectis ciliaris*); 65cm
Indian threadfish (*A. indicus*); 1.5m
Golden trevally (*Gnathanodon speciosus*); 1.1m
Giant trevally (*Caranx ignobilis*); 1.7m
Black jack (*C. lugubris*); 91cm
Bluefin trevally (*C. melampygus*); 80cm
Bigeye jack (*C. sexfasciatus*); 85cm
Leatherback (*Scomberoides lysan*); 70cm

Ikan layang
Selar bentong
Kuwe rambut (*hair*)
Kuwe rambut (*hair*)
Kuwe macan (*tiger*)

Dayah nyumbah (Ba)

Lasi (*forbidden eating*), lima jari (*five fingers*); manok (Ba)

Rainbow runner (*Elagatis bipinnulatus*); 1.2m
Greater amberjack (*Seriola dumerili*); 1.9m
Silver pompano (*Trachinotus blochii*); 1.1m

Sunglir; uroh-uroh (Ba); suru (Bu)
Bangaya (Ba)

Mojarras (Gerreidae)
Common mojarra (*Gerres argyreus*); 19cm

Ikan kapas-kapas (*cotton*)

Snappers (Lutjanidae)
Blue-lined sea bream (*Symphorichthys spilurus*); 50cm
Black-and-white snapper (*Macolor macularis*); 50cm
Black snapper (*M. niger*); 60cm
River snapper (*Lutjanus argentimaculatus*); 70cm
Red snapper (*L. bohar*); 80cm

Bambangan, gerot-gerot; sulayasa (Ba)
Dayah sangai (Ba)
Kakap
Ikan tanda-tanda (*signs, markers*)

Ikan merah (*red fish*), jenaha, kakap; ahrang (Ba)

Blackspot snapper (*L. ehrenbergi*); 26cm
Flametail snapper (*L. fulvus*); 35cm
Humpback snapper (*L. gibbus*); 42cm
Bluelined snapper (*L. kasmira*); 26cm
Onespot snapper (*L. monostigmus*); 45cm

Dapa

Fusiliers (Caesionidae)
Yellowtail fusilier (*Caesio cuning*); 23cm
Lunar fusilier (*C. lunaris*); 26cm
Yellowback fusilier (*C. teres*); 27cm
Bluestreak fusilier (*Pterocaesio tile*); 22cm
Three-striped fusilier (*P. trilineata*); 13cm

Pisang-pisang, lalosi
Ekor kuning (*yellowtail*); bulek kuneh (Ba)

Sweetlips and Grunts (Haemulidae)

Ikan gerot-gerot, raja bau (*smell*), raja caci, pepondok.

Slatey sweetlips (*Diagramma pictum*); 78cm
Sulawesi sweetlips (*Plectorhinchus celebecus*); 41cm
Clown sweetlips (*P. chaetodonoides*); 60cm
Goldman's sweetlips (*P. goldmanni*); 60cm

Kerong-kerong (Ba); kokoreh (Bu)

Laundung (Ba)
Balekeh (Ba)

Oriental sweetlips (*P. orientalis*); 72cm — Balekeh (Ba)
Spotted sweetlips (*P. picus*); 70cm — Lepeh (Ba)
Yellow-ribbon sweetlips (*P. polytaenia*); 70cm — Gaiji

Threadfin breams (Nemipteridae)
Black-and-white spinecheeks (*Scolopsis lineatus*); 20cm
Redfin mid-water bream (*Pentapodus macrurus*); 30cm — Suelala (Ba)

Emperors (Lethrinidae) — Lencam, ketambak, asunan
Yellowspot emperor (*Gnathodentex aurolineatus*); 21cm — Lalanga (Ba)
Bigeye emperor (*Monotaxis grandoculus*); 45cm
Ambon emperor (*Lethrinus amboinensis*); 57cm
Blackspot emperor (*L. harak*); 50cm
Longnose emperor (*L. olivaceus*); 84cm — Sikuda; lausa (Ba); anduping (Bu)

Goatfishes (Mullidae) — Biji nangka (*jackfruit seed*), jangut kuni-
Yellowstripe goatfish (*Mulloides flavolineatus*); 36cm — ran (*yellow beard*), ikan kambing
Yellowfin goatfish (*M. vanicolensis*); 31cm — (*goat fish*); jajango (Ba); salmoneti,
Dash-dot goatfish (*Parupeneus barberinus*); 50cm — matadung (Bu)
Multibarred goatfish (*P. multifasciatus*); 24cm

Sweepers (Pempherididae)
Pigmy sweep (*Parapriacanthus ransonneti*); 6cm

Chubs (Kyphosidae)
Snubnose chub (*Kyphosus cinerascens*); 37cm

Batfishes (Ephippidae) — Gebel, ikan bawal, ikan bendera (*flag*)
Orbiculate batfish (*Platax orbicularis*); 47cm — Gebel bunder
Pinnate batfish (*P. pinnatus*); 37cm — Gebel asli (*native*)
Round-faced batfish (*P. tiera*); 41cm — Gebel biasa (*ordinary*)

Butterflyfishes (Chaetodontidae) — Kepe-kepe, ikan kupu-kupu (*butterfly*),
Threadfin butterflyfish (*Chaetodon auriga*); 15cm — ikan daun-daun (*leaves*), kiper laut
Baroness butterflyfish (*C. barronessa*); 11cm — [Note: Colorful reef fishes in general,
Bennett's butterflyfish (*C. bennetti*); 15cm — butterflyfish, angelfish, damselfish:
Saddleback butterflyfish (*C. ephippium*); 17cm — ikan karang (*coral*), ikan prong or
Klein's butterflyfish (*C. kleinii*); 11cm — ikan hias (*ornamental*), ikan cincin
Lined butterflyfish (*C. lineolatus*); 24cm — (*ring*)]
Raccoon butterflyfish (*C. lunula*); 16cm
Meyer's butterflyfish (*C. meyeri*); 14cm
Ornate butterflyfish (*C. ornatissimus*); 15cm
Spotnape butterflyfish (*C. oxycephalus*); 17cm
Raffles' butterflyfish (*C. rafflesii*); 11cm
Red-finned butterflyfish (*C. trifasciatus*); 12cm
Vagabond butterflyfish (*C. vagabundus*); 16cm
Copperband butterflyfish (*Chelmon rostratus*); 18cm — Kepe-kepe monyung asli (*native, true*)
Longnose butterflyfish (*Forcipiger flavissimus*); 18cm — Kepe-kepe monyung palsu (*false*)
Big longnose butterflyfish (*F. longirostris*); 18cm
Pyramid butterflyfish (*Hemitaurichthys polylepis*); 13cm
Bannerfish (*Heniochus acuminatus*); 20cm
Bannerfish (*H. diphreutes*); 19cm
Pennant bannerfish (*H. chrysostomus*); 13cm
Masked bannerfish (*H. monoceros*); 18cm
Singular bannerfish (*H. singularis*); 24cm
Humphead bannerfish (*H. varius*); 15cm

Angelfishes (Pomacanthidae) — Injel (*"angel"*), ikan kupu-kupu (*butterfly*),
Three-spot angelfish (*Apolemichthys trimaculatus*); 26cm — edo (Ba)
Bicolor angelfish (*Centropyge bicolor*); 14cm — Injel biru-kuning (*blue and yellow*)
Dusky angelfish (*C. bispinosus*); 10cm
Lemonpeel angelfish (*C. flavissimus*); 8cm
Keyhole angelfish (*C. tibicen*); 15cm — Injel hitam (*black*)

Pearlscale angelfish (*C. vrolikii*); 8cm
Blackspot angelfish (*Genicanthus melanospilos*); 15cm
Regal angelfish (*Pygoplites diacanthus*); 21cm — Injel lurik (*type of striped cloth*)
Blue-ring angelfish (*Pomacanthus annularis*); 30cm
Emperor angelfish (*P. imperator*); 30cm — Kaiser, beluston, betman (*"batman"*)
Blue-girdled angelfish (*P. navarchus*); 20cm — Injel piyama (*yes, "pyjamas"*)
Semicircle angelfish (*P. semicirculatus*); 29cm
Six-banded angelfish (*P. sextriatus*); 38cm
Blue-faced angelfish (*P. xanthometopon*); 32cm — Beluston, beluboran

Damselfishes (Pomacentridae) — Asan, giru
Sergeant-major (*Abudefduf vaigiensis*); 17cm — Bonang-bonang, sersan major
Golden damsel (*Amblygliphidodon aureus*); 10cm
Staghorn damsel (*A. curacao*); 9cm
Skunk anemonefish (*Amphiprion akallopisos*); 9cm — For all anemonefishes: Klon (*"clown"*),
Orange-fin anemonefish (*A. chrysopterus*); 13cm — klon asan, giru prong, gemutu, ikan
Clark's anemonefish (*A. clarkii*); 10cm — jamur (*mushroom*); kinsang (Ba)
Red saddleback anemonefish (*A. ephippium*); 11cm
Tomato anemonefish (*A. frenatus*); 11cm
Dusky anemonefish (*A. melanopus*); 9cm
Clown anemonefish (*A. ocellaris*); 8cm
Pink anemonefish (*A. perideraion*); 8cm
Saddleback anemonefish (*A. polymnus*); 10cm
Orange anemonefish (*A. sandaracinos*); 11cm
Reef chromis (*Chromis agilis*); 8cm — For all *Chromis* spp.: Gucia, betok laut,
Yellow-speckled chromis (*C. alpha*); 9cm — kapas-kapas (*cotton fleece*)
Ambon chromis (*C. amboinensis*); 6cm
Yellow chromis (*C analis*); 14cm
Black-axil chromis (*C. atripectoralis*); 9cm
Bicolor chromis (*C. margaritifer*); 6cm
Blue-green chromis (*C. viridis*); 7cm
Blue devil (*Chrysiptera cyanea*); 6cm
Blue-spot damsel (*C. oxycephala*); 7cm
Three-striped dascyllus (*Dascyllus aruanus*); 7cm
Black-tailed dascyllus (*D. melanurus*); 7cm
Reticulated dascyllus (*D. reticulatus*); 6cm
Three-spot dascyllus (*D. trimaculatus*); 11cm — Dakocan (*black puppet*), giru bolong
Black damsel (*Neoglyphidodon melas*); 13cm — (*pierced*), giru gete-gete
Java damsel (*N. oxyodon*); 12cm
Behn's damsel (*N. nigroris*); 9cm
Neon damsel (*Pomacentrus coelestis*); 7cm
Lemon damsel (*P. moluccensis*); 6cm
Peacock damsel (*P. pavo*); 9cm
Spine-cheek anemonefish (*Premnas biaculeatus*); 17cm
Farmerfish (*Stegastes lividus*); 13cm
Dusky farmerfish (*S. nigricans*); 12cm

Wrasses (Labridae) — Keling (small wrasses). Nuri-nuri (*a type*
Lyretail hogfish (*Bodianus anthoides*); 24cm — *of parrot*) (large wrasses). Gigi anjing
Axilspot hogfish (*B. axillaris*); 16cm — (*dog's tooth*) (tuskfishes). Lamboso;
— lampah (Ba) (hogfishes).
Red-breasted wrasse (*Cheilinus fasciatus*); 28cm — Besiparai (Ba)
Napoleon wrasse; humphead wrasse (*C. undulatus*); — Napoleon; langkoeh, angkeh (Ba)
    1.8m; total length to 2.3m
Ringtail wrasse (*C. unifasciatus*); 38cm
Slingjaw wrasse (*Epibulus insidiator*); 30cm
Clown coris (*Coris aygula*); 1m
Yellowtail coris (*C. gaimard*); 35cm — Keling merah putih (*red-white*)
Bird wrasse (*Gomphosus varius*); 18cm
Two-tone wrasse (*Thalassoma amblycephalum*); 12cm
Lunar wrasse (*T. lunare*); 18cm
Bicolor cleaner wrasse (*Labroides bicolor*); 10cm — Ikan doktor (*doctor fish*)
Bluestreak cleaner wrasse (*L. dimidiatus*); 9cm — Ikan doktor (*doctor fish*)

Parrotfishes (Scaridae)
Bumphead parrotfish (*Bolbometopon muricatum*); 1m
Bicolor parrotfish (*Cetoscarus bicolor*); 60cm
Filament-finned parrotfish (*Scarus altipinnis*); 41cm
Blue-chin parrotfish (*S. atropectoralis*); 42cm
Bleeker's parrotfish (*S. bleekeri*); 39cm
Festive parrotfish (*S. festivus*); 34cm
Yellowfin parrotfish (*S. flavipectoralis*); 21cm
Blue-barred parrotfish (*S. ghobban*); 57cm
Java parrotfish (*S. hypselopterus*); 26cm
Pale-nose parrotfish (*S. psittacus*); 27cm
Rivulated parrotfish (*S. rivulatus*); 34cm
Redlip parrotfish (*S. rubroviolaceus*); 48cm
Bullethead parrotfish (*S. sordidus*); 26cm

Ikan kakatua (*cockatoo*); pelo, mogoh (Ba)
Ankeh (Ba); Loong (Bu)
Mogoh (Ba)

Mullets (Mugilidae)
Fringelip mullet (*Crenimugil crenilabis*); 50cm
Engel's mullet (*Valamugil engeli*); 15cm
Mullet (*V. speigleri*)

Belanak, tikus-tikus (*mice*), kuro, sumbal
Ikan janggut (*beard*); depoh (Ba)
Bunteh (Ba)

Barracudas (Sphyraenidae)
Great barracuda (*Sphyraena barracuda*); 1.7m
Blackfin barracuda (*S. genie*); 1.5m
Arrow barracuda (*S. novaehollandiae*); 50cm

Senuk, alu-alu, barakuda
Pangaluang (Ba)

Sandperches (Pinguipedidae)
Sandperches (*Parapercis* spp.); approx. 14cm

Blennies (Blenniidae)
Bicolor blenny (*Ecsenius bicolor*); 8cm
Red-spotted blenny (*Istiblennius chrysospilos*); 11cm
Cleaner mimic blenny (*Aspidontus taeniatus*); 10cm
Scale-eating blenny (*Plagiotremus tapienosoma*); 12cm

Dragonets (Callionymidae)
Mandarinfish (*Synchiropus splendidus*); 5cm

Dartfishes (Microdesmidae)
Zebra dartfish (*Ptereleotris zebra*); 10cm
Decorated dartfish (*Nemateleotris decora*); 7cm
Firefish (*N. magnifica*); 5cm

Gobies (Gobiidae)
Prawn gobies (various); ave. 7cm
Gorgonian goby (*Bryaninops amplus*); 5cm
Coral gobies (*Gobiodon* and *Paragobiodon* spp.); ave.
  4cm
Mudskipper (*Periophthalmus kalolo*); 10cm

Beladok cina

Beladok

Surgeonfishes (Acanthuridae)
Ringtail surgeonfish (*Acanthurus blochii*); 32cm
Clown surgeonfish (*A. lineatus*); 24cm
Whitecheek surgeonfish (*A. nigricans*); 16cm
Powder-blue surgeonfish (*A. leucosternun*); 20cm
Orangeband surgeonfish (*A. olivaceus*); 25cm
Mimic tang (*A. pyroferus*); 19cm
Thompson's surgeonfish (*A. thompsoni*); 19cm
Convict tang (*A. triostegus*); 21cm
Yellowfin surgeonfish (*A. xanthopterus*); 43cm
Striped bristletooth tang (*Ctenochaetus striatus*); 20cm
Goldring surgeonfish (*C. strigosus*); 14cm
Tomini surgeonfish (*C. tominiensis*); 10cm
Hepatus tang (*Paracanthurus hepatus*); 20cm

Surgeonfishes—Botana; kadodoh (Ba).
  Unicornfishes—Gutana; kumai (Ba).
Botana kasur (*mattress*)

Kecamata (*eyeglasses*)

Angka enam (*the numeral 6*)

Brown tang (*Zebrasomas scopas*); 15cm
Sailfin tang (*Z. veliferum*); 30cm
Whitemargin unicornfish (*Naso annulatus*); 1m
Humpback unicornfish (*N. brachycentron*); 90cm
Spotted unicornfish (*N. brevirostris*); 60cm   Kumai tandoh (Ba)
Sleek unicornfish (*N. hexacanthus*); 75cm
Orangespine unicornfish (*N. literatus*); 31cm
Humpnosed unicornfish (*N. tuberosus*); 60cm
Bluespine unicornfish (*N. unicornis*); 70cm
Bignose unicornfish (*N. vlamingii*); 50cm

Tetpai tambako (*makes you "drunk"*) (Ba)

Moorish Idol (Zanclidae)   Ikan bendera (*flag*), gayam, moris idol
Moorish Idol (*Zanclus cornutus*); 14cm

Rabbitfishes (Siganidae)   Baronang, bihang, masadar; uhi, bulawis
         (Ba); belawis (Bu); bete-bete (M)
Foxface (*Siganus [Lo] volpinus*); 18cm   Berah (Ba)
Seagrass rabbitfish (*S. canaliculatus*); 23cm   Lingkis, bulawis samo
Coral rabbitfish (*S. corallinus*); 23cm
Pencil-streaked rabbitfish (*S. doliatus*); 20cm   Kea-kea
Golden rabbitfish (*S. guttatus*); 33cm   Baronang lada; berah (Ba)
Lined rabbitfish (*S. lineatus*); 34cm
Scribbled rabbitfish (*S. spinus*); 23cm   Bulawis jantang (Ba)
Double-barred rabbitfish (*S. virgatus*); 20cm

Tunas and mackerels (Scombridae)   Tuna (tunas and billfish), tongkol (little
         tunas, makerels), tenggiri (makerels)
Frigate mackerel (*Auxis thazard*)   Tongkol
Double-lined mackerel (*Grammatorcynos bilineatus*);   Andeh-andeh (Ba)
    60cm
Dogtooth tuna (*Gymnosarda unicolor*); 2m   Bambuloh (Ba); pakukul (Bu)
Striped mackerel (*Rastrelliger kanagurta*); 35cm   Kembung lelaki
Narrow-barred king mackerel (*Scomberomorus com-*   Tenggiri
    merson); 2.2m
Skipjack tuna (*Katsuwonus pelamis*)   Cakalang
Albacore (*Thunnus alalunga*)   Albakor
Yellowfin tuna (*T. albacares*)   Madidihang, pane
Southern bluefin tuna (*T. maccoyii*)
Bigeye tuna (*T. obesus*)
Longtail tuna (*T. tonggol*)   Abu-abu (*ashes*)

Flatfishes (Bothidae)   Kalankan, ikan lidah (*tongue*)
Peacock flounder (*Bothus mancus*); 40cm
Black-spotted sole (*Aseraggodes melanostictus*); 5cm

Triggerfishes (Balistidae)   Triger, ikan tato, ikan tatul (*wound*);
         ampala (Ba); pogo (Bu); sunga (M)
Orange-striped triggerfish (*Balistapus undulatus*); 23cm   Kauk; popogo batu (Ba); kau (Bu)
Clown triggerfish (*Balistoides conspicillum*); 25cm   Triger kembang (*flower*), triger ceplok
         (*polkadot*); ampala bulunti (Ba)
Titan triggerfish (*B. viridescens*); 63cm   Triger sisir (*comb*); ampala gila (*crazy*) (Ba)
Grey triggerfish (*Melichthys niger*); 28cm
Black triggerfish, red-tooth triggerfish (*Odonus niger*);   Triger abu-abu (*ashes*)
    29cm
Yellow-margined triggerfish (*Pseudobalistes flavo-*
    marginatus); 53cm
Undulate triggerfish (*P. fuscus*); 41cm   Triger liris (*batik pattern*)
Picasso triggerfish (*Rhinecanthus aculeatus*); 20cm   Triger matahari (*sun*)
Rectangular triggerfish (*R. rectangulus*); 18cm   Triger segi tiga (*triangle*)
Blackbelly Picasso triggerfish (*R. verrucosa*); 19cm

Filefishes (Monacanthidae)   Bulusan babi (*pig*), hayam
Scribbled filefish (*Aluterus scriptus*); 71cm

Barred filefish (*Cantherhines dumerili*); 25cm
Wire-net filefish (*C. pardalis*); 20cm
Longnose filefish (*Oxymonacanthus longirostris*); 10cm
Blackbar filefish (*Pervagor janthinosoma*); 11cm

Trunkfishes (Ostraciidae)

Longhorn cowfish (*Lactoria cornuta*); 30cm

Cubefish (*Ostracion cubicus*); 31cm
Spotted trunkfish (*O. meleagris*); 15cm
Reticulate boxfish (*O. solorensis*); 10cm

Ikan buntel kotak (*swelled box*); pogo, lumis, kepe (Ba)

Ikan buntel tanduk (*horn*); cocoring (Ba); kabila, tatumbu (Bu)

Puffers (Tetradontidae)
Whitespotted puffer (*Arothron hispidus*); 45cm
Map puffer (*A. mappa*); 54cm
Guineafowl puffer (*A. melagris*); 40cm
Dog-faced puffer, black-spotted puffer (*A. nigro-punctatus*); 27cm
Star puffer (*A. stellatus*); 90cm
Ambon sharpnose puffer (*Canthigaster amboinensis*); 10cm
Crowned sharpnose puffer (*C. cornata*); 10cm
Spotted sharpnose puffer (*C. solandri*); 9cm
Valentini's sharpnose puffer (*C. valentini*); 8cm

Ikan buntel (*swelling*)

Gurisang (Ba)

Porcupinefishes (Diodontidae)
Porcupinefish (*Diodon hystrix*); 80cm

Ikan duren (*spiky, delicious fruit*); konkeh (Ba); landah (Bu)

Other animals

Sea snakes (famlly Hydrophiidae)
Colubrine sea snake (*Laticauda colubrina*)
Yellow-bellied sea snake (*Pelamis platurus*)

Ular laut

Sea turtles (order Chelonia)
Loggerhead (*Caretta caretta*)
Green turtle (*Chelonia mydas*)
Leatherback turtle (*Dermochelys coriacea*)
Hawksbill turtle (*Eretmochelys imbricata*)

Penyu
Penyu tempayan (*large water jar*)
Penyu hijau (*green*), penyu daging (*meat*)
Penyu belimbing (*like a starfruit*)
Penyu sisik (*tortoiseshell*), penyu kembang

Dugong (order Sirenia)
Dugong (*Dugong dugon*)

Dugung

Whales (order Cetacea)
Shortfin pilot whale (*Globicephala macrorhynchus*)
Great killer whale (*Orcinus orca*)
Pygmy killer whale (*Feresa attenuata*)

Ikan paus (*pope fish*)
Temu bela (Lamalera)
Seguni

Striped dolphin (*Stenella coeruleoalba*)
Spinner dolphin (*S. longirostris*)
Common dolphin (*Delphinus delphis*)
Bottlenose dolphin (*Tursiops truncatus*)

Lumba-lumba (all dolphins)
Timu kira (Lamalera language)

Lumba-lumba berhidung botol (*bottlenose*)

Pygmy sperm whale (*Kogis* spp.)
Sperm whale (*Physeter catodon*)

Lodan, kotal lema

Minke whale (*Balaenoptera acutorostrata*)
Sei whale (*B. borealis*)
Bryde's whale (*B. edeni*)
Blue whale (*B. musculus*)
Fin whale (*B. physalus*)
Humpback whale (*Megaptera novaeangliae*)

Kararu
Kararu
Kararu
Ikan paus biru (*blue*)
Kararu

Further Readings

In addition to a good guide, a diver is probably most interested in a fish identification book, to help make some order out of the more than 2,500 species swimming around the reefs of Indonesia. Two excellent resources recently became available.

Tropical Reef-Fishes

Tropical Reef-Fishes Of The Western Pacific—Indonesia And Adjacent Waters, by Rudie H. Kuiter is the first extensive guide to the reef fishes of Indonesia. It is in press as this is being written, although we have seen galleys.

This compact, handsome book is a manageable 300 pages long, and includes 1,300 excellent color photographs, illustrating 1,027 species including males, females and juveniles, where color or morphological differences exist. *Tropical Reef-Fishes* covers more than 50 families of reef fishes, just about every species you are likely to see around Indonesia's reefs down to about 30 meters.

Each family receives a brief description, headed by a large photo and followed by several smaller ones, usually six to the page. The common names are Australian usage (Kuiter lives in Australia). Kuiter is one of the world's leading authorities on Pacific reef fishes, being the principal author of the description of a half-dozen new species and associate author for a dozen more. Some of these new species are included in this book.

Because of space constraints, however, not all families are listed. In particular, there is nothing on sharks, rays and some of the roving lagoon species, and pelagic species are skipped over lightly. Some of these, of course, are of great interest to the diver. Still, it is an indispensable work.

Micronesian Reef Fishes

Micronesian Reef Fishes: A Practical Guide to the Identification of the Inshore Marine Fishes of the Tropical Central and Western Pacific, 2d ed., by Robert F. Myers, also belongs in the library of every diver in Indonesia. While Myers has not sought to write a book about Indonesian species, there is a great deal of overlap in the faunas of the two regions, and well over 90 percent of the species discussed can be found in Indonesia.

Myers' book is a model of accuracy and detail, with clear color photos of more than 1,000 species, complete meristics, and a dense 50–100 word description of the habitat and behavior of each species. A large number of black-and-white photos of preserved specimens and line drawings are particularly useful, showing such details as the location of cirri and mouth shapes where it is important in identification.

Myers covers the sharks and rays, and a number of other families Kuiter leaves out. Still, Kuiter's book describes 15–20 more butterflyfish, and 30 more damsels. The best solution is to get both.

Other Works of Interest

The grandfather of all Indonesian fish guides is of course Bleeker's Atlas Ichthyologique. It is still very accurate, although not even close to being portable, or even available.

Another very valuable book that became available as we were in production is Gerald R. Allen's *Damselfishes of the World.* This fine book describes and illustrates some 321 damselfish, all that are currently known, including 16 new species. Full meristics, and range and habitat descriptions of all the species are included.

The most available series of books on Indo-Pacific reef life in the United States are those put out by Tropical Fish Hobbyist publications in New Jersey. Unfortunately, however, these books are almost universally awful. They are really badly edited, with misidentified photos and poor organization.

Unfortunately, we were unable to find any books on the rich invertebrate life of Indonesian reefs as thorough and compact as the above-mentioned fish books. We have listed some below, however, that may prove helpful.

Fishes

Allen, Gerald R. *Butterfly And Angelfishes Of The World.* New York: Wiley Interscience, 1979.

——*Damselfishes of the World.* Hong Kong: Mergus, 1991. (Distributed in the United States by Aquarium Systems, 8141 Tyler Blvd., Mentor OH 44060.)

Allen, Gerald R. and Roger C. Steene. *Reef Fishes Of The Indian Ocean* (Pacific Marine Fishes, Book 10). Neptune, N.J.: T.F.H. Publications, 1988.

Bleeker, Pieter. *Atlas Ichthyologique des Indes Orientales Neerlandaises* (9 volumes). Amsterdam, 1877. (Dr. Bleeker's classic "Atlas." Out of print and very valuable. Look for it at a good library.)

Burgess, Warren E. *Atlas Of Marine Aquarium Fishes.* Neptune, N.J.: T.F.H. Publications, 1988. (Full of inaccuracies and misidentified photos; no scientific value.)

Burgess, Warren E. and Herbert R. Axelrod. *Fishes of the Great Barrier Reef* (Pacific Marine Fishes, Book 7). Neptune, N.J.: T.F.H. Publications. 1975.

——*Fishes of Melanesia* (Pacific Marine Fishes Book 7). Neptune, N.J.: T.F.H. Publications, 1975.

Carcasson, R. H. *A Guide To Coral Reef Fishes Of The Indian And West Pacific Regions.* London: Collins,

1977. (Out of date, hard to recognize fishes from the drawings.)

Kuiter, Rudie H. *Tropical Reef-Fishes Of The Western Pacific—Indonesia And Adjacent Waters.* Jakarta: Gramedia, 1992. (Excellent, see text above.)

Myers, Robert F. *Micronesian Reef Fishes: A Practical Guide to the Identification of the Inshore Marine Fishes of the Tropical Central and Western Pacific, 2d ed.* Guam: Coral Graphics, 1991. (Excellent, see text above. Order through Coral Graphics, P.O. Box 21153, Guam Main Facility, Barrigada, Territory of Guam 96921.)

Nelson, J.S. *Fishes Of The World.* New York: John Wiley and Sons, 1984.

Piesch, Ted and D.B. Grobecker. *Frogfishes Of The World.* Stanford, CA: Stanford University Press, 1987.

Randall, John E., Gerald R. Allen and Roger Steene. *Fishes of the Great Barrier Reef and the Coral Sea.* Bathhurst, Australia: Crawford House Press, University of Hawaii Press, 1990.

Sawada, T. *Fishes in Indonesia.* Japan International Cooperation Agency, 1980.

Schuster W.H. and R.R. Djajadiredja. *Local Common Names For Indonesia Fishes.* Bandung, Java: N.V. Penerbit W. Van Hoeve, 1952.

Weber, M. and de Beaufort, L.F. *The Fishes Of The Indo-Australian Archipelago* (11 volumes, 404–607 pages each). Leiden, E.J. Brill. 1913–1962.

Invertebrates

Debelius, Helmut. *Armoured Nights of the Sea.* Kernan Verlag, 1984.

Ditlev, Hans A. *A Field-Guide to the Reef-Building Corals of the Indo-Pacific.* Klampenborg: Scandinavian Science Press, 1980. (Good, compact volume.)

Randall, Richard H. and Robert F. Myers. *Guide to the Coastal Resources of Guam, vol. 2: the Corals.* Guam: University of Guam Press, 1983.

Usher, G.F. "Coral Reef Invertebrates In Indonesia." IUNC/WWF Report, 1984.

Walls, Jerry G., ed. *Encyclopedia of Marine Invertebrates.* Neptune, N.J.:T.F.H. Publications, 1982. (The text of this 700-page book is often good. There are the usual mistakes with photos, however, and many of the names have not kept up with recent changes. A preponderance of the illustrations are Caribbean.)

Wells, Sue, *et al,* eds. *The IUNC Invertebrate Red Data Book.* Gland, Switzerland: International Union for Conservation of Nature and Natural Resources, 1983.

Wood, Elizabeth M. *Corals of the World.* Neptune, N.J.: T.F.H. Publications, 1983.

Reef ecology

Darwin, Charles. *The Structure and Distribution of Coral Reefs.* Tucson, AZ: University of Arizona Press, 1984.

——*The Voyage of the Beagle.* New York: Mentor (Penguin), 1988.

George, G. *Marine Life.* Sydney: Rigby Ltd, 1976 (also: New York: John Wiley & Sons).

Goreau, Thomas F., Nora I. Goreau and Thomas J. Goreau. "Corals and Coral Reefs," *Scientific American* vol. 241, 1979.

Henry, L.E. *Coral Reefs of Malaysia.* Kuala Lumpur: Longman, 1980.

Randall, Richard H. and L.G. Eldredge. "A Marine Survey Of The Shoalwater Habitats Of Ambon, Pulau Pombo, Pulau Kasa and Pulau Babi." Guam: University of Guam Marine Laboratory, 1983.

Salm, R.V. and M. Halim. *Marine Conservation Data Atlas.* IUNV/WWF Project 3108, 1984.

Soegiarto, A. and N. Polunin. "The Marine Environment Of Indonesia." A Report Prepared for the Government of the Republic of Indonesia, under the sponsorship of the IUNC and WWF, 1982.

Umbgrove, J.H.F. "Coral Reefs of the East Indies," *Bulletin Of The Geological Society of America,* vol. 58, 1947.

Wallace, Alfred Russel. *The Malay Archipelago.* Singapore: Oxford University Press, 1986.

Wells, Sue, *et al. Coral Reefs Of The World* (3 volumes). Gland, Switzerland: United Nations Environmental Program, 1988.

Whitten, Anthony J., Muslimin Mustafa and Gregory S. Henderson. *The Ecology of Sulawesi.* Yogyakarta, Java: Gadjah Mada University Press, 1987. (Though not exclusively or even particularly marine in focus, a very interesting work.)

Wyrtri, K. "Physical Oceanography of the Southeast Asian Waters, Naga Report Vol. 2." La Jolla, CA: University of California, Scripps Institute of Oceanography, 1961.

Conservation

Barnes, R. H. *et al.* "Observations and Research on the Cetacean Fishery of Lembata, Indonesia." World Wildlife Fund Project 1428, 1980.

Chia, L.S. and C. MacAndrews eds. *Southeast Asian Seas: Frontiers For Development.* Singapore: McGraw Hill, 1981.

Heslinga, G.A. and F. Perron. "Palau Giant Clam Hatchery." ICLARM, Manila. 1983

Petocz, Ronald G. *Conservation and Development in Irian Jaya.* Leiden: E.J. Brill, 1989. (Useful, if rather brief and policy-oriented in its descriptions. Limited to Irian Jaya.)

Ruddle, K. and R.E. Yohannes, eds. *The Traditional Knowledge and Management of Coastal Systems in Asia and the Pacific.* Jakarta: UNESCO/ROSTEA, 1985.

Index